INTRODUCTION TO ECONOMICS OF AGRICULTURAL DEVELOPMENT

McGraw-Hill Series in Agricultural Economics

CONSULTING EDITOR

Peter J. Barry, *University of Illinois*

Norton and Alwang: Introduction to Economics of Agricultural Development

INTRODUCTION TO ECONOMICS OF AGRICULTURAL DEVELOPMENT

George W. Norton
Jeffrey Alwang

Virginia Polytechnic Institute and State University

McGRAW-HILL, INC.

New York St. Louis San Francisco Auckland Bogotá
Caracas Lisbon London Madrid Mexico Milan Montreal
New Delhi Paris San Juan Singapore Sydney Tokyo Toronto

This book was set in Times Roman by Better Graphics, Inc.
The editors were Anne C. Duffy and John M. Morriss;
the production supervisor was Al Rihner.
The cover was designed by Rafael Hernandez.
Project supervision was done by Tage Publishing Service, Inc.
Arcata Graphics/Halliday was printer and binder.

**INTRODUCTION TO ECONOMICS
OF AGRICULTURAL DEVELOPMENT**

1 2 3 4 5 6 7 8 9 0 HAL HAL 9 0 9 8 7 6 5 4 3 2

ISBN 0-07-047922-4

Library of Congress Cataloging-in-Publication Data

Norton, George W.
    Introduction to economics of agricultural development / George W.
Norton, Jeffrey Alwang.
      p.   cm. — (McGraw-Hill series in agricultural economics)
    ISBN 0-07-047922-4
    1. Agriculture—Economic aspects.   I. Alwang, Jeffrey R.
II. Title.   III. Series.
HD1415.N67   1993
338.1—dc20   92-35127

ABOUT THE AUTHORS

GEORGE W. NORTON is Professor of Agricultural Economics at Virginia Polytechnic Institute and State University (Virginia Tech) and senior fellow at the International Service for National Agricultural Research (ISNAR). He completed his BS at Cornell University and his Ph.D. at the University of Minnesota. He has been on the faculty at Virginia Tech since 1980 and was a visiting professor at Cornell from 1987 to 1988. Professor Norton has taught undergraduate and graduate international agricultural development courses at Virginia Tech since 1981. He has worked in several developing countries, and served as a Peace Corps volunteer in Colombia from 1971 to 1973. He was a consultant for WINROCK from 1977 to 1978, assisting the Sisseton-Wahpeton Sioux Indian Tribe with tribal farm planning.

JEFFREY ALWANG is Assistant Professor of Agricultural Economics at Virginia Tech. He received BA and MS degrees from the Pennsylvania State University, and a Ph.D. from Cornell University. He has been on the faculty of Virginia Tech since 1989. He teaches graduate courses in international development and dynamic optimization. Professor Alwang has worked in several developing countries. He served as a Peace Corps volunteer in Paraguay from 1979 through 1982.

To Our Families

CONTENTS

PREFACE

Hunger, massive population growth, and poverty are among the most critical problems of our time, and many solutions to them have been suggested. It is now generally agreed that agricultural development has a key role to play, that economic interactions among nations are increasingly important, and that agricultural development requires both improved technologies and improved institutions. However, the complex development process must be tailored to each country's resource base and stage of development. The challenge in studying the economics of agricultural development is to build a broad view of the problem, and to bring economic theory to bear on both the development of agriculture and on the means for utilizing agricultural surpluses to further overall economic development. The goal of this book is to help students and other interested practitioners understand agricultural development and acquire the analytical skills that will enhance their capability to solve development problems.

This book interprets for undergraduates the economic theory found in graduate-level development texts. It also illustrates the importance of modifying that theory to account for imperfect information and for the willingness of people to exploit others. These modifications provide important insights for development policy and help explain why some countries develop while others are left behind. This book stresses the importance in agricultural development of enhanced information flows. It covers such topics as sustainability of the natural resource environment, macroeconomic policies, causes of and solutions to external debt problems, the roles of women in agricultural development, and the effects of foreign aid—topics not found in less comprehensive agricultural development text books.

INTENDED AUDIENCE

Introduction to Economics of Agricultural Development is designed as a comprehensive text for a first course in the economics of agricultural development. We were motivated to write it after having taught undergraduate students for several years the economics of agricultural development without a readily accessible textbook targeted at that audience. Hence, this book is aimed at undergraduate students who have only a course in introductory economics as prerequisite. Because such students frequently represent a wide variety of disciplines, economic jargon is kept to a minimum and is explained where necessary. A second audience for the book is those who work for public and private international development organizations.

ORGANIZATION OF THE BOOK

Introduction to Economics of Agricultural Development contains five major sections. Part One considers the many dimensions of the world food-income-population problem in both a human and an economic context. Chapter 1 summarizes key dimensions of the world food situation, describes the interrelationships among poverty, food production, and hunger, and discusses the meaning of economic development. Chapter 2 examines forms of, causes of, and solutions to hunger and malnutrition. Chapter 3 reviews basic economic principles and relates them to the demand for and supply of food in developing countries. Chapter 4 explores basic facts and issues related to population growth and to rural-to-urban migration.

With the severity and dimensions of the food-income-population problem identified, Part Two describes theories of economic development that have been suggested as potential solutions as well as the role of agriculture in those theories. Chapter 5 both presents economic concepts related to agricultural production and discusses the six basic sources of economic growth and the economic transformation that occurs as development proceeds. Chapter 6 reviews economic development theories and stresses the importance of tailoring a development strategy to the resource base and stage of development of a particular country. Chapter 7 describes the food and fiber, labor, capital, foreign exchange, market demand, and rural welfare contributions of agriculture.

Although Part Two establishes the importance of agriculture, it is difficult to design means for improving agriculture without first having a basic understanding of existing agricultural systems. Hence, Part Three provides students with an overview of traditional farming and agricultural systems in less-developed countries. Chapter 8 describes common characteristics of traditional agriculture and presents two case studies that illustrate these characteristics. Chapter 9 explores differences in agricultural systems, factors that influence the types of systems, and the crucial roles of women in agriculture.

With the importance of agriculture established in Part Two and the nature of existing agriculture considered in Part Three, Part Four then examines agricultural development theories and the elements, both technical and institutional, required for improving the agricultural sector. In Chap. 10, alternative agricultural development theories are summarized, with emphasis on the theory of induced innovation. However, the implications for that theory of transactions costs and collective action are explored. The need to build on, but also to modify, our current agricultural development theories is stressed. Means for enhancing information flows and for generating enlightened self-interest are discussed. Chapter 11 considers the meaning of land tenure and the need for land reform; Chap. 12 examines the nature of, causes of, and solutions to environmental problems related to agriculture; Chap. 13 focuses on the importance of access to inputs and credit. Rural money-markets and government credit policies are discussed. Chapter 14 considers how and why governments intervene in agricultural markets and stresses the role of government in providing marketing infrastructure and information. Chapter 15 discusses the critical role of agricultural research in generating improved technologies and institutions, the organization and transfer of agricultural research, and the roles of education and agricultural extension.

Part Five moves beyond the agricultural sector and considers international trade, foreign aid, and macroeconomic forces and policies that feed back on agricultural development. Chapter 16 explores why countries trade and explores trade problems and potential solutions. Chapter 17 examines macroeconomic policies in developing countries and their relationships to agriculture. Causes of, effects of, and solutions to external debt problems are addressed. Chapter 18 identifies the rationale for and types of foreign assistance to agriculture. Positive and negative effects of food aid are considered. Finally, Chap. 19 summarizes and integrates various components of the book. Future prospects for agricultural development are assessed, and ways that individuals can help solve the food-poverty-population problem are suggested.

ACKNOWLEDGMENTS

Many people have helped us write this book through their teaching or research collaboration. A special debt is owed to Martin Abel, Randy Barker, Brady Deaton, Sr., Bill Easter, John Mellor, Philip Pardey, Terry Roe, Vernon Ruttan, Ed Schuh, Dan Sisler, Dan Taylor, and Insan Tunali. The encouragement and assistance of our colleagues at Virginia Tech are gratefully acknowledged. We couldn't ask for a more friendly and helpful place to work. We especially want to thank our former Department Head, Herb Stoevener, for his support and advice; Sandra Batie, Leonard Shabman, and Waldon Kerns for reviewing parts of the manuscript; Mary Holliman and Tony Caruso for editorial assistance; Brady Deaton, Jr. for preparation of maps; numerous undergraduate students who have read and provided feedback on draft chapters; and the many graduate students we have worked with over the years. We want to thank the International Service for National Agricultural Research and the Department of Agricultural Economics at Cornell University for their sabbatical support when part of the book was first drafted. We appreciate the typing assistance of Rhonda Blaine.

We would like to thank the following reviewers for McGraw-Hill for their helpful comments and suggestions: Peter Barry, University of Illinois; Brady

Deaton, University of Missouri, Columbia; Walter P. Falcon, Stanford University; Steven C. Kyle, Cornell University; Marshall Martin, Purdue University; C. Ford Runge, University of Minnesota; Stephen C. Schmidt, University of Illinois; Stephen M. Smith, Pennsylvania State University; and Philip F. Warnken, University of Missouri, Columbia. We appreciate the encouragement and assistance of McGraw-Hill Agriculture Editor, Anne Duffy.

Finally, a special thanks goes to Debra Robertson who typed endless drafts of the manuscript and prepared all the artwork with exceeding patience and good humor.

George W. Norton

Jeffrey Alwang

PART ONE

DIMENSIONS OF WORLD FOOD AND DEVELOPMENT PROBLEMS

Rural family in Colombia.

INTRODUCTION

Most hunger is caused by a failure to gain access to the locally available food or to the means to produce food directly.

Timmer, Falcon, and Pearson[1]

THIS CHAPTER

1 Examines the basic dimensions of the world food situation
2 Discusses the meaning and purpose of economic development
3 Identifies the key role of agriculture in economic development

OVERVIEW OF THE FOOD-POVERTY-POPULATION PROBLEM

One of the greatest challenges facing the world is to find solutions to problems of hunger and poverty in less-developed countries. Despite concerted development efforts since World War II, millions of people remain ill-fed, poorly housed, underemployed, and afflicted by a variety of illnesses. These people must regularly endure the pain of watching their loved ones die prematurely, often from preventable causes. Also, in many countries the natural resource base is being rapidly degraded, with potentially serious implications for the well-being of future generations.

[1] C. Peter Timmer, Walter P. Falcon, and Scott R. Pearson, *Food Policy Analysis* (Baltimore: Johns Hopkins University Press, 1983), p. 7.

Why do these problems continue, how severe are they, and what are their fundamental causes? What can agriculture do to help solve the problems and how might agriculture itself be improved? To what extent do relatively rich nations influence agriculture, the environment, and economic conditions in relatively poor nations and vice versa? These are some of the questions addressed in this book.

Much has been learned over the past four decades about the roles of improved technologies, rural infrastructure, education, agricultural policies, macroeconomic policies, and international trade and aid in agricultural development. These lessons and other potential solutions to development problems are examined herein from an economic perspective. The need to modify standard economic theory to incorporate the key role of enhanced information flows in guiding institutional change is stressed. Such modification is made necessary by the social, cultural, and political changes that accompany the development process. This modified economic model can provide insights into why some economies develop while others are left behind. The current chapter begins with an overview of the world *food-poverty-population problem*.

World Food and Income Situation

Are people hungry because the world does not produce enough food? No. In the aggregate, the world produces a surplus of food. If the world's food supply were evenly divided among the world's population, each person would receive substantially more than the minimum amount of nutrients required for survival. The world is not on the brink of starvation. Population has increased roughly 50 percent over the past 20 years, but food production has grown even faster.

If total food supplies are plentiful, why do people die from hunger-related causes every year? At its most basic level, hunger is a poverty problem. Only the poor go hungry. They go hungry because they cannot afford food or cannot produce enough of it themselves. The very poorest groups tend to include: families of the unemployed or underemployed landless laborers; the elderly, handicapped, and orphans; and persons experiencing temporary misfortune due to weather, agricultural pests, or political upheaval. Thus, hunger is for some people a chronic problem and for others a periodic or temporary problem. Many of the poorest people live in rural areas.

Hunger is both an individual problem related to the distribution of income and food within countries and a national and regional problem related to the geographic distribution of food, income, and population. Approximately half of the world's population lives in nations in which annual per capita incomes (total income divided by the number of people) average less than $500. These nations are found primarily in Asia and Africa. Most of the world's poor and hungry live in Asia. However, severe hunger and poverty problems exist in many Sub-Saharan African and some Latin American countries.

Woman and child in Ethiopia.

While hunger and poverty are found in every region of the world, Sub-Saharan Africa is the only major region where per capita food production has experienced a downward trend for the past 20 years. As Fig. 1-1 shows, per capita food production in Africa has fallen since 1970. Over the same period, the Latin American and Asian regions have experienced relatively steady increases. Per capita calorie availability is below minimum nutritional standards in many Sub-Saharan countries. Low agricultural productivity (farm output divided by farm inputs), wide variations in yields due to natural, economic, and political causes, and rapid population growth have combined to create a very precarious food situation in these countries.

Annual variation in food production has been a serious problem as well, particularly in Sub-Saharan Africa (Fig. 1-1). This variation has caused periodic famines in individual countries, particularly when the production problems have been compounded by political upheaval or wars that have hindered international relief efforts. Production variability causes wide price swings that reduce food security for millions who are on the margin of being able to purchase food. If the world is to eliminate hunger, it must distinguish among

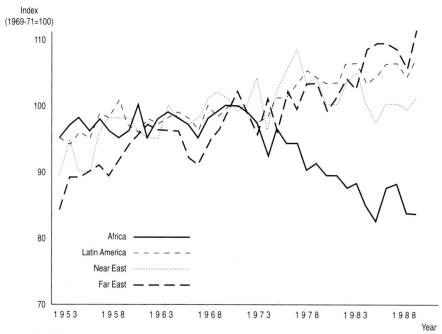

FIGURE 1-1
Index of per capita food production. (*Source: FAO Production Yearbook,* various years.)

solutions needed for short-term famine relief, those needed to reduce commodity price instability (or its effects), and those needed to reduce long-term or chronic poverty problems.

Malnutrition

Hunger is most visible to people in developed countries when a drought or other disaster results in images in the news of children with bloated bellies and bony limbs passively enduring the pain of extreme hunger. Disturbing as such images are, they represent only the tip of the malnutrition iceberg. Less conspicuous, but perhaps more pernicious due to the large number of people suffering and dying, is chronic malnutrition. While accurate figures of the number of malnourished in the world are not available, and even good estimates depend on the definition used, a conservative estimate is that roughly one-sixth of the world's population suffers from chronic or severe malnutrition associated with food deprivation. More than 10 million people, many of them young children, die each year from causes related to inadequate food consumption.

Increasing per capita food production has allowed more of the world's population to eat better. But for those in the lower income groups, the situation has become more difficult. The absolute number of malnourished people in the world has increased over time because of high birth rates and growing populations in poor countries.

Health

People born in developing countries live, on average, 15 years less (in Sub-Saharan Africa, 26 years less) than those born in developed countries. Health problems, often associated with poverty, are responsible for most of the differences in life expectancies. Mortality rates for children under age five are particularly high, often 10-20 times higher than in developed countries (Fig. 1-2). Though countries with high rates of infant mortality are found in all regions, Sub-Saharan African countries are particularly afflicted. The band of high infant mortality stretching from the Atlantic coast across Africa to Somalia on the Indian Ocean covers some of the poorest and most undernourished populations in the world.

Poverty affects health by limiting people's ability to purchase food, housing, medical services, and even soap and water. Inadequate public sanitation and high prevalences of communicable diseases are also closely linked with poverty. A major health problem, particularly among children, is diarrhea, usually caused by poor water quality. According to the World Bank, 5 to 10 million children die each year from causes related to diarrhea. Respiratory diseases account for an additional 4 to 5 million deaths, and malaria another million. Many people have never been vaccinated against such common—but preventable—diseases as polio and measles, although vaccination rates for children under one year old did increase sharply worldwide during the 1980s. Basic health services are almost totally lacking in many areas; on average, there are ten times as many people per doctor and per nurse in low-income countries as there are in the developed countries.

Another growing health problem is acquired auto-immune deficiency syndrome (AIDS). The disease is particularly difficult to contain in many African countries because of the ease of its heterosexual spread, lack of education about the disease, and little use of protective birth control devices.

Population Growth

How important is population growth to the food-poverty-population problem? It is very important, and will continue to be so at least for the next 50 years. Population is growing less than 1 percent per year in developed economies, but 2 percent per year in developing countries, and 3 to 4 percent in many Sub-Saharan African countries. These higher growth rates place pressure on available food supplies in many low-income countries. It is argued that the world, and particularly the least-developed countries, should concentrate more on slowing population growth than on increasing food production. Such sug-

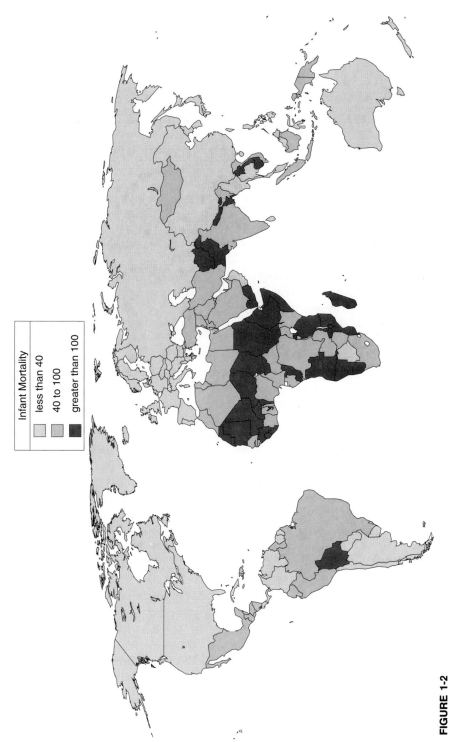

FIGURE 1-2
Infant mortality rates (per 1000 live births). (*Source:* Constructed with data from the World Bank, *World Development Report*, New York: Oxford University Press, 1991.)

Infant Mortality

less than 40

40 to 100

greater than 100

Young boy in Nepal.

gestions ignore the facts that population growth and food production are closely linked and that changing either in a major way takes time, as discussed in Chap. 4. It is clear that continual increases in food production are needed, because regardless of how successful are efforts to control population growth, world population will not stabilize for many years.

Global Interdependence

Food and economic systems in less-developed countries are affected by the international economic environment far more today than they were 15 to 20 years ago. Trade and other economic policies abroad and at home, along with oil price shocks, have combined to increase both the instability of and the opportunities for improving the food and economic security of developing countries.

International trade in agricultural products (as with other products) grew rapidly in the 1970s, building on improvements in transportation and information systems. As exports and imports of farm products constitute a higher proportion of agricultural production and consumption, effects of domestic agricultural policies aimed at influencing the agricultural sector are altered. World prices become more important to farmers than they were previously, and possibilities for maintaining a nation's food security at the aggregate level are improved. However, production and policy changes abroad also tend to have a greater effect on domestic agriculture as international trade grows. While the need for food production self-sufficiency has been reduced, the need to be price competitive with other countries has grown.

International capital (money) markets, through which currencies flow from country to country in response to differences in interest rates and other factors, have become as important as, and perhaps more important than, trade to the food and economic systems in less-developed countries. Certainly, the volume of international financial transactions far exceeds the international flows of goods and services. Capital flows affect the values of national currencies in foreign exchange markets. The foreign exchange rate, or the value of one country's currency in terms of another country's currency, is an important determinant of the price a nation receives for exports or pays for imports. Changes in the world foreign exchange system itself in the early 1970s increased the speed with which changes in the relative values of currencies occur in response to underlying changes in national economies or in macroeconomic (monetary and fiscal) policies.

Changes in monetary or financial markets have become more important for another reason as well. During the 1970s, less-developed countries increased their rate of borrowing from both public and private sources in developed countries. Latin American countries borrowed particularly heavily. In some cases, the borrowing was necessitated by sharp increases in the cost of oil imports. Banks and governments in developed countries were very willing to lend. As interest rates rose in the early 1980s, these loans became difficult to repay. Many countries reduced their rate of government spending in efforts to service this debt, and this decrease in turn reduced economic growth rates, creating further hardships for the poor. The need for foreign exchange to repay external debts has also increased the importance of exports for less-developed countries, and this increased importance of exports has forced some developing countries to reexamine their trade and exchange rate policies. At the same time, new technologies have been changing the possibilities that countries have for producing and trading particular products.

Food Prices

Food prices in the world have trended down for several years. The constant dollar international prices of maize, rice, and wheat, the world's major foodgrains are shown in Fig. 1-3. Since historical peaks in the mid-1970s, prices of all three grains have declined. Rice prices have fallen the most. This trend is both good and bad because prices affect economic growth and social welfare in a contradictory fashion. Lower food prices benefit consumers and stimulate industrial growth but can lower agricultural producer incomes and reduce employment of landless workers. To the extent that lower prices reflect lower producer costs, perhaps due to adoption of improved technologies, income reductions to producers may be mitigated. Future food price trends depend on the relative importance of *demand* shifts, resulting primarily from changes in population and income, compared to *supply* shifts, resulting from a variety of forces, particularly new technologies.

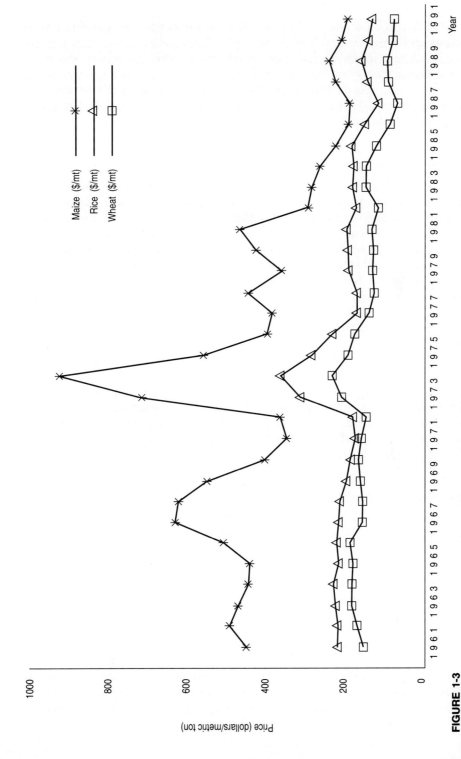

FIGURE 1-3
World prices of major feedgrains, in constant 1985 dollars. (*Source:* World Bank, International Economics Department, International Commodity Markets Division.)

Instability in local and world food prices is another problem affecting food security and hunger in developing countries. The three grains shown in Fig. 1-3 have exhibited sizable year-to-year price shifts. This instability was most severe during the 1970s. Food price fluctuations directly affect the well-being of the poor, who spend a high proportion of their income on food. Governments are finding that food price instability increases human suffering and also threatens political stability.

Environmental Degradation

As populations grow, environmental problems become more severe. Deforestation, farming of marginal lands, overgrazing, and misuse of pesticides have contributed to soil erosion, desertification, poisoning of water supplies, and even climatic changes. The problems are particularly severe in parts of Africa but exist in every region of the world. Some degradation is intentional, but most is the unintended result of people and governments seeking means of solving immediate food and economic crises, often at the cost of long-term damage to the environment. Some of this damage may compromise the ability of a country to raise incomes in the long run. When people are hungry, it is hard to tell them to save their resources for the future. However, many potential solutions exist which are consistent with both short-term increases in food production and long-term goals of simultaneously sustaining or improving environmental quality while raising incomes.

The preceding overview provides brief highlights of some of the dimensions of the food-income-population problem. These and other problems are discussed in more depth in subsequent chapters, and alternative solutions are suggested. First, however it is important to consider what we mean when we talk about development.

MEANING OF DEVELOPMENT

The term *development* defies precise definition but basically refers to improvement in the standard of living of the entire population of a given country or region. Development is a process with many economic and social dimensions, but requires, as a minimum, rising per capita incomes, eradication of absolute poverty, and reduction in inequality over the long term. The process is a dynamic one, including not only changes in the structure and level of economic activity, but also increased opportunities for individual choice and for improved self-esteem.

Development is often a painful process. There is a wide body of evidence that in the early stages of development inequality and absolute poverty may even increase. There is often dramatic social upheaval with traditional ways of life being displaced, existing social norms being challenged, and increasing pressures for institutional and political reform. The landscape of an economy or a culture changes during this transition.

As concern over environmental degradation in developing countries grows, many have begun to argue that for development to be meaningful, it must be "sustainable." The World Commission on Environment and Development defines sustainable development as "development that meets the needs of the present without compromising the ability of future generations to meet their own needs."[2] Thus, the term "development" encompasses not only an economic growth component, but distributional components, both for the current population and for future generations.

Measures of Development

Although development is difficult to define, it is often necessary to measure it in order to assess the impacts of particular programs, to establish criteria for foreign assistance, and for other purposes. Because of its several dimensions, single indicators of development can be misleading. Measures are needed that are consistent with the objective of raising the standard of living broadly across the population. Average per capita income is frequently used as a measure (Fig. 1-4). Is it a good measure?

Average per capita income is not the perfect measure for several reasons, but finding an alternative development indicator that can incorporate each dimension of development is impossible. Because development is multidimensional, collapsing it into a single index measure requires placing weights on different dimensions. Average per capita income is a poor measure even of the economic dimensions because it misses the important distributional elements of development and is a crude measure of the average level of living. It underestimates income in low- compared to high-income countries by neglecting to count many household goods and services produced in less-developed countries.

Alternative multidimensional development indicators have been suggested. One of the oldest is a level of living index proposed by Bennett that weights 19 indicators for which data are available.[3] Examples of indicators include caloric intake per capita, infant mortality rates, number of physicians per 1000 of total population, and years of schooling. Weighting schemes are subjective, however, and average per capita income is highly correlated with many of the indicators. Consequently, average per capita income, measured as gross national product (GNP) or gross domestic product (GDP) per capita is usually employed as a first approximation; then measures such as income distribution, literary rates, life expectancy, and child mortality are examined. Even these supplementary indicators can be misleading due to regional disparities within countries.

[2] World Commission on Environment and Development, *Our Common Future* (New York: Oxford University Press, 1987), p. 43.
[3] See M. K. Bennett, "International Disposition in Consumption Levels," *American Economic Review,* vol. 41, September 1951, pp. 632–649.

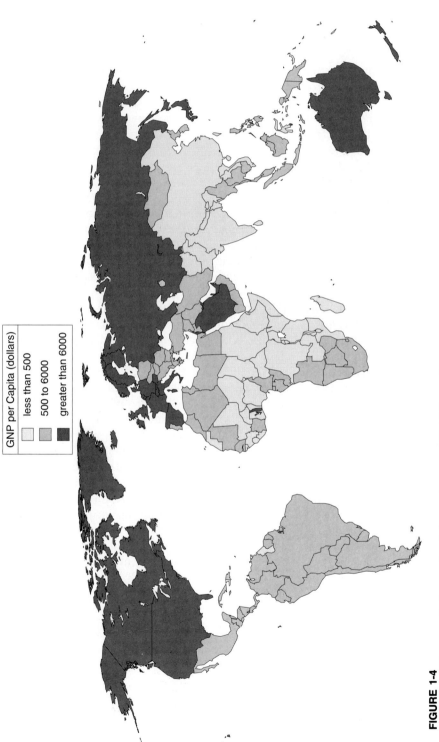

FIGURE 1-4

Incomes (GNP) per capita. Income levels frequently are used to define and measure development. (*Source:* Constructed with data from the World Bank, *World Development Report,* New York: Oxford University Press, 1991.)

GNP per Capita (dollars)

- less than 500
- 500 to 6000
- greater than 6000

Several studies have called for the GNP income measure itself to be modified to account for depreciation or appreciation of natural resource-based assets, particularly forests.[4] This modification may be possible once natural resource accounting procedures are further refined.

Incomes and Development

Poverty and low incomes are most frequently associated with underdevelopment, while growing per capita incomes should indicate increasing levels of development. As discussed above, increasing average incomes may not necessarily mean more development, because the distribution of this income often determines whether poverty and inequality are diminished. Some of the relationships between poverty and inequality are discussed in Box 1-1.

Numerous measures of inequality and the extent of poverty exist. These are discussed later in the book. If, as is argued above, the meaning of development contains some element of poverty reduction or increased equality of income distribution, then clearly the incomes of the poor and destitute should be raised during the development process.

When policies are undertaken to promote development, different effects on the incomes of the poor result. Some people benefit, but often some do not, and, at times, incomes fall for certain population groups. It is important to consider the winners and losers in the development process. Income distributions and changes in them are indicators of the impact of development policies on different groups in society.

Values and Development

Value judgments or premises about what is or is not desirable are inextricably related to development economics. The fact that we call the world food-income-population *situation* a food-income-population *problem* is itself a value judgment. Concerns for economic and social equality, the *eradication* of poverty, and the *need* to improve education all derive from subjective beliefs about what is good and what is not.

Even if people share the same set of beliefs and values, they may attach different weights to the individual beliefs and values within that set. Because there is no correct set of weights, people may not agree about appropriate solutions to development problems, even if the suggested solutions appear conceptually sound in terms of leading to their intended impacts.

Most policy suggestions would result in goth gainers and losers. In some cases, the gainers could compensate the losers, but sometimes they could not,

---

[4] See Salah El Serafy and Ernst Lutz, "Environmental and Natural Resource Accounting," Chap. 3, in Gunter Schramm and Jeremy Warford, (eds.), *Environmental Management and Economic Development* (Baltimore: Johns Hopkins University Press, 1989), for a summary of the concept known as natural resource accounting.

BOX 1-1

POVERTY AND INEQUALITY

Poverty may be roughly defined as the failure to achieve certain minimum standards of living. By its very nature, poverty refers not just to *averages,* but to *distributions.* Poverty is not, however, synonymous with inequality; countries with perfect equality could contain all rich or all poor people. Measurement of poverty requires three steps: determining an appropriate measure or indicator, deciding on its minimum level, and counting the number or percentage of families falling below it. Alternatively, a measure of degree or intensity of poverty would indicate the amount by which families fall below the poverty line.

While poverty refers to some level or position with respect to a measure such as income, inequality refers to the distribution of that measure among a population. For example, evidence from 21 developing countries indicates that, on average, 6 percent of household income is received by the poorest 20 percent of the households, whereas 48 percent of household income is received by the richest 20 percent. In some countries the extremes are even more dramatic. It is possible for poverty to decrease in a country during the development process, but for inequality to increase, at least for a period of time.

---

and often they do not. Because affected groups have differing political strengths within society, economic and social development policies cannot be separated from the political process. These realities must be considered if development policies are to succeed.

ROLE OF AGRICULTURE

There are many alternative development paths or strategies. The strategy followed by an individual country at a particular point in time is, or at least should be, influenced in part by its resource endowments and stage of development. Some countries with vast oil and mineral resources have generated capital for development by exporting those resources. Others have chosen to emphasize cash crop exports such as coffee, cocoa, and tea. Some have focused on industrial exports, while others have stressed increases in basic food production. The optimal development path will vary from country to country, but the choice of an inappropriate path, given the existing resource endowments and stage of development, can result in long-term stagnation of the economy.

There are numerous examples of countries choosing the wrong development path and paying the price. Argentina, a country well-endowed with land resources, chose a development path in the 1940s and 1950s that stressed industrialization and virtually ignored agriculture. The result was that agricultural exports, previously an important component of economic growth, stagnated in the 1950s, and foreign exchange shortages prevented the imports of capital goods needed for industrialization. Economic growth slowed dramatically as a result. India is another country whose potential for agriculture-driven growth was subverted by a disproportionate emphasis on industrialization in the 1950s and 1960s.

Agriculture is not very productive in most low-income countries. Early in the development process much of the population is employed in agriculture, and a high percentage of the national income is derived from that sector (see Table 1-1). As development proceeds, population grows and per capita income increases. As incomes grow, more food is demanded; either agricultural production or imports must increase. Because agriculture commands so many of the resources in most low-income countries, few funds are available for importing food or anything else unless agricultural output grows.

The capacity of the agricultural sector to employ an expanding labor force is limited. As incomes continue to rise, the demand for nonfood commodities grows as well. Therefore, economic development requires an economic or structural transformation of the economy involving relative expansion of non-

TABLE 1.1
RELATIONSHIP AMONG PER CAPITA NATIONAL INCOME, THE PROPORTION OF NATIONAL INCOME IN AGRICULTURE, AND THE PROPORTION OF THE LABOR FORCE IN AGRICULTURE, SELECTED COUNTRIES, 1986

Country	Per capita national income	Agriculture GDP as a percentage of total GDP	Percentage of active labor force in agriculture
Ethiopia	120	46	76
Bangladesh	160	47	82
Tanzania	240	40	80
Niger	260	54	79
India	270	28	58
Kenya	300	28	75
Indonesia	500	23	52
Bolivia	540	20	50
Zimbabwe	620	12	56
Honduras	740	27	58
Thailand	810	23	72
Colombia	1,230	19	22
Brazil	1,810	11	33
Mexico	1,850	9	32
Argentina	2,350	9	11
Greece	3,680	15	33
Spain	4,840	7	13
Italy	8,550	6	8
France	10,710	4	6
Japan	12,850	3	7
Canada	14,090	4	4
United States	17,500	6	2

Source: U.S. Department of Agriculture, *World Agricultural Trends and Indicators, 1970–1988,* Economic Research Service Statistical Bulletin No. 781, Washington, D.C., June 1989.

agricultural sectors. The agricultural sector must contribute food, labor, and capital to that expansion. It also provides a market for nonagricultural goods.

This economic transformation is illustrated in Table 1-1. Agriculture accounts for a large percentage of total income, and an even larger percentage of total employment for the lower income countries. A steep decline in agricultural employment relative to the rest of the economy seems to occur at about $1000 per capita income. The contribution of agriculture to national income declines from 40 to 52 percent for the lower-income countries, to 20 to 30 percent for the middle-income range, and down to 15 percent or below for the highest income countries.

The initial size and the low productivity of agriculture in most developing countries suggest an opportunity for raising national income through agricultural development. Because of the initial size of, and low per capita income in the agricultural sector, there is real scope for improving the distribution of income and enhancing the welfare of a major segment of the population through agricultural development.

Improving Agriculture

How can agriculture be improved to facilitate its role in providing food and contributing to overall development? There are still areas of the world, particularly in parts of Latin America and Africa, where land suited for agricultural production is not being farmed. Most increases in agricultural production will have to come, however, from more intensive use of land currently being farmed. Such intensive use will require improved technologies generated through research as well as improved irrigation systems, roads, market infrastructure, and other investments. It will require education and changes in institutions such as land tenure systems, input and credit policies, and pricing policies (Box 1-2).

One of the keys to agricultural development is to improve information flows. In primitive societies, information is basically available to all, and inappropriate activities are constrained by social and cultural norms. As development begins to proceed and economies become more complex, information needs increase but traditional forms of information transmission are incapable of meeting these needs. Modern information systems are slow to develop, creating inequalities in access to new information. Those with greater access than others can take advantage of this situation to further their own welfare, often at the expense of overall agricultural and economic development.

Some changes required to foster broad-based and sustainable development require institutional changes and capital investments. Capital investments necessitate savings. Such savings are channelled into private and public investment, the latter to build the infrastructure needed for development. Saving requires striking a balance between present and future levels of living because it requires abstention from current consumption. Means must be sought to reduce this potential short-run versus long-run conflict during the development

BOX 1-2

HISTORICAL PERSPECTIVE ON AGRICULTURAL DEVELOPMENT

The historical progression of agricultural development can be broadly broken into four distinct periods. From the time that they first appeared on earth until the "invention" of settled agriculture, roughly 10,000 years B.C., human beings hunted and gathered their food. A combination of climatological changes and over predation of large game following the end of the last Ice Age created conditions for settled agriculture. People, first in the Middle East, began collecting the grains of wild plant-precursors of modern barley, wheat, and rye, and planting them. This collection and planting of grains marked the end of agriculture's first period.

Agriculture's second period began with the invention of settled agriculture and proceeded through the founding and evolution of the traditional means of crop and animal production, many of which exist today. These systems evolved responding to population pressures and resource bases and to the relative scarcity of different factors of production. The wide variety of agricultural systems found around the developing world is testimony to the resourcefulness with which traditional farmers adapt to pressures they face.

The third period of agricultural development, propelled by scientific knowledge and industrial growth, began in the middle of the nineteenth century. This period was marked by the mechanization of agriculture, the development of more efficient crop varieties and animals strains, the application of science to develop chemical fertilizers and pest controls, and the creation of industry and infrastructure to integrate agriculture into the modern economy. The expansion of agricultural output has largely been a product of more intensive production on existing land.

The creation and maturing of institutions—government policies, legal structures, marketing structures, etc.—help define the fourth period of agricultural development. In developing countries, some of the failures to benefit from the scientific revolution of the third period can be clearly attributed to institutional failure. Development efforts focus on improving the institutional environment to promote agricultural growth. Education and the creation of marketing infrastructure, as well as policy reforms to create incentives for farmers, are all part of this institutional revolution. Responsive institutions to generate, disseminate, and promote technologies are a critical part of this fourth period.

process. However, certain types of investments necessary for development, such as education, provide both short- and long-run benefits, as do investments in technologies and industries that are employment-intensive.

Agriculture and Employment Interactions

Agricultural development can provide food, labor, and capital to support increased employment in industry and can stimulate demand in rural areas for employment-intensive consumer goods. Because of their comparative advantage in labor-intensive production, many developing countries will need to import capital-intensive goods, such as steel and fertilizer, and export labor-intensive consumer goods and certain types of agricultural goods. Countries that fail to match an employment-oriented industrial policy with their agricultural development policy will fail to realize the potential income and employment benefits of agricultural development.

SUMMARY

Some of the basic dimensions of the world food-poverty-population problem were examined. The aggregate world food situation was reviewed, and questions such as who the hungry are, and why they are hungry even though the world produces a surplus of food, were addressed. The significance of population growth and of a series of forces in the global economy that influence developing countries were stressed.

The meaning and measures of development were discussed and that the importance of development problems and the desirability of suggested solutions depend on value judgments. While alternative development strategies exist, agriculture has an important role to play in overall development in most developing countries. Development will require a complex set of improved technologies, education, and institutions, and an employment-oriented industrial policy.

IMPORTANT TERMS AND CONCEPTS

Agricultural productivity
Development
Enhanced information flows
Environmental degradation
Food-poverty-population problem
Food price instability
Foreign exchange rates
Health problems

Institutions
International capital markets
International trade
Measures of development
Population growth
Structural transformation of the
  economy
Sustainability
Technology

LOOKING AHEAD

In order to visualize more clearly the relationships among food supplies, food demand, population growth, and nutrition, it is important to examine facts, scientific opinion, and economic theory. We make this examination in the remaining chapters of Part One in this book. We turn first in Chap. 2 to the causes and potential solutions to hunger and malnutrition problems.

QUESTIONS FOR DISCUSSION

1 Are people hungry because the world does not produce enough food?
2 Has food production in developing countries kept pace with population growth there?
3 Is malnutrition more widespread today than in the past?
4 What are some factors that will influence the price of food over the next 10 to 20 years?
5 Is there any hope of bringing more land into production to help increase food production?

6 Why is agricultural development particularly important in less-developed countries?

7 Approximately what proportion of the world's population lives in countries with per capita income less than $500?

8 What is development? To what extent are values important when discussing development issues?

9 Is average per capita income a good measure of level of living?

10 Why is most of the labor force engaged in agriculture in many less-developed countries?

11 Does economic development require expansion of the nonagricultural sector in low-income countries?

12 What is the conflict between increasing near- versus long-term levels of living in developing countries?

13 What are the major health problems in developing countries and what are their primary causes?

14 How fast is population growing in developing countries?

15 Why has international agricultural trade become more important over the past 20 years?

16 Why have international capital markets become more important to developing countries over the past 20 years?

17 Why might low food prices be both good and bad?

18 Why has environmental degradation become an increasing problem in developing countries?

19 Why might developing countries want to import capital-intensive goods?

RECOMMENDED READINGS

Gittinger, J. Price, Joanne Leslie, and Caroline Hoisington, (eds.), *Food Policy: Integrating Supply, Distribution, and Consumption* (Baltimore: Johns Hopkins University Press, 1987), especially pp. 11–88.

Lappe, Frances Moore, and Joseph Collins, *World Hunger: Twelve Myths* (New York: Grove Press, 1986).

Latham, Michael C., "International Nutrition Problems and Policies," in M. Drosdoff, (ed.), *World Food Issues,* Cornell University, Center for Analysis of World Food Issues, Ithaca, N.Y., January 1987, pp. 55–63.

Mellor, John W., *The New Economics of Growth* (Ithaca, N.Y.: Cornell University Press, 1976), especially pp. 1–21.

Stevens, Robert D. and Cathy L. Jabara, *Agricultural Development Principles: Economic Theory and Empirical Evidence* (Baltimore: Johns Hopkins University Press, 1988), Chap. 1 and pp. 31–41.

The Hunger Project, *Ending Hunger: An Idea Whose Time Has Come* (New York: Praeger Publishers, 1985).

Timmer, C. Peter, Walter P. Falcon, and Scott R. Pearson, *Food Policy Analysis* (Baltimore: Johns Hopkins University Press, 1983), especially pp. 3–17.

Todaro, Michael P. *Economic Development in the Third World* (New York: Longman, 1989), especially Chaps. 1, 2, and 3.

U.S. Department of Agriculture, *Can We End Hunger?* U.S. Department of Agriculture, Office of International Cooperation and Development, Washington, D.C., September 1981.

World Bank, *World Development Report* (New York: Oxford University Press), see Volumes for 1982, 1986, and 1990.

CHAPTER 2

FOOD SUPPLIES AND NUTRITION

For hunger is a curious thing: at first it is with you all the time, waking and sleeping and in your dreams, and your belly cries out insistently, and there is a gnawing and a pain as if your very vitals were being devoured, and you must stop it at any cost, and you buy a moment's respite even while you know and fear the sequel. Then the pain is no longer sharp but dull, and this too is with you always, so that you think of food many times a day and each time a terrible sickness assails you, and because you know this you try to avoid the thought, but you cannot, it is with you. Then that too is gone, all pain, all desire, only a great emptiness is left, like the sky, like a well in drought, and it is now that the strength drains from your limbs, and you try to rise and find that you cannot, or to swallow water and your throat is powerless, and both the swallow and the effort of retaining the liquid taxes you to the uttermost.

Markandaya[1]

THIS CHAPTER

1 Examines different forms of hunger and malnutrition: their magnitudes, consequences, and measurement
2 Describes the principal causes of hunger and malnutrition
3 Identifies some potential solutions to hunger and malnutrition problems

---

[1] Kamala Markandaya, *Nectar in a Sieve* (New York: New American Library, 1954), p. 91.

HUNGER, MALNUTRITION, AND FAMINE

Hunger is the silent crisis of the world. In times of famine, it may tear at the heartstrings as media attention belatedly focuses on its dramatic effects. But to most people in the developed world most of the time, it is an invisible problem, somewhere out there. Hunger has many types. The most extreme hunger is severe calorie and protein undernutrition during a famine. However, more pervasive is chronic undernutrition and malnutrition caused by poverty, illness, ignorance, maldistribution of food within the family, and seasonal fluctuations in access to food. We begin our discussion of hunger by examining its dimensions and consequences.

Famines

Famine is marked by an acute decline in access to food that occurs in a definable area and has a finite duration. This lack of access to food usually results from crop failures, often in successive years, due to drought, flood, insect infestation, or war. During a famine, food may actually be present in the affected area, but its price is so high that only the wealthy can afford it. Food distribution systems may break down so that food cannot reach those who need it.

Famines have occurred throughout history. In recent years, their prevalence has been greatest in Sub-Saharan Africa, but famines also occurred in Kampuchea (formerly Cambodia) in 1979, Bangladesh in 1974, in India in 1966 to 1967, and China in 1959 to 1961. The latter was the worst famine of the 20th century and resulted in an estimated mortality of at least 16 million people.[2]

Famine is the extreme on the hunger scale because it causes severe loss of life and concurrent social and economic chaos over a relatively short period of time. As access to food falls, people begin by borrowing money and then selling their assets in order to acquire money to purchase foods. Subsistence farmers sell their seed stocks, livestock, plows, and even land. Landless laborers and other poor groups lose their jobs, or face steeply higher prices for food at constant wages. As the famine intensifies, whole families and villages migrate in search of relief. The telltale signs of acute malnutrition and, eventually, sickness and death appear (see Box 2-1).

Fortunately, there is evidence that progress is being made against famine. Although there are large variations in annual food production in individual countries and world population continues to grow, the frequency and intensity of famines is decreasing due to improved information and transportation networks, increased food production and reserves, and dedicated relief organizations. Much of the starvation we see during famines today occurs in areas where transportation systems are particularly poor and where political upheaval thwarts relief efforts.

[2] See John W. Mellor and Sarah Gavian, "Famines, Causes, Prevention, and Relief," *Science,* vol. 235, January 30, 1987, pp. 539–545.

BOX 2-1

NATURAL DISASTER AND FAMINE IN BANGLADESH[a]

From June to September 1974, severe flooding of the Brahmaputra River in Bangladesh led to large-scale losses of the dry-season rice crop and created pessimism about the prospects for the transplanted spring crop. The price of rice doubled in fewer than three months during and after the floods. Two months after this sudden upturn in rice prices, unclaimed dead bodies began to be collected in increasing numbers from the streets of Dacca, the capital city. Similar collections were reported throughout the countryside. The government of Bangladesh officially declared a famine in September 1974. Estimates of the final death toll vary widely, but most agree that more than 1 million people died of starvation or related causes during and after the famine.

The absence of sufficient food stocks clearly hindered the government's efforts to provide relief. Inadequate relief stocks should not, however, be confused as a cause of the famine; the evidence clearly shows that in 1974 there were adequate food grains available in Bangladesh to avoid famine. This same evidence shows that the districts most affected by the famine even had increased availability of food per person compared to prior years.

What, then, caused the famine? Landless laborers and farmers with less than half an acre of land were most severely affected by the famine. These groups, whose only true asset was their labor power, found that the value of their labor declined greatly relative to the price of rice. The flood did not immediately affect food supply since the lost crop would not have been harvested until the next year anyway. It did, however, greatly lower employment opportunities. Lower wages combined with higher rice prices were the root causes of the 1974 Bangladesh famine.

[a] Most of this material is drawn from Amartya K. Sen, *Poverty and Famines: An Essay on Entitlement and Deprivation* (New York: Oxford University Press, 1981).

Chronic Hunger and Malnutrition

As devastating as famines are, they account for only a small fraction of hunger-related deaths. Famines can be attacked by relief agencies in a relatively short period of time if world food surpluses exist and upheaval in the afflicted country does not hamper relief efforts. Chronic hunger and malnutrition affect a much greater number of people and are more difficult to combat.

Although no accurate figures on the prevalence of malnutrition exist, the World Health Organization (WHO) estimates that a half-billion people suffer from protein and calorie deficiencies and perhaps an equal number suffer from malnutrition caused by inadequate intakes of micronutrients (iron, vitamin A, and iodine, etc.).[3] Thus 15 to 20 percent of the world's population suffers from some form of malnutrition. The estimated prevalence of different forms of

[3] See Michael C. Latham, "Strategies for the Control of Malnutrition and the Influence of the Nutritional Sciences," in J. Price Gittinger, Joanne Leslie, and Caroline Hoisington, (eds.), *Food Policy: Integrating Supply, Distribution, and Consumption* (Baltimore: Johns Hopkins University Press, 1987), pp. 330–345, for a more detailed discussion of the prevalence of malnutrition.

malnutrition is summarized in Table 2-1. Malnutrition does not affect all segments of the population equally. Preschool children and pregnant and nursing women are particularly vulnerable to the dangers of malnutrition.

Serious malnutrition in developing countries reflects primarily under-nourishment—a shortage of food—not an imbalance between calories and protein. The availability of calories per capita by country is illustrated in Fig. 2-1. Many of the countries with very low per capita calorie availability are found in Sub-Saharan Africa. A close, but not perfect, correspondence exists between low calorie availability and the low-income countries identified in the previous chapter. Before the early 1970s, the major nutritional problem was believed to be the shortage of protein. Although dietary protein is important, most nutritionists now believe that when commonly consumed cereal-based diets meet energy (calorie) requirements, it is likely that most protein needs will be satisfied. Quantity of food, particularly calories, is now the overriding concern. It is often possible to reduce protein and micronutrient deficiencies with rather small investments and changes in diet once calorie consumption is adequate.

Nevertheless, there are areas where calorie intake is adequate but protein or micronutrient intake is deficient. Regions where diets are based on staples such as cassava or sugar rather than cereals are more likely to be deficient in protein even if calories are adequate. Iodine deficiency is common in regions far from the sea, for example parts of the Andes mountains in South America. Iron deficiency is a particularly serious problem among women of child-bearing age all over the world, and vitamin A deficiency is common in several countries.

TABLE 2-1
ESTIMATED NUMBER OF PEOPLE AFFECTED BY PREVENTABLE MALNUTRITION, WORLDWIDE

Deficiency	Morbidity owing to malnutrition	Prevalence of morbidity (millions)	Group most affected	Mortality per year
Protein and energy	Stunted growth	500	Ages 0–6	—
	Clinical cases of kwashiorkor and marasmus	1	Ages 1–4	10 million[a]
Iron	Anemia	350	Women 18–45	—
Vitamin A	Blindness	6	All ages and sexes	750,000[b]
Iodine	Goiter	150	All ages and sexes	—
	Cretinism	6	All ages and sexes	—

[a] Diarrhea is often the eventual cause of death.
[b] Deaths caused by reduced resistance to disease.
Source: Latham, Michael C., "Strategies for the Control of Malnutrition and the Influence of the Nutritional Sciences," in *Food Policy: Integrating Supply, Distribution, and Consumption,* J. Price Gittinger, Joanne Leslie, and Caroline Hoisington (eds.), (Baltimore: Johns Hopkins University Press, 1987), p. 331.

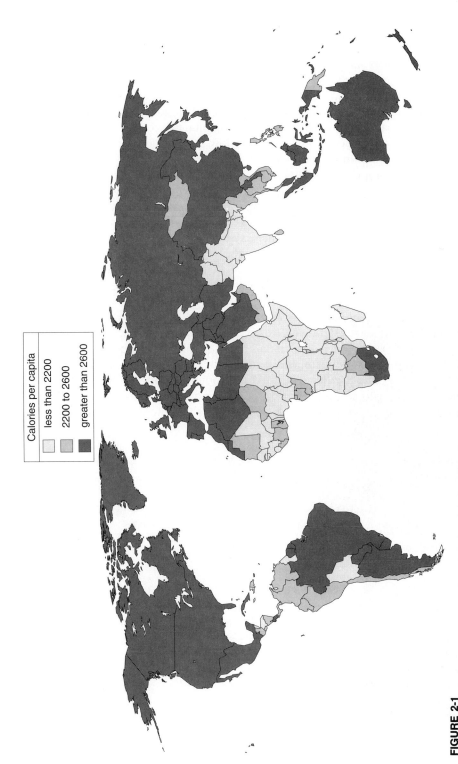

FIGURE 2-1
Daily calorie availability per capita. (*Source:* Constructed with data from the World Bank, *World Development Report 1991*, New York: Oxford University Press, 1991.)

Calories per capita

less than 2200

2200 to 2600

greater than 2600

Consequences of Hunger and Malnutrition

Stunted growth, reduced physical and mental activity, muscle wastage, increased vulnerability to infections and other diseases, and, in severe cases, death are the most common consequences of calorie deficiencies. Death most frequently results from dehydration caused by diarrhea, whose severity is closely linked to malnutrition. Chronic protein malnutrition results in stunted growth, skin rash, edema, and change of hair color. A diet relatively high in calories but low in protein can result in an illness known as kwashiorkor, while a diet low in both calories and protein can result in an illness known as marasmus. People can live about a month with kwashiorkor, 3 months with marasmus; 7 to 10 million people die each year from the two diseases.[4]

Iron deficiency anemia affects muscle function and worker productivity. Vitamin A deficiency is a leading cause of childhood blindness and often results in death due to reduced disease resistance. Iodine deficiencies cause goiter and cretinism.

Mother Teresa with malnourished child in India. (J.P. Laffont/Sygma)

[4] Latham, op. cit.

There is little question that hunger and malnutrition result in severe physical and mental distress even for those who survive the infections and diseases. Malnutrition can affect the ability of a person to work and earn a decent livelihood, as mental development, educational achievement, and physical productivity are reduced. People with smaller bodies because of inadequate childhood nutrition are paid less in agricultural jobs in many countries. Lower earnings tend to perpetuate the problem across generations.

Measuring Hunger and Malnutrition

Measuring the extent of hunger and malnutrition in the world is difficult. Disagreement surrounds definitions of adequate caloric and protein requirements while data on morbidity and mortality reflect the combined effects of sickness and malnutrition.

Nutritional assessments are usually attempted through food balance sheets, dietary surveys, anthropometric surveys, clinical examinations, and administrative records. Food balance sheets place agricultural output, stocks, and imports on the supply side and seed for next year's crops, exports, animal feed, and wastage on the demand side. Demand is subtracted from supply to derive an estimate of the balance of food left for human consumption. That amount left can be balanced against the Food and Agricultural Organization of the United Nations' (FAO) tables of nutritional requirements to estimate the adequacy of the diet. This method provides rough estimates at best, due to difficulties in estimating agricultural production and wastage in developing countries.[5]

Food balance sheets provide only a picture of average food availability. Malnutrition, like poverty, is better measured if the distribution of food intake or of other indicators also is measured. Average national food availability can be adequate, while malnutrition is prevalent in certain geographic areas, or among particular population groups. Even within families, some members may be malnourished while others are not. To measure malnutrition accurately, information on households or individuals is required.

This information can be obtained from dietary or expenditure surveys and from clinical or field measurements of height, weight, body fat, and blood tests. These methods are expensive and are seldom administered on a consistent and widespread basis for an entire country. They can be effective, however, in estimating malnutrition among subgroups of the population. Since preschool children are most vulnerable to nutritional deficiencies, random surveys targeted at either their food intakes or anthropometry (body measurements) can provide a good picture of the extent of malnutrition. Another procedure for estimating the extent of malnutrition is to utilize existing data in hospital, health service, and school records. Anthropometric information from these records

---

[5] See Jean Mayer, "The Dimensions of Human Hunger," *Scientific American: Food and Agriculture* (San Francisco: W. H. Freeman, 1976), pp. 14–23 for additional discussion.

can be compared with standards. Unfortunately, these statistics can be biased because the records for rural areas are scarce, the poor are the least likely to have sought medical attention, and the quality of the information in the records is uneven. For example, many countries in Latin America record the heights, weights, and ages of first-year elementary school children. Unfortunately, many members of the poorest populations groups—particularly native Americans—do not attend school. Estimates of the percentage malnourished among school-aged children generally understate the true problem. In summary, one reason why malnutrition is misunderstood is that its measurement is so difficult.

CAUSES OF HUNGER AND MALNUTRITION

A variety of factors contribute to hunger and malnutrition, but inadequate income is certainly the most important. If people, for whatever reason, provide too few goods and services that others want, they lack income to buy food and they go hungry. Even in times of famine, decreased purchasing power rather than absolute food shortages is often the major problem, as food may be available in nearby regions. Incomes in the affected area have declined so that people cannot afford to buy food from unaffected areas. The World Bank estimates that redistributing just 2 percent of the world's output would eliminate malnutrition.[6]

Figure 2-2 contains a schematic diagram of the determinants of nutritional status. Factors affecting income and productive assets determine how much food can be purchased or consumed by the family. Total food purchases and consumption do not, however, tell the entire story. Health status and family food preparation, along with how food is distributed among members of the family, help determine how food available to a family is related to individual nutritional status.

Health and Malnutrition

Poverty's interaction with malnutrition is often compounded by infectious diseases and parasites that reduce appetites, cause malabsorption of food, or result in nutrient wastage due to fever and other metabolic processes. Health problems and malnutrition exhibit a synergistic relationship: infections and parasites lead to malnutrition while malnutrition can impair the immune system, thus increasing the risk of infection and the severity of the illness.[7] Measles, parasites, intestinal infections, and numerous other health problems

[6] World Bank, *World Development Report 1980* (New York: Oxford University Press, 1980), p. 61.
[7] See Joanne Leslie, "Interactions of Malnutrition and Diarrhea: A Review of Research," in J. Price Gittinger, Joanne Leslie, and Caroline Hoisington, (eds.), *Food Policy: Interacting Supply, Distribution, and Consumption* (Baltimore: Johns Hopkins University Press, 1987), pp. 335–370 for additional discussion.

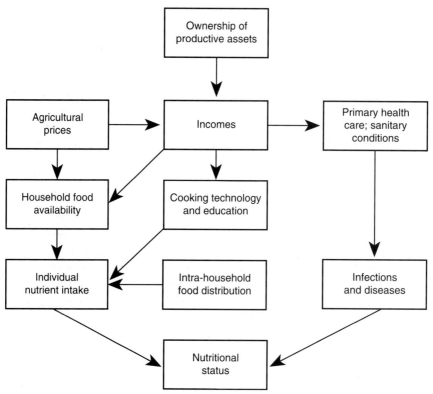

FIGURE 2-2
Determinants of individual nutritional status.

are prevalent in developing countries. Many of these health and sanitation problems lead to diarrhea, which in turn can lead to dehydration and death. Health is determined by, among other things, the sanitary facilities of the household. These in turn are affected both by family assets and income, and by government programs. There is room for optimism related to many childhood diseases. The World Health Organization reports that, because of sustained efforts to vaccinate children, the majority of the world's children under one year old were vaccinated against six common childhood diseases in 1990. This coverage in immunizations against measles, polio, diptheria, pertussis, tetanus, and tuberculosis rose from approximately 20 percent worldwide in the 1970s.

Poor Nutritional Practices

Ignorance of good nutritional practices, maldistribution of food within the family, and excessive demands on women's time can all contribute to malnutrition. The results of studies that have examined each of these factors provide conflicting evidence as to their importance. Each factor is undoubtedly significant in some areas of the world but not in others. For example, in parts of Northern India and Bangladesh, evidence indicates that adult males receive a disproportionate share of food in the family compared to young females, but this is not universally the case.[8] Problems that appear to be related to ignorance, and are in fact discriminatory, are sometimes related to culture and often to poverty.

There is evidence that whether the male or female controls income and assets within a family helps determine how food is distributed. Likewise, there is strong evidence that increased educational opportunities for women are linked both to improved nutritional practices and more equitable distribution in the family.

Seasonal and Cyclical Hunger

Many people in developing countries move in and out of a state of malnutrition. There are hungry seasons, hungry years, and hungry parts of the life cycle. A given individual may or may not survive these periods and frequently experiences lasting physical, mental, and emotional impacts if he or she does survive.

Hungry seasons occur because of agricultural cycles. In the weeks or months preceding a harvest, food can be in short supply. This normal seasonality can be exacerbated if crops in a particular year are short. In certain seasons of the year, particularly the rainy seasons, disease and infection are more common. Likewise, droughts, floods, and insect infestations happen in some years but not in others. Young children are vulnerable, in part due to dangers associated with diarrhea. Pregnant and lactating women experience extra nutritional demands on their bodies while the elderly suffer disproportionately as well, particularly if they lack the support of their children.

SOLUTIONS TO HUNGER AND MALNUTRITION PROBLEMS

Solutions to hunger and malnutrition vary depending on the types and causes of the problem. Famine relief strategies will differ from solutions to chronic hunger and malnutrition. Unfortunately, there is no magic bullet. A concentrated effort on a variety of fronts is required to eliminate hunger.

Raising Incomes

Reducing poverty is central to any long-term strategy to alleviate malnutrition in the world. For subsistence farmers, this implies raising productivity levels, increasing the access to land, or creating opportunities to migrate to off-farm employment. For the population in general, it implies a need for increased

---

[8] See Michael Lipton, "Variable Access to Food," in J. Price Gittinger, Joanne Leslie, and Caroline Hoisington, (eds.), *Food Policy: Interacting Supply, Distribution, and Consumption* (Baltimore: Johns Hopkins University Press, 1987), pp. 385–392.

employment opportunities combined with higher productivity per person. The latter requires rapid growth in jobs and in capital per job in the non-farm sector. Enhanced education, an investment in human capital, will also increase productivity and incomes. Equal access to jobs and expanded economic opportunities in impoverished regions within countries can also help reduce poverty. Economic growth without increased employment for the poorest segments of the population will do little to reduce hunger. Programs to increase employment and earning opportunities for women are particularly important, as these opportunities place downward pressures on birth rates (for reasons discussed in Chap. 4).

Agricultural Production

Increased income or food consumption by the poor is unlikely in most developing countries unless agricultural production increases. Increased production not only raises the incomes of poor farmers, but can lower the price of food, making it possible for the poor to purchase larger quantities. Hence, methods for increasing food production are a major focus of this book. Increased use of purchased inputs, improved marketing and credit institutions, improved agricultural policies, enhanced education, effective agricultural research, and development of infrastructure such as roads, storage, and irrigation systems are particularly important.

Food Intervention Programs

Food price subsidies, supplementary feeding programs, and food fortification can each help reduce nutritional deficiencies. Few developing countries have come close to eliminating malnutrition without some combination of these practices. At the same time, these programs alone cannot solve problems of chronic malnutrition.

General food price subsidies were used in Sri Lanka for several years and helped relieve malnutrition and extend life expectancy to a remarkable degree. However, food price subsidies are expensive, and even Sri Lanka decided to cut back its general subsidy, which lowered prices for all consumers, and instead to target specific groups. A study by the International Food Policy Research Institute (IFPRI) of the Sri Lankan food stamp scheme indicates that the targeted subsidies did reduce program costs substantially, but had mixed results in reaching the poor.[9] Food price subsidy schemes sometimes lower prices, thereby reducing incentives for domestic food production.

Several countries have instituted supplementary feeding programs for vulnerable groups such as children and pregnant and nursing mothers. In some

---

[9] Neville Ediringhe, "The Food Stamp Scheme in Sri Lanka: Costs, Benefits, and Options for Modification," International Food Policy Research Institute, Research Report No. 58, Washington, D.C., March 1987, pp. 1–85.

cases these programs provide food to be consumed in a specific location such as in schools or health centers, while in others food may be consumed at home. In either case, while total family food consumption rises, that of the food recipient usually grows by less then the total donation. Some food is shared with family members. The evidence on supplementary feeding programs indicates that they often are associated with measurable improvements in nutritional status, but they tend to be expensive for the benefits received. Administration of these projects can be very difficult.[10] In some cases, these programs have been assisted with food aid from other countries as discussed below.

Another major food intervention program is the fortification of food by adding specific nutrients to food during processing. The most successful example of fortification are programs that add iodine to salt to prevent goiter. Vitamin A also has proven relatively inexpensive to add to foods such as tea, sugar, margarine, monosodium glutamate, and cereal products. Attempts have been made to fortify food with iron to prevent anemia, but reducing iron deficiency anemia has proven to be a complex problem. In general, the effectiveness of adding nutrients to food is reduced by the fact that the poor buy few processed foods, there is often cultural resistance to the fortified product, and the cost of fortification is prohibitive. In many cases, the "fortified" food has been shown to have no more nutrients than unfortified foods; quality control can be prohibitively expensive in developing countries.

Health Improvements

Programs to improve sanitation, reduce parasitic infections, and prevent dehydration caused by diarrhea can reduce malnutrition and mortality substantially. For example, oral rehydration therapy, which involves the use of water, salt, and sugar in specified proportions to replace fluid lost during diarrhea, can significantly reduce diarrhea-related deaths. Investments in sanitation services, such as potable water and latrine construction, help improve water quality, and, when combined with effective education programs, can significantly improve nutritional status. Improvements in health services including immunization programs can reduce the incidence and intensity of diseases that contribute to malnutrition.

Political, Social, and Educational Changes

Political stability can help alleviate both famine conditions and chronic hunger. The famine in Ethiopia in 1983 to 1984 was exacerbated substantially by political upheaval that hampered relief efforts. Because programs to curb

---

[10] See George H. Beaton and Hossein Ghassemi, "Supplementary Feeding Programs for Young Children in Developing Countries: A Summary of Lessons Learned," in J. Price Gittinger, Joanne Leslie, and Caroline Hoisington, (eds.), *Food Policy: Integrating Supply, Distribution, and Consumption* (Baltimore: Johns Hopkins University Press, 1987), pp. 413–428.

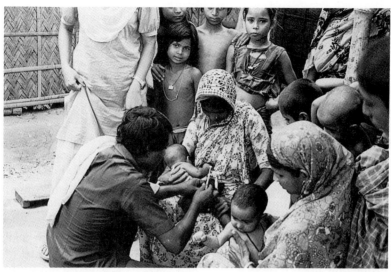

Infant immunization in Bangladesh.

chronic hunger and malnutrition require long-term commitments, they are necessarily rendered less effective by political instability. Responsible political action can improve income distribution in a country, thereby reducing poverty and malnutrition.

Social, cultural, and educational factors also come into play. For example, declining rates of breastfeeding in some countries have contributed to malnutrition as substitutes often are less nutritionally complete, are often watered down, and in some cases are even unsanitary. In other cases, breastfeeding continues too long without the addition of needed solid foods. While social and cultural factors change slowly, and economic factors influence decisions, education can help. In fact, few consumption practices are totally unaffected by education. Nutrition education programs, especially when combined with income-generating projects or efforts to increase a family's access to nutrients, such as home gardening, have been shown to lead to improved nutritional status.

International Actions

A variety of international actions can help alleviate both famine and chronic malnutrition. Because increased incomes are so important to improved nutrition, opening of markets in more developed countries, price stabilization and insurance schemes, and debt relief are all actions that can help, especially in the long run. Foreign assistance can provide short-run relief and also facilitate a long-run development program.

Reduced barriers by developed countries to imports from developing countries will enable low-income nations to gain greater access to world markets.

The foreign exchange earned can be used for development efforts and food imports when needed.

Price stabilization is important to reduce the wide fluctuations in incomes received by farmers and the periodic high prices faced by consumers. International food reserves and price-stabilizing policies are less expensive means of achieving food security than individual countries trying to maintain adequate food reserves for lean years. International insurance-type schemes can reduce variations in foreign exchange earnings (see Chap. 16).

Debt relief is a dire need in many countries, particularly in Latin America and parts of Africa. Attempts to reduce internal consumption to repay foreign debts have hindered efforts to raise incomes and address nutritional problems in several countries. It is in the long-run best interests of both developed *and* developing countries to share some of the burden of adjustments required to reduce the debt problem (see Chap. 17).

Foreign assistance includes food aid as well as technical and financial assistance. Gifts and loans of food at low interest rates can help solve part of the hunger problem if the food assistance is properly administered. Food aid can relieve short-term famines and be used in supplementary feeding programs and in other activities, such as food for work programs, to help generate wealth in developing countries. Financial and technical assistance can help developing countries expand their capital bases and improve methods for producing food and other products.

SUMMARY

In this chapter, the types and consequences of hunger and malnutrition were examined. Even though it is difficult to measure accurately the extent of hunger and malnutrition in the world, it is known that chronic malnutrition affects more people than do famines. Malnutrition results in reduced physical and mental activity, stunted growth, blindness, anemia, goiter, cretinism, mental anguish, and death.

The causes of hunger are many, but virtually all these causes are related to poverty. Infections, diseases and parasites, poor nutritional practices, and seasonal variability in food supplies all contribute to the severity of malnutrition. Solutions to hunger and malnutrition include raising incomes; increasing agricultural production in developing countries; food intervention programs; improving health systems; political, social, and educational changes; and a series of international activities such as food aid and other foreign assistance, debt relief, opening of foreign markets, and price stabilization.

IMPORTANT TERMS AND CONCEPTS

Anthropometry
Chronic malnutrition
Debt relief

Kwashiorkor, marasmus, goiter,
  anemia, and cretinism
Maldistribution of food

Dietary surveys	Oral rehydration therapy
Famine	Political upheaval
Food aid	Price stabilization
Food balance sheets	Protein and calorie deficiency
Food fortification	Seasonal and cyclical hunger
Food price subsidies	Supplementary feeding programs
Foreign assistance	Vitamin and mineral deficiency

LOOKING AHEAD

Hunger and malnutrition imply a need for food but not necessarily a demand for food unless that need is backed by purchasing power. Food demand is influenced by income, prices, population, and tastes and preferences. In the next chapter we will examine tools that can help measure or project the extent to which various demand factors affect food consumption. We will explore how demand interacts with supply to determine prices. The tools discussed are the first of a set of theories and methods presented in this book that can improve your ability to analyze and not just observe food and development problems and policies.

QUESTIONS FOR DISCUSSION

1 Is famine more widespread today than in the past?
2 Is protein deficiency a more severe problem in developing countries today than is calorie deficiency? Why or why not?
3 If people in the United States moved to a diet in which they consumed more grain and less meat, would there be more food for people in poor countries of the world? Why or why not?
4 What are the principal causes and consequences of hunger?
5 How do we measure the adequacy of food availability in a country?
6 What are some solutions to hunger and malnutrition problems?
7 Why and how does political upheaval contribute to famine?
8 What are the major interactions between health and nutritional problems?

RECOMMENDED READINGS

Gittinger, J. Price, Joanne Leslie, and Caroline Hoisington, (eds.), *Food Policy: Integrating Supply, Distribution, and Consumption* (Baltimore: Johns Hopkins University Press, 1987), Chap. 24–34.
Markandaya, Kamala, *Nectar in a Sieve* (New York: New American Library, 1954).
Mayer, Jean, "The Dimensions of Human Hunger," *Scientific American: Food and Agriculture* (San Francisco: W. H. Freeman, 1976), pp. 14–23.
Mellor, John W., and Sarah Gavian, "Famine, Causes, Prevention, and Relief," *Science*, vol. 235, January 1987, pp. 539–545.
Sen, Amartya K., *Poverty and Famines: An Essay on Entitlement and Deprivation* (New York: Oxford University Press, 1981).

The Hunger Project, *Ending Hunger: An Idea Whose Time Has Come* (New York: Praeger Publications, 1985), pp. 6–17.

Timmer, C. Peter, Walter P. Falcon, and Scott R. Pearson, *Food Policy Analysis* (Baltimore: Johns Hopkins University Press, 1983), pp. 19–34.

World Bank, *World Development Report 1980* (New York: Oxford University Press, 1980), pp. 59–64.

World Bank, *Poverty and Hunger,* Washington, D.C., 1986.

CHAPTER 3

FOOD DEMAND
AND ITS INTERACTION
WITH SUPPLY

Rather than a race between food and population, the food equation should be viewed as a dynamic balance in individual countries between food supply and demand.

J. W. Mellor, and B. F. Johnston[1]

THIS CHAPTER

1 Discusses the concept of effective demand and the relative importance of income, population, preferences, and prices in determining the demand for food as development occurs
2 Explains the importance of income elasticities and price elasticities of demand for projecting consumption patterns and for development planning
3 Describes the determinants of supply and how supply interacts with demand over time to determine price trends

EFFECTIVE DEMAND FOR FOOD

The need for food and the effective demand for food are related but distinct concepts. Food needs correspond to the nutrient consumption required to maintain normal physical and mental growth in children and to sustain healthy

[1] John W. Mellor and Bruce F. Johnston, "The World Food Equation: Interrelations Among Development, Employment, and Food Consumption," *Journal of Economic Literature*, vol. 22, June 1984, p. 533.

bodies and normal levels of activity in adults. The effective demand (often called simply demand) for food is the amount of food people are willing to buy at different prices given their disposable income. Because effective demand is related to income or purchasing power, any analysis of food consumption must consider the effects of both income and price changes.

In this chapter, we consider the means for analyzing food demand changes. The goal is to help you assess the likely impacts on consumption resulting from changes in economic circumstances. Food demand analysis also can help you understand the effects of price and income changes on food consumption at the macro or country level. Changes in food prices affect producer incentives as well. We begin our study of food demand by examining its major determinants.

Determinants of Food Demand

The quantity demanded of food, or of any specific commodity, at a point in time generally bears an inverse relationship to price. This inverse relationship is often called the *law of demand*. As price increases, less quantity is demanded; when price falls, more quantity is demanded. The schedule of amounts demanded at different prices traces out a demand curve (Fig. 3-1).

The slope and location of a demand curve are determined primarily by population, per capita income and the distribution of that income among socioeconomic groups, prices of other goods, and sociological and demographic factors such as tastes, habits, customs, and the degree of urbanization. Changes in any of these factors cause the demand curve to shift, as shown by the shift from curve 1 to curve 2 in Fig. 3-1. This shift results in a different quantity demanded at a given price. For example, rapid population growth in developing countries can be a major factor causing the demand curve to shift out (to the right). Population growth, which varies substantially by country, is discussed in detail in the next chapter.

A rise in per capita *real* income in developing countries is frequently associated with a sizable increase in total food demand. Real income is money income divided by a suitable price index to take inflation into account. The effect of income growth on food demand can be more important than the effect of population growth at certain stages of development. Only in very-high-income countries is income growth relatively unimportant as a determinant of the rate of growth of food demand. Even in a country like the United States, however, income substantially influences the demand for food by low-income consumers.[2]

The effect of income growth on demand also varies by commodity. Because the influence of income on food demand is not constant across countries,

---

[2] The Associated Press reported that a five-year old boy in Texas won a contest in a local department store. He was given the choice of a bicycle or $50. He hesitated for a moment, but he took the $50. His father was out of work and his family needed the money for food. A bicycle is a luxury to a hungry child. (*Syracuse Herald American*, November 22, 1987).

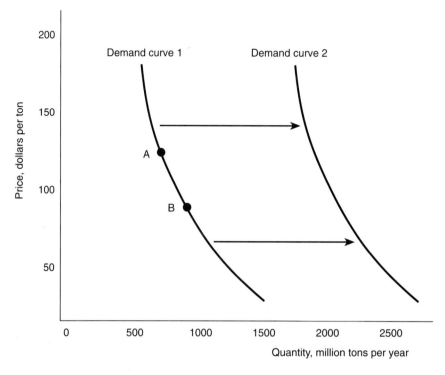

FIGURE 3-1
Hypothetical demand curve for a commodity. A reduction in the price of the commodity, all other things being equal, will cause a movement along a demand curve, say from point A to point B, and an increase in quantity demanded. Changes in the determinants of demand—population, income, prices of other goods, and preferences—can cause a shift in demand, say from demand curve 1 to demand curve 2 or vice versa.

within countries, or by commodity, it is important to have a measure of the sensitivity of demand for food and for particular goods to changes in income. The measure used is called the *income elasticity of demand*.

Income Elasticity of Demand

The income elasticity of demand is defined as the percentage by which the quantity demanded of a commodity will change for a given percentage change in income, other things remaining constant.[3] For example, when per capita income increases by 1 percent, if quantity demanded of a commodity increases by 0.3 percent, its income elasticity of demand is 0.3. Typically, for a very low-

---

[3] If we let n_1 = the income elasticity of demand for good 1, ΔQ_1 = change in quantity demanded for good 1, and ΔI = change in income, then:

$$n_1 = \frac{\%\Delta Q_1}{\%\Delta I} = \left(\frac{\Delta Q_1}{\Delta I}\right)\left(\frac{I}{Q_1}\right).$$

income country, the elasticity of demand for food as a whole is around 0.8 while for a very high-income country it is around 0.1. This difference in income elasticities means that changes in income have a much larger relative impact on food demand in low-income countries than in high-income countries.

Variation in Income Elasticities

Income elasticities of demand vary systematically by commodity, by income levels, and by groups within society. The latter particularly reflects differences due to urbanization, culture, and preferences.

Poor people spend the bulk of their income (at times as much as 80 percent) and a high proportion of any income increases on food. As people reach higher income levels, they spend smaller proportions of their income and smaller percentages of income increases on food. This change in the proportion of the family's budget spent on food, or Engel's law, says that as income increases, people spend a smaller proportion of their total income on food. The fact that income elasticities of demand for food decline as income increases is related to this change in budget proportions. Engel's law is illustrated graphically in Fig. 3-2 which shows the percentage of total income spent on food for a number of countries with different per capita incomes. The distinct downward slope demonstrates Engel's law. A graph could be constructed for income groups within countries to illustrate the same point.

Engel's law reflects, in part, the limited capacity of the human stomach, but note that total expenditures on food can continue to rise even as the proportion of the budget spent on food declines. Some additional quantities of food may be purchased. In addition to this, more expensive foods tend to be consumed as incomes rise. Higher priced calories substitute for starchy staples. A wider variety of foods is demanded and more proteins are added as a higher quality diet is desired. This diversification of food consumption, or Bennett's law, says that, as incomes grow, less is spent on starchy staples such as cassava and yams.

The diversification of food consumption with rising incomes reflects the fact that income elasticities vary by commodity. Estimated income elasticities of demand in Sub-Saharan Africa for a range of commodities are shown in Table 3-1. Estimated income elasticities for several specific countries and commodities are presented in Table 3-2. Note that income elasticities for animal products are higher than for food grains and root crops. Wheat and rice elasticities tend to be higher than those of coarse grains, while roots and tubers have consistently small elasticities. There are substantial variations in income elasticities across countries, reflecting, in part, differences in income and in preferences for foods. For example, the income elasticity of demand for beef is low in Latin America compared to Africa, partly because initial levels of beef consumption are high in Latin America.

Income elasticities for most foods range between 0 and 1. Economists call these goods *normal*. Those goods with income elasticities greater than 1 are

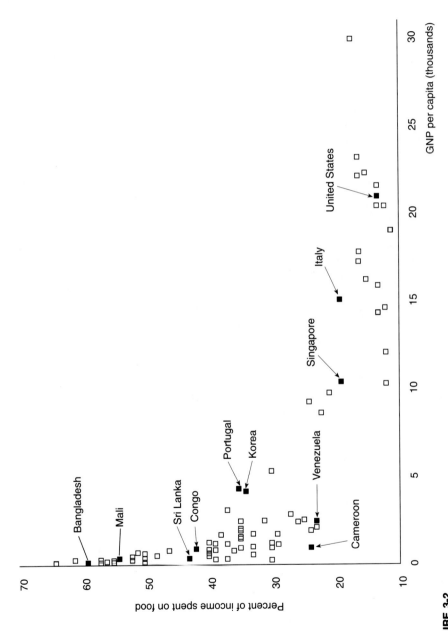

FIGURE 3-2
Relationship between per capita income and percentage of income spent on food, most countries (selected countries labeled).

TABLE 3-1
SELECTED INCOME ELASTICITIES OF DEMAND FOR AGRICULTURAL COMMODITIES IN SUB-SAHARAN AFRICA

Region	Wheat	Rice	Maize	Millet	Roots and tubers	Pulses
The Sahel	0.92	0.93	0.46	0.15	−0.04	−0.14
West	0.87	0.65	0.15	0.09	0.12	0.42
Central	0.55	0.93	0.66	0.28	−0.21	0.14
Eastern	0.51	0.58	0.28	0.01	0.29	0.02
Southern	1.46	0.56	0.35	0.17	−0.15	−0.002

Source: Cheryl Christensen and others, "Food Problems and Prospects in Sub-Saharan Africa: The Decade of the 1980's," U.S. Department of Agriculture, Economic Research Service, Foreign Agricultural Research Report Number 166, Washington, D.C., August 1981.

called *superior* and represent foods which can be thought of as luxuries in the diet in a particular country. If the income elasticity is less than 0, the goods are called *inferior* as consumption of them actually declines as income increases.

The fact that income elasticities vary by commodity means that increases in income will result in an asymmetrical expansion in demand for different commodities. The demand for some commodities will expand by a greater percentage than that for others. Depending on the nature of commodity supply, this asymmetric expansion can cause different pressures on commodity prices. These changes in commodity prices can influence which crops producers grow and can help determine the direction of development.

TABLE 3-2
SELECTED INCOME ELASTICITIES OF DEMAND FOR CEREALS AND LIVESTOCK PRODUCTS IN VARIOUS COUNTRIES

Country	Cereals	Beef	Pork	Poultry	Cow's milk	Eggs
Brazil	0.15	0.58	0.29	0.64	0.45	0.55
Egypt	0.04	0.80	0.70	1.30	1.00	0.70
India	0.25	1.20	0.80	1.50	0.80	1.00
Indonesia	0.29	1.50	0.80	1.50	0.20	1.20
Kenya	0.35	1.00	0.70	1.20	0.59	1.30
South Korea	0.09	0.80	0.73	1.00	0.49	0.80
Malaysia	0.14	0.49	0.41	0.87	0.57	0.73
Mexico	−0.10	0.59	0.49	0.93	0.68	0.59
Nigeria	0.17	1.20	1.00	1.00	1.20	1.20
Philippines	0.22	1.20	0.93	1.00	1.50	1.00
Thailand	0.06	0.56	0.47	0.50	0.80	0.50
Turkey	−0.05	0.80	0.50	1.20	0.80	0.80

Source: J. S. Sarma, "Cereal Feed Use in the Third World: Past Trends and Projections to 2000," International Food Policy Research Institute, Research Report No. 57, Washington, D.C., December 1986, p. 64.

Price Elasticities of Demand

Growth in income and population are major factors shifting the demand for
agricultural products. The quantity demanded of a good also changes in response to a change in its own price. That price response can be represented by
movements along the demand curve in Fig. 3-1, such as movement from point
A to point B. The degree of response is measured by the (own) *price elasticity
of demand*, which is defined as the percentage change in quantity demanded of
a commodity given a one percent change in its price, other things remaining
unchanged.[4] For example, an own-price elasticity of -0.5 means that with a
1 percent change in price, the quantity demanded will change in the opposite
direction by 0.5 percent. Own-price elasticities are typically negative. If the
own-price elasticity of demand is greater (in absolute value) than 1, the demand
is said to be elastic. If it is equal to -1, it is said to have unitary elasticity. If it
is less than 1, it is said to be inelastic. In a graph such as shown in Fig. 3-1, an
elastic demand has a relatively lower slope than an inelastic demand.

Price elasticities of demand are useful for projecting demand changes that
might result from policies that manipulate prices or from supply shifts. *Cross-
price elasticities*, which represent the percentage change in quantity consumed
of one commodity for a one percent change in the price of another commodity,
holding all else equal, also are important.[5] If the cross-price elasticity of
demand is greater than zero, the two commodities are said to be *substitutes*. If
the cross-price elasticity is equal to zero, the commodities are unrelated and if
it is less than zero they are called *complements*.

When the price of a commodity changes, the change in relative prices causes
most consumers to adjust the composition of the commodity bundle they
purchase so that they buy less of the good that increased in price. This
substitution is known as the *substitution effect*. Also, if the price of a commodity increases, the real purchasing power of a given amount of income is
reduced, causing demand to change because of an *income effect*. In most cases,
this income effect is a second factor that reduces demand for the commodity
experiencing the price increase.[6] For inferior goods, however—commodities

[4] If we let E_1 = price elasticity of demand for good 1, ΔQ_1 = change in quantity demanded, and
ΔP_1 = change in price, then:

$$E_1 = \frac{\%\Delta Q_1}{\%\Delta P_1} = \left(\frac{\Delta Q_1}{\Delta P_1}\right)\left(\frac{P_1}{Q_1}\right).$$

[5] If we let E_{12} = the cross price elasticity for commodity 1 as the price of commodity 2 changes,
ΔQ_1 = the change in quantity demanded of commodity 1, and ΔP_2 = the change in price of
commodity 2, then:

$$E_{12} = \frac{\%\Delta Q_1}{\%\Delta P_2} = \left(\frac{\Delta Q_1}{\Delta P_2}\right)\left(\frac{P_2}{Q_1}\right).$$

[6] If the consumer is also a producer of the good, which is often the case in rural areas of
developing countries, this income effect can be positive. Commodity price increases can actually
raise disposable income by increasing farm profits. This profit effect can be important when
examining price responses among agricultural households which both consume and produce goods.

Cassava in Thailand.

such as potatoes and cassava—the income effect may work in the opposite direction and partially offset the reduced consumption induced by the relative price change.

A price increase for a good will increase the consumption of substitutes, and decrease the consumption of complements. Part of these consumption changes are caused by changes in relative prices and part of them are due to income effects. Because the income elasticity of demand for food is large for low-income consumers and because they spend a high proportion of their income on food, low-income consumers often make larger adjustments in their commodity purchases than do high-income consumers when food prices change.

Obtaining Elasticity Estimates

The theoretical effects of changes in consumer behavior discussed above have important implications for food policies and nutrition in less-developed countries. The food-policy analyst, however, would like to have not only the theory but actual estimates of the sizes of the income elasticities, own-price elasticities, and cross-price elasticities of demand for various commodities. For example, if a policymaker wants to project domestic food demand and the increased production or imports needed to meet that demand, the income elasticity of demand for food is one of the pieces of information needed. If an estimate of the effect on the calorie and protein intakes of the poor resulting from a decrease in the price of rice is needed, it is important to have the own-price elasticity of demand for rice and the cross-price elasticities of demand between rice and other major foods in the country, disaggregated by income group.

How are elasticity estimates obtained? There are several approaches, and the appropriate procedure to use depends on the data available and the questions being asked.[7] One type of data that may be available is national aggregate data on consumption, production, trade, and prices. Often these data are published by international sources for several countries. If data are available on the same factors for several countries or for several regions in one country for one period of time, they are called *cross-sectional data*. If data are available for the same factors for one country for several years, they are called *time-series data*. Often we have combined cross-sectional and time-series data, that is, time-series data for the same factors for a number of countries at the aggregate level. These aggregate data are not very useful for studying short-term consumption behavior for commodities within countries because tastes and preferences vary by country. However, the data may be helpful in making long-term projections.

Sometimes, household-level, cross-sectional data are obtained by sampling consumers in a large number of households to obtain information on income, expenditures on different commodities, prices paid, and educational levels and other demographic characteristics. Occasionally the data are collected over time as well, although not often because of the cost involved. If one is interested in microeconomic issues associated with consumer behavior for different income groups, these household-level data are preferred.

Data (aggregate or household-level) are usually analyzed graphically and then in a statistical or *econometric* (statistical model which incorporates economic theory) model containing a set of demand equations. These equations include variables for the factors mentioned above. Elasticities are calculated from the estimated coefficients in the model. Once these elasticities have been calculated, they can be used for a variety of policy and planning purposes.

For some countries, there are serious deficiencies in aggregate and household-level data. Often these data are unreliable or even nonexistent. Policy analysts who have little time or money to collect new data and estimate a model sometimes rely on relationships from economic theory to obtain rough approximations of missing elasticities. For example, there is a useful working assumption (called the *homogeneity condition*) that the sum of the own-price elasticity, the income elasticity, and the cross-price elasticities of demand for a commodity is equal to zero.[8] Typically, the sum of the cross-price elasticities for a commodity is greater than zero and the own-price elasticity is negative. Therefore, the absolute value of the own-price elasticity of demand is usually larger

---

[7] See C. Peter Timmer, Walter P. Falcon, and Scott R. Pearson, *Food Policy Analysis* (Baltimore: Johns Hopkins University Press, 1983), pp. 48–56, for additional but brief discussion of approaches for obtaining elasticities. More detailed information is provided in several textbooks on consumer demand analysis.

[8] That is, for the ith commodity out of T commodities,

$$E_i + n_i + \sum_{\substack{j=1 \\ i \neq j}}^{T} E_{ij} = 0.$$

than the income elasticity of demand. One may have an estimate of the income elasticity of demand but not the own-price elasticity. The homogeneity condition can be used to obtain a rough estimate of the size of the price elasticity of demand given that income elasticity and assumptions about cross-price elasticities. The homogeneity condition is just one example of the use of demand theory.

USING CONSUMPTION PARAMETERS FOR POLICY AND PLANNING

The purpose of obtaining income and price elasticities is to assist with policy analyses and planning. A variety of questions can be answered with the help of these elasticities. For example, what will happen to the consumption of rice, wheat, sugar, or meat when income rises? What will happen to the aggregate demand for food? How will the demand for different commodities change as absolute and relative prices change? What will be the effects of price and income policies on the poor? The answers to these questions help policymakers anticipate future demand changes and production needs, and provide information for designing price and income policies (see Box 3-1).

Income-Induced Changes in the Mix of Commodities Demanded

For commodities with high income elasticities, demand increases substantially with income. Therefore, policymakers may want to support research or use other means for encouraging increased production of those commodities. Otherwise, prices will rise or imports increase in response to this demand growth.

Many highly income-elastic commodities such as milk and vegetables have high nutritional value. However, some goods with relatively high nutritional

---

BOX 3-1

TOTAL DEMAND VERSUS PER CAPITA DEMAND

Food demand projections are usually made for one of two purposes. First, total demand projections are made to estimate food requirements needed to meet demands. If supplies do not expand by the same proportion as the demand growth, then food prices will rise. Rising prices could especially hurt low-income consumers. Increased supplies have to come either through increases in production, or increases in food imports.

A second reason demand projections are made is to forecast demand (or consumption) *per capita*. Previously, we have seen how per capita food and nutrient consumption and nutrition are interrelated. If population grows at a faster percentage rate than does demand, then demand per capita will fall even though demand itself will grow. In order to increase demand per capita, per capita income must grow. Thus, the links between population, food demand, and income are critical for development planning.

Cattle in Colombia.

value have low income elasticities. If a government wants to increase consumption of a good with a low income elasticity, it may have to resort to educational or subsidy programs. Educational programs help change people's perceptions about physical (nutrient) needs and the amount of these needs the food provides. These programs essentially lower the costs associated with acquiring information about nutrient needs and food nutrient content.

At the world level, differences in income elasticities by commodity imply that as average per capita income grows over time, there will be a relative shift in demand toward agricultural commodities with high income elasticities. Many of these are high protein foods such as livestock products. One can also expect the grains fed to livestock, such as corn, to increase in demand relative to food grains such as rice. These types of changes have already been occurring and have been documented by Pinstrup-Andersen.[9]

Another impact of these patterns of income elasticities is that the average income elasticity of demand for food grains will decrease as development occurs. Small income elasticities are associated with small price elasticities of demand. With these decreased price elasticities, increased production of food grains would put sharp downward pressure on their prices. Lower prices should help poor consumers who continue to spend a large share of their budget on food grains, but may force many of the farmers producing these grains to switch to other commodities or to leave agriculture.

[9] See Per Pinstrup-Andersen, "Changing Patterns of Consumption Underlying Changes in Trade and Agricultural Development," a paper prepared at the International Food Policy Research Institute for presentation at the meeting of the International Trade Research Consortium, CIMMYT, El Batan, Mexico, December 1986.

Changes in Aggregate Food Demand as Development Proceeds[10]

The demand for food is influenced by population, per capita income, prices, and preferences. As development proceeds, the two primary factors shifting the demand for food outward are increases in population and in per capita income. Consequently, the simple relation $D = p + ng$, where D = rate of growth in the demand for food, p = rate of population growth, n = income elasticity of demand for food, and g = rate of increase in per capita income, captures these two major forces shifting the aggregate demand for food over time.

In the above equation, population influences food demand in two ways. First, as presented by the term p, it causes a proportional increase in demand. However, per capita income equals total income divided by population. Therefore, the net effect of population growth will not be a proportional increase in demand because population growth also slows the rate of per capita income growth, assuming total income remains unchanged.

At the extreme, if income does not expand at all with increased population, the drop in per capita income will almost completely nullify the direct effect of population growth. For example, developing countries often experience a population growth rate of 3 percent per year during the early stages of development. The income elasticity of demand for food may be as high as 0.9. If total income remains constant, then per capita income will decline by 3 percent and the rate of growth of demand will be $D = 3 + 0.9(-3) = 0.3$.[11]

On the other hand, if per capita income is growing at 3 percent per year while population is also growing at 2.5 percent (rates that are not uncommon in middle-income developing countries), even if the income elasticity of demand for food drops to 0.7, the rate of growth in demand for food would be 4.6 percent per year. Few countries have been able to maintain such a rate of growth in agricultural production over time. Thus, food imports may be needed to meet growing demands.

These examples ignore the fact that income growth in most less-developed countries is heavily dependent on agricultural output. If agricultural output fails to grow, per capita income will grow very slowly. As development proceeds, the proportion of employment and of total national income derived from agriculture declines. Even so, total per capita income in the country still may be affected by the rate of growth of agricultural production because agriculture provides food, capital, and a market for the non-agricultural sector. These issues will be more fully discussed in subsequent chapters.

The determinants of food demand are interrelated; but as development proceeds, certain patterns tend to hold for some of these factors (see Ta-

---

[10] The material in this section draws heavily on John W. Mellor, *Economics of Agricultural Development* (Ithaca, N.Y.: Cornell University, 1966), pp. 73–79.

[11] The negative consequences of such a scenario should be obvious: total demand will increase by 0.3 percent but *per capita* demand will decline by 2.7 percent.

TABLE 3-3
COMPARISON OF GROWTH OF DEMAND FOR AGRICULTURAL GOODS,
HYPOTHETICAL CASES

Levels of development	Rate of population growth	Rate of per capita income growth	Income elasticity of demand	Rate of growth in demand
Very low income	2.5	0.5	1.0	3.0
Low income	3.0	1.0	0.9	3.9
Medium income	2.5	4.0	0.7	5.3
High income	2.0	4.0	0.5	4.0
Very high income	1.0	3.0	0.2	1.3

Adapted from John W. Mellor, *Economics of Agricultural Development* (Ithaca, N.Y.: Cornell University Press, 1966), p. 78.

ble 3-3). As incomes increase, population growth rates generally increase slightly at first as death rates decline. For a number of reasons discussed in the next chapter, population growth rates eventually decline as income continues to grow. The rate of per capita income growth is frequently highest in the middle-income countries, and the income elasticity of demand for food declines continually as income grows. The result is that the rate of growth in food demand is highest for middle-income countries. These are the countries which are most likely to need food imports. Data for the past 20 years indicate that middle-income countries have frequently exhibited the largest increase in per capita income and food imports even though they have also experienced the largest increases in agricultural production.[12]

Price Effects on Demand

Price elasticities of demand help policy analysts anticipate demand changes, including shifts in consumption from one commodity to another, when relative prices change. These changes can have important nutritional implications. Price elasticities also help predict the effects of government policies. The ability to predict these price effects is important because prices play contradictory roles in the market. Low agricultural prices can benefit consumers and stimulate industrial growth, but can reduce farm income and the employment of landless laborers. The responses of consumers to price changes also influence the cost to the government of alternative policies.

[12] See, for example, Kenneth L. Bachman and Leonardo A. Paulino, "Rapid Food Production in Selected Developing Countries: A Comparative Analysis of Underlying Trends, 1961–76," International Food Policy Research Institute, Research Report No. 11, Washington, D.C. October 1979; and Leonardo Paulino "Food in the Third World: Past Trends and Projections to 2000," International Food Policy, Research Institute Research Report No. 52, Washington, D.C., June 1986.

INTERACTIONS OF SUPPLY WITH DEMAND

If markets operate freely with numerous buyers and sellers, supply interacts with demand to determine the quantity supplied and demanded as well as the price. *Supply* may be defined as the amounts of a product that will be offered for sale in a market at each specified price during a specified period of time (see Fig. 3-3).

A given supply curve assumes that the following factors are held constant: (1) technology of production (the way the good is produced), (2) price of inputs used in production, (3) prices of products that may be substituted in production, and (4) number of sellers in the market. Changes in these factors can cause the supply curve to shift left or right. For food as a whole, changes in technology are a major factor causing shifts in supply over time. A new technology that lowers the cost of production will shift the supply curve down to the right (such as from supply curve 1 to supply curve 2 in Fig. 3-3).

FIGURE 3-3
Hypothetical supply curve for a commodity. An increase in the price of the commodity, all other things being equal, will cause a movement along a supply curve, say from point A to point B, and an increase in quantity supplied. Changes in the determinants of supply—technology, input prices, other output prices, number of sellers—can cause a shift in supply, say from supply curve 1 to supply curve 2 or vice versa.

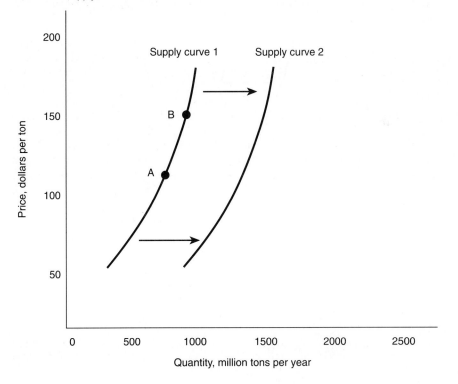

Price and Policy Implications

The rate of growth or decline in agricultural prices over time depends on the net effects of supply and demand shifts (see Fig. 3-4). Because of outward shifts of the demand curve caused by population and income growth, it is unlikely that agricultural prices will experience major declines resulting from supply shifts in a country during the early stages of development.[13] If the supply curve for food shifts out very little, population- and income-driven demand growth could lead to some price increases. However, these increases are also likely to be small because of the close relationship between agricultural production increases and income growth during the early stages of development. As noted earlier, it is difficult to get large increases in income, and therefore effective demand, without corresponding increases in agricultural production.

FIGURE 3-4
Hypothetical supply and demand curves for a commodity. Changes in determinants of demand—for example, income and population—can cause a shift in demand while changes in the determinants of supply—for example, technology—can cause a shift in supply. Whether price increases or decreases (A is higher or lower than B) depends on the relative size of shifts of supply and demand and the slopes of the curves.

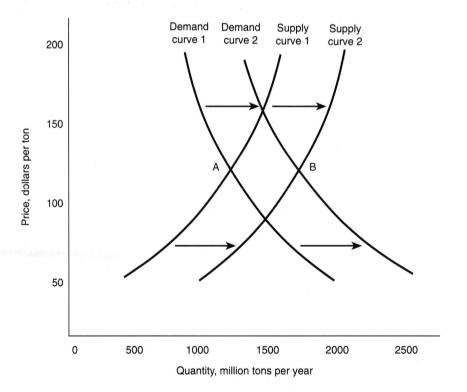

[13] However, there may be substantial local or regional variation (see Box 3-2).

BOX 3-2

MARKETS AND REGIONAL PRICE VARIATION

Developing countries are often characterized by poor transportation systems, sparsely populated areas, or isolated pockets of high population densities, and poor means of knowing what economic conditions exist in these isolated regions. Because of these factors, regional food markets tend to be isolated and independent. Prices can vary widely from region to region, with little relationship to average national prices and quantities, or to those prices prevailing in markets in large cities. In addition, local prices tend to be much more variable than national prices since, with few market participants, changes in behavior by small numbers of participants can affect prices.

The consequences of these market problems can be severe. High regional food prices lead to less ability to meet consumption needs for given incomes. High variability in prices causes uncertainty, and hinders the ability to make plans. Both of these factors worsen the national distribution of welfare, and can cause isolated pockets of poverty. Increases in national supply will do little to improve this distribution.

Regional supply differences caused by high marketing costs due to poor transportation systems can only be improved by investments in infrastructure. Poor information can also cause these differences when the costs associated with gathering price and demand information impairs the effectiveness of the marketing system. Measures to enhance information flows include telecommunications systems that transmit market information.

Other important determinants of the effect of supply and demand shifts on agricultural prices are the elasticities of supply and demand. The more elastic the supply curve (the flatter it is in Fig. 3-4), the less prices will change as demands grow. Open economies (those where imports and exports are common) tend to be characterized by more elastic commodity supplies. One means of minimizing demand-induced price increases is to permit food imports. Another is to increase the responsiveness of the food production sector.

The expected relative stability in food prices during the early stages of development (except as prices are affected by short-run phenomena such as weather) implies a need to place emphasis on policies to shift out the agricultural supply curve and to raise incomes rather than on pricing policies. Thus, the focus of public investment needs to be where the return is highest, whether it is in agriculture or the nonagricultural sector. And, programs that increase the real income of the poor, such as food aid, may be worthwhile. Because it is difficult to increase the incomes of the poor without increasing employment, the country may need to focus investments on labor-intensive commodities and industries.

As development proceeds, incomes grow, and demand shifts outward, the possibilities for rapid increases in food prices arise even in countries experiencing rapid growth in agricultural production. The reasons for this were discussed earlier and illustrated in Table 3-2. Middle-income countries experiencing rapid rates of income growth are likely to need increased agricultural imports.

Eventually, when high income levels are reached, the income elasticities of demand for food and population growth rates are likely to be small. These small income elasticities relieve the upward pressure on food prices but create the potential for food surpluses and low farm prices. Agricultural policies at this stage tend to be concerned with easing the cost of adjusting large portions of the labor force out of agriculture, directing producers into those commodities for which the country has a relative advantage in world markets, and stabilizing domestic farm prices, which are now more heavily influenced by swings in world prices.

The existence of these many structural changes in the market for agricultural goods suggests a strong need to tailor development policies to each country's stage of development. It also suggests a need for each country to consider the stages of development of other countries in the world when making projections about future demands for agricultural products.

SUMMARY

The effective demand for food is determined by the physical and psychological need for food combined with the ability to pay for it. This demand is influenced by prices, population, income and preferences. The level of per capita income is a major determinant of food demand in low-income countries. The income elasticity of demand for food varies systematically by income level, by commodity, and by group within a country. The income elasticity of demand for food declines as development proceeds, and shifts in consumption occur from starchy staples to higher protein foods. Own- and cross-price elasticities of demand are useful for projecting demand changes, both absolute and relative changes among commodities. Several procedures are available for obtaining income and price elasticities. It is the middle-income developing countries that experience the most rapid rates of growth in demand for food.

IMPORTANT TERMS AND CONCEPTS

Aggregate versus household data
Bennett's law and why it holds
Contradictory role of agricultural
  prices
Cross-price elasticity of demand
Cross-sectional versus time-series
  data
Econometric model
Effective demand
Elastic versus inelastic demands
Engel's law and why it holds
Factors that shift the demand
  curve
Factors that shift the supply curve
Homogeneity condition and its use

Income effect
Income elasticity of demand
Law of demand
Major determinants of long-run price
  trends
Normal, superior, and inferior
  goods
Own-price elasticity of demand
Stage of development
Substitutes and complements
Substitution effect
Supply
Use of aggregate versus household-
  level data

LOOKING AHEAD

Rapid population growth over the past few years has dramatically increased the world's population and made the task of raising per capita income and reducing hunger in some countries more difficult. Population growth is influenced by many factors, and several policies have been tried or suggested for controlling it. The rate of migration from rural to urban areas has increased in many countries, as has the proportion of the world's population living in urban areas. In the next chapter, you will learn about the dimensions of population growth and migration, including implications for food consumption and natural resource use. You will examine population and migration projections and policies for the future.

QUESTIONS FOR DISCUSSION

1 As incomes increase, do people spend greater, smaller, or the same proportion of their income on food?
2 Distinguish between an income elasticity of demand and a cross-price elasticity of demand.
3 What tends to happen to the income elasticity of demand for food as the per capita income of a nation increases? Why?
4 To estimate the effect on the calorie and protein intake of a population resulting from a decrease in the price of rice, why is it important to know something about the cross-price elasticities of demand between rice and other major foods in the country?
5 Assume the price elasticity of demand for eggs in India is -0.75. By what percentage would the price of eggs have to change to increase egg consumption by 15 percent?
6 Do you expect the price of food in the world to be higher or lower 10 years from now? To answer this question, draw a graph with supply and demand curves and show how you expect the curves to change over time and why.
7 If population is growing at 2.6 percent per year, the income elasticity of demand for food is 0.6, and per capita income is growing at 4 percent per year, what would be the growth in demand for food per year, assuming prices remain constant?
8 What tends to happen to the mix of foods consumed as per capita income in a country increases? Why?
9 If agricultural development is successful at increasing the level of per capita food production in several less-developed countries over the next 10 years, why might these same countries become less self-sufficient in food (have to import more food than before) during that period of time?
10 Assume you have the following cross-price elasticities for a particular country:

Commodity	Cross-price elasticity
Rice and beans	-0.35
Rice and wheat	0.40
Rice and chicken	-0.10
Rice and milk	-0.05
Rice and other goods	0

a You are a planner for the country represented above and you want to increase the consumption of rice by 6 percent to improve calorie intake of the population.

The income elasticity of demand for rice is 0.4. Use the information above and the homogeneity condition to determine the necessary percentage change in the price of rice.

b If rice consumption increases by 6 percent, what else besides the calories obtained from rice would you need to consider when assessing the impact on calorie consumption?

11 What distinguishes the need for food from the effective demand for food?

12 Which of the following factors shift primarily the demand curve and which factors shift primarily the supply curve: per capita income changes; new technologies; population growth; tastes and preferences; prices of inputs used in production; prices of other goods consumed; prices of substitute goods in production?

13 Why is there a close relationship between agricultural production growth and a nation's income growth during the early stages of development?

14 Even if agricultural production increases rapidly, why is it unlikely that countries in early stages of development will experience major price decreases as a result?

15 Why do middle-income countries experiencing rapid rates of growth in food production often need food imports while very poor countries that are experiencing slower rates of food production growth do not?

RECOMMENDED READINGS

Bachman, Kenneth L. and Leonardo A. Paulino, "Rapid Food Production in Selected Developing Countries: A Comparative Analysis of Underlying Trends, 1961–76," International Food Policy Research Institute, Research Report 11, Washington, D.C., October 1979.

Mellor, John W., *Economics of Agricultural Development* (Ithaca, N.Y.: Cornell University Press, 1966), Chap.4.

Mellor, John W., "Third World Development: Food, Employment, and Growth Interactions," *American Journal of Agricultural Economics*, vol. 64, May 1982, pp. 304–311.

Mellor, John W. and Bruce F. Johnston, "The World Food Equation: Interrelations Among Development, Employment, and Food Consumption," *Journal of Economic Literature*, vol. 22, June 1984, pp. 531–574.

Paulino, Leonardo A., "Food in the Third World: Past Trends and Projections to 2000," International Food Policy Research Institute, Research Report 52, Washington, D.C., June 1986.

Pinstrup-Andersen, Per, "Food Prices and the Poor in Developing Countries," Chap. 20 (pp. 282–292), in J. P. Gittinger, J. Leslie and C. Hoisington, (eds.), *Food Policy: Integrating Supply, Distribution, and Consumption* (Baltimore: Johns Hopkins University Press, 1987), pp. 282–292.

Stevens, Robert D. and Cathy L. Jabara, *Agricultural Development Principles: Economic Theory and Empirical Evidence* (Baltimore: Johns Hopkins University Press, 1988), pp. 41–49.

Timmer, C. Peter, Walter P. Falcon, and Scott R. Pearson, *Food Policy Analysis* (Baltimore: Johns Hopkins University Press 1983), pp. 35–76.

CHAPTER 4

POPULATION AND MIGRATION

Rapid population growth is associated, at household and national levels, with slower progress in raising living standards, especially for the poor.

World Development Report 1984[1]

THIS CHAPTER

1 Presents basic facts about the distribution of the world's population, the rate of population growth, and the consequences of rapid population growth
2 Explains the determinants of population growth and policies which can affect that growth
3 Examines causes and implications of migration from rural to urban areas

BASIC FACTS ABOUT POPULATION GROWTH

The human race dates back about 3 million years. During more than 99 percent of this time there was virtually zero population growth. Average life expectancy was 20 to 25 years, and world population probably never exceeded 10 million people. After agriculture replaced hunting and gathering of food, around 6000 to 8000 B.C., population began to grow more quickly because

[1] World Bank, *World Development Report 1984* (New York: Oxford University Press, 1984), p. 184.

larger numbers of people could be supported by food production. By the year 1 A.D., there were about 300 million people and by 1650, 500 million.[2]

Population began to grow more rapidly during the industrial revolution in the eighteenth century and really accelerated after World War II when populations in developing countries began to grow dramatically. World population reached 1 billion around 1800, 2 billion in 1930, and 3 billion in 1960. It grew to 4 billion in 1975, 5 billion in 1986 and will exceed 6 billion before the year 2000, based on its current growth rate of about 1.7 percent per year (see Fig. 4-1).[3]

The rate of population growth in the world peaked at 2.0 percent in 1965 and has declined since then to its current rate. However, population itself will continue to grow for many years since the future number of parents will be much larger than the current number because of the rapid population growth in the recent past.

Distribution of the World Population

Neither the rate of population growth nor population density is constant across countries. The countries with the highest and lowest population growth rates in mid-1991 are shown in Table 4-1, and the ten most populous nations and their population densities are shown in Table 4-2. Syria, Kenya, and Zambia led the world with annual growth rates of 3.8 percent. Six of the ten countries with the fastest growing populations were found in Sub-Saharan Africa. The two most populous countries are China and India, with 37 percent of all the world's population. Seven of the ten most populous countries are developing countries. As a group, developing countries account for more than three-fourths of the world's population and 90 percent of the annual increase.[4] The distribution of the world's population and population growth rates are illustrated in Figs. 4-2 and 4-3.

Among developing regions, Asia has both the largest population (two-thirds of the developing-country population) and the highest average *population density* (people per square kilometer). While average population densities are much lower in Africa and Latin America, some countries in some parts of these regions have very dense populations in relation to the capacity of their natural resource bases to sustain people in agriculture. Consequently, larger and rapidly growing populations are creating problems in those regions as well.

Consequences of Rapid Population Growth

Rapid population growth is a problem for most developing countries because it imposes a strain on the natural resource base, increases pressures for jobs, reduces food production gains per capita, contributes to pollution, and strains

[2] Elaine M. Murphy, *World Population Toward the Next Century*, Population Reference Bureau, Inc., Washington, D.C., November 1981, p. 2.

[3] If we multiply 5 billion by 1.017 and multiply the resulting number by 1.017, and so on, until we get 6 billion, it would take about 11 years.

[4] World Bank, *World Development Report 1991* (New York: Oxford University Press, 1991), pp. 254–255.

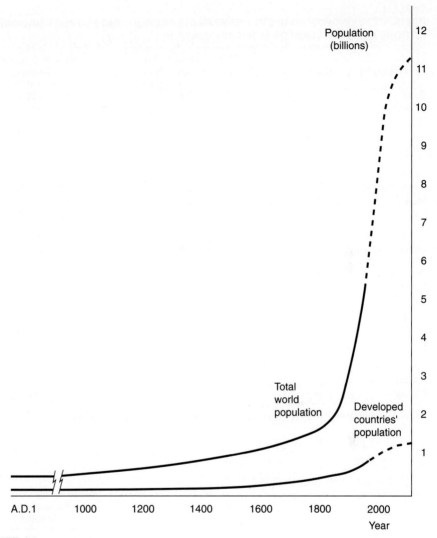

FIGURE 4-1
Past and projected world population, A.D. 1 to 2150. (*Source:* World Bank, *World Development Report 1984*, New York: Oxford University Press, 1984, p. 3.)

the capacity of schools and other social services. While it would be an over-simplification to say that population growth is the root cause of natural resource problems, unemployment, and so forth, it certainly intensifies these problems.

A larger population does provide some benefits. It is less costly per person to deliver some health and sanitation services in more densely populated areas. Increased population expands the size of the market for goods and the supply of labor. On the other hand, rapid population growth increases the number of young people not yet working and complicates the task of educating them.

TABLE 4.1
POPULATION GROWTH RATES IN THE WORLD'S FASTEST AND SLOWEST GROWING NATIONS (WITH 8 MILLION OR MORE POPULATION)

Fastest growing nations	Annual growth rate (percentage, 1991)	Mid-1991 population (millions)
Syria	3.8	12.8
Kenya	3.8	25.2
Zambia	3.8	8.4
Tanzania	3.7	26.9
Côte d'Ivoire	3.5	12.5
Uganda	3.5	18.7
Yemen	3.5	10.1
Saudi Arabia	3.4	15.5
Malawi	3.4	9.4
Iran	3.3	58.6

Slowest growing nations	Annual growth rate (percentage, 1991)	Mid-1991 population (millions)
Hungary	−0.2	10.4
Germany	0.0	79.5
Italy	0.1	57.7
Bulgaria	0.1	9.0
Belgium	0.1	9.9
Greece	0.1	10.1
United Kingdom	0.2	57.5
Czechoslovakia	0.2	15.7
Spain	0.2	39.0
Portugal	0.2	10.4

Source: Population Reference Bureau, Inc., *1991 World Population Data Sheet,* Washington, D.C., 1991.

TABLE 4.2
THE WORLD'S MOST POPULOUS NATIONS

Nation	Mid-1991 population (millions)	Population density (people/km²)
China	1151	120
India	859	260
USSR	292	13
United States	253	27
Indonesia	181	94
Brazil	153	18
Japan	124	331
Nigeria	123	132
Pakistan	118	146
Bangladesh	117	806
Total (10 nations)	3371	59
Total (world)	5384	40

Source: Population Reference Bureau, Inc., *1991 World Population Data Sheet,* Washington, D.C., 1991.

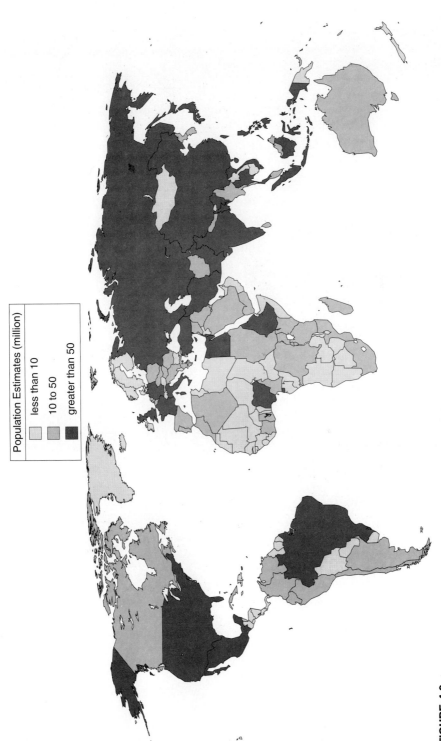

FIGURE 4-2
Population estimates, 1991. *Source: World Bank, World Development Report 1991 (New York: Oxford University Press, 1991), pp. 204–205.*

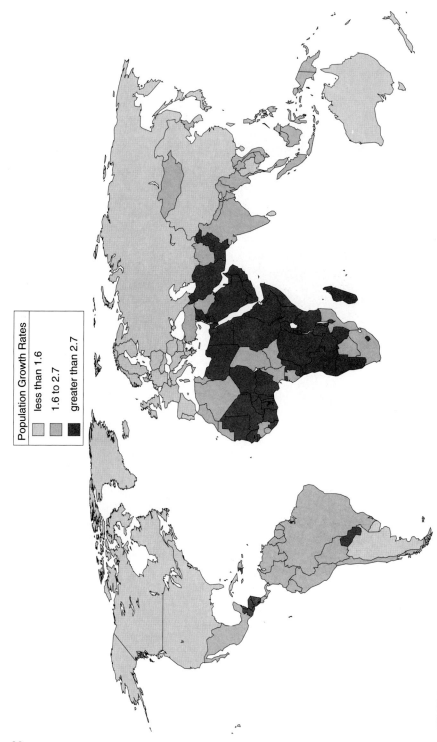

FIGURE 4-3
Population growth rates (percentage annual), 1991. *Source:* Population Reference Bureau, 1991 World Population Data Sheet.

Population Growth Rates

less than 1.6

1.6 to 2.7

greater than 2.7

Large numbers of very young children relative to working-aged people cause increased current consumption and reduced savings and investment (see Box 4-1). The impacts of rapid population growth on schooling can be particularly important. Since about 25 percent of the people in developing countries are of school age, compared to 15 percent in typical developed countries, equal amounts of budget outlay for education translate either to low expenditures per pupil or low enrollment rates. Inadequate investments in either physical or human capital will hurt the long-run possibilities for development.

The argument that most countries need more population to provide labor and markets is not very compelling, given the abundance of unskilled labor

---

BOX 4-1

POPULATION PROFILES, GROWTH AND MOMENTUM

The age distribution of the people in a country has a major impact on the future rate of growth of its population. The population pyramid is a tool that demographers use to describe this distribution. Shown below are two population pyramids, one for developed Sweden and the other for developing Pakistan.

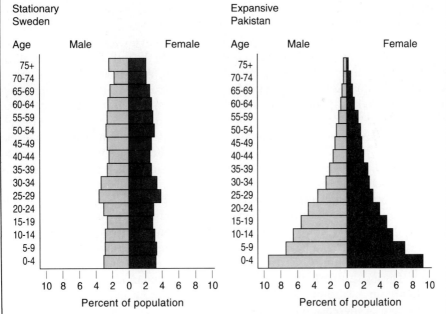

The broad base on the Pakistan pyramid means that there is population growth "momentum" which will cause population to grow, even if fertility, or the number of children that each family has, falls immediately to replacement levels. As the large number of people in the younger age groups in Pakistan reach child-bearing age, the number of births will rise dramatically, even if the number of births per couple falls. Sweden has a relatively even age distribution, and the country is unlikely to experience large increases in population.

Source: The Hunger Project, *Ending Hunger: An Idea Whose Time Has Come* (New York: Praeger Publications, 1985), p. 30.

relative to capital in many countries and the fact that increased consumption of manufactured goods is heavily dependent on per capita income growth.

Hunger, famine, and poverty were serious problems long before population began its rapid rise. However, the population explosion has made it difficult for some countries to invest and has magnified the lack of social justice in others.

CAUSES OF FERTILITY CHANGE AND POPULATION GROWTH

Population growth occurs for the world as a whole when births exceed deaths.[5] Years ago, births and deaths were both high, on the order of 40 to 50 every year per 1000 people in the population. About half of the deaths occurred before age ten, and death rates fluctuated from year to year with contagious diseases and with variations in food supplies.

Population began to grow more rapidly during the industrial revolution because death rates began to decline (see Fig. 4-4). Technological and economic progress resulted in improved nutrition and health, which reduced infant deaths and extended life expectancy. Initially, birth rates remained high; falling death rates combined with high birth rates led to population growth. Birth rates eventually began to fall in developed countries around 1875 and declined steadily for the next 100 years. This eventually led to a slowing of population growth in those countries.

In currently developing countries, death rates have declined more rapidly than they did in the now-developed countries due to the introduction of medical and public health improvements, mostly following World War II—antibiotics, sanitation, immunization, insecticides that controlled malaria-bearing mosquitos, and oral rehydration methods for infants and children. Many of these improvements were created in the developed countries and exported to developing countries through international aid programs. Food aid also reduced the death toll during droughts and other disasters.[6] Fortunately, birth rates also began to decline in developing countries beginning in the late 1950s, for reasons discussed below.

The historical demographic patterns for developed and developing countries shown in Fig. 4-4 have repeated themselves in country after country. A *demographic transition* typically occurs in which an initial period of high birth and death rates (and a relatively stable population size) is followed by a period in which both death and birth rates decline but the death rate declines more rapidly. During this period, rapid and increasing population growth rates occur. Eventually, in a third phase, birth rates decline more rapidly than death rates and the rate of increase in population decreases.

The fact that this demographic transition has been observed in many countries in the past does not, of course, guarantee that it will be observed in the future. While death rates are declining for nearly all countries for reasons

[5] Population in individual countries also depends on immigration and emigration.
[6] Murphy, op. cit., p. 3.

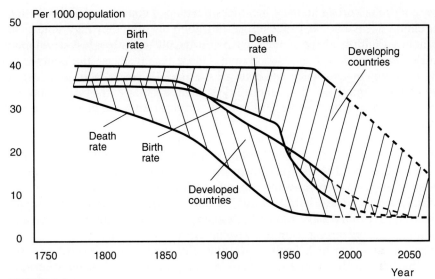

FIGURE 4-4
Trends in births and deaths, 1775–2050. (*Source:* World Bank, *World Development Report 1980*, New York: Oxford University Press, 1980, p. 64.)

previously described, birth rates are still extraordinarily high for many. Therefore, we need to examine the causes of fertility (birth rate) changes and consider policies that might influence those changes.

Causes of Fertility Changes

Family size is largely determined by parental motivation, and this motivation reflects rational, and in many cases, economic decisions. Tastes, religion, culture, and social norms all play a role; yet evidence suggests that differences in economic factors as well as family planning education and access to birth control play the major roles.[7]

People receive pleasure and emotional satisfaction from children. Thus there is a consumption benefit from having children, and in poor societies there may be little competition from other consumption goods. It costs time and money to raise children, but these costs (both out of pocket and in terms of earnings foregone while caring for children) may be relatively low, especially in rural areas.

Children are also an investment. This investment value increases the benefits associated with having children. They frequently work during childhood. In rural areas they gather firewood, collect water, work in the field, move livestock, and do other chores. In urban areas, a child's ability to contribute work to the family is more limited; however, income opportunities exist for very

---

[7] World Bank, *World Development Report 1980* (New York: Oxford University Press, 1980), p. 66.

young children in urban areas of most less-developed countries (LDCs). When older children leave home, especially if they go to the city, they may send cash back home. Children also provide security during old age. Most less-developed countries have no social security system. These benefits raise the number of desired children in less-developed countries, especially among poor families. In many of these countries, child mortality is high, so that extra births may be necessary to ensure that the desired number survive. All these factors increase birth rates.

As people obtain more education and earn more money, they delay marriage, learn more about family planning, often prefer fewer but healthier children, no longer need the income from their children's work, and have more alternative uses for their time and money. An increase in per capita income is inherently a rise in the human value of time. A rise in the value of time, particularly if women have expanded employment opportunities outside the household, creates strong incentives to have fewer children.

Thus, poverty and high fertility are mutually reinforcing. Quantitative research has shown that social and economic factors such as income, literacy,

Brother and sister, Bogota, Colombia.
(J.P. Laffont/Sygma)

and life expectancy accounted for as much as 60 percent of the variation in fertility changes among developing countries from 1960 to 1977. The strength of family planning programs accounted for an additional 15 percent.[8]

Birth rates may not decline immediately as incomes begin to increase. Indeed, economic development may weaken social and cultural forces that were holding birth rates below the biological maximum.[9] For example, in parts of Africa, customs have held husband and wife apart during nursing of the children, thus leading to fewer pregnancies. However, continued increases in income eventually exert strong pressures for lower birth rates, especially as society becomes more urbanized. Urbanization increases the cost of raising children and reduces some of the benefits associated with them, such as firewood and water gathering. Finally, urbanization results in greater availability of goods that substitute for children.

Policies That Influence Population Growth

Virtually everyone favors public and private actions to reduce death rates, but measures to reduce birth rates are more controversial. The controversy arises because some question the cost-effectiveness of family planning programs and others find efforts to control fertility in conflict with their strongly held values and beliefs. Family planning programs in at least one major country appear to have been coercive, and some argue that more people are needed to provide labor and domestic markets.

Those who argue for public actions to help curb birth rates argue that the public costs (schools, hospitals, pollution, etc.) associated with large families exceed the social benefits. Therefore society has a right to at least inform its citizens of ways to control births. There is evidence from countries that have had strong family planning programs, such as Colombia and Indonesia, that these programs can be effective.[10]

China combined educational programs, social pressure, and economic incentives to reduce rates of birth. These were effective, but many people consider China's family planning program too strong; they particularly object to the use of abortion to control family size. These critics can point to less-coercive educational programs that appear to have been equally effective in Sri Lanka, in parts of India, and in other countries.

Measures to improve income growth and distribution, develop social insurance and pension programs, and expand education and employment opportunities for women are all likely to help reduce birth rates. These efforts take time, however, which is why the policy debate often centers around family

---

[8] World Bank, *World Development Report 1980*, pp. 65–66.
[9] Mellor, op. cit, p. 49.
[10] World Bank, *World Development Report 1984*, p. 9.

planning issues. Increased populations make all these programs more expensive and difficult to implement, so that current investments in family planning will save money in the long run. There is evidence that most people in developing countries consider the fertility rates in their countries too high, and only a few consider them too low.[11]

Future Population Projections

The World Bank projects that world population will stabilize around the year 2150 at about 11 billion people.[12] Most of the growth until this time will be concentrated in the developing countries. However, future population projections are uncertain. The above projection assumes that fertility will decline to replacement levels in developing countries between the years 2005 and 2045, an assumption that, in some respects, appears optimistic given the current low levels of income in many countries. However, experience of the past few decades has shown that both mortality and fertility can be brought down more quickly than projected by increasing incomes, education, and family planning.[13]

RURAL-TO-URBAN MIGRATION

While total population in developing countries grew roughly 2.1 percent annually from 1980 to 1989, urban population grew at an annual rate of more than 3.5 percent.[14,15] According to a United Nations survey, natural population increases in urban areas account for 60 percent of this growth rate, and another 8 to 15 percent is attributable to reclassification of rural areas to urban areas.[16] Therefore, at least 25 percent of the rapid growth in urban areas is caused by migration from rural to urban areas. Because a large proportion of the migrants are of child-bearing age, a sizable part of the "natural increase" in urban populations also can be attributed to recent migrants. The percentage of urban population growth due to migration is highest in those countries in the early stages of development. Let's examine the causes and consequences of this massive population movement.

[11] The Hunger Project, *Ending Hunger: An Idea Whose Time Has Come* (New York: Praeger, 1985), p. 30.

[12] World Bank, *World Development Report 1984*, p. 7.

[13] These population projections do not consider some potentially important unknowns such as the future path of the AIDS virus, particularly in Africa. Furthermore, small changes in the projected fertility rates of China and India can have major effects on the total projection.

[14] World Bank, *World Development Report 1991*, pp. 255 and 265. Urban growth rates were even higher in the lowest-income countries.

[15] The world's largest cities are increasingly found in the developing countries. Twelve of the 15 largest cities in the world are likely to be in less-developed countries by the year 2000. Mexico City is expected to be the largest city with a population projection exceeding 30 million people.

[16] World Bank, *World Development Report 1984*, p. 97.

Hospital in the Philippines, newborn nursery. (David Burnett/Contact)

Causes of Rural-to-Urban Migration

Rural-to-urban migration is, in a broad sense, a natural reflection of the economic transformation from agriculture to industry which economies undergo during the development process. As we discuss in Chap. 6, the process of industrialization increases the demand for labor in the manufacturing and service sectors. In the early stages of development, much of this labor must come from the rural areas.

By and large, people move to urban areas because they expect increased economic opportunities. Landlessness and rural poverty, natural calamities, lack of educational opportunities, unequal services, and other factors come into play as well. Although living costs are higher in urban areas, migrants are searching for a better standard of living; they are pushed out of rural areas by poverty and desperation, and pulled to the cities by hope and opportunity.

The vast majority of people who migrate to cities perceive that the benefits of the move exceed its costs (these costs include foregone rural income and the cost of the move), or they would not make the move. Migrants tend to be young, disproportionately single, and better educated than the average of those left behind. The first two of these characteristics tend to lower the costs of the move, while the third raises the benefits. Better-educated people can expect higher returns (wages) in urban areas. A substantial majority of migrants to large cities in developing areas has relatives or friends already living there, a fact that tends to lower the cost of the move.

Rural-to-urban migration has been persistent despite rising unemployment rates in urban areas. The likely reasons for this persistence are that workers consider both rural-urban wage differentials and the probability of obtaining a job (which is often much less than 100 percent) and still perceive that they will be made better off by moving. Many of these migrants realize it is unlikely that they will obtain a high-paying or "formal" job immediately, but they are willing to work in low-paying jobs such as selling goods on street corners, "watching over" parked cars, or doing some other job in the "informal" sector. For some of these migrants, these high-paying jobs may come only to their children, and then only if the children receive a better education than their parents.

The importance of educational opportunities and other public services cannot be overlooked as reasons for rural-to-urban migration. In many countries, an urban political bias has created a large disparity between the levels of services, including quality of public education, in rural and urban areas. Furthermore, and perhaps more important, the political bias extends to economic policies such as pricing policies. Food prices are often kept artificially low

Many of the migrants to Dhaka, Bangladesh seek work as bicycle rickshaw drivers.

(through policies discussed later in this book). This policy helps urban consumers but discourages investment in food production and lowers incomes in rural areas. These distortions help explain some of the attractions of cities.

Consequences of Rural-to-Urban Migration

Urbanization per se is not a problem. There are economies of scale resulting from the concentration of suppliers and consumers for both industry and public services. The problem arises when cities become "too large, too quickly," especially when rural-to-urban migration increases the urban population at a rate faster than industry, schools, sewage systems, and so forth, can expand. The result is substandard housing, poor sanitation, and lack of other services for recent migrants (see Box 4-2). While migrants have been shown to be assets to the cities, the ever-expanding shanty towns that surround almost all large cities in less-developed countries attest to the growing disparities that occur

---

BOX 4-2

MEXICO CITY: AN EXAMPLE OF RAPID URBAN GROWTH

In 1950, only seven urban centers of the world had populations exceeding 5 million. This number rose to 34 in 1980, and it is estimated that by 2025, 93 cities will hold more than 5 million, with 80 of these located in currently less-developed countries. The situation in Mexico City, whose population more than tripled (from 5 to 16 million) between 1965 and 1990, is an example of some of the strains imposed by over-rapid urbanization.

The growth of Mexico City outstripped the growth in the availability of services. The city opened an ultramodern subway system in 1969, began large-scale construction of housing in the early 1970s, and inaugurated a deep-drainage sewer system that was hailed as an engineering marvel in 1975. Despite these costly investments, the subway and other transportation systems are hopelessly overloaded, 30 percent of the families in the city live in single rooms, and fully 40 percent of houses lack sewerage. Congestion and air pollution caused the government to prohibit use of one-fifth of the city's 2.5 million private cars each day of the week. Water is pumped into the city from as far away as 50 miles; rainwater and sewage are pumped out. The sewer system is so overtaxed that sewers back up and overflow into the streets during downpours. The city's garbage dumps are overflowing, and some 17,000 people earn their livelihood by picking garbage at the public dump.

Rural-to-urban migration continues in spite of these problems, with about 400,000 rural Mexicans moving to Mexico City each year. The hope of a better life provides a strong pull. While roughly 23 percent of the country's population lives in the city, 40 percent of the GDP is produced there, and more than one-third of the factory and commercial jobs and two-thirds of the vast national bureaucracy is located in the capital. Rural Mexico is extremely poor, with high rates of malnutrition, low literacy, and poor services even compared to the capital.

Source: Bart McDowell, "Mexico City: An Alarming Giant," *National Geographic*, vol. 166, August 1984, pp. 38–78.

within cities if urbanization occurs too rapidly. Many people live in absolute squalor, often without sewage systems and sometimes in garbage dumps. The fact that people are willing to live in these areas highlights the poverty and lack of opportunity in many rural areas.

Evidence suggests that farm output has not been affected greatly by the loss of migrants to urban areas. In some cases, the migrants remit money back to relatives in rural areas. However, there are rural areas in the world that have suffered because the brightest and most educated workers have migrated.

Governments have employed many approaches to the task of slowing down rural-to-urban migration. Some countries are restricting migration, implementing resettlement schemes, and providing services to smaller towns and cities. It appears, however, that unless the urban bias in economic policies is removed and economic development proceeds to the point where living conditions improve in rural areas, rural-to-urban migration will continue in many countries at a rate faster than is socially optimal.

SUMMARY

The current world population of more than 5.3 billion is growing at an annual rate of 1.7 percent, an extremely high rate by historical standards. The developing world is experiencing a population explosion caused by rapid decline in death rates due to improved health and nutrition. While birth rates have begun to decline due to higher incomes, family planning, education, and other factors, world population is likely to continue to grow for the next 160 years. Effective measures to control population growth should consider the economics of fertility and how different economic and social policies affect childbearing decisions. Rural-to-urban migration is proceeding at a rapid rate in many developing countries as migrants seek to achieve higher standards of living. Rapid urbanization has caused a strain on public services, pollution, and other problems.

IMPORTANT TERMS AND CONCEPTS

Birth rates and death rates	Family planning
Causes of fertility changes	Population density
Causes of rural-to-urban migration	Population distribution
Characteristics of migrants	Population growth
Consequences of rapid population growth	Rural-to-urban migration
	Urban political bias
Demographic transition	Why death rates decline

LOOKING AHEAD

This chapter concludes our overview of several dimensions of the world food-income-population problem. Hunger and development problems are both severe and complex. We move now to a set of three chapters which examine economic theories that have been used in attempts to identify the heart of the development process. We begin in the next chapter with a discussion of important factors related to production growth. Subsequent chapters then incorporate these factors into development theories.

QUESTIONS FOR DISCUSSION[17]

1 Has population increased at a fairly constant rate since prehistoric times?
2 What is the current world population and how fast is it growing? When will it stop growing?
3 At present growth rates, how long will it take to add 1 billion people to the world population?
4 Why is population increasing more rapidly today in LDCs than it did during early stages of development in Europe and the United States?
5 What are the major determinants of birth rates in LDCs?
6 What are the impacts of rapid population growth?
7 What policies can be used to help reduce population growth?
8 Are population growth rates more likely to increase or decrease over the next 15 years?
9 Which are the fastest and slowest growing countries in the world (in terms of population)?
10 What proportion of the world's population lives in Asia?
11 Why are we seeing rapid rural-to-urban migration in many developing countries?
12 What are the consequences of rapid rural-to-urban migration?
13 Describe the characteristics of the most common type of migrant.
14 How can high fertility be viewed as a consequence of poverty as well as a cause of it?
15 Describe the demographic transition that tends to occur as development takes place and why it occurs.

RECOMMENDED READINGS

Brown, Lester R. *State of the World 1987* (New York: W. W. Norton and Company, 1987), pp. 20–56 (and the most current issue of this annual publication).

Coale, Ansley J., "Recent Trends in Fertility in Less Developed Countries," *Science*, vol. 221, August 26, 1983, pp. 828–832.

Ghatak, Subrata, *An Introduction to Development Economics* (New York: Allen and Unwin, 1986), pp. 183–219.

Johnson, D. Gale, and Ronald D. Lee, *Population Growth and Economic Development: Issues and Evidence*, (Madison, Wis.: University of Wisconsin Press, 1987).

Mellor, John W., *Economics of Agricultural Development* (Ithaca, N.Y.: Cornell University Press, 1966), pp. 47–55.

Murdock, William W., *The Poverty of Nations* (Baltimore: Johns Hopkins University Press, 1980), pp. 15–92.

Murphy, Elaine M., *World Population Toward the Next Century*, Population Reference Bureau, New York, November 1981.

---

[17] Some of these questions are taken from Murphy, op. cit.

Notestein, Frank W., "Population: The Long View," in Theodore W. Schultz, (ed.), *Food for the World*, (Chicago: University of Chicago Press, 1945) (Notestein was the originator of the Demographic Transition Theory.)

Population Reference Bureau, *World Population Data Sheet*, Washington, D.C., 1991 (or the most current issue of this annual publication).

The Hunger Project, *Ending Hunger: An Idea Whose Time Has Come* (New York: Praeger Publications, 1985), pp. 22–56.

Todaro, Michael P., "A Model of Labor Migration and Urban Employment in Less Developed Countries," *American Economic Review*, vol. 59, 1969, pp. 138–148.

World Bank, *World Development Report 1984* (New York: Oxford University Press, 1984). (See also pp. 64–70 in the 1980 volume and the tables at the end of the latest volume of this annual report.)

PART TWO

DEVELOPMENT THEORIES AND THE ROLE OF AGRICULTURE

Rice in Peru. Agriculture is important in theories of economic development.

CHAPTER 5

SOURCES OF ECONOMIC GROWTH

Economic growth depends ultimately on the impact of productive resources and the efficiency with which they are used.

Maddison[1]

THIS CHAPTER

1 Presents the concept of a production function and illustrates how it can be used to describe the way in which factors of production are combined to produce goods
2 Identifies the six basic sources of economic growth
3 Describes the economic transformation, involving a relative decline in the size of agriculture compared to the nonagricultural sector, that occurs as economic development proceeds

RELATING INPUTS TO OUTPUTS

The quantity, quality, and organization of a country's basic production resources are central to its economic growth and development. We begin by examining how economists characterize the way resources are combined to produce outputs. Understanding this characterization is important for subsequent interpretation of economic development theories.

---

[1] Angus Maddison, *Economic Progress and Policy in Developing Countries* (New York: W. W. Norton and Co., 1970), p. 34.

Production Functions

Production requires resources or inputs such as labor, natural resources, and tools or other capital items. These inputs are often called factors of production. Production also requires that these factors be combined by a producing unit that can organize their use to obtain desired goods and services.

A description of the way in which factors of production are combined to produce goods and services is commonly called a *production function.* A production function describes, for a given technology, the different output levels that can be obtained from various combinations of inputs or factors of production.

If only one input is allowed to vary (say labor) while other inputs are held fixed (say land and capital), a mapping like that shown in Fig. 5-1 can be used to illustrate the effects of different levels of the input on output. The resulting production function is also referred to as a *total product curve.* If the levels of the fixed inputs change, the relationship between the variable input and output also will change. This change can be represented by a shift in the total product curve.

If two inputs are allowed to vary (say labor and capital) with all others (land) held fixed, the resulting production function can be illustrated as in Fig. 5-2. In this case, each curve (called an *isoquant*) represents a different level of output;

FIGURE 5-1
Total product produced with one variable factor.

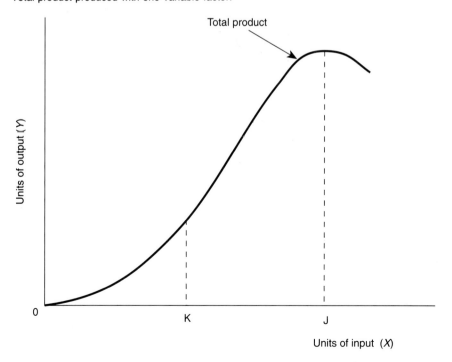

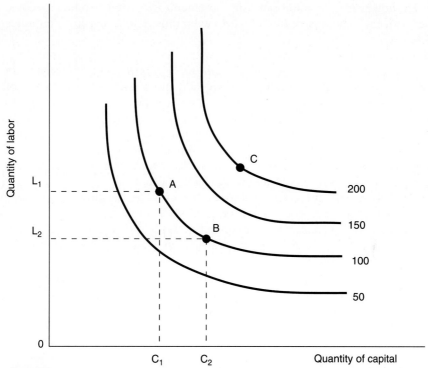

FIGURE 5-2
A production function with two variable inputs.

curves higher and to the right represent greater output levels than curves lower and to the left. For example, point C represents a higher output level (200 units) than points A or B (100 units).

The isoquant that represents 100 units of output illustrates that the same level of output can be produced with different combinations of labor and capital (combination A versus combination B). Thus, if a country has abundant labor and little capital it might produce using the combination of labor and capital represented by A. If it has abundant capital and little labor, it might produce at B. The isoquant through points A and B shows all the different combinations of labor and capital that can be used to produce 100 units of output. It also tells us how easy it is to substitute labor for capital in the production of that output. When isoquants are very curved, inputs are not easily substituted for each other. Straighter isoquants imply easier substitution.

Marginal Product

The production function in Fig. 5-1 shows how total product increases as units of labor are added, holding all other inputs constant. Up to K units of labor, each successive unit adds more to total product than did the previous units.

After K, however, the additions (or increments) to total product become smaller with each successive unit of labor, even though total product continues to increase.

The decrease in increments of output with successive units of input illustrates what economists call the *law of diminishing returns*. This law says: "In the production of any commodity, as we add more units of one factor of production to a fixed quantity of another factor (or factors), the additions to total product with each subsequent unit of the variable factor will eventually begin to diminish." What is diminishing is the marginal output gain or *marginal product* of the factor (labor in Fig. 5-1).[2] As discussed below, the law of diminishing returns has important implications for countries experiencing rapid population growth with a fixed natural resource base.

A marginal product curve can be derived from Fig. 5-1 to show the *changes* in total product for each successive unit of input. The marginal product curve corresponding to the production function in Fig. 5-1 is shown in Fig. 5-3. To the left of K, the slope of the total product curve is increasing (Fig. 5-1); thus the marginal product curve is rising (Fig. 5-3). To the right of K, the marginal product curve falls. If total product eventually ceases to rise at all as more labor is applied, the marginal product goes to zero; this is point J on the total and marginal product curves. Marginal productivity is very important because marginal productivity helps determine payments to factors of production, such as wages paid to labor. In addition, the marginal productivity of an input, together with prices of outputs and inputs, determines the demand for the input.

SOURCES OF ECONOMIC GROWTH[3]

Why are we interested in factors of production and production functions? We can see from Figs. 5-1 and 5-2 that one of the major ways that economic growth can occur is by an increase in the amounts of inputs used in production. While production functions usually refer to a particular type of output (say corn, or automobiles), one can think of an aggregate production function relating total inputs to total output or total national product. Additional inputs can move a country out its aggregate production function to higher isoquants and higher levels of output. Therefore, (1) *population growth* (which affects labor availability), (2) expanded use of *natural resources,* and (3) *capital accumulation* are three major elements in the development process. These sources of growth cause movement along a given production function.

---

[2] The marginal product of an input is equal to the slope of the total product curve, or $\Delta Y / \Delta X$, where Δ represents a small change. Therefore, anything affecting this slope changes the marginal product.

[3] See Richard T. Gill, *Economic Development, Past and Present* (Englewood Cliffs, N.J.: Prentice-Hall, 1973), Chap. 1, for a more detailed discussion of ideas presented in this section.

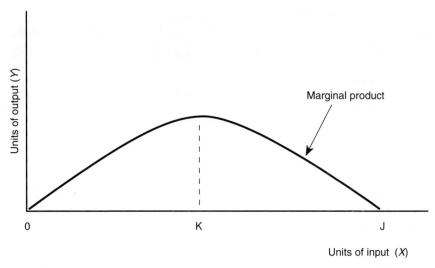

FIGURE 5-3
Marginal product curve derived from the total product curve in Fig. 5-1. Diminishing marginal productivity occurs after point K.

A second means of spurring economic growth is to change the way in which a country uses its factors of production, increasing the amount of output produced by these inputs. These output increases can result from better organization of production or from shifts in the production function. New technology can shift the total product curve upward so more output is produced per unit of inputs. There are three ways to get increased output per unit of input: (1) increases in scale or specialization, (2) increases in efficiency, and (3) technological progress. Movements along a given production function versus shifts in the function are illustrated in Box 5-1.

Let's examine each of the six sources of economic growth.

Population Growth

Increasing population means a greater supply of labor. Over the long span of history, population growth has undoubtedly been the major source of output growth in the world. People worked with primitive tools and more people meant more output, even if output per person remained roughly the same. Modern economic growth and development presupposes rising output *per capita*. But population growth is a mixed blessing because, while there are more productive hands, there are more mouths to feed.

What determines whether the net effect of population growth on a country's level of per capita output will be positive or negative? First, if population

BOX 5-1

SOURCES OF GROWTH AND THE PRODUCTION FUNCTION

Production functions characterize the relationship between inputs and outputs. Growth in output can come within the existing technology (production function) or by changing to a new technology (shifting the production function). The diagrams below illustrate this difference.

Increased inputs (population growth, more extensive use of natural resources, and capital accumulation) are shown as movement along the existing production function. More input $(X_1 \rightarrow X_2)$ leads to more output $(Y_1 \rightarrow Y_2)$. Improvements in technical efficiency also occur in the context of existing technology. At point A, inputs are used to produce less than the efficient level of output (point B). Thus, movement from a point underneath the production function to a point on the function produces more output with the same amount of input.

The right-hand diagram illustrates that technological progress implies a shift upward in the production function. Here, more output is achieved with the same amount of all inputs.

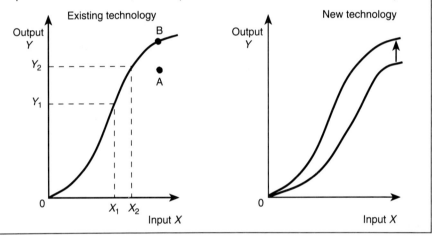

growth means an increasing number of children relative to adults, then the number of consumers is growing faster than the number of producers and the effect will be negative. If population growth results from extending the productive life of workers, the effect may be positive.

Second, if the country has ample resources in the location in which population growth occurs, the effect is more likely to be positive. A situation in which there is plenty of land or human-made capital is very different from one in which there is a dense population in a limited area and little capital. If labor is added to a fixed resource base, the smaller that base the sooner the law of diminishing returns takes effect. Diminishing returns to labor may become a serious problem if population grows very rapidly in a country with little increase in natural resources or capital.

Third, population growth can have the positive effect of providing a larger market for domestically produced goods. However, unless economic growth occurs due to other factors as well, these people may not have income to spend on the products.

Honduran children.

Natural Resources

Natural resources—including land and its associated soil, water, forests, and minerals—have played an important role in the economic development of most countries. The extension of the frontier in the United States brought more resources into production and helped create wealth. Similar expansions occurred in other countries. Will natural resources continue to be an important source of economic growth or will they be a limitation to future growth?

Some have argued that Earth is like a spaceship, that its natural resource capacity is finite. There is only so much land and, indeed, we see increasing problems with soil erosion, deforestation, and overgrazing. Increased combustion of fossil fuels releases carbon into the atmosphere and depletes a finite supply of these resources. Water resources are exploited to their fullest potential (or overexploited) in many places.

Others have suggested that technologies change and in essence create new resources. As petroleum becomes scarce, for example, we see an increase in the development of alternative energy sources. In this view, resource constraints will be limiting only if science and technology cease to advance, and there is no reason such advances should cease.

Which argument is correct? There is little question that land itself is limited and that the opening of new uninhabited fertile lands will be much less important to future economic growth in most countries than it has been historically. It is also clear that many resources, particularly forests and minerals, are being rapidly depleted in many countries and are thus becoming less available to stimulate growth than they once were.

However, a critical issue for many countries is not absolute physical exhaustion of resources, but rather the attainment of an orderly transition from one

A plow can be a sizable capital investment for a farmer in Thailand.

resource-using regime to another. There are adjustment costs to be borne during these transitions and, in many cases, costs of damages from pollution. Also the ownership distribution of natural resources is often unequal. These issues are discussed further in Chap. 12; the point here is that even if natural resources do not pose a serious constraint to economic growth in many countries, neither will they provide as great a source of growth as they did in the past.[4] There may be some exceptions to the latter statement with respect to certain mineral-rich countries.

Capital Accumulation

Capital may be defined as a country's stock of human-made contributions to production consisting of such items as buildings, factories, bridges, paved roads, dams, machinery, tools, equipment, and inventory of goods in stock. Capital, as we refer to it here, means human-made physical items and not money, stocks and bonds, etc. It refers to private physical goods but also public investments in physical infrastructure.

Capital accumulation is the process of adding to this stock of buildings, machinery, tools, bridges, etc. Another name for capital accumulation is investment. Capital investment is important because it can increase the amount of machinery and tools per worker, thereby increasing the output or marginal product per worker. A higher marginal product per worker usually leads to a higher income per worker.

[4] For additional discussion of the future role of natural resources in economic development, see Robert Repetto, *World Enough and Time* (New Haven, Conn.: Yale University Press, 1986).

Capital accumulation is also related to the possibilities of making changes in the scale of technology of production. Furthermore, the process of capital accumulation involves a choice between consumption today and investing for future economic growth. The choices of how much to invest and in what types of capital have important implications for the rate and direction of economic development. As will be argued throughout this text, investment should be guided along an appropriate path by signals (prices and policies) that reflect the true scarcity of resources.

Scale and Specialization

Increases in input levels (land, labor, and capital) accounted for much economic growth prior to the nineteenth century. However, evidence suggests that changes in the ways goods are produced have been the engine of modern economic growth for many if not most countries (again, with the exception of certain mineral-rich countries).

One type of organizational change involves increases in scale and specialization of production. Changes in scale and specialization are interrelated; as firms, for example, increase in size, they are often more able to achieve specialization. Division of labor can make workers more efficient as they become proficient at just a few tasks. Also, as markets expand, the possibilities of mass-producing goods enable firms to achieve efficiency gains in both production and marketing. Increased scale of production and specialization allows more output per unit of input and, hence, growth.

Efficiency Improvements

Another type of organizational change that can lead to economic growth is improved production efficiency. Improved efficiency simply means getting more for the same inputs by allocating them in a better way.

Efficiency can be divided into different types. First, *market efficiency* relates to the degree to which the market is competitive. Second, *technical efficiency* relates to the degree to which firms are producing on the production function as opposed to below or inside it. For the same amounts of inputs, some firms obtain higher output levels than others due to differences in management and effort, and perhaps to other reasons (see Box 5-1). Third, *price or allocative efficiency* relates to the degree to which firms, operating on their production functions, employ the correct amounts of inputs to equate their marginal revenue to their marginal cost of obtaining the last unit of output.

Market efficiency relates to the type of economic system and the degree of monopolistic power within it. A country or sector of an economy that has a relatively free market with many buyers and sellers so that prices are not influenced by relatively few economic agents, has greater market efficiency than a country or sector that has a few people controlling prices. Technical and

price efficiency relate to the ability of producers to effectively use the resources available to them, given a particular technology and a particular price
regime.

Two types of government activities can affect efficiency and thus contribute
directly to economic growth. Investment in infrastructure such as roads and
communications can improve market efficiency. At the same time, as new
markets become available for producers, education can enhance their ability to
manage their resources and respond to prices. Thus, more education improves
technical and price efficiency, though its impact on the latter is probably more
important.

Technological Progress

The organization of production can also be changed through technological
progress, that is, using different production technologies to get more output for
the same inputs. Technological progress can be thought of as a shift upwards in
the production function. For example, new higher-yielding seeds may cause
production to go up for the same quantity of all inputs. The quantity demanded
of individual inputs may increase or decrease following the introduction of a
new or improved technology (see Box 5-2).

If the same resources provide more output, the value of output per unit of
resources rises, and this rise can lead to increases in per capita income.
Resources can also be freed up to provide new types of goods. The phenomenon of technological progress is not new but has been occurring for many
years. What is new is the rapidity with which new technologies are being
developed.

Modern technological progress is the result of both *applied science* and *new
knowledge* in the basic sciences. Furthermore, improvements in *education*
have contributed to the generation of new technologies and have prepared
economic agents (e.g., farmers) to receive those technologies. Thus, education
is itself an important source of economic growth inextricably linked with
technological progress and, of course, with the quality of labor. Part of the
economic benefits of education is derived from improved quality of workers,
part from improved quality of management, and part from education's contribution to producing new or improved technologies.[5]

Relative Importance of Growth Elements

It is difficult to quantify the relative importance of the individual sources of
growth because of differences across countries and over time. Nevertheless,

---

[5] Education can of course have other benefits associated with the capacity to develop new
institutions and with many noneconomic factors.

BOX 5-2

TECHNOLOGICAL PROGRESS AND THE DEMAND FOR INPUTS

The relationship between inputs and outputs changes when new technologies are adopted. Therefore, different quantities of inputs may be employed following adoption of new technologies. Input demand is determined by three factors: the price of the output, the relative costs of inputs, and the production technology. These factors determine the value of marginal product of the input (VMP), or the output price times the marginal product of the input.

Depending on the nature of the shift of the production function, the marginal product of a specific input may change. If output and input prices remain unchanged, input demand will be determined by this change in marginal product. The marginal productivity grows following technical change in the left-hand graph below. Therefore, the demand for the input increases. Total productivity increases but marginal productivity declines in the right-hand graph. In this case, the input demand declines. Without examining how the marginal product of an input changes with technology, it is impossible to predict how demands for inputs change. This fact has important implications for development, as full employment of labor is usually a development goal. Technological change in agriculture can increase, decrease, or not affect the demand for labor, and hence employment.

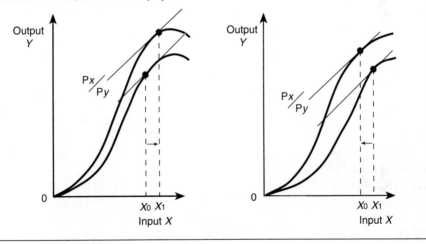

over the past 50 years, among the factors that have contributed to growth by moving out along the production function (population growth, natural resources, capital accumulation), capital accumulation has undoubtedly been the most important. This is particularly true for the agricultural sector when growth is placed on a per capita basis.

Among the other three sources of growth, evidence suggests that technological progress (together with improvements in education) has been the most important. There is little question that one of the keys to development is discovering how to facilitate technological progress. Another key is to properly choose the appropriate technologies to develop.

THE ECONOMIC TRANSFORMATION[6]

In the next chapter, we discuss how the various sources of growth have been incorporated into alternative theories of economic development. Some of these theories prescribe necessary interactions between agriculture and the non-agricultural sectors if development is to take place. Before examining development theories, you should recognize the *economic transformation* that occurs in all economies as economic growth proceeds. The economic transformation is an increase in the size of the nonagricultural sector relative to agriculture. As development occurs, agricultural employment declines relative to employment in the nonagricultural sector, the value of agricultural production as a proportion of total output falls, and expenditures on agricultural products constitute a smaller proportion of consumer budgets. Figures 5-4 and 5-5 show how agricultural output relative to total output, and agricultural employment relative to total employment shrink as GNP per capita grows. Let's consider why this transformation occurs, what affects its rate, and what its implications are for the role of agriculture in development.

Causes of the Economic Transformation

In low-income countries, labor productivity is low and people, out of necessity, spend a high proportion of their income on food. At low stages of development, high percentages of the total population in a country are employed in agriculture. Consequently, the economies of low-income countries are predomi-

An improved wheat variety is an example of an improved technology in Nepal.

[6] For additional discussion of many of these issues, see Mellor, op. cit., Chap. 2.

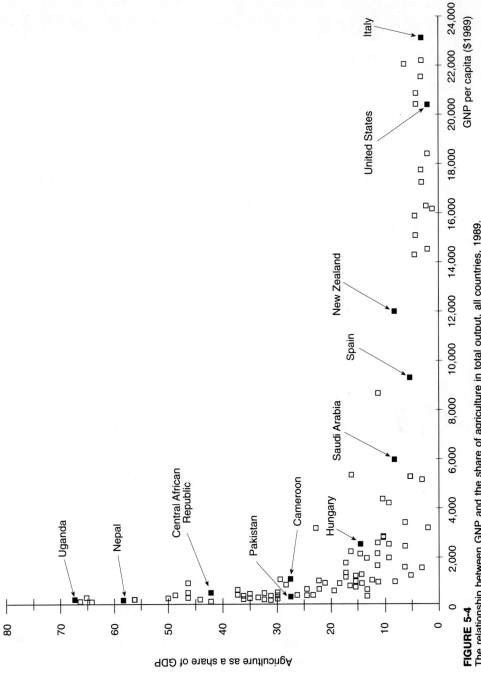

FIGURE 5-4
The relationship between GNP and the share of agriculture in total output, all countries, 1989.
The downward sloping relationship illustrates the structural transformation of the economy.

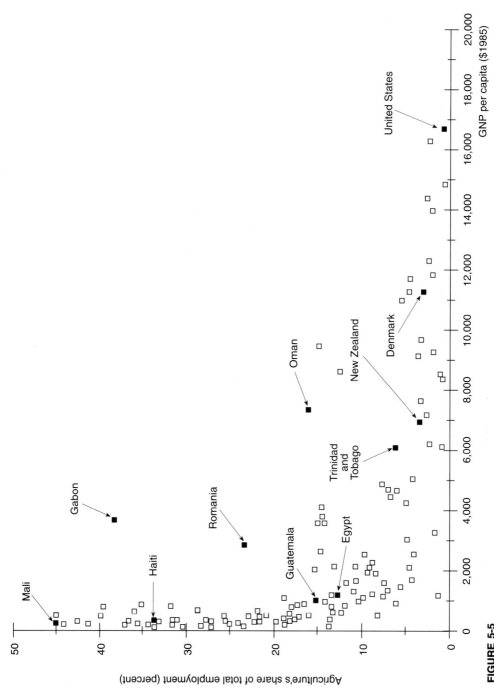

FIGURE 5-5
Agricultural employment as a share of total employment versus GNP/capita, 1985.

nantly agricultural. Many of the nonagricultural goods that are available are produced in farm households and in small villages.

As the productivity of labor and other factors increases, incomes rise and people begin to spend a larger proportion of their income on nonfood items.[7] This consumption change occurs primarily because the income elasticity of demand for food is less than 1.0 and tends to decline as income grows. Declining income elasticities mean that for each percentage increase in income, progressively lower proportions are spent on food. These changes in demands for agricultural and nonagricultural product mean that, as development proceeds, relatively more labor inputs and other resources are devoted to the nonagricultural sector.

The initial low productivity in agriculture often means a high potential for increasing the productivity in that sector, particularly as capital accumulation and technological progress occur. Technological progress shifts out the agricultural supply curve against a relatively inelastic demand curve, reducing total returns to resources in agriculture including labor. Consequently, the decline in agriculture's share of total employment is often greater than what would be suggested by income elasticities alone.

This tendency for a declining share of employment in agriculture creates an adjustment problem that is exacerbated by the fact that birth rates are usually higher in rural areas than in urban areas. Pressures are created for rural-to-urban migration, since most nonagricultural employment is found in urban areas.

The economic transformation also proceeds because the industrial sector finds it easier to specialize than does the agricultural sector. This difference in ease of specialization is due in part to the nature of factor proportions in agriculture, which dictates a higher proportion of land to be combined with labor than is the case in industry. Industry is able to geographically concentrate its labor more than is agriculture. Furthermore, industry in general experiences lower transportation costs than does agriculture. These factors mean that economies of size as a source of growth benefit industry more than agriculture. These and other factors reinforce the inevitable economic transformation.[8] The existence of the transformation does not imply that improving agricultural productivity is unimportant to overall development but merely that expansion of the nonagricultural sector is an inevitable companion of economic development.

Factors Influencing the Rate of Economic Transformation

The rate of economic transformation depends on the rate of growth of the total labor force, the proportion of the labor force initially in agriculture, and the rate

---

[7] See the discussion of Engel's law in Chap. 3.

[8] Several of these "other" factors include government policies at home and abroad that discriminate against the agricultural sectors in particular countries.

of growth of nonfarm job opportunities. The rate at which the proportion of the labor force in nonagricultural employment increases is given by the difference between the rates of growth of the total labor force and the labor force in nonagricultural employment. Thus, if the labor force grows 2 percent per year and nonfarm employment opportunities grow 4 percent per year, the proportion of the labor force in nonfarm employment grows 2 percent per year. As we will see in the next chapter, the rate of transformation depends on whether agriculture is the residual claimant of labor, or whether the nonfarm sector offers higher wages than agriculture does, and whether or not productivity in agriculture has increased sufficiently to allow workers to leave it without sacrificing food production (or food can be obtained cheaply enough on the international market).

With a given rate of population growth, the smaller the initial proportion of the labor force in the nonfarm sector, the greater must be the rate of growth of nonfarm employment to cause a decline in agricultural employment. Thus, even if the proportion of the labor force in the nonfarm sector is growing rapidly, countries in the early stages of development are unlikely to absorb into the nonfarm sector all the increased labor that accompanies population growth. To illustrate, if the total labor force is growing 3 percent per year and only 30 percent of the labor force is in the nonfarm sector, nonfarm employment would need to grow 10 percent (3 percent divided by 0.3) to absorb all the increased labor into the nonfarm sector.

Implications for Agriculture

The absolute and relative sizes of the agricultural labor force change as development proceeds. If the economic transformation process proceeds too slowly, average farm size and per capita income in agriculture will decline. Since land is essentially fixed, population growth, if it is largely confined to the agricultural sector, will create smaller farms. Because of diminishing returns, productivity and income will fall. The rate of transformation, especially in the early stages of development, depends on the rate of agricultural growth, so that food and capital can be transferred to the nonagricultural sector. This transfer is discussed in detail in the next chapter.

The existence of an economic transformation implies that labor will bear adjustment costs. These costs will be reduced if farmers and their children have received adequate formal education. Dispersion of certain types of industries into smaller cities and towns throughout the country also may ease the adjustment costs by limiting widespread migration to capital cities.

SUMMARY

Production functions describe, for a given technology, the different amounts of product that can be obtained from various combinations of factors of production. An isoquant shows different combinations of two inputs which can be used to produce the same level of output given a particular technology. The marginal product shows the change in output that occurs for a one-unit change in an input. The law of diminishing returns has important implications as population increases against a fixed land base.

There are six basic sources of economic growth. The first three (population growth, natural resources, and capital accumulation) can cause movements along a production function for a given technology. The last three (scale and specialization, efficiency improvements, and technological progress) represent changes in the organization or the way outputs are produced. Technological progress causes the production function to shift upward. Capital accumulation and technological progress have been the most important sources of economic growth in recent years for most countries.

The size of the agricultural sector relative to the nonagricultural sector declines as economic development proceeds. This economic transformation occurs, among other reasons, because the income elasticity of demand for food is less than 1.0 and because productivity increases in agriculture free up resources for nonagricultural production. The rate of growth of the total labor force, the proportion of the labor force initially in agriculture, and the rate of growth of nonfarm job opportunities determine the rate of economic transformation. This transformation has important implications for agriculture.

IMPORTANT TERMS AND CONCEPTS

Capital accumulation
Economic efficiency
Economic transformation
Education
Input demands
Isoquant
Law of diminishing returns
Marginal product

Natural resources
Nonfarm job opportunities
Population growth
Production function
Scale and specialization
Sources of economic growth
Technological progress
Total product curve

LOOKING AHEAD

The sources of growth discussed above relate to whole economies, to sectors within economies, and to individual firms (including farms). Various theories have been proposed to explain how the sources of growth have been or could be combined to transform economies from low to higher standards of living. We examine these theories in the next chapter. In subsequent chapters we consider how these growth factors can affect firms within the agricultural sector.

QUESTIONS FOR DISCUSSION

1 What is meant by the term 'factors of production'?
2 What are the three major factors of production and how do they relate to the major sources of economic growth?

3 What is the law of diminishing returns and what might be its significance in relation to population growth?

4 Will natural resource limitations be a serious restriction to future economic growth and/or growth in food production?

5 What is capital accumulation and why is it important to development?

6 Why are specialization, efficiency, and technological progress important to agricultural and economic development?

7 Why is an economic transformation inevitably associated with economic development?

8 What factors determine the rate at which an economy becomes transformed from an agricultural to a mixed economy with significant nonagricultural as well as agricultural activities?

9 If the total labor force were growing 2 percent per year and 50 percent of the labor force were in agriculture, how fast would nonagricultural employment need to expand in order to hold the number of people employed in agriculture constant? Why is this important?

10 What are the implications of the economic transformation for the agricultural sector?

RECOMMENDED READINGS

Anderson, Kym, "On Why Agriculture Declines with Economic Growth," *Agricultural Economics,* vol. 3, no. 1, October 1987, pp. 195–207.

Gill, Richard T, *Economic Development: Past and Present* (Englewood Cliffs, N.J.: Prentice-Hall, 1973), Chap. 1.

Johnston, Bruce, "Agriculture and Structural Transformation in Developing Countries: A Survey of Research," *Journal of Economic Literature,* vol. 8, no. 2, 1970, pp. 369–404.

Maddison, Angus, *Economic Progress and Policy in Developing Countries* (New York: W. W. Norton and Co., 1970), pp. 34–62.

Mellor, John W., *The Economics of Agricultural Development* (Ithaca, N.Y.: Cornell University Press, 1966), see Chap. 2.

Ridker, Ronald, and Elizabeth Cecelski, "Resources, Environment, and Population," *Population Bulletin,* vol. 34, no. 3, Population Reference Bureau, Washington, D.C., 1979, pp. 1–43.

CHAPTER 6

THEORIES OF ECONOMIC DEVELOPMENT

. . . theoretical views have changed in response to experience and deeper understanding of development processes, and it is instructive to gain some appreciation of the progress which development theory has made.

Colman and Nixson[1]

THIS CHAPTER

1 Reviews different theories of economic development suggested over time and the role these theories assign to agriculture
2 Describes how development theories and experience have led to alternative development strategies
3 Discusses how experience with alternative development strategies has led to a recognition of the need to tailor a strategy to the resource base and stage of development of a particular country. It considers the importance of agriculture, technological progress, employment-intensive strategies, and international markets to development

DEVELOPMENT THEORIES

In the previous chapter, we identified the major sources of economic growth and discussed the inevitable structural transformation that accompanies economic development. We turn now to theories that attempt to explain how these

[1] David Colman and Frederick Nixson, *Economics of Change in Less Developed Countries* (Oxford: Philip Alan, 1978), p. 19.

potential sources of growth can be integrated into a transformation process that produces sustained increases in living standards.

The search for a general theory of economic development has received economists' attention for two centuries. Some of the resulting theories have involved formal (graphical or mathematical) economic models. Others have provided descriptions of the stages or structural changes that countries tend to experience as development proceeds. Still others have identified international relationships that are hypothesized to stimulate or impede economic progress in less-developed countries. In the following sections, we examine the historical progression of these theories (emphasizing the more prescriptive and formal models) before considering their implications for development strategies.[2]

Classical Model

In the late eighteenth and early nineteenth centuries, *classical* economists such as Adam Smith, John Stuart Mill, Thomas Robert Malthus, and David Ricardo developed a theory of growth that relied heavily on three of the factors (population growth, natural resources, and capital accumulation) discussed in the last chapter. In its simplest form the theory proceeds as follows. There are two broad types of people: workers, whose only asset is their labor, and capitalists, who own land and capital. Given a certain amount of labor, just enough wages are paid to cover workers' subsistence. If a new invention or some other favorable event creates an increase in production, a surplus (i.e., the difference between the value of total production and total consumption or wages) is generated which is then accumulated by capitalists. Such accumulation increases the demand for labor, and, with given population, in the short run wages tend to rise. As wages exceed the level of subsistence, population grows, generating an increase in demand for food. But, if high quality land is essentially fixed, the rise in food demand is met by bringing lower-quality land into production. The price of food rises to cover the higher cost of production on lower-quality land. The effects of increased population (supply of labor) and higher-priced food drive the real wage, or the wage paid divided by food prices, back to the subsistence level, and the rate of population growth declines.

Thus, in the classical model, diminishing returns to increments of labor applied to a relatively fixed supply of high-quality land, and higher costs of production on lower-quality land, represent a constraint to growth so that living standards remain at subsistence levels. If technological progress occurs, the situation may change temporarily but not permanently.

---

[2] This section on development theories draws heavily on Yujiro Hayami and Vernon W. Ruttan, *Agricultural Development: An International Perspective* (Baltimore: Johns Hopkins University Press, 1985), Chap. 2. See also Richard T. Gill, *Economic Development: Past and Present* (Englewood Cliffs, N.J.: Prentice-Hall, 1973), Chap. 2; and Subrata Ghatak, *An Introduction to Development Economics* (London: Allen and Unwin, 1986), Chaps. 2 and 3 for additional discussion and interpretation.

History has shown that the classical model underestimates the role of technological progress. It also fails to consider factors that tend to lower birth rates as economic growth occurs. It oversimplifies the forces influencing wages (e.g., trade unions) and the complexity of the sharing or distribution objective found in many societies. Nevertheless, as we will see below, certain aspects of the classical model had a significant influence on subsequent theories of economic development.

Growth Stage Theories

A second approach to economic development theory has been to categorize the growth process into successive stages through which countries must pass as they develop. While the suggested sets of stages have been based on different principles, most growth stage theories have attempted to emphasize that economic development involves a structural (economic and/or social) transformation of a country. Some of the analyses of growth stages have been more descriptive than theoretical, but most have been designed with public policy implications in mind.

In the nineteenth century, Frederick List, a German economic historian, developed a set of stages based on shifts in occupational distribution. His five stages were savage, pastoralism, agriculture, agriculture and manufacturing, and agriculture-manufacturing-commerce. List believed that progress in agriculture was dependent on strong export demand or domestic industrial development. He felt the latter had the most potential as a source of agricultural and total economic growth. He called for *import substitution* policies to protect infant domestic industries so they could grow and replace what otherwise might be imported. This suggestion has appealed to many politicians and industrialists in developing countries but has been controversial among economists for reasons discussed below.

Another nineteenth-century German, Karl Marx, visualized five stages of development based on changes in technology, property rights, and ideology. His steps were primitive communism, ancient slavery, medieval feudalism, industrial capitalism, socialism, and communism. He felt that class struggles drive countries through these stages. One class possesses the land, capital, and authority over labor while the other possesses only labor. Class struggles occur because economic institutions allow the exploitation of labor. Prior to reaching the final stage, labor is never paid its full value. For example, if wages rise in the fourth stage (industrial capitalism), labor is replaced by machines, thereby creating a body of unemployed workers that brings wages back down. Because capitalists derive their profits from labor, more machines and fewer laborers mean lower profit rates. The pressure of lower profits leads to more exploitation, more unemployment, mass misery, and eventually revolution. Labor then gains control over all means of production under communism.

Marx's ideas have received the most attention in those developing countries where the economic division between the haves and have-nots is the sharpest.

Aside from ideological considerations, his writings are of contemporary interest because of the role he attached to technological progress in influencing economic institutions.[3] Marx also viewed economies of scale in both agriculture and industry as major sources of growth. He felt that small peasant farms should be eliminated and the peasants employed in industry.

The concept of stages of growth reemerged in the 1930s to 1950s when Alan Fisher and later Colin Clark developed a theory with three stages of growth. In Clark's formulation, agriculture is dominant in the first stage, manufacturing grows relative to agriculture in the second, and "tertiary" or service industries grow the fastest in the third stage. Economic growth is achieved by increases in output per worker in any sector and by transfer of labor from sectors with low output per worker to those with higher output per worker. Fisher linked the transition from stage to stage to advances in science and technology.

The final major growth stage theory was developed by W. W. Rostow during the 1950s. He identified five stages through which, in his view, all countries must pass: traditional society, the preconditions for takeoff, the takeoff, the drive to technological maturity, and the age of high mass consumption.

Rostow felt that deceleration, or a slowdown in the rate of growth in sectoral production, is the normal path for a sector, due to several factors on both the supply and demand sides. Achieving growth involves discovering how to offset that decline. He stressed capital accumulation and suggested that technology plays an important role in the emergence of leading sectors. Declining price and income elasticities of demand eventually dampen the growth rates of leading sectors, transforming them into declining sectors.

Rostow's ideas received little attention until the early 1960s, following the publication of his second book.[4] During the 1950s, economists and policymakers were more enamored with a growth model developed by economists Roy Harrod and Evsey Domar. The Harrod-Domar model stresses that the rate of growth of national income is related positively to the national savings rate and negatively to the nation's capital/output ratio. In other words, in order to grow, a country must save and invest, but the rate at which it grows for any given level of savings and investment depends on how productive that investment is, which in turn can be measured by the inverse of the capital/output ratio.

Unfortunately, while the Harrod-Domar model rightly identified capital accumulation as a potential source of growth, it neglected other important elements of the development process. It led policymakers in certain developing countries, such as India in the 1950s and 1960s, to place heavy reliance on capital-intensive industrial growth while the need for mobilizing labor and improving agriculture was neglected.

---

[3] Hayami and Ruttan, op. cit., p. 17.
[4] W. W. Rostow, *The Stages of Economic Growth* (Cambridge: Cambridge University Press, 1960).

Dual-Economy Models

A third set of development theories also emerged in the 1950s and 1960s called *dual-economy* (or two-sector) theories. Dualism theories attempt to explain why development may or may not proceed in a society characterized by two sectors, a large traditional sector and a smaller, more modern sector.

Sociological Dualism

One dual-economy theory, called *sociological dualism,* was developed by the Dutch economist J. H. Boeke to explain why the Dutch colonial period failed to induce economic development in Indonesia. Boeke argued that economic activity in the West and in Western enclaves in the East is motivated by economic needs, but economic activity in the East is motivated by social needs.[5] The implication is that it is useless to introduce new ideas, new institutions, and new technologies into Eastern societies. Sociological dualism provided a rationalization for emphasizing industrial development and ignoring agriculture.

Enclave Dualism

A second dual-economy theory, *enclave dualism,* was developed by Benjamin Higgins and Hla Myint.[6] Higgins and Myint attempted to explain why, in developing countries, small enclaves of modern society remain surrounded by a sea of traditional society. These developed enclaves are oriented toward extraction of primary commodities in mining and on plantations and exportation of those commodities to developed countries. The modern sector imports labor-saving technology from abroad. There is little development of the traditional sector, only exploitation of its resources. The implication is that unless developing countries explicitly focus their development efforts on the traditional sector, broad-based development will not occur.

Labor-Surplus Dual-Economy Models

Sociological and enclave dualism models have been called "static" because they attempt to explain what the situation is but not how to change it. "Dynamic" dual economy models that attempt to explain how less-developed

---

[5] See Hayami and Ruttan, op. cit., pp. 22–23; and J. H. Boeke, *Economics and Economic Policy of Dual Economies as Exemplified by Indonesia* (New York: Institute of Pacific Relations, 1953).

[6] Benjamin Higgins, "The Dualistic Theory of Underdeveloped Areas," *Economic Development and Cultural Change,* vol. 4, 1955-1956, pp. 99–115; Hla Myint, *The Economics of Developing Countries* (London: Hutchinson University Library, 1964), pp. 69–84. Higgins strongly disagreed with the validity of Boeke's theory.

countries might improve their economic situations were developed by several economists beginning with W. Arthur Lewis' *labor surplus* theory.[7]

A simplified version of the labor-surplus dual-economy model, as refined by several economists, can be illustrated using the total and marginal product curves shown in Fig. 6-1. This version of the model is designed to relate most closely to the situation in large labor-surplus but relatively natural-resource-poor countries in which domestic (as opposed to international) characteristics of the economy dominate. The model could potentially represent (albeit roughly) the situation in a country such as India or China.

The model borrows its two-sector representation from the static dual-economy models, includes the same three sources of growth (population growth, natural resources, and capital accumulation) as well as some of the dynamics found in the classical model, and then illustrates the potential for using surplus labor and technological progress in agriculture to achieve overall economic growth. The model assumes the existence of a large population in the traditional agricultural sector, for which the marginal product of labor is below the wage rate. There is disguised unemployment or underemployment in the sense that if the people who appear to be working were removed, production would not drop (in the Lewis and Fei and Ranis versions of the model) or would drop very little (in the Jorgenson version).[8] In other words, labor is applied in the agricultural sector into stage II (Jorgenson) or stage III (Lewis and Fei and Ranis) in the upper left-hand graph in Fig. 6-1; or to the right of N_3 or N_2 in the lower left-hand graph. The wage rate in agriculture (W) is assumed to approximate the average productivity of labor in that sector (Lewis and Fei and Ranis) or is determined in an intersectoral labor market (Jorgenson). Land is fixed. Wages in the modern industrial sector are assumed to be higher than in the agricultural sector in order to attract labor out of agriculture. Firms in the modern sector hire labor up to the point at which the marginal product of labor equals the wage rate. Initially this is the point P_0 in the lower right-hand graph of Fig. 6-1. Labor in industry is hired up to L_0 at the wage P.

The essence of the development process in this kind of economy is the transfer of labor from agriculture, where it adds nothing or little, to the industrial sector, where it creates a profit that can be used for further economic growth and development. In the lower right-hand graph in Fig. 6-1, total wages initially paid to labor in industry equal the area PP_0L_0O while profits equal the area qP_0P. This profit, or part of it, is reinvested in capital items such as equipment, machinery, and buildings—items that make labor more productive.

---

[7] See W. Arthur Lewis, "Economic Development with Unlimited Supplies of Labor," *Manchester School of Economics and Social Studies,* vol. 22, May 1954, pp. 139–191; John C. Fei and Gustav Ranis, *Development of the Labor Surplus Economy* (Homewood, Ill.: Irwin, 1964); Dale W. Jorgenson, "The Development of a Rural Economy," *Economic Journal,* vol. 71, June 1961, pp. 309–334; John C. Fei and Gustav Ranis, "Agriculture in Two Types of Open Economies," *Agriculture in Development Theory,* Lloyd G. Reynolds, (ed.), (New Haven, Conn.: Yale University Press, 1975), pp. 355–372.

[8] Lewis, op. cit.; Fei and Ranis, op. cit.; Jorgenson, op. cit.

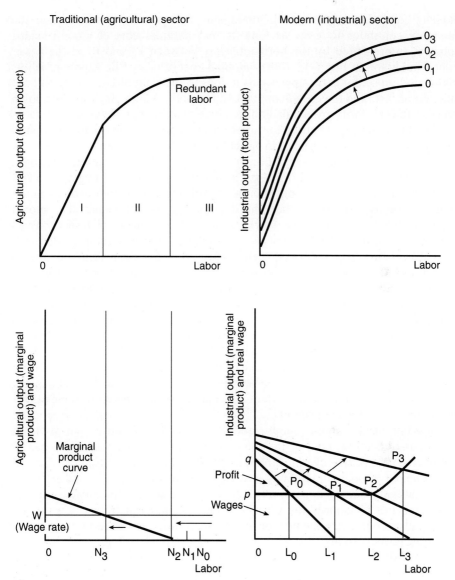

FIGURE 6-1
Graphical representation of labor-surplus dual-economy model.

This greater productivity shifts the total product produced by labor in industry upward (see the upper right-hand graph of Fig. 6-1) and the corresponding marginal product of labor (demand for labor) out to the right (see the lower right-hand graph of Fig. 6-1).

This shift in the marginal product of labor in industry creates more profits, which can be reinvested in capital to increase the marginal product of labor in industry (and the demand for labor) again. The process continues and the economy continues to grow as long as the marginal cost of labor remains constant (represented by the horizontal line between P_0 and P_2 in the lower right-hand graph in Fig. 6-1). If the marginal cost of labor (the supply of labor) to the modern sector turns upward, as it does to the right of L_2, profits will not increase as fast, and the growth in demand for labor by industry will slow down because fewer profits are available for reinvesting in capital items.

Why might the supply curve for labor turn up and the demand for labor stop shifting out? First, surplus labor in agriculture might be used up so industry has to offer higher wages to attract labor from agriculture. In fact, if fewer than N_2 workers are used in agriculture, then agricultural output will begin to fall as more labor is removed. Second, if population is increasing and incomes in the industrial sector are rising, then the demand for food is rising. The model assumes that as the first few workers move to the industrial sector from agriculture, there will be a savings or surplus of food in agriculture, which can be sent to them in the industrial sector. However, if there is little increase in agricultural production associated with continued increase in population and income, then agricultural prices will eventually rise relative to industrial prices. This rise, in turn, will raise the wage at which employers will be able to obtain workers from agriculture for industry, will cause the supply curve for labor to turn up, and will slow down or stop development.

The major implication of this model is that growth can only be self-sustaining if agriculture experiences productivity increases. A path of balanced growth of both the traditional and modern sectors is needed for sustained development. Jorgenson argues that these productivity increases in agriculture depend primarily on technological progress.

The labor-surplus dual-economy model, like any model, has weaknesses due to oversimplification. One of the most common criticisms is that the model ignores the cost of transferring labor and food to the industrial sector when, in fact, transportation and marketing costs can be substantial. A second criticism is that, although many do, not all developing economies have excess labor. Third, the model ignores the possibility of international trade. Fourth, the model fails to recognize the cost of resources used in conducting research and educating farmers to produce more and facilitate adoption of new technologies.

Despite these limitations, the dual-economy model described above does provide useful insights into both the role of agriculture and the need for improving agricultural productivity in many countries if development is to occur and be sustained. Subsequent studies have removed some of the limitations from the models just described.[9] A particularly useful contribution was the extension of the dual-economy model to an open-economy (i.e., allowing

[9] See Allen C. Kelley, Jeffrey G. Williamson, and Russell J. Cheetham, *Dualistic Development: Theory and History* (Chicago: University of Chicago Press, 1972); John C. Fei and Gustav Ranis, "A Model of Growth and Employment in the Open Dualistic Economy: The Cases of Korea and Taiwan," *Journal of Development Studies* vol. 11, January 1975, pp. 32–63; Avinash Dixit, "Growth Patterns in a Dual Economy," *Oxford Economic Papers,* vol. 22, July 1970, p. 233.

international trade) situation. For example, Fei and Ranis adopted the dual-economy model to labor-surplus but natural-resource-poor countries (such as Taiwan and Korea) and to natural-resource-rich countries (such as much of Latin America, Thailand, Malaysia, and the Philippines).[10] They point out that natural-resource-poor but open economies eventually reach a point at which labor-intensive industrial exports replace traditional agricultural exports and the countries switch from being net exporters to net importers of agricultural commodities. On the other hand, countries with more abundant natural resources may continue to export agricultural products from the more-developed portions of the agricultural sector, using the foreign exchange earnings to develop the domestic nonagricultural sector. That sector can then produce goods consumed domestically that substitute for imports. These countries may move beyond this type of growth in the long run, but not for several years.

Dependency Theories

In the 1950s and 1960s, yet another perspective or set of development theories emerged, which focused on forces in the international economic system that impede economic development. The most descriptive term for this set of theories is the *dependency view*.[11] This theory in its broadest sense is a type of dual-economy theory of the world economy with the developed countries (and modern enclaves in less-developed countries) forming the modern sector or *center* and the less-developed countries and regions forming the traditional sector or *periphery*.

The dependency view has many branches (see Box 6-1), but its distinguishing feature is that because the center has greater economic power than the periphery, it is able to develop *at the expense of the periphery*. The lack of development in less-developed countries is a product of the same forces that had led to development in the more-developed countries. As less-developed countries become more integrated into the world economy, they open themselves up to increased exploitation by the developed countries. Increased integration of the rural traditional sector into the market increases poverty in that sector.

---

[10] John C. Fei and Gustav Ranis, "A Model of Growth and Employment in the Open Dualistic Economy: The Cases of South Korea and Taiwan," op. cit.; John C. Fei and Gustav Ranis, "Agriculture in Two Types of Open Economies," *Agriculture in Development Theory,* op. cit.

[11] Yujiro Hayami and Vernon W. Ruttan, *Agricultural Development: An International Perspective,* argue that the dependency view can be thought of as incorporating a range of perspectives including the unequal exchange concepts of the Latin America structuralist school led by Raúl Prebish, *The Economic Development of Latin America: Toward a Dynamic Development Policy for Latin America,* United Nations, New York, 1963; the Marxist underdevelopment perspective led by Paul A. Baran, *The Political Economy of Growth* (New York: Monthly Review Press, 1957); Andre Gunder Frank, "The Development of Underdevelopment," *Monthly Review,* vol. 18, September 1966, pp. 17–31; and Theotonio Dos Santos, "The Structure of Dependence," *American Economic Review,* vol. 60, 1970, pp. 231–236; as well as the subsequent agrarian political economy perspective of Alain de Janvry, *The Agrarian Question and Reformism in Latin America* (Baltimore: Johns Hopkins University Press, 1981).

BOX 6-1

THE EVOLUTION OF THEORIES OF UNEQUAL DEVELOPMENT

One approach to dependency rejects the possibility of capitalist development, basing this rejection on neo-Marxist theories of unequal development. Marx devoted little attention to economic development, yet his description of the expansionist drive of capitalism led to the prediction that similar patterns of growth would emerge throughout the world. Subsequent Marxist writers advanced different versions of this thesis, arguing that declining rates of profit in the developed world (and other factors) encouraged flows of capital into backward regions. Unequal development referred to this *faster* rate of growth in the periphery accompanying this expansion.

In 1928, much of this Marxist theory was reversed; Kuusinen hypothesized that capitalist development was detrimental to the periphery, and that through imperialism, the capitalist center was developing at the expense of the periphery. Some said that this state of affairs was caused by an alliance between international capitalists and feudal oligarchies. Others, particularly Baran and Sweezy, attributed the negative impacts of capitalist expansion to the existence of monopoly capital in the center which allowed it to extract a surplus from the periphery.

This central thesis of the incompatibility of capitalist expansion into the periphery with economic development led to the conclusion by Frank and others that development can only be achieved by breaking with the capitalist economy. Thus, the hypothesis of underdevelopment was used, especially in Latin America, as a rationalization for a socialist revolution, an idea that received widespread support following the Cuban Revolution. Other non-Marxist versions of dependency theory led to different conclusions, such as a need to quickly industrialize using government interventions to correct international market imperfections. These dependency theories promote "forced industrialization" within the capitalist system. Unequal development, a radical version of the very broad dependency school, holds that the only possible path of development is outside the capitalist system.

Sources: Alain de Janvry, *The Agrarian Question and Reformism in Latin America* (Baltimore: Johns Hopkins University Press, 1981), especially pp. 9–23; Gabriel Palma, "Dependency: A Formal Theory of Underdevelopment of a Methodology for the Analysis of Concrete Situations of Underdevelopment?" *World Development,* vol. 6, 1978, pp. 881–924.

The policy implication of the dependency view is that less-developed countries and regions should attempt to become self-sufficient unless the international economic system is reformed and unless domestic political changes, perhaps caused by a revolution, lead to increased equity within countries.

Dependency theories have been attacked by some for lacking rigor and formality in the analyses presented. Most would agree that many colonies suffered economically as a result of economic dependence on foreign powers, which directed production toward external rather than domestic needs. Several countries have also suffered the effects of foreign and domestic monopoly power in particular industries. However, several less-developed countries, heavily dependent on international markets (such as South Korea, Taiwan, and Brazil), have achieved substantial growth over time. There is little question that dependency has and does exist. Empirical evidence seems to suggest, however, that growth rates have been higher over the past 30 years in those countries that encouraged exports and foreign investment by opening their economies to the international market. It appears that the solution to the international dependency problem is not withdrawal from the economic system, but more selective dealings with developed countries, including policies to thwart monopolistic power of foreign investors.

More Recent Development Thinking

In the 1950s and 1960s, economists had moved from whole-economy, one-sector development models to two-sector models. In the 1970s, economists devoted increased attention to firm-level and people-level issues associated with development. Spurred in part by advances in agricultural productivity as a result of new crop varieties and other technologies, economists explored the sources and processes of technical and institutional innovations in agriculture. Persistent poverty even in rapidly growing countries led to increased attention to distributional issues, particularly in rural areas. The fact that most of the rapidly growing LDCs were pursuing outward- or export-oriented strategies focused attention on the role of international markets. The fact that much of Africa experienced declining growth rates during the 1970s while other regions grew, highlighted the need to consider regional differences.

While no general theory of development emerged in the 1970s, there was some reason for optimism in many developing countries as they entered the 1980s. During the 1970s, partly fueled by increasing commodity prices, economic growth was strong in many regions of the developing world. However, worldwide recession in the early 80s, increased foreign debt problems in many countries, and outright famine in several Sub-Saharan African countries brought home the fact that sustained development would continue to be difficult, even for those countries that had begun to experience improved economic conditions.

Rather than a general theory of development, what has emerged is a set of alternative strategies based on earlier theories and experience and the recognition that the developing world is far from homogeneous. Debates have begun to center around appropriate strategies for particular countries given their stage of growth, resource base, asset-ownership patterns, and institutional structures. In the rest of this chapter we examine more closely several components of these strategies and the insights into their merits provided by previous development experience.

FROM THEORY TO ALTERNATIVE STRATEGIES

The concept of a *development strategy* implies a long-term road map that encompasses a series of fundamental decisions with respect to sector emphasis (agriculture versus industry), factor use (capital-led versus employment-led growth), international market orientation (inward versus outward), concern for growth versus distribution, and the roles of the private versus the public sector.

Many of these decisions present sharply conflicting choices that individual countries must make when designing their particular development strategies. The appropriate path for a particular country depends on its starting characteristics and global economic conditions.

Industry versus Agriculture

The question of whether to channel public and private investments into the agricultural or industrial sectors has been asked by policymakers for many decades. Several economists in the 1950s and 1960s advocated strategies of *balanced* growth across sectors in the economy, sometimes calling for a *big push* on all sectors at once.[12] Those who argued for *unbalanced* growth often implied the need for an industrial emphasis.[13] Others stressed the importance of agriculture in overall economic development.[14] History has shown the naivete of prejudging the need for balanced growth and a big push (which implies that gradualism is not likely to lead to development). Investment opportunities at any point in time in a particular country are usually unequal across sectors, and countries have experienced growth without a big push on all sectors at once. However, it is equally naive to assume that growth must be unbalanced or stress the industrial sector.

In most countries, agriculture is initially the dominant sector containing most of the resources, therefore it cannot be ignored. However, in others, primary oil and mineral products are major resources to be exploited. As growth occurs, one sector may decline and another take the lead. Many countries find it most fruitful to invest in productivity-enhancing agricultural technologies in the early and middle stages of development because that is where the people and natural resources are concentrated, and food is a major item in the consumer budget. Once development reaches a certain point, the relative importance of agriculture declines, as it has in countries like Taiwan and South Korea over the past few years.

Capital- versus Employment-Led Growth

The importance of capital accumulation to development and the implicit need to increase capital-intensity if labor productivity is to increase, should not be confused with the need to allocate capital broadly in the economy. Scarce capital must be allocated to increase the productivity of the *bulk of the labor force* if real wages are to increase. If capital is concentrated in a few large-scale

---

[12] Ragnar Nurske, *Problems of Capital Formation in Underdeveloped Countries* (New York: Oxford University press, 1953); Paul Rodenstein-Roden, "Notes on the Theory of the Big Push," in Howard S. Ellis, (ed.), *Economic Development for Latin America* (London: MacMillan, 1951).

[13] Albert O. Hirschman, *The Strategy of Economic Development* (New Haven: Yale University Press, 1958).

[14] Bruce F. Johnston and John W. Mellor, "The Role of Agriculture in Economic Development," *American Economic Review*, vol. 51, September 1961, pp. 566–593.

industries, particularly if the products of the industry could have been imported, then less employment, lower labor productivity, and slower overall growth will be achieved than is potentially possible. While some intermediate products such as electric power can only be produced in relatively large-scale capital-intensive industries, other products manufactured by large-scale capital-intensive industries such as fertilizer and steel can be imported. Capital can then be dispersed more broadly in the industrial sector and also used to provide basic infrastructure such as roads, schools, hospitals, etc., as well as manufactured goods for mass domestic consumption.

Several countries have suffered the consequences of poor capital allocation decisions. Mellor points to India as a classic example.[15] The surpluses generated through agricultural productivity increases have not been utilized effectively to create sufficient employment in industry. Consequently, India has experienced the unhappy situation of producing food surpluses for the country as a whole (and even exporting food) while masses of underemployed people suffer from malnutrition. Many other countries would benefit from a more employment-led strategy to development.[16]

Inward- versus Outward-Led Growth

A persistent debate in the development literature has centered around the merits of an inward (import-substitution, self-sufficiency) oriented strategy versus an outward (international trade, export promotion) oriented strategy.[17] Some have argued that developing countries are hurt by trade because they produce mainly primary products (agricultural and mineral) for which prices decline over time relative to the manufactured products they import. This deterioration in the *terms of trade* is believed to be generated by (1) low price and income elasticities of demand for primary products compared to manufactured products, (2) slow productivity growth in primary product production, and (3) monopolistic elements in the production of products imported by developing countries while primary products are produced competitively. In addition, the colonial heritage in several developing countries included the export of certain primary products to developed countries with the profits

[15] John W. Mellor, *The New Economics of Growth* (Ithaca, N.Y.: Cornell University Press, 1976).

[16] John W. Mellor, "Agriculture on the Road to Industrialization," in John P. Lewis and Valeriana Kallab, (eds.), *Development Strategies Reconsidered,* (New Brunswick, N.J.: Transaction Books, 1986).

[17] For views in favor of an inward strategy see Raúl Prebish, *Towards A New Trade Policy for Development* (New York: United Nations, 1964); Ragnar Nurske, *Equilibrium and Growth in the World Economy* (Cambridge, Mass.: Harvard University Press, 1962); and Gary Fields, "Employment Income Distribution and Economic Growth," *Economic Journal,* vol. 94, March 1987, pp. 74–83. For views in favor of an outward strategy, see Anne O. Krueger, *Trade and Employment in Developing Countries: Synthesis and Conclusions* (Chicago: University of Chicago Press, 1982); and Jagdish N. Bhagwati, "Rethinking Trade Strategy," *Development Strategies Reconsidered,* John P. Lewis and Valeriana Kallab, (eds.), (New Brunswick, N.J.: Transaction Books, 1986).

Bananas have been a controversial export for several developing countries.

going to foreign companies or to small groups of elites in the developing countries. Recent proponents of an inward strategy have also argued that countries following an inward-oriented path suffer less from debt crises, protectionist pressures in the developed countries, and the adverse effects of high wages due to labor market imperfections.

The impact of inward-directed strategies depends largely on the policies used to implement the strategy. Policies such as overvalued exchange rates, import restrictions, and explicit export taxes, which discourage exports and stimulate substitution of domestically produced goods for imports, have generally been shown to be counterproductive. They lead to distortions in resource prices, create monopoly profits, high government budget deficits and, usually, inflationary pressures. On the other hand, policies that support production of foods for internal consumption via research, infrastructure, and other public investments can be called inward-oriented, yet are not associated with some of the distortions caused by measures typically used to promote import-substitution.

Proponents of outward strategies argue that by removing the bias against exports, countries can achieve significant economic benefits from specialization and comparative advantage, from the import of products manufactured by highly capital-intensive industries abroad, and from the stimulus to employment provided by reduced pressures to concentrate capital and higher wages in a limited number of highly capital-intensive industries.[18] Economies of scale

[18] The concept of comparative advantage is discussed in detail later in this book, but it basically means that a country will maximize its economic gains from production if it concentrates on what it produces best relative to other goods and countries and then trades for those goods it produces less well.

can be achieved due to enlargement of the effective market size. Some countries that have been successful at promoting export-led growth have, in fact, also relied on government interventions in exporting industries.

There are theoretical arguments that support either position. However, over the past 30 years, empirical evidence seems to weigh in favor of an outward-looking strategy which *biases the economy neither for nor against exports.*[19] There is evidence that policies often used to create an inward-looking strategy can lead to inefficiency. The economic efficiencies sacrificed in attempts to insulate a country from world market forces can be significant. Open markets expose a country to the effects of protectionist policies and interest rate fluctuations abroad. However they also offer insurance against risks originating at home.

Growth versus Equity

The persistence of abject poverty even in countries experiencing rapid rates of economic growth has spurred a debate over the appropriate focus of development efforts. Since, by our earlier definition (and value judgment), there is no real development unless standards of living are raised for the entire population, most of us would accept the notion that removal of abject poverty is the highest goal of economic development.[20]

While there is little disagreement that abject poverty should be removed, there are several competing ideas on how to do it. Essentially three general approaches have been suggested, sometimes in combination. The first is to make direct transfer payments (money, goods, services) from the more well-to-do to the poor. The second is for the country to concentrate entirely on growth as a goal, no matter who receives the income. The hope is that part of the benefits will trickle down to the poor. The third approach is to direct specific efforts toward raising the productivity of the poorest segments of society during the growth process.

Direct transfer payments are difficult for developing countries to afford unless obtained as grants from international sources. The most important role of direct transfers can occur (1) during short-run weather-induced famines or other emergency situations and (2) among the perpetually disadvantaged elderly, orphaned, and handicapped.

---

[19] Several detailed statistical analyses of the relationship between outward-looking strategies and economic growth have been conducted. For example, a study by Rata Ram, "Exports and Economic Growth in Developing Countries: Evidence from Time Series and Cross-Section Data," *Economic Development and Cultural Change,* vol. 36, October 1987, pp. 51–72 found that for a sample of 88 developing countries, the relationship between exports and growth was positive for more than 80 percent of the countries.

[20] Abject poverty can be defined in various ways, but certainly the World Bank's suggestion of an annual per capita income of U.S. $50 in 1960 purchasing power can be accepted as a minimum definition (almost one billion people live below that level). See Irma Adelman, "A Poverty-Focused Approach to Development Policy," in John P. Lewis and Valeriana Kallab, (eds.), *Development Strategies Reconsidered* (New Brunswick, N.J.: Transactions Books, 1986).

The majority of the poor, however, are the unemployed and underemployed rural landless. Even unskilled urban workers are usually better off than the rural landless. The landless live close to the margin and may fall below it during bad crop years. Therefore the important question is whether the benefits of growth will trickle down to the poor or whether development efforts must be directed at the poor.

There is little question that rapid growth means that some benefits are captured by the poor. However, the income distribution usually tends to worsen (become more unequal) during the initial stages of growth unless specific efforts are directed toward incorporating the poor into productive development activities. Furthermore, asset ownership, particularly land, and education affect the distribution of development benefits. Countries that begin with a more equal distribution of assets tend to experience growth with equity more than others. And, growth itself can be affected by the wider spread of assets, institutional changes, and employment-creating activities.

The mere widening of the income distribution as development occurs is not as much a concern as what happens to income *levels* of the poor. However, neither the level nor the distribution of income will be improved for the poor in most countries unless they have improved access to assets such as land and to education which can make their primary asset, labor, more productive during the growth process. Development strategies that increase employment opportunities and promote the supply of wage goods (mainly food) will have the best chances for reducing poverty under virtually all circumstances.

Private versus Public

The appropriate role for the public sector in economic development has been sharply debated, particularly over the past decade. Often, the debate has been influenced by philosophical or political differences of opinion which go beyond economics. However, even when there is agreement on the appropriate strategy to achieve growth and on the distribution of development benefits, there is room for debate over the most efficient mix of public and private resources to maximize growth and achieve that distribution.

Most agree that preserving economic incentives for individuals is vital to achieving economic development. Activities by the public sector can sometimes distort those incentives. Public activities can also be costly because of leakages in the tax and subsidy system due to both administrative costs and corruption.

However, public activities are essential for many purposes if public welfare is to be maximized. Some vitally important goods and services are *public goods* in the sense that the private sector would have insufficient incentive to produce them if the public sector did not. Public goods tend to be those with *free rider* problems. By this we mean that if one firm produces that good or service, many others receive the benefits without having to pay the cost. Also, public involvement is often required to ensure health and safety of the population.

As economies grow and become more complex, an individual, a group of people, or a country can gain unfair advantage at the expense of others if the public sector is not involved to design and enforce new institutional arrangements or property rights. In primitive economies, information gathering, negotiating, supervising, and enforcing contracts are performed on a very personal basis. As countries develop, the costs associated with these activities grow. Substitute institutional arrangements are needed to lower those *transactions costs*.[21] Otherwise, even if new technologies are available, growth is hindered by an inefficient and often inequitable institutional structure.

Philosophical and political opinions of the appropriate roles of the public and private sectors often swing from one period of time (decade) to another with little consideration of the likely implications for economic development. The 1980s saw a swing toward increased interest in privatizing development efforts while the 1960s and 1970s saw greater interest in the role of the public sector. While this is a broad generalization, it appears that in neither case were the underlying economic implications adequately assessed, rather the policies tended to be guided by political ideologies.

LESSONS FROM DEVELOPMENT THEORY AND EXPERIENCE

Experience with alternative development theories and strategies has led to a recognition of the need to tailor the development strategy to the resource base, stage of development, and institutional setting of the particular country. In addition, certain lessons with respect to the importance of agriculture, asset ownership, education, technological and institutional change, employment, and international markets have been learned.

Resource Mix, Institutional Setting, and Stage of Development All Matter

The particular resource mix of a country is extremely important to the choice of a development strategy. Maximum use of abundant resources (in some cases labor, in others minerals, in others land, etc.) must be achieved while new technologies and institutional improvements should be designed to save scarce resources. The fact that resources can vary by region within a country may require development strategies to differ spatially within nations.

Size, asset ownership patterns, institutional structures, and sociopolitical conditions must be considered as well. For example, highly skewed asset distributions affect both incentives for savings and investment and the distribution of economic growth. Asset distribution patterns need to be changed in several countries if development is to proceed. However, these changes must be accompanied by improved institutional arrangements to lower the transac-

---

[21] See Douglas North, "Institutions, Transactions Costs, and Economic Growth," *Economic Inquiry,* vol. 25, 1987, pp. 415–428.

tions costs that encouraged those patterns to develop in the first place. Institutional changes that enhance information flows are particularly important.

It is clear that countries do pass through different stages of development, although those stages may not be the particular ones identified previously in the literature. While it is unlikely that all countries experience exactly the same stages, it is clear that agriculture does represent a high proportion of national income and employment during the very early stages of development and that manufacturing and service sectors gradually increase in importance as development occurs.

Stages occur within sectors as well, with different sources of growth taking the lead over time. The implication is that there is no single development strategy that will serve for all developing countries, even for those with the same resource base, at a point in time or across regions.

Agriculture Matters

For most developing countries, agricultural development matters for overall economic development. Prior to the 1960s, development strategies emphasized capital-intensive industrial growth. For a period in the 1970s, concern that agricultural development would skew income away from small-scale farmers and tenants led to calls for integrated rural development projects. Unfortunately, these projects tended to be complex, often lacked integration with national support structures, frequently diverted personnel and other resources away from broad-based agricultural development, and ignored the need for more fundamental institutional changes.[22]

It is now clear that agricultural development, spurred in part by education, the adoption of new technologies, and institutional improvements, can help stimulate broad-based economic development. The agricultural sector provides food, it supplies labor for industry, it directly and indirectly generates capital, including foreign exchange, and it provides a market for nonagricultural-goods-based services. Agricultural development can potentially provide a direct increase in rural welfare.

Employment Matters

When agricultural development has not been associated with concurrent concern for employment, this development has stimulated less overall economic development than would be possible. Agricultural development has sometimes led to reduced food imports and growing food stocks even though people remain hungry. Mellor's call for an employment-oriented strategy which stresses research, education, roads, rural electricity, and, most important, low-

---

[22] The projects correctly identified the need to develop local institutions, but illustrated the dangers of spreading scarce public resources too thin on isolated projects which lack a national research base.

capital intensity industries makes a lot of sense. A rural sector with growing income can provide a large domestic market for locally produced non-agricultural goods and services.[23]

International Market Matters

International markets for goods and capital can have a major influence (at times good, at times bad) on development. These markets provide the potential for LDCs to exploit comparative advantage and specialization in production, and they allow for international transfers of capital. The development performance of several countries was positively influenced by expanding exports and capital inflows in the 1960s and 1970s and negatively influenced by weak export markets and massive foreign debts in the 1980s.

It appears that many countries that experienced severe debt problems during the 1980s, still benefitted in net from their outward orientation. One reason is that they will never repay part of the debt. Another is that the outward orientation placed pressure on some of those countries to use resources in a manner that approximated their opportunity costs. It is also clear, however, that the belt tightening undertaken by many countries to repay debts has caused severe economic stress among the poor.

The importance of international markets to developing countries highlights the significance of domestic and trade policies of developed countries in influencing LDC growth rates. High interest rate and protectionist policies in developed countries can have severe negative effects on developing countries.

SUMMARY

The classical model of economic growth stressed the importance of diminishing returns to labor as a constraint to growth. Growth-stage theories attempted to categorize the growth process into successive stages through which all countries must pass as they developed. Dual-economy models attempted to explain why development might or might not proceed in a society characterized by a large traditional sector and a smaller more modern sector. Dual-economy models provided useful insights into both the role of agriculture and the need for improving agricultural productivity. Dependency theorists felt that increased exploitation of developing countries occurred as they become more integrated into world markets.

Alternative development strategies have emerged over the past 20 years. Many economists now argue for the need to incorporate agriculture into development plans, to focus on employment-intensive growth, to open up the economy to international markets, to redistribute assets when asset ownership is highly skewed, and to raise the productivity of the poorest segment of society. The appropriate roles of both public and private sectors must be identified. The

---

[23] Mellor, op. cit.

logical development strategy for a particular country depends on the resource mix, stage of development, and institutional structure of the country. New institutional arrangements will have to be designed in a number of countries to enhance information flows and lower the transactions costs that accompany development but cause it to become self-limiting.

IMPORTANT TERMS AND CONCEPTS

Capital-led growth	Income distribution
Center and periphery	Institutional arrangements
Classical model	Integrated rural development
Comparative advantage	Labor-surplus dual-economy
Dependency theory	Open versus closed economy
Employment-led growth	Public good
Enclave dualism	Resource mix
Export-led growth	Sociological dualism
Growth stage theory	Stage of development
Growth versus equity	Terms of trade
Harrod-Domar model	Transactions costs
Import substitution	

LOOKING AHEAD

In this chapter, the roles of agriculture in economic development were mentioned along with the need for particular countries to tailor their development strategies to their resource bases and stages of development. In the next chapter, we examine in detail the several roles that agriculture can play in countries with different resource bases. We consider how those roles differ for countries at different stages of development and how they change as an individual country moves through various stages.

QUESTIONS FOR DISCUSSION

1 What is the major factor which is hypothesized to constrain economic growth in the classical model?
2 Distinguish among the major growth-stage theories of development. Why are they or are they not useful development theories?
3 Distinguish between sociological and enclave dualism. Why are these dual economy models called "static?"
4 What are the major features of the labor-surplus dual-economy model and what are its primary weaknesses?
5 Why might the wage rate eventually increase in the industrial sector in the labor-surplus dual-economy model?
6 What implications does technological change in the agricultural sector have in the labor-surplus dual-economy model?

7 What is the distinguishing feature of dependency theories? What are the policy implications of dependency theories? Why have dependency theories been criticized?

8 Why is agricultural development important in most developing countries?

9 What is employment-led growth and why is employment important to development?

10 What are the arguments for and against inward- versus outward-oriented development strategies?

11 What are the three general approaches that have been suggested for alleviating abject poverty?

12 Why might both the private and public sectors have important roles to play in development?

13 List several lessons from development theory and the experience of developing countries.

RECOMMENDED READINGS

Colman, David, and Frederick Nixson, *Economics of Change in Less Developed Countries* (Oxford: Philip Alan, 1978), Chap. 2.

Fei, John, and Gustav Ranis, *Development of the Labor Surplus Economy* (Homewood, Ill.: Irwin, 1964).

Fei, John, and Gustav Ranis, "Agriculture in Two Types of Open Economies," in Lloyd G. Reynolds, (ed.), *Agriculture in Development Theory* (New Haven, Conn.: Yale University Press, 1975), pp. 352–372.

Ghatak, Subrata, *An Introduction to Development Economics* (London: Allen and Unwin, 1986), Chaps. 2 and 3.

Gill, Richard T., *Economic Development: Past and Present* (Englewood Cliffs, N.J.: Prentice-Hall, 1973), Chap. 2.

Hayami, Yujiro, and Vernon W. Ruttan, *Agricultural Development: An International Perspective* (Baltimore: Johns Hopkins University Press, 1985), Chap. 2.

Johnston, Bruce F., and John W. Mellor, "The Role of Agriculture in Economic Development," *American Economic Review,* vol. 51, 1961, pp. 571–581.

Lewis, W. Arthur, "Economic Development with Unlimited Supplies of Labor," *Manchester School of Economics and Social Studies,* vol. 22, May 1954, pp. 139–191.

Lewis, John P., and Valeriana Kallab, (eds.), *Development Strategies Reconsidered,* (New Brunswick, N.J.: Transaction Books-Rutgers, 1986).

Mellor, John W., *The New Economics of Growth: A Strategy for India and the Developing World* (Ithaca, N.Y.: Cornell University Press, 1976).

North, Douglas, "Institutions, Transactions Costs, and Economic Growth, *Economic Inquiry,* vol. 25, 1987, pp. 415–418.

Rostow, W. W., *The Stages of Growth* (Cambridge: Cambridge University Press, 1960).

THE ROLE OF AGRICULTURE IN ECONOMIC DEVELOPMENT

The fact that countries, like people, as they grow richer spend a declining fraction of their incomes on food and devote a diminishing proportion of their man hours to agriculture, does not imply that improved productivity in agriculture is unnecessary for economic growth.

Millikan and Hapgood[1]

THIS CHAPTER

1 Describes the specific contributions of agriculture to economic development
2 Discusses how alternative resource bases, stages of development, world economic conditions, political systems, and asset ownership patterns affect the contributions of agriculture to broad-based economic growth and development

POTENTIAL CONTRIBUTIONS OF AGRICULTURE TO DEVELOPMENT

Several of the development theories described in Chap. 6 prescribe, at least implicitly, an important role for agriculture in economic development. Because of differences in resource bases, stages of development, and conditions across countries, agriculture's precise role will vary from country to country. Let's examine in detail the potential contributions of agriculture, and explore the conditions under which particular contributions are likely to be most important.[2]

---

[1] Max F. Millikan and David Hapgood, *No Easy Harvest: The Dilemma of Agriculture in Underdeveloped Countries* (Boston: Little, Brown and Company, 1967), p. 1.
[2] These contributions were described in a classic article several years ago by John W. Mellor and Bruce F. Johnston, "The Role of Agriculture in Economic Development," *American Economic Review*, vol. 51, no. 4, September 1961, pp. 566–593.

Food and Fiber

Growing population, rising incomes that accompany economic development, and a high proportion of income increases spent on food and fiber make increased food and fiber production a key contribution of agriculture to economic development. Food has often been called a *wage good* because wage labor spends such a high proportion of its income on food that food prices have a major impact on real wages.[3] If food production fails to keep pace with demand in early stages of development, food prices tend to rise, nominal wage rates are forced up, profits and investment decline, and growth and employment stagnate.

Rising food prices can be a major cause of inflation in low-income countries, where typically over half of total consumption expenditures are for food. Food imports can relieve these price pressures, but limited foreign exchange may constrain that option. Therefore, food production for domestic markets is one of the primary contributions of agriculture to overall economic development.

Labor

One of the major conclusions from the labor-surplus dual-economy model was that transfers of surplus labor from agriculture to industry can provide a source of economic growth. There is little question that the bulk of labor for industrial development must be drawn from the agricultural sector in the early stages of development. Obtaining that labor is seldom a problem if productivity increases occur in agriculture (see Box 7-1). In fact, given a dynamic agriculture, surplus labor will be released at a growing rate without sacrificing food production. A balanced path of development requires that these laborers be absorbed in a productive capacity by industries. Thus, capital formation in the industrial sector should be channeled into labor-intensive industries to promote employment growth. Ensuring that capital accumulation occurs in labor-intensive industries so as to generate employment sometimes is a problem.

BOX 7-1

THE CONTRIBUTION OF LABOR AND LABOR-SAVING TECHNOLOGIES

The need to release labor from agriculture should not be confused with a need to develop labor-saving technologies for agriculture. Maximum *productive* employment in both agriculture and industry should be sought. Technologies that improve labor productivity in agriculture are necessary, as are investments in rural infrastructure. Investments in rural education simultaneously enhance labor's productivity in agriculture and its potential to work in industry. These investments help smooth the flow of agricultural labor to industry.

---

[3] Real wages are the nominal wage, or the actual wage paid, divided by a cost-of-living price index.

Women, here shown transplanting rice in Thailand, are an important component of the labor force in most developing countries.

Historically, many countries have chosen a development path that favors investment in capital-intensive heavy industries. They do so for several reasons, including national prestige, which is thought to be enhanced by heavy industrial production, and an innate capital bias associated with import-substitution policies. These countries often are disappointed by the results of such programs. Because capital-intensive industries cannot absorb sufficient labor, increased urban unemployment and stagnating demands follow.

Capital

Capital requirements for economic development are enormous. Capital is needed for factories and machinery; for certain types of agricultural inputs; for infrastructure such as roads, schools, and electric power facilities; and for urban housing. For most countries, the major source of that capital is domestic savings.[4] Because during the early stages of development agriculture is the largest sector, domestic savings must come primarily from agriculture, except in countries with large earnings from petroleum or mineral exports.

In general, voluntary savings in less-developed countries are insufficient to provide the amount of capital necessary for development. Low levels of income, inadequate rural financial institutions, and the fact that saving requires

---

[4] Foreign aid and foreign investment are other potential capital sources. Except for a few small countries such as Nepal or Grenada, foreign aid is unlikely to be the major source of capital. Foreign investment can play a major role in some cases, but usually implies either foreign control or a future commitment for repayment (thus requiring future domestic savings).

current consumption to be sacrificed, all limit savings. Hence, developing countries are required to use various devices to "squeeze" agriculture to mobilize capital.[5]

How can countries secure this flow of capital out of agriculture? There are four basic means: taxes, relative declines in agricultural prices, direct capital formation within the sector, and direct investment in industry by people in agriculture.[6] Agricultural taxation has played a key role in generating capital for development in several countries. Land taxes were an important source of capital in Japan's economic development (see Box 7-2).[7] Thailand, Ghana, Argentina, and several other countries currently rely on agricultural export taxes. Other major types of taxes include income and labor taxes.

Land taxes are appealing because they are fixed taxes and therefore do not discourage production. They are relatively easy to administer and can be made progressive (relatively higher for people with greater wealth). However, land taxes are direct and obvious, sometimes associated with prior colonial history, and hence difficult to institute. Often there is substantial political pressure against land taxes, especially in societies where wealth and political power are directly associated with land ownership. Export taxes are easier to institute and administer. They have the serious deficiency, however, of taxing *marginal* production, and, hence, discouraging production. Income taxes tend to be difficult to administer in developing countries. Labor taxes are common for local public works projects.

A relative decline in the price of agricultural commodities compared to industrial commodities (decline in the terms of trade) is an important means of transferring capital from agriculture to industry in many countries. This relative decline in agricultural prices helps keep food prices low, which in turn increases profits and facilitates capital investment in industry. Where this decline in the terms of trade has occurred as a result of lower production costs due to technical change in agriculture, these transfers have not been particularly onerous. Where the decline has been brought about by forced deliveries at low prices (historical examples can be found in the Soviet Union, India, and Egypt) or by implicit taxes on agriculture resulting from over-valued foreign exchange rates (historical examples can be found in several Latin American countries), growth rates of both agriculture and industry have suffered.

Shifting the terms of trade against agriculture requires the agricultural supply curve to shift by more than demand. Lowering the terms of trade for agriculture may be difficult to achieve in the early and middle stages of development because of rapid demand shifts caused by population and income

---

[5] See Wyn F. Owen, "The Double Development Squeeze on Agriculture," *American Economic Review*, vol. 56, March 1966, pp. 43–70.

[6] John W. Mellor, *Economics of Agricultural Development* (Ithaca, N.Y.: Cornell University Press, 1966), p. 84.

[7] Ohkawa, K. and H. Rosovsky, "The Role of Agriculture in Modern Japanese Economic Development," in Carl Eicher and Lawrence Witt (eds.), *Agriculture and Economic Development* (New York: McGraw Hill, 1964).

BOX 7-2

AGRICULTURE AND ECONOMIC DEVELOPMENT IN JAPAN

The contribution of agriculture to Japan's economic progress is a widely cited example of the role agriculture can play in development. Japanese agricultural output grew at slightly less than 2 percent annually from the Meiji Restoration in 1868 until World War II, yet capital outflows from agriculture were substantial.

Between 1888 and 1902, agriculture provided 27 percent of the total capital used for investment in the nonagricultural sector. From 1903 to 1922, agriculture still provided 23 percent of nonagricultural capital formation. Flows of labor out of agriculture provided 67 percent (from 1888 to 1900) and 79 percent (from 1901 to 1920) of the increase in non-agricultural labor during these early stages of development. Farm products, particularly tea leaves and silk cocoons, were raw materials for industrial expansion, while food imports were virtually nil during the early years of development.

PERCENTAGE COMPOSITION OF JAPANESE GOVERNMENT TAX TAKE

Year	Land tax	Excise tax	Income tax	Business tax	Miscellaneous
1870	73.9	—	—	—	26.1
1880	72.9	10.0	—	—	17.1
1890	51.7	21.8	1.4	0.4	24.8
1900	24.6	28.6	3.4	3.8	39.5
1910	15.9	18.7	6.6	6.8	51.9
1920	6.2	31.6	16.0	9.8	36.3
1930	4.8	37.4	14.2	7.9	35.8

Source: Gustav Ranis, "The Financing of Japanese Economic Development," chap. 2, in *Agriculture and Economic Growth: Japan's Experience*, Kazushi Ohkawa, Bruce F. Johnston, and Hiromitsu Kaneda, (eds.), (Princeton, N.J.: Princeton University Press, 1970), p. 433.

The flow of capital from agriculture to industry was largely enforced by a land tax, which, especially during the first decades of development, was the most prominent source of government revenue. During the first quarter century of development, taxes accounted for a very large percentage of these capital flows, but later voluntary savings played a much larger role than forced taxation. These voluntary savings were stimulated by widespread availability of savings banks, especially in rural areas, moral suasion on the part of the government, and a regressive tax structure that put more income in the hands of people with higher propensities to save.

Evidence also suggests that the flow of labor out of agriculture had a more significant impact on Japanese economic development than did the flow of capital. Both of these flows were made possible by the impressive technological progress in agriculture that increased productivity and rural incomes, and created a surplus to be extracted.

Source: World Bank, *World Development Report 1986* (New York: Oxford University Press, 1986), p. 81; and Ranis, op cit.

growth. However, even agricultural production increases that are smaller than demand shifts can help reduce the relative rise in agricultural prices and dampen upward pressure on wages and downward pressure on capital formulation.

The third means of raising capital from agriculture, direct capital formation within the sector, relates both to local infrastructure development and to creating agricultural linkages to input and processing markets. Examples of local infrastructure development include terracing of rice paddies, building of farm-level irrigation systems, clearing of land, development of orchards and plantations, and other capital items constructed with human labor. By stimulating this internal investment, more capital funds (savings) are made available to the industrial sector.

The fourth means of securing capital from agriculture, direct investment by agriculture in industry, has been important in those countries with effective rural financial institutions such as Japan, Taiwan, and South Korea. As rural incomes grow, so do rural savings. Policies to promote formal rural savings and to ease barriers to capital flows from rural to urban areas help this form of capital transfer.

Foreign Exchange

Foreign exchange is needed for the import of key raw materials and capital goods. Also, with the collapse in borrowing from foreign private creditors during the 1980s, many less-developed countries have been forced to generate trade surpluses to pay off external debts. The agricultural sector is often called upon to make significant contributions to these foreign exchange needs.

Many LDCs have relied on exports of agricultural commodities as their major source of foreign exchange. Others have attempted to reduce their foreign exchange needs by increasing agricultural production to displace imports of food. Import displacement that occurs without protectionist policies can be a viable strategy, particularly for countries with rapidly expanding domestic demand for food. However, if that displacement occurs as a result of overvalued exchange rates or other trade restrictions, development may be slowed.

There are gains from specializing in particular agricultural commodities for export, but there are dangers as well, such as cyclical price fluctuations and rising protectionism in international markets. We will discuss trade issues in more detail in Chap. 16.

Market Demand

One problem facing the industrial sector as it attempts to expand is the overall size of the domestic market. Economies of scale in the production of industrial products often mean that large markets (demands) are needed. As incomes rise in agriculture, the potential is created for a substantial expansion of domestic demand for consumer goods and agricultural inputs. Even though agriculture requires relatively few inputs from industry, the consumption demand generated by growing agricultural productivity provides a strong linkage to, and markets for, the nonagricultural sector. These linkages cause multipliers whereby increased output in agriculture leads to increased incomes in the nonagriculture sector (Box 7-3).

BOX 7-3

MEANS FOR FOSTERING THE MARKET DEMAND CONTRIBUTION

This market demand contribution of agriculture can be fostered in three ways. First, and most obvious, rising incomes in agriculture create a large potential market for domestically produced industrial goods. Second, investments in infrastructure in rural areas will help not only in the transportation of agricultural output to urban areas and for export, but also will facilitate the marketing of industrial output in rural areas. Finally, in order to exploit the market potential of rural areas, industry should be encouraged to produce the types of goods that rural consumers (and producers) want.

A study of the linkages between agriculture and the demand for nonfarm goods in India showed that each dollar of agricultural income creates $.70 of value-added in the nonfarm economy.[8] Agricultural development offers the potential for rapid growth in domestic demand for labor-intensive goods and services.[9]

Rural Welfare

Agricultural development can have significant direct impacts on rural welfare. If productivity is increased, farmers receive benefits both through increased home consumption and through the income generated from farm product sales.

If agricultural development programs include asset redistribution in countries where asset ownership is highly skewed, poverty reductions can occur for reasons in addition to those associated with sectoral growth. Finally, if agricultural growth stimulates nonfarm growth and employment, landless labor can benefit from those employment opportunities. Farm income is largely spent on domestically produced goods, some of which come from the modern sector and some of which are produced in rural cottage industries. These expenditures cause spillovers (multipliers) which benefit nonagricultural families. In the long run, many farmers will also receive income from nonfarm employment.

Although in the very early stages of development agriculture is not the only productive sector in rural areas, it is certainly the dominant sector. Even in developed countries, where agriculture's share of total rural economic activity is relatively small, rural welfare is closely linked to the fate of agriculture. In less-developed countries a stagnant agriculture can lead to increased rural poverty, accelerated migration from rural to urban areas, and, in extreme cases, famine. Thus, since such a large portion of the population is found in rural areas, the rural welfare contribution of agriculture is vital to national welfare.

---

[8] C. Rangarajan, "Agricultural Growth and Industrial Performance in India," International Food Policy Research Institute, Research Report No. 33, Washington, D.C., 1982.

[9] John W. Mellor, *The New Economics of Growth* (Ithaca, N.Y.: Cornell University Press, 1976).

Agricultural development increases the demand for agricultural imputs such as this human-powered rice thresher.

THE CONTRIBUTION OF AGRICULTURE UNDER ALTERNATIVE DEVELOPMENT CONDITIONS

The six major contributions of agriculture to economic development—(1) food and fiber, (2) labor, (3) capital, (4) foreign exchange, (5) market demand, and (6) rural welfare—will not be received in all countries at every stage of development. The importance of particular contributions will vary with the resource base and development stage of a nation. It also will vary with world economic conditions and be influenced by the political system and asset ownership patterns of the country. Let's examine the circumstances under which particular contributions are most significant.

The Influence of Resource Differences and Stages of Development

Countries with productive natural resource bases will usually benefit from programs designed to stimulate the potential food and fiber contributions of agricultural development, at least in the early to middle stages of development. While this situation is representative of many countries in the world, some— for example, certain countries in the Middle East—have a natural advantage in oil and mineral production and often stress agriculture to a lesser degree. Others, primarily small urban, natural-resource-poor countries, such as Hong Kong and Singapore, concentrate on industrial production. In most countries, as development proceeds beyond a certain point, the food and fiber contribution of agriculture becomes relatively less important than its other contributions.

The significance of agricultural productivity growth in freeing up labor for the industrial sector will be greatest in labor-scarce countries and during the early stages of development. The relative importance of agriculture in providing labor for development has been reduced in many countries in recent years with the emergence of large numbers of underemployed people around the fringes of major cities.

The importance of the potential capital contribution of agriculture remains strong, particularly in the least-developed countries and in the large countries in Asia such as China, India, and Indonesia. As countries (particularly small countries) move into the middle stage of development, agriculture's role in generating or saving foreign exchange often grows and becomes critical. Middle-income countries tend to experience substantial yearly increases in the demand for food and fiber resulting from the effects of higher incomes accompanied by relatively high income elasticities of demand for those goods. If this demand is not met by domestic production, sizable increases in imports can result. Thus, the role of domestic producers in meeting these demands assumes greater importance.

The market contribution of agriculture is especially critical during the early and middle stages of development. It is at this time when fledgling domestic industries will be least likely to succeed in international markets. A high proportion of the population is still employed in agriculture, and thus rural areas potentially provide the largest market. The expanding urban informal sector in many low- to middle-income countries produces goods and services that are primarily consumed domestically. Higher incomes in agriculture can potentially have large income and employment multipliers in this informal sector. If the informal sector has access to credit, new technologies, and improved infrastructure so that it can supply goods to meet increasing domestic rural demands, the possibility exists for agriculture to provide a major contribution to expanding the domestic market for goods and services from that sector. Eventually, as development proceeds, the relative size of the rural market falls, and so does the market contribution of agriculture.

The rural welfare contribution of agricultural development will be highest in the early stages of development when the agricultural sector contains a large proportion of the population. While the direct welfare contribution may decline as development proceeds, it remains relatively important even after a country achieves a very high level of development.

The Influence of World Economic Conditions and Domestic Economic Policies

The interdependence of nations through capital and goods markets mean that economic conditions abroad can have important effects on domestic economic growth and development. The cyclical nature of fluctuations in commodity prices and aggregate income levels in the developed world means that the role of agriculture in a developing country is influenced in a cyclical fashion by events outside the domestic economy. These cyclical fluctuations have had an especially important impact on agriculture's contribution to foreign exchange earnings. High variability in international prices means increased uncertainty related to foreign exchange availability, and foreign exchange availability, in turn, affects the ability to import needed goods.

During the 1960s and 1970s, several developing countries expanded their exports to more-developed countries. Others took the opposite strategy. They adopted policies that led to overvalued exchange rates, borrowed heavily from foreign private and public sources, and imported goods, all of which adversely affected parts of their agricultural sectors while inflationary pressures grew. In the early 1980s, worldwide recession and high interest rates, caused primarily by economic policies in more-developed countries, led to lower agricultural commodity prices and contributed to debt crises in less-developed countries. Protectionist sentiments increased in more-developed countries, and international markets for manufactured goods became highly competitive.

The above series of events forced several less-developed countries to undertake drastic domestic stabilization policies to control inflation while attempting to generate trade surpluses to avoid defaulting on foreign loans. Exchange rates were devalued and government expenditures reduced. Trade surpluses have been generated principally by reducing imports. These policies have in some cases had a high social cost in terms of increased unemployment, falling real wages, and greater income inequality.[10]

The implications for agriculture of these events are that agriculture's contributions to food and fiber production for domestic markets, to foreign exchange generation, and to market demand creation for nonfarm consumer goods have become more important, relative to its labor contribution. Currency devaluations in particular, since they raise the prices of imported goods relative to domestically produced goods, have opened up opportunities for displacing imported foods and fiber without the need for protectionist policies. Scarce foreign exchange can then be reserved for capital goods, which are essential in many cases for the growth of the modern industrial sector. This expansion of domestic agricultural production means increased incomes in rural areas, which can increase domestic demand for goods from the nonfarm sector as well.

Some countries will be able to expand their agricultural exports, despite continuing protectionist policies in developed countries. Such expansion is particularly possible for those countries exporting products such as coffee, tea, and cocoa, which tend not to compete with agricultural products in developed

---

[10] Squire, Lyn, "Introduction: Poverty and Adjustment," *World Bank Economic Review*, vol. 5(2), 1991, pp. 177–186.

countries. Other countries may have to wait for cyclical changes in commodity prices to enable them to compete abroad, unless they have made rapid progress in improving their agricultural productivity. In summary, world economic conditions which change from time to time interact with domestic economic policies to influence the relative importance of agriculture's diverse contributions to development.

The Influence of Alternative Political Systems and Asset Ownership Patterns

The six contributions of agriculture to economic development are relevant irrespective of the type of political system or the distribution of assets in the country. Nevertheless, the levels of those contributions and the mechanisms for extracting them are a function of the political system and asset ownership patterns.

Food and fiber under the communist system in the former Soviet Union historically was extracted through required deliveries to the nonfarm sector. Food and fiber prices were kept low relative to nonfarm prices, thereby facilitating capital formation in industry.[11] Under the Chinese system, rural labor played a major role in both farm and nonfarm direct capital formation through building of infrastructure and working at low wages in nonfarm jobs in rural communes. Rural welfare has been directly increased through increased food availability, and the demand has expanded for locally produced, nonfarm goods. In other words, agricultural development can play similar roles in command and market systems even though the functioning of the systems differs.

A variety of asset ownership patterns, particularly in land, is found in both market and nonmarket systems. In some countries, a substantial proportion of agricultural assets is concentrated in the hands of a few. This fact has important implications for production incentives, the distribution of benefits from agricultural development, and the contributions of agriculture to overall economic development. When production takes place on a relatively few large plantations, the food and fiber contribution may be reduced relative to the foreign exchange contribution. This reduction may, in turn, diminish agriculture's market demand, domestic capital, and rural welfare contributions as well.

When reforms take place in the ownership patterns of land and other fixed assets, the contributions of agriculture to development tend to change in both the short and the long runs. When land ownership becomes more equal, additional quantities of food and fiber are consumed in rural areas and agriculture's food and fiber contribution to development of industry may be reduced in the short run. At the same time, this additional rural consumption

---

[11] Owen, op. cit., p. 46.

directly increases rural welfare. In the long run—with adequate credit, marketing, and other reforms—the surplus marketed to the nonfarm sector often increases. Land reform often increases the domestic capital contribution of agriculture to development and eventually increases the market demand contribution. Other implications of asset distribution patterns and the transactions costs associated with alternative patterns are discussed in detail in Chaps. 10 and 11. The main point here is that those patterns do influence the relative importance of agriculture's various potential contributions to development.

SUMMARY

Agriculture contributes food and fiber, labor and capital, and foreign exchange toward overall economic development. Agricultural development increases the market demand for non-farm goods and services and provides direct improvements in rural welfare. The capital contribution is secured through taxes, relative declines in agricultural prices, direct capital formation in the rural sector, and investment by the agricultural sector in industry. Differences in resource bases and stages of development influence the relative importance of agriculture's various contributions. World economic conditions, the structure of the political system, and asset ownership patterns each influence the role of agriculture in economic development.

IMPORTANT TERMS AND CONCEPTS

Agricultural taxation
Asset ownership patterns
Capital contribution
Debt crisis
Domestic savings
Employment multipliers
Food and fiber contribution
Foreign exchange contribution
Import displacement
Infrastructure

Interdependence of nations
Labor contribution
Market demand contribution
Overvalued exchange rates
Role of agriculture
Rural welfare contribution
Stabilization policies
Terms of trade
Urban informal sector
Wage good

LOOKING AHEAD

This chapter concludes the section of the book that describes alternative economic development theories and the role of agriculture in those theories. We made the point in Part One of this book that serious income, hunger, and population problems exist in the world. In Part Two, we made the point that alternative development theories exist, that these theories have evolved over time, and that agriculture has an important role to play in economic development. In the third part of the book we will examine the nature of traditional agriculture and compare several agricultural systems, and examine the role of women in those systems. We will present suggestions for improving agriculture in later chapters of the book. First, however, it is useful to consider the current situation and we begin in Chap. 8 by exploring the characteristics of traditional agriculture.

QUESTIONS FOR DISCUSSION

1 What are the six major contributions of agriculture to economic development?
2 What are the primary means of marshalling capital from the agricultural sector?
3 What are the principal forms of agricultural taxation and what are their advantages and disadvantages?
4 Why must domestic savings initially come from the agricultural sector?
5 Agriculture may contribute to capital formation by providing agricultural commodities in such quantities as to cause a relative reduction in agricultural compared to nonagricultural prices. How might this relative price reduction help generate capital?
6 Why is it difficult to shift the terms of trade against agriculture in the early to middle stages of development?
7 What are some examples of direct capital formation within the agricultural sector?
8 How can agriculture make a net contribution to a country's foreign exchange?
9 How does agricultural development improve rural welfare?
10 Why might the labor contribution be less important than agriculture's other contributions in many countries today?
11 Why might an overvalued exchange rate discourage domestic agricultural production?
12 Why might the market demand contribution of agriculture increase as agriculture becomes more developed?
13 Why might middle-income countries tend to experience substantial increases in the demand for food and fiber?
14 How do world economic conditions influence the contributions of agriculture to development?
15 What major events in the world economy over the past 20 years have affected developing countries?
16 How might a highly concentrated land ownership pattern affect the contributions of agriculture to economic development?

RECOMMENDED READINGS

Johnston, Bruce F., and John W. Mellor, "The Role of Agriculture in Economic Development," *American Economic Review*, vol. 51, 1961, pp. 566–593.

Mellor, John W., *Economics of Agricultural Development* (Ithaca, N.Y.: Cornell University Press, 1966), Chaps. 5, 6 and 7.

Millikan, Max F. and David Hapgood, *No Easy Harvest: The Dilemma of Agriculture in Underdeveloped Countries* (Boston: Little, Brown and Company, 1967).

Murdock, William W., *The Poverty of Nations* (Baltimore: Johns Hopkins University Press, 1980), Chap. 7.

Owen, Wyn F., "The Double Development Squeeze on Agriculture," *American Economic Review*, vol. 56, 1966, pp. 43–70.

Rangarajan, C., "Agricultural Growth and Industrial Performance in India," International Food Policy Research Institute, Research Report No. 33, Washington, D.C., 1982.

Reynolds, Lloyd G., *Agriculture in Development Theory* (New Haven, Conn.: Yale University Press, 1975), Chap. 1 by L. Reynolds, and Chap. 12 by H. Myint.

THREE

TRADITIONAL AGRICULTURE AND COMPARATIVE AGRICULTURAL SYSTEMS

Traditional farm in Nepal.

CHAPTER 8

TRADITIONAL AGRICULTURE

In low-income countries, peasant agriculture tends to be characterized by low levels of utilization of certain resources, low levels of productivity, and relatively high levels of efficiency in combining resources and enterprises.

Mellor[1]

THIS CHAPTER

1 Describes the common characteristics of traditional agriculture
2 Identifies the particular roles of livestock in traditional farming systems
3 Discusses the implications that the characteristics of traditional farming systems have for agricultural development

CHARACTERISTICS OF TRADITIONAL AGRICULTURE

As we have already discussed, the world food-income-population problem is serious, and the solution to this problem depends in part on agricultural development. Before we discuss means for fostering agricultural development, we need to be aware of the current condition of agriculture in developing countries. Without this awareness, it is impossible to understand the types of changes needed to promote the development of agriculture, and how these changes will affect the people involved. In this chapter we examine some general characteristics of traditional agriculture. Then in Chap. 9 we compare specific types of agricultural systems, some types more developed than others.[2]

---

[1] John W. Mellor, *Economics of Agricultural Development* (Ithaca, N.Y.: Cornell University Press, 1966), p. 134.
[2] Agricultural systems include production practices, or *how* things are produced, as well as the types of enterprises, or *what* things are produced.
[3] Mellor, op. cit., p. 133.

The term *traditional agriculture* conveys part of its own meaning. The word "traditional" means "to do things the way they have usually been done." Because natural resources, culture, history, and other factors vary from place to place, the way things have usually been done also differs greatly from one location to another. And, because conditions change, no type of farming system, no matter how traditional, is ever completely stable. Nevertheless, farms in traditional agricultural systems do have several common characteristics.

Intermixing of Farm and Family Decisions

Traditional agriculture takes several forms, but small peasant farms predominate in most developing countries. Business decisions on these farms are generally intermixed with family or household decisions. The importance of the family and the close relationship between production and consumption decisions occur because much of the labor, management, and capital come from the same household. A sizable proportion of the production is consumed on the same farm or at least in the same community where it is produced.

This intermixing of production and consumption decisions, along with the low levels of income common among peasant farms, adds an element of conservatism to family farming.[3] A farm disaster usually means a family disaster. Consequently, traditional farms often use crop varieties and breeds of livestock that have proven dependable under adverse conditions, such as low levels of fertility or rough terrain, even if yields or productivities are modest.

For example, cassava is commonly grown on a portion of a traditional farmer's land. Cassava grows slowly, but on relatively poor soils, and under a variety of weather conditions. It is a root crop that can be pulled out of the ground at various times of the year to meet calorie needs when other foods may be short.

Traditional farms consume most of their products at home. However, the surplus they trade or sell connects them to the local market. Consequently, traditional farms are influenced by market price relationships in their decisions to allocate family resources. Sometimes, traditional farms are called subsistence farms. The surplus traded or sold by traditional farms varies from country to country, region to region, and farm to farm, but few of these farms are entirely subsistence farms in the sense that they consume all they produce. However, many are *semisubsistence*, consuming part and selling part. The percentage of the total output that is marketed may be planned or unplanned.

Labor and Land Use

Traditional farms generally are very small, usually only 1 to 3 hectares. Labor applied per hectare planted, however, tends to be high. In many areas, land is a limiting factor and is becoming more limiting over time as populations continue

A traditional farm in Peru.

to grow. Labor is often underemployed during certain times of the year, while the capital assets that do exist are fully exploited. Much sharing of work and income occurs on traditional farms so there is little open unemployment during slack times. This sharing means that the individual's implicit wage, at times, may be determined by the average rather than the marginal productivity of labor, as mentioned in Chap. 6. Family farm members also may supplement their incomes by working off the farm part time, often on larger farms.

Although family labor is important, traditional farms may hire some labor as well, at least during the busy times of the year. Low wages caused by high underemployment in peasant agriculture create incentives to hire laborers. That is, traditional farmers can hire labor or buy a small amount of leisure and enhance their social status at relatively low cost. Therefore the people with the lowest economic and social status are not the owners of small traditional farms, but the landless workers hired by those farmers.

Seasonality

Labor use in traditional agriculture tends to exhibit marked seasonal variation corresponding to agricultural cycles. During slack seasons, those immediately following planting or preceding harvest, labor may be abundant. However, during peak seasons, especially during weeding and harvest, labor is in short supply. Wages often exhibit similar seasonal fluctuations.

The seasonal nature of agricultural production also causes seasonal variations in consumption and nutritional status. Because storage facilities may be lacking and mechanisms for saving and borrowing infrequent, consumption patterns tend to follow agricultural cycles. It is common to find "lean seasons," when consumption is low and short-run malnutrition high, especially immediately prior to harvest (see Box 8-1).

Productivity and Efficiency

Traditional farms are characterized by low use of purchased inputs other than labor. Yields per hectare, production per person, and other measures of productivity tend to be low. These factors do not mean, however, that traditional farms are inefficient. As T. W. Schultz points out, traditional farms tend to be *poor but efficient.*[4] Why?

The crop varieties, power sources, methods for altering soil fertility, and certain other factors available to traditional farms constrain productivity growth and hence returns to labor and traditional types of capital. Efficiency, as measured by equating marginal returns to resources in alternative uses, is high. In other words, given the technologies available to traditional farmers, they tend to do a good job of allocating resources. The implication is that just reallocating the resources they currently have will not have a major impact on output.

It makes sense that with static levels of technology, physical conditions, and factor costs, farmers would gradually become very efficient at what they do. It is when conditions are changing rapidly that many of the mistakes in resource allocation occur. Also, one must be careful not to equate lack of education (another common characteristic in traditional agriculture) with lack of intelligence.

A situation with low use of certain inputs, low productivity, but high economic efficiency under static conditions has important implications if productivity is to be increased. First, new technologies can help to change the production possibilities available to farmers. Second, education may be needed to help farmers learn to adjust resource use to changing conditions so as to maintain their high levels of efficiency. However, under the static conditions of traditional agriculture, education will do little to improve productivity, since peasant producers are already relatively efficient.

Rationality and Risk

Traditional farmers are economically rational. They are motivated to raise their standard of living while, of necessity, they are cautious. Traditional farmers are not adverse to change, but proposed changes must fit into their current farming

---

[4] Theodore W. Schultz, *Transforming Traditional Agriculture* (Chicago: University of Chicago Press, 1964), p. 38.

BOX 8-1

SEASONAL MIGRATION: A RATIONAL RESPONSE

Seasonal weather patterns cause traditional farmers to adopt production and consumption patterns that help smooth variations. Seasonality also induces migration as people search for employment opportunities and food. Other seasonal causes of migration are trade and marketing, cultivation of secondary landholding, and pasturing cattle. Seasonal migration is a worldwide phenomenon. In some rainfed areas of Africa, 30 to 40 percent of the economically active population migrates, while in rural Nepal as much as 30 percent of the households have at least one member who migrates.

Why does seasonal migration occur? During the lean season, labor demands are low, incomes are stretched, and food can be in short supply. Other rural regions may have crop conditions (either because of different environmental factors or because of different crop technologies or irrigation) that alter the agricultural calendar and create demands for workers. The large plantations that are common for many export crops also demand labor on a seasonal basis. Seasonal rural-to-urban migration involves workers migrating to towns, cities, and mines in search of work. These reasons combine to push migrants out of regions where their labor is temporarily in surplus and pull them into areas with high demands for labor.

There is now overwhelming evidence that seasonal migration is not inefficient nor is it caused by factors such as imperfect labor markets. It is a natural adaptation to highly seasonal agricultural cycles and can smooth family incomes and consumption. Seasonal migration also provides insurance; in the event of a crop failure family income can be maintained in the short run by migration.

Seasonal labor flows have benefited countries by minimizing labor shortages in harvest times. Exports of cocoa and coffee from forest regions of Western Africa are largely made possible by seasonal migrants who provide labor during harvest. Other regions of the world have seen their total production possibilities shift outward as labor moves to fill seasonal gaps.

Source: Material was largely drawn from Sahn, David E., (ed.), *Causes and Implications of Seasonal Variability in Household Food Security* (Baltimore: Johns Hopkins University Press, 1987).

---

systems without altering too abruptly the methods they have developed over time to reduce risk and spread out the demand for labor (Box 8-2).

One mechanism by which traditional farmers in many countries have spread risk is by exchanging labor and other resources through joint and extended families. By joint and extended families we mean relatives (and sometimes friends) beyond parents and their children. In many countries, there is a substantial degree of sharing, which not only adds to social status but spreads risk. Some of these sharing arrangements and ties that bind extended families together may deteriorate as development proceeds, creating a need for new institutional arrangements to spread risk and in some cases to constrain anti-social behavior.

BOX 8-2

THE NATURAL ENVIRONMENT CAN BE CRUEL TO TRADITIONAL FARMERS

"That year the rains failed. A week went by, two. We stared at the cruel sky, calm, blue, indifferent to our need. We threw ourselves on the earth and we prayed. I took a pumpkin and a few grains of rice to my Goddess, and I wept at her feet. I thought she looked at me with compassion and I went away comforted, but no rain came.

"Perhaps tomorrow," my husband said. "It is not too late."

We went out and scanned the heavens, clear and beautiful, deadly beautiful, not one cloud to mar its serenity. Others did so too, coming out, as we did, to gaze at the sky and murmur, "Perhaps tomorrow."

Tomorrows came and went and there was no rain. Nathan no longer said perhaps; only a faint spark of hope, obstinately refusing to die, brought him out each dawn to scour the heavens for a sign.

Each day the level of the water dropped and the heads of the paddy hung lower. The river had shrunk to a trickle, the well was as dry as a bone. Before long the shoots of the paddy were tipped with brown; even as we watched, the stain spread like some terrible disease, choking out the green that meant life to us.

Harvesting time, and nothing to reap. The paddy had taken all our labour and lay now before us in faded, useless heaps. . . .

Then, after the heat had endured for days and days, and our hopes had shrivelled with the paddy—too late to do any good—then we saw the storm clouds gathering, and before long the rain came lashing down, making up in fury for the long draught and giving the grateful land as much as it could suck and more. But in us there was nothing left—no joy, no call for joy. It had come too late."

Source: Kamala Markandaya, *Nectar in a Sieve* (New York: New American Library, 1954), p. 76, 81–82.

THE ROLE OF LIVESTOCK

Livestock play many vitally important roles in traditional farming systems. Unfortunately, these roles are sometimes misunderstood by outsiders who may question the desirability of improving animal productivity in developing countries. There is little question that when crops and livestock directly compete for the same resources, it is usually more efficient for humans to consume grain than it is to feed the grain to livestock and consume meat. However, in most traditional farming systems, livestock consume little grain, and meat production is often one of the least important roles of livestock. Let's consider several of the more important roles of livestock.[5]

---

[5] See Sterling Wortman and Ralph Cummings, Jr., *To Feed This World* (Baltimore: Johns Hopkins University Press, 1978), p. 38, for additional discussion of the role of livestock in traditional agriculture.

Buffers and Extenders of the Food Supply

Farm animals provide a special protection to farm families, acting as a buffer between the family and a precarious food supply. Animals are like a savings bank. Farmers can invest surpluses in them, they grow, and they can be consumed or sold during crop failures.

In most of traditional agriculture, livestock do not directly compete with crops because they eat crop residues, feed off steep slopes and poor soils, and generally consume materials which "extend" the food supply. Many types of animals are ruminants (e.g. cattle, goats, sheep, buffalo) that eat grass and other forages that humans cannot and can then convert the forages to products for human consumption.

Of course livestock make an important contribution to extending the quality of the diet as well, by providing meat, milk, and eggs. Small amounts of these high-protein foods can have a significant impact on human health.

Fertilizer, Fuel, Hides and Hair

Animal manure is vitally important as a source of both fertilizer and fuel in several countries. For example, in the remote hills of Nepal, it is difficult to obtain chemical fertilizer. Animal manure adds both fertility and organic matter to the soil. In countries where wood is scarce, animal dung is dried and burned for fuel. In many countries, these two uses of animal manure compete. Dung that is burned cannot be used to increase soil fertility. In India and other

A cow is a type of savings bank in Kenya.

Farmer plowing with bullock in Thailand.

countries, methane digesters have been developed, and the gas produced is used for cooking, and the residual nitrogen applied to crops.

Few livestock products are wasted in traditional society. Clothing and blankets are made from animal hides and hair of not only cattle and sheep, but buffalo, goats, and other livestock.

Power and Transport

In many countries, livestock are the principal source of power. They plow the fields, transport products to market, and carry out processing tasks like grinding sugarcane. In some remote areas, animals help to market crops by eating grain and other plant products and then walking to market.

Tractors are a very recent phenomenon in the world. The large investments needed to purchase tractors make them prohibitively expensive for traditional farmers. And, on the steep slopes and rough terrain in parts of some developing countries, it will be many years, if ever, before mechanical power replaces animal power.

Social and Cultural

Livestock, particularly cattle and goats, are highly valued in some societies for social and cultural reasons. A family's social status may be measured by the number of animals it owns.[6] Cattle are given as gifts during ceremonial occa-

---

[6] In nomadic societies where no individual family owns the land, animal ownership is almost the only criterion available for measuring social status.

sions. While livestock serve major economic functions, they also serve these other social and cultural functions as well. Of course, it is possible that the social and cultural values placed on livestock have evolved over the years because of their importance as capital and income-earning assets.

TRADITIONAL FARMING AND AGRICULTURAL DEVELOPMENT

One of the striking characteristics of farms in developing countries is their diversity. In this section we examine more closely two specific case studies in different parts of the world, Nigeria and the Philippines. These two cases demonstrate both this diversity and some common features of semisubsistence agriculture. The cases also illustrate regional differences. Farms in much of Sub-Saharan Africa are still very traditional whereas farms in many parts of Asia and the Pacific already have begun to intensify and modernize. These examples illustrate several implications important for understanding agricultural development.

Case 1—Nigeria

David Norman conducted a careful study of the production and decision-making behavior of traditional farmers in the Zaria region of Northern Nigeria.[7] He found that land in the communities he studied, although traditionally a communal asset, was allocated by a system of user rights for a certain period of time. These rights were allocated very unequally; the smallest farms averaged 2.2 hectares and the large farms, 6.7 hectares.

The average family had seven members. Polygamy was common. Some types of family units were simple families with one adult male and wives and children. Other units were composite families with two or more adult males and several wives and children. Most of the farm work was undertaken by family members (71 percent) and, unlike that of many areas in Africa, most of it was completed by adult males (75 percent); less than 1 percent was completed by females. Females provided less farm labor than in most parts of Africa due to their Moslem religion. The rest of the work was completed by children and hired labor.

Interestingly, about 47 percent of the average male adult's time was spent on off-farm occupations. Uneven distribution of rainfall created seasonal fluctuations in labor use. Roughly 55 percent of the annual labor use on farms occurred between May and August. Although there was an abundant supply of labor in many months, it was short in June and July.

Investments in tools and equipment were extremely low, only $6.50 per farm in 1967 dollars. More than three times this amount was invested in livestock.

[7] See David W. Norman, "Economic Rationality in Traditional Hausa Dryland Farmers in the North of Nigeria," in Robert D. Stevens (ed.), *Tradition and Dynamics in Small-Farm Agriculture*, (Ames: Iowa State University Press, 1977).

Little purchased fertilizer was used, and seed was saved from the previous year's harvest or purchased, sometimes with borrowed money. Most of the borrowing that occurred, however, was for household consumption.

About half the cultivated area was devoted to cereals. Millet, sorghum, and cowpeas were the most important food crops. Groundnuts, sugarcane, and cotton were the main cash crops. Many crops were grown together in mixtures. Sometimes as many as six crops were grown together. Only 24 percent of the total cultivated area was single-cropped. Millet-sorghum was the most common mixture but many different combinations were found. Differences in growth periods and harvesting dates appeared to account for some of the crop mixtures. Crop mixing helped spread labor demand over a longer period.

Norman asked farmers about the reasons for the mixed cropping patterns he observed. Farmers indicated that they grew mixed crops both to maximize the return to their scarcest resource, land, and to reduce risk. He calculated costs and returns and found that, except for sugarcane, mixtures did return more per hectare. He calculated the variation in income for different cropping patterns and found that mixtures also provided relatively stable income compared to single crops.

Income per family was $287 in 1967 dollars, including nonfarm income, which represented 24 percent of the total. Forty percent of the crops was sold for cash, and the remainder consumed or used for seed. Savings were very low.

In comparing the three villages in the study area, Norman found that use of labor and fertilizer per hectare was higher in the villages where, because of access to transportation, population density was highest; more land was left fallow in remote areas. Less off-farm employment occurred in the most remote

Mixed cropping in Africa.

village, and high-valued sugarcane was grown in the villages closest to the road.

What are some conclusions and implications from the study? First, levels of input usage, productivity, and income per family were very low. Economic inefficiency, however, was high. Farmers were reasonably successful at maximizing income while attempting to ensure a stable food supply.

The fact that farmers' incomes were relatively low indicates a need for higher productivity; their low incomes also reduced their ability to take many chances with newer practices if those practices involve risk. The prevalence of mixed cropping suggests the need to tailor new technologies to the farming system and not just to the needs of one crop. Finally, infrastructure, such as roads, appeared to be useful for raising incomes.

Case 2—The Philippines

Yujiro Hayami and his associates conducted an intensive study of a typical rice-producing village in the Philippines.[8] They used household record-keeping and interview surveys to gather information on flows of goods and services from farming and other activities in the village of Tubuan on the Southern coast of Laguna de Bay. What they found was a village in the midst of transition from traditional farming to more intensive and modern farming methods. The results of their study illustrate some of the potential gains and many of the problems facing households and villages as they attempt agricultural development.

Tubuan had a population of 550 people and a growth rate of 4.3 percent per year at the time of the study in the mid 1970s. Sixty-one percent of the population was under 21. The cultivated land area in the village was relatively constant; farm size was shrinking, and the number of landless households was increasing. More than 80 percent of these households had nuclear families with one married couple and their children. Several of the larger families were extended families with grandparents. Women were engaged in both household and farm work and had as much education as their male counterparts.

The labor utilization rate, or the percentage of total time spent working, was only 70 percent of capacity, reflecting the seasonality of rice production. Half of all labor was hired, 40 percent was family labor, and the rest was exchange of labor among farms in the village. Ninety-five percent of all off-farm work occurred within the village, primarily in rice farming.

Total land area in the village was 131 hectares, of which 111 were in rice and the rest in coconuts. Villagers lived in a total of 95 houses located in a coconut grove surrounded by rice paddies. They owned only 30 percent of the coconut land but were allowed to live there in exchange for clearing the undergrowth between the trees. They leased the rice paddies for a fixed lease and owned

[8] See Yujiro Hayami, *Anatomy of a Peasant Economy: A Rice Village in the Philippines*, Los Banos, Laguna, Philippines: International Rice Research Institute, 1978.

only 2 percent of the rice land. Most of the land was owned by absentee landlords. Most of the rice farms were 1 to 3 hectares; only four local farmers owned any land.

A major change occurred in the village in 1958 with the arrival of the national irrigation system. With water and the new varieties of rice that arrived in the late 1960s, rice yields per field more than doubled between 1958 and 1974. Power tillers replaced carabaos in land preparation, and by 1974 there were 21 tillers in the village. Many of the smaller farmers had their land tilled by those who had tillers. Without exception the villagers adopted the new rice varieties. Landless workers (those who did not lease land) owned weeding implements because that gave them better opportunities for employment. While rice farming and growing coconuts were the major farming activities, a major sideline was raising ducks.

Incomes were $1164 per household, or $197 per person, based on information collected in 1975 to 1976. Twenty-seven percent of total consumption expenditures was for home-produced goods and 73 percent for outside purchases. Savings ranged from 8 percent of income for landless peasants to 28 percent for operators of "large" farms. More than 95 percent of investments was from household savings.

The average household had a net worth of $3148, or $534 per person. Landless workers, however, had net worths of only $235 per household and $49 per person.[9] More than 90 percent of all assets in the village was in the form of leases for land which had value because of land scarcity.

Institutional arrangements were changing over time, in part due to new technologies. Land reform had converted farms from share-tenancy arrangements to fixed leases at a rental rate of 25 percent of the average harvest for three normal years preceding the conversion. Higher yields due to irrigation, new plant varieties, fertilizers, and other new methods caused the system of hiring laborers for harvest to change. Under the traditional farming practices, hired labor received one-sixth of the harvest for its harvesting work. With the new system, to receive this one-sixth share, labor also had to weed earlier in the season. The increased yields more than compensated workers for their larger workload.

The introduction of mechanical technologies and the subsequent land reform aggravated the inequality in the village. The major source of income inequality was identified as unequal ownership of tenancy (lease) titles. Increased opportunities and incomes for landless workers helped dampen this inequality.

What are some of the development implications of the Philippine case? First, traditional agriculture can be rapidly changed through the introduction of new technologies such as irrigation and improved crop varieties. These changes tend to raise production and average income levels. Migration into areas experiencing economic growth is common.

---

[9] Landless workers had smaller families, on average, than tenant farmers.

The new varieties were adopted by all farmers in Tubuan, but the power tillers were purchased only by the larger farms. Biological technologies such as new varieties tend not to worsen the income distribution within a village, while mechanical technologies often do because of the capital needed to purchase the latter.

When land is limited, there is a need to increase production per hectare and to diversify into activities such as poultry and perhaps other livestock that do not require much of the scarce land resource. The landless workers benefitted from income increases generated through employment, but there was need for more nonfarm employment. If the landless are to benefit in the long run, they need either land or education combined with jobs. The labor-contracting procedures proved to respond flexibly to the changing needs of the farmers.

Land reform did not reduce the income inequality in the village, in part because the land itself was never redistributed. Only the leasing system was restructured. The lower-priced leases combined with increased incomes per hectare meant that the leases themselves became more valuable. Higher incomes usually get bid into the value of fixed or scarce assets as in this case. In summary, the village standard of living increased but inequality remained. There was a need for more new technologies, additional institutional changes related to land, and more off-farm employment opportunities.

Reinforcing Positive Change in Traditional or Semisubsistence Agriculture

Traditional farms are efficient but poor. As population continues to grow, poverty increases. Agriculture must change if the situation is to improve. But change brings the danger of increasing income disparities. The distribution of income generated through new plant varieties and power tillers will be affected by asset distribution patterns and institutions which govern the rules of behavior in society.

The Nigerian case illustrates the need for new technologies but also the importance of their meshing with the current farming system. Risks must be spread. Institutions that substitute for the prior sharing arrangements must be created. Improved transportation should facilitate development.

The Philippines case illustrates that some institutional changes may exacerbate rather than improve income disparities if improperly conceived. It also illustrates one of the problems beginning to face certain Asian countries, the need to diversify out of rice. While rice will remain the dominant agricultural commodity, certain types of livestock production become increasingly attractive because of both changing consumer demands as incomes grow and the need to intensify labor use. Additional education and nonfarm employment opportunities are becoming important elements in an overall development strategy.

SUMMARY

Traditional agriculture is diverse, but traditional farms have some common characteristics. Traditional agriculture is generally characterized by small peasant farms in which farming and family decisions are intermixed. Traditional farm families consume, sell, or trade most of their products locally. Their labor use and land area per farm are small, but labor input per hectare is high. Hired labor is often important. These product and labor sales and purchases mean that farmers are, in general, closely linked to the local economy and respond to market signals. Productivity and use of purchased inputs are low but efficiency is high. Traditional farmers are rational but risk averse. They often live in extended or joint families. Livestock play many roles, including extending the food supply; providing a buffer against poor harvests; improving the quality of the diet; generating fertilizer, fuel, hides, and hair. They also provide power and transport and meet social and cultural needs. Traditional farms differ by region, and as farms change some people, particularly the landless, may be left behind unless new technologies are accompanied by improved institutions and education.

IMPORTANT TERMS AND CONCEPTS

Asset distribution pattern
Biological technologies
Buffers and extenders
Diversification
Institutional arrangements
Intermixing of farm and family
 decisions
Joint and extended families
Landless labor

Mechanical technologies
Mixed cropping
Off-farm employment
Poor but efficient
Rational but cautious
Role of livestock
Seasonality
Semisubsistence farms
Traditional agriculture

LOOKING AHEAD

A wide variety of agricultural systems are found in the world. These systems evolve over time. In the next chapter we examine the factors that influence the type of farming systems found in a particular country at a point in time. The importance of technical, human, institutional, and political factors is discussed. Several common types of agricultural systems are described and the significant roles of women and children are highlighted.

QUESTIONS FOR DISCUSSION

1 Why might traditional farms be fairly conservative or slow to change from current practices?

2 Are traditional farms subsistence farms?

3 Why are livestock important in many traditional farming systems?

4 Distinguish between productivity and efficiency. Why do traditional farms tend to have high levels of efficiency? Why do they tend to have low or high levels of productivity?

5 What factors influence resource allocation on traditional farms? If a farmer fails to adopt a new, apparently more profitable, farming practice, is he or she irrational?

6 If traditional farmers use resources efficiently, why should we be concerned with raising productivity by increasing the use of new technologies?

7 Are the farmers who own 1 to 3 hectares the poorest people in rural communities in developing countries?

8 Why are joint and extended families still important in many developing countries?

9 Why are farm and household decisions often inseparably linked in developing countries?

10 Why are institutional changes often as important as technological changes for agricultural development?

11 Why do farmers practice mixed cropping? Are agricultural diversification and mixed cropping synonymous?

12 Summarize the development implications from the Nigerian and Philippine case studies.

13 Why is hired labor often important in traditional or semisubsistence agriculture?

14 Why was there less off-farm employment in the Philippine case than in the Nigerian case?

15 Why are new biological technologies often more important than new mechanical technologies for fostering agricultural development?

16 Why did land reform in the Philippine village fail to reduce income inequality?

17 Why is agricultural diversification becoming increasingly important in many Asian countries?

RECOMMENDED READINGS

Ghatak, Subrata and Ken Ingersent, *Agriculture and Economic Development* (Baltimore: Johns Hopkins University Press, 1984).

Hayami, Yujiro, *Anatomy of a Peasant Economy: A Rice Village in the Philippines*, Los Banos, Laguna, Philippines: International Rice Research Institute, 1978.

Hopper, W. David, "Allocation Efficiency in a Traditional Indian Agriculture," *Journal of Farm Economics*, vol. 47, 1965, pp. 611–625.

Mellor, John W., *Economics of Agricultural Development* (Ithaca, N.Y.: Cornell University Press, 1966), Chap. 8.

Norman, David W., "Economic Rationality of Traditional Hausa Dryland Farmers in the North of Nigeria," in Robert D. Stevens (ed.), *Tradition and Dynamics in Small-Farm Agriculture* (Ames: Iowa State University Press, 1977).

Schultz, Theodore W., *Transforming Traditional Agriculture* (New Haven, Conn.: Yale University Press, 1964).

Stevens, Robert D. and Cathy L. Jabara, *Agricultural Development Principles: Economic Theory and Empirical Evidence* (Baltimore: Johns Hopkins University Press, 1988), Chap. 8.

Wharton, Clifton R., "The Economic Meaning of Subsistence," *Malayan Economic Review*, vol. 8, 1963, pp. 46–59.

Wolgin, J. M., "Resource Allocation and Risk: A Case Study of Smallholder Agriculture in Kenya," *American Journal of Agricultural Economics*, vol. 54, 1975, pp. 622–630.

Wortman, Sterling and Ralph Cummings, Jr., *To Feed This World* (Baltimore: Johns Hopkins University Press, 1978).

CHAPTER **9**

COMPARATIVE AGRICULTURAL SYSTEMS AND THE ROLE OF WOMEN

The agricultural pattern that has emerged in each area is in part the result of ecological factors—a particular combination of climate and soil—and in part the result of economic and cultural factors in the society that grows the crops.

Loomis[1]

THIS CHAPTER

1 Identifies factors that influence the agricultural systems found in a particular country at a point in time
2 Explores the differences in farming systems found in various parts of the world
3 Discusses the roles of women and children in farming systems

DETERMINANTS OF FARMING SYSTEMS

The farming systems in each region of the world show considerable variety. Farming systems are differentiated by how production is organized, by the nature of technologies employed, and by the types of crops and livestock produced. Each system consists of a small number of dominant crops (or livestock) and numerous minor crops (or livestock). Let's examine the primary determinants of the prevailing systems before classifying and describing them. We must understand agricultural systems if we are to improve them.

[1] Robert S. Loomis, "Agricultural Systems," *Scientific American*, September 1976, p. 69.

Technical, institutional, and human factors determine the type of agricultural system. These sets of factors interact at each location and point in time to provide a unique environment for agricultural production (Fig. 9-1). When these factors remain constant in a particular geographic area for several years, the farming system that evolves represents a long-term adaptation to that environment. Economic development can introduce rapid changes in several of the underlying factors, thus placing pressure on the existing system.

Technical Determinants of Farming Systems

Technical elements, including both physical and biological factors, determine the potential types of crop and livestock systems. Physical factors including climate, land, water control, capital items, and distance to markets are unique to each location; although water control and other capital items can be altered through investments and new technologies over time. For example, the nomadism, discussed below, that prevails in many arid regions of the world, represents an adaptation to harsh climates. However, the introduction of wells has encouraged more settled farming or ranching activities in parts of these nomadic areas. Likewise, the introduction of irrigation into the Philippine community described in Chap. 8 led to subtle but significant changes in the way production was organized in the village.

Biological factors including pests, crop species, and livestock species are even more susceptible to modification. In the short run, however, these factors play a major role in defining the prevailing agricultural system. The existence of the tse-tse fly in areas of the African humid tropics has created farming systems that are dramatically different from those in similar climates where the fly does not exist. Animal traction is not an option in areas where the tse-tse fly is common. Technologies to control the fly can help spread animal traction and alter traditional farming relations.

Institutional and Human Determinants of Farming Systems

Institutional and human elements influencing farming systems are characterized by both exogenous (externally controlled) and endogenous (internally controlled) factors. Factors largely outside the control of individual farmers include marketing systems, social and cultural norms and beliefs, population density, market opportunities, and off-farm employment opportunities. For example, high population densities in many South Asian countries are partly responsible for the very different farming systems employed there as compared to the systems found in the relatively low-density areas of sub-Saharan Africa and Southeast Asia (see Table 9-1).

A large variety of politically determined institutions such as pricing policies, credit policies, macroeconomic policies, trade policies, and land-tenure systems is also important. Land ownership patterns are highly skewed in many countries. In areas of Central America, for example, large commercial farms

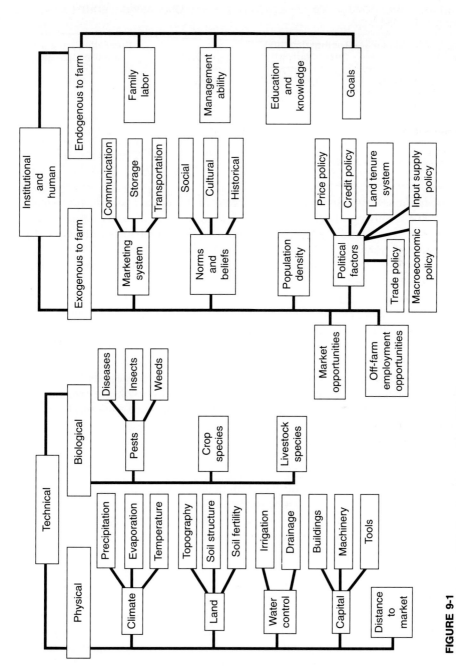

FIGURE 9-1
Major determinants of the farming system at a point in time.

TABLE 9-1
LAND AREA AND POPULATION DENSITIES IN SUB-SAHARAN AFRICA, SOUTH ASIA, AND SOUTHEAST ASIA

Region	Total agricultural area (000 km²)	Arable area (%)	Population/agricultural area (people/km²)
Sub-Saharan Africa	1,262	6.7	291
South Asia	2,021	57.3	416
Southeast Asia	461	16.9	296

Source: International Food Policy Research Institute/International Service for National Agricultural Research (IFPRI/ISNAR), "Towards a New Agricultural Revolution: Research, Technology, Transfer, and Application for Food Security in Africa" (The Hague, Netherlands: International Service for National Agricultural Research, 1991), p. 15.

and plantations exist alongside small peasant subsistence and semisubsistence farms. The farming practices used in these areas are significantly influenced by the distribution of land. In some areas of the world, people have only use rights (e.g., the communal areas of Zimbabwe). The political system itself may dictate collectives, communes, or private property as the prevailing organizational system for land use.

Endogenous or farmer-controlled determinants of agricultural systems include family labor, management ability, education, knowledge, as well as the goals farmers are striving for. The riskiness of agricultural production, particularly in arid, rain-fed regions has forced farmers to adapt their practices to ensure survival. These adaptations are determined, in part, by the farmers' degree of risk aversion. Any of these exogenous or endogenous factors can change over time. New technologies and population growth are two particularly important determinants of how and in what direction agricultural systems change over time.

MAJOR TYPES OF FARMING SYSTEMS

While the specific type of farming system in use depends on a large number of factors (Fig. 9-1), Duckham and Masefield have grouped farming systems into three basic types: shifting cultivation, pastoral nomadism, and settled agriculture (Fig. 9-2).[2] Settled agriculture includes many subtypes. Let's briefly examine each of these systems.

Shifting Cultivation

Shifting cultivation is an old form of agriculture still practiced in many parts of the world. As the name implies, it involves shifting to a new piece of land when the fertility of the original patch runs out or when weeds and other pests take

[2] See Alec N. Duckham and G. B. Masefield, *Farming Systems of the World* (London: Chatto and Windus, 1970).

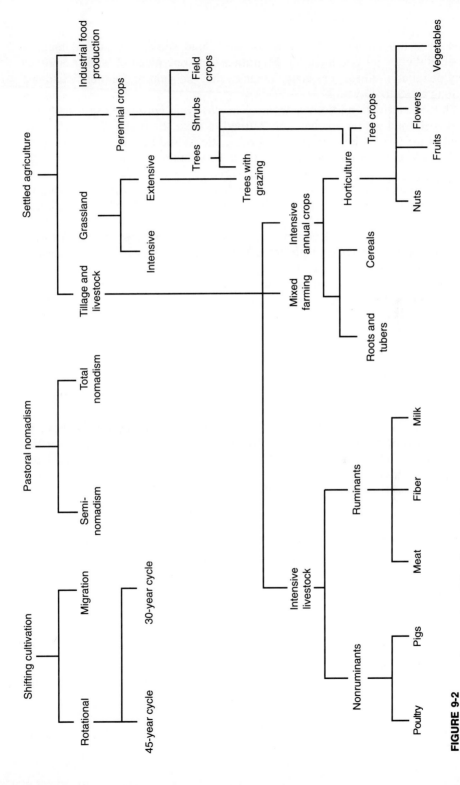

FIGURE 9-2
Example of a classification of world farming systems.

over. The movement may be fast or slow, and sometimes animal manure extends the use of one location. Migration from one piece of land to another may be random, linear, or cyclic. When cyclic, the rotation frequency can last as long as 30 to 45 years.

Shifting cultivation also has been called *slash and burn* because usually the land is slashed with a machete and burned to clear the brush. Capital investment in the farm is low; machetes, digging sticks, and hoes being the primary tools. Typical crops include corn, millet and sorghum, rice, and roots. Usually the crops are mixed. Occasionally the cleared area is used for perennial crops. Shifting cultivation is practiced on about 20 percent of the world's exploitable soils, particularly in Africa and Latin America. It is popular where population pressures are not too severe.

Shifting cultivation is frequently associated with the insecure control over the land, either because of absentee (or government) ownership or unclear tenure status. It has been linked to soil erosion and other environmental problems in several developing countries, partly because there are few incentives to invest in practices that maintain soil fertility. In the Dominican Republic, for example, shifting cultivation on government-owned land led to a loss of forest cover and extensive erosion.

Pastoral Nomadism

Pastoral nomadism involves people who travel, more or less continuously, with herds of livestock. Pastoral nomads have no established farms, but often follow well-established traditional routes. Although there are probably only about 15 million pastoral nomads in the whole world, they occupy an area larger than the entire cultivated area in the world. They are especially prevalent in the arid and semi-arid tropics (see Fig. 9-3). Some examples include the Masai of Kenya and Tanzania, the Hima of Uganda, the Fulani of West Africa, the Bedouin of the Eastern Mediterranean, and the nomads of Mongolia.

Pastoral nomadism can be total or partial. In the latter case, the nomads have homes and some cultivation for part of the year. Typically five or six families will travel together with 25 to 60 goats and sheep or 10 to 25 camels. Sometimes they own cattle as well. The livestock eat natural pasture and their productivity is quite low.

Pastoral nomadism can lead to a variety of problems. Because the grazing takes place on common land, there is a tendency for overgrazing because every individual farmer wishes to maximize his or her number of animals. As the number of animals increases, the grazing areas deteriorate and incomes shrink. There is little scope for technical improvement, and serious problems arise in years of drought. As the human population grows, additional pressures are placed on the resource base supporting the nomadic system.

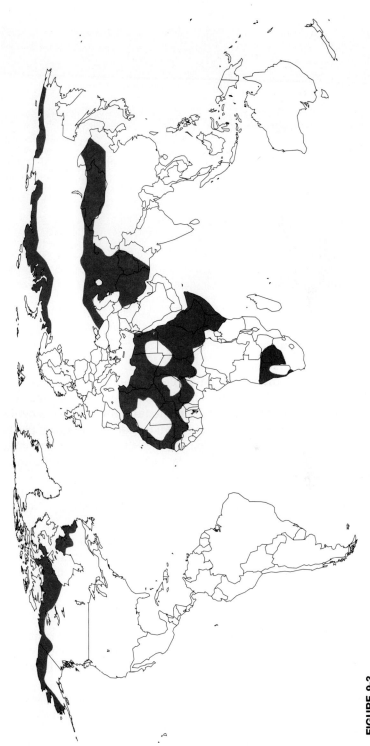

FIGURE 9-3
Limits of nomadism worldwide. (*Source: Andreae Bernd, Farming, Development and Space,*
New York: Walter de Gruyter, 1981.)

Nomads are common in the northern half of Africa.

Settled Agriculture

Settled agriculture represents a variety of agricultural systems including mixed farming systems, intensive annual crops, intensive and extensive livestock systems, and perennial crops. These farming systems are the survivors of an enormous amount of human experimentation. Systems have evolved that produce a relatively high and certain return in storable products per unit of effort. As discussed above, the environment as well as distance to market are major factors influencing the choice of the system as well as the individual commodities for particular locations.

Mixed farming usually involves a mixture of crops and livestock. Few farming systems consist of just one commodity. However, what is meant by mixed farming is the integration of crops and livestock production such that multiple commodities are grown at the same time on the same land. As mentioned in Chap. 8, mixed farming is common in traditional agriculture because it produces relatively high returns while minimizing risk, makes efficient use of labor and land, and helps maintain fertility. Good management is required to coordinate the various farming activities.

Intensive annual crops are extremely important in the world. About 70 percent of the cultivated area of the world is planted to the major grain crops, which include wheat, rice, and corn. Other important annual crops are barley, millet, sorghum, roots, tubers, vegetables, and pulses. Pulses include such crops as beans, soybeans, peas, and peanuts.

Perennial crops are grown and harvested over several years and include crops such as cocoa, coffee, bananas, and sugarcane. Some of these crops are grown in large plantations but often in very small farms as well, even in the same country. They tend to produce high-value products that are often exported.

Intensive livestock systems include both *ruminants* (for example, cattle, buffalo, sheep, and goats) that produce milk, meat, fiber, dung, and other products, and *nonruminants* (for example, pigs and poultry) that are particularly important for their meat and eggs. These animals are often fed grains in addition to pasture and forage. In a few countries, intensive livestock systems can involve carefully managed grasslands or pasture.

Extensive livestock systems include a wide variety of grazing systems on semi-arid range, high and cool mountain pastures, wet lowlands, and more. Livestock may graze on leaves as well as grass.

In summary, there are a large number of crops and livestock systems, many of which have been relatively productive or at least well suited to their environment. As population expands and other conditions change, a particular system may no longer be adequate and is forced to change (see Box 9-1). Few systems are static for very long today, and several offer potential for improved productivity.

The Influence of the Political System

In Fig. 9-1, political factors were listed as significant determinants of farming systems, including land tenure systems. The political system can dictate a private property, collective, commune, or other type of land tenure system. When systems such as collectives and communes restrict farmers' freedom to manage and respond to market signals, waste, inefficiency, and production disincentives can become serious problems. Attempts have been made within these systems, for example in China, to create individual incentives through point systems and bonuses for exceeding quotas. However, these have been less effective than price incentives.

In recent years, China has experimented with increased market incentives and as a result has experienced significant increases in agricultural production (see Box 9-2). Adoption of new technologies and use of purchased inputs such as fertilizer have increased substantially. These changes have occurred very rapidly in China causing important ramifications for world markets. Remember that China has more than 1 billion people and less than one-half hectare per farm worker. Rice production predominates but livestock, particularly pork, are very important.

Government policies other than rules governing land tenure affect farming systems. Price policies that favor certain products over others or promote the use of different inputs can have a strong impact on the types of crops planted, on how long they are grown, and even on the degree to which traditional farmers interact with markets. Policies affecting the value of the land create incentives for more or less investments in land. These incentives can change farming practices dramatically. Population programs can influence population densities, which in turn help determine the particular agricultural system.

BOX 9-1

POPULATION DENSITY AND AGRICULTURAL SYSTEMS

The intensity of land utilization varies worldwide, and there is a close relationship between this intensity and the density of population in a particular region. Boserup hypothesized that pressure from increasing population has caused a shift in recent decades from more extensive to more intensive systems. This classification scheme traces a continuum from shifting cultivation to settled agriculture:

1 Forest fallow cultivation: one to two year planting of plots followed by a 20 to 25 year fallow period.
2 Bush fallow cultivation: 6 to 10 year fallow period. Periods of uninterrupted cultivation may be as short as 1 to 2 years, or as long as 5 to 6 years.
3 Short fallow cultivation: fallow lasts one or a couple of years.
4 Annual cropping: land is left uncultivated only between the harvest of one crop and the sowing of the next.
5 Multicropping: the most intensive system of land use; the land bears two or more successive crops every year.

Boserup hypothesized that increased population densities put pressure on food production systems to increase outputs. The successively more intensive systems require increased labor inputs for weeding and cultivation, and more varied farming implements. In forest fallow cultivation, only an axe is needed, and as the fallow period is shortened, implements such as hoes, plows, and even irrigation systems are used.

Different patterns of land use exist within similar agroclimatic zones. For example, the land used for intensive cultivation in parts of Nigeria is remarkably similar to the land used for long fallow cultivation in the same country. Thus, Boserup concluded that humans not only adapt to the climatic conditions they face, but actually change the relationship between the conditions and agricultural output by using methods that enhance soil fertility. These adaptations are mostly influenced by rates of population growth.

Source: Ester Boserup, *The Conditions of Agricultural Growth* (London: Allen and Unwin, 1965), especially Chap. 1, pp. 15–22.

In summary, the major types of farming systems in the world include shifting cultivation, pastoral nomadism, and several types of settled agriculture. These systems, particularly settled agriculture, can be affected in a major way by the political system in the country, which dictates private or public control over land use. Other government policies influence agricultural systems both directly and indirectly.

THE ROLES OF WOMEN IN FARMING SYSTEMS

Women have key roles to play in farming systems throughout the world. Women are involved not only in household chores and child rearing in rural areas but are a major source of labor for food production and account for a large proportion of economic activity.

BOX 9-2

CHINESE AGRICULTURAL SYSTEMS

In the rural areas of China prior to 1979, the agricultural production system was organized according to guidelines established in the national agricultural plan. Farming operations were organized into collective teams of 20 to 30 households; these teams were required to sell fixed quantities of output to the government at set prices. Quantities produced in excess of the quotas were also surrendered to the government. The collectives had some freedom to adjust inputs, but the acreage planted to each crop was determined by government planners.

   This rigid system led to stagnation in agricultural output. Between 1957 and 1978, per capita grain production grew at a 0.3 percent annual rate, while soybean and cotton production per capita *declined*, respectively, by 3.0 and 0.6 percent annually. In 1978, rural incomes were virtually identical to levels of 20 years earlier. This poor performance of the agricultural sector had important implications in a country where 80 percent of the population resides in rural areas.

   In 1978, the government decided to introduce the *Household Responsibility System*, which restored individual households as the basic unit of farm operation. Under this system, a household leases a plot of land from the collective, and, after fulfilling a state grain procurement quota, can retain additional output. This output can be consumed or sold to the government. The households have flexibility to determine acreage for individual crops. At the same time, the government prices of agricultural commodities were increased, and the prices paid for above-quota grain production were increased substantially above quota prices. As a result of these reforms, grain output rose at a 4.9 percent annual rate between 1979 and 1984, while soybeans, cotton, and meat output rose at annual rates of 4.1, 18.7, and 10.1 percent, respectively. These reforms led to a wholesale change in the Chinese agricultural system; by 1983 over 97 percent of the collective teams in China had been converted to the new system.

   Sources: Justin Y. Lin, "The Household Responsibility System Reform and the Adoption of Hybrid Rice in China," *Journal of Development Economics,* vol. 36(2), 1991, pp. 353–373; Ehou Junhua, "Economic Reform: Price Readjustment (1978–87)," *Chinese Economic Studies,* vol. 24(3), Spring 1991, pp. 6–26.

Dual Roles of Women

With the notable exception of strongly Islamic societies, women play two major roles in the rural areas of the vast majority of developing countries. First, they have household responsibilities for child rearing, food preparation, and other chores. Second, they are paid or unpaid workers in agriculture or off the farm. They produce food, they process food, they preserve food, and they prepare food. They work in the fields, they tend livestock, they thresh grain, and they carry produce to market. In many areas, women manage the affairs of the household and the farm. They sell their labor to other farms and sometimes migrate to plantations. They work in small industries and in the informal sector, producing goods and services for sales locally or beyond. In many cases, the true extent of involvement of women in agriculturally related activities is underestimated because, when surveys are taken, women often describe their

Woman thrashing wheat in Nepal.

principal occupation as housewife. They are then counted as economically inactive. This "invisibility" of female employment has led to policies and programs that ignore women and sometimes adversely affect them.

Involvement in farm production may be seasonal, particularly in Asia where, in many countries, women assume major responsibilities for harvesting, both on their own farms and as paid labor on other farms. The role of women varies by region and with size of farm as discussed below.

Regional Differences

Women play the largest role in farming in Africa. In many African countries nearly all the tasks connected with food production are left to women. Men may tend livestock or produce cash crops. In Malawi, for example, over two-thirds of those working full time in farming are women.[3] In areas of Africa where men migrate to work elsewhere, the entire administration of the household is often left to women (Box 9-3). Women are important to agriculture in most areas of the world. Households headed by women make up 20 to 25 percent of rural households in developing countries, excluding China and Islamic societies.[4] In Latin America, women typically care for animals, particularly chickens and pigs, while tending garden vegetables and other food crops. In sugar and fruit producing areas, especially in the Caribbean, women work as

[3] Janice Jiggins, "Gender-Related Impacts and the Work of the International Agricultural Research Centers," Consultative Group for International Agricultural Research (CGIAR) Study Paper Number 17, World Bank, Washington, D.C., 1986.
[4] Ibid.

BOX 9-3

GENDER DIVISION OF LABOR IN BOTSWANA

A study of traditional farms in Central Botswana uncovered illuminating differences in the division of labor by gender. Because men have opportunities to work in Botswanan mines, a large porportion of rural households are headed by females (40 percent in this study). In agricultural areas, land is held communally by the village, and both men and women can obtain rights to cultivate the land. Mostly sorghum, but also maize, cowpeas, and melon varieties are grown on 4 to 5 hectare plots. Livestock, particularly cattle, are very important.

In all aspects of economic activity there is a stark differentiation between male and female roles. In crop production, men traditionally plow and maintain the fields, women sow the seeds, weed, harvest, and thresh. Men and boys almost exclusively tend and milk livestock (mostly cattle and goats), while women manage the chickens, used mostly for home consumption. Women brew and sell sorghum beer, and beer sales can produce substantial amounts of household income.

Women provide virtually all of the household maintenance. Time spent gathering firewood, fetching water, cooking, and in other household chores accounts for 68 percent of the women's total time. Men allocate only 10 percent of their total time to household chores. Even so, women provide 38 percent more time for agricultural fieldwork than do men. Women provide 48 percent of the total hours worked by members of the household, while men account for 22 percent, and the children the rest.

Source: Doyle C. Baker with Hilary Sims Feldstein, "Botswana: Farming Systems Research in a Drought Prone Environment, Central Region Farming Systems Research Project," chap. 3, in Hilary Sims Feldstein and Susan V. Poats, (eds.) *Working Together Gender Analysis in Agriculture. Vol. I: Case Studies,* (Westford, Conn.: Kumarian Press, 1989), pp. 43–75.

---

cash laborers on plantations, and, thus, provide a substantial proportion of household income. In Asia, many examples of female farming systems are known.[5] In Nepal, it is estimated that women on subsistence farms produce 50 percent of household income; men and children produce 44 and 6 percent, respectively.[6]

Determinants of the Roles of Women in Agriculture

Social, cultural, and religious factors; population pressures; farming techniques; off-farm job activities; colonial history; and many other factors determine the role of women in farming systems. Sometimes in areas with apparently similar physical conditions, women assume very different roles. As off-farm job opportunities, population pressures, and farming techniques change, so too does the role of women.

---

[5] Ester Boserup, *Women's Role in Economic Development* (London: George Allen and Unwin, 1970).

[6] Meena Acharya and Lynn Bennett, "Women and the Subsistence Sector. Economic Participation and Household Decision Making in Nepal," World Bank Staff Working Paper Number 526, Washington, D.C., World Bank, 1982.

Shifting cultivation with hand labor tends to lend itself more to female labor than does settled cultivation with a plow. For countries with low population densities, adequate food could be raised without using male labor in farming. Men used to spend their time felling trees, hunting, and in warfare.[7] In areas where agriculture has changed from shifting cultivation to settled agriculture and cash crops, men typically do more work than previously, but often the role of women in farmwork still dominates.

The shift to the plow and draft animals has made a difference in the amount of male labor used in some areas, and long standing differences in farming techniques undoubtedly account for many of the regional gender differences in farm labor. In regions of intensive cultivation on small irrigated farms, for example in several Asian countries, men, women, and children must work hard to generate enough production on a small piece of land to support themselves. Work is mostly done by hand. In contrast, on some larger farms, more tasks may be mechanized and women may devote a higher percentage of their time to housework. In some areas, mechanization has displaced female labor and has tended to lower their status, since housework is often underappreciated compared to farmwork.

Increased integration of peasant farmers into the labor market has increased the importance of women's role in agriculture, because it is often the males who find outside wage work. In some countries, males may work away from the household for several weeks or months at a time. In Lesotho, for example, the result has been that 70 percent of households are headed by women.[8]

Policy Implications

Why is it important to recognize the role of women in farming systems? Woman may assume major responsibilities in agriculture, but why do we draw attention to this fact? First, gender is important as one of the several socioeconomic characteristics that influence the adoption of new technologies. If women are important in agriculture, their opinions must be sought when designing new technologies. The impact of these technologies on the relationship between men and women should be considered. Females must receive education and guidance from extension services. If women are making farming decisions, they must have access to credit and to inputs.

Women often have inadequate access to credit for a number of reasons. First, in many societies women lack legal status necessary to enter into contracts. Second, only very infrequently do women hold title to land, often necessary as collateral for loans. Third, there seems to be a bias against women in the administration of credit programs.

It is likely that most new technologies are relatively gender neutral, and we see some efforts on the part of many public extension systems to reach women

---

[7] Boserup, op. cit.
[8] Jiggins, op. cit.

Colombian women receiving instructions on how to vaccinate a chicken.

farmers.[9] However, lack of female access to credit and purchased inputs in many countries makes many new technologies gender-biased. Furthermore, women often grow food crops that are minor in terms of value of production but are important in the diets of families on small farms.[10] Agricultural research often neglects these crops, and this neglect may have adverse effects on nutrition. Also, because extension services are still highly male in most countries, communication with female farmers can often be inhibited.

The relative importance of gender in influencing agricultural development must be kept in perspective, but it also should not be ignored. The impacts of credit, technology and other agricultural policies on women have been exacerbated by discriminatory land reform and settlement policies.[11] In Latin America, where land reform and settlement schemes often have been designed to benefit "heads of households," women have been, by convention, excluded. In Ethiopia and Tanzania, rights to lands have been bestowed on men. In Asia, specifically the settlement schemes in Indonesia, Papua New Guinea, and Sri Lanka, land was only given to male heads of households. Inadequate access to

[9] In The Gambia, research on rice was expected to increase women's incomes, since women were the primary producers. Instead, following the introduction of the new technologies, the men took over this production. See Joachim von Braun, Detlev Puetz, and Patrick Webb, "Irrigation Technology and Commercialization of Rice in The Gambia: Effects on Income and Nutrition," International Food Policy Research Institute, Research Report No. 75, Washington, D.C., 1989.

[10] Food and Agriculture Organization, "Women in African Food Production and Security," in J. Price Gittinger, Joanne Leslie, and Caroline Hoisington (eds.), *Food Policy: Integrating Supply Distribution and Consumption* (Baltimore: Johns Hopkins University Press, 1987).

[11] See United Nations Centre for Social Development and Humanitarian Affairs, *1989 World Survey on the Role of Women in Development* (New York: United Nations, 1989), especially pp. 91–93.

land, worsened by government policies, when combined with problems of access to credit can hinder women's ability to participate in agricultural development. Given the large role that women play in developing country farming systems, efforts that ignore or discriminate against women have distorting effects and diminish chances of success.

Role of Children

Children also are a major source of farm labor in every region of the world, and their tasks expand with each year of their age. They typically begin by following a parent or sibling into the field and rapidly become involved in hoeing, weeding, harvesting, and other tasks. They feed and otherwise care for animals. They, particularly boys, may work as low-paid farm laborers on other farms. Young girls often care for younger brothers and sisters to free their mother for other work. Farm children throughout the world take on major farm responsibilities at a very young age.

Boy breaking ground in India.

SUMMARY

Farming systems in the world exhibit considerable variability. Both technical and human factors determine the types of farming systems. Technical factors include both physical and biological factors. Institutional and human factors are characterized by both externally and internally controlled forces. The major farming systems of the world can be grouped into three classes: shifting cultivation, pastoral nomadism, and settled agriculture. Settled agriculture represents a variety of agricultural systems including mixed farming systems, intensive annual crops, intensive and extensive livestock systems, and perennial crops. Women and children play important roles in agriculture, particularly in Africa. Social, cultural, religious, technological, off-farm employment, historical, and other factors determine the role of women in farming systems. The importance of women in agriculture has implications for credit and input policies, for the generation and extension of new technologies, and for land reform policies.

IMPORTANT TERMS AND CONCEPTS

Determinants of the role of women
  in agriculture
Dual role of women
Farming systems
Human determinants of farming
  systems
Implications of the role of women in
  agriculture
Intensive annual crops
Livestock systems
Mixed farming system

Pastoral nomadism
Perennial crops
Political determinants of farming
  systems
Regional differences in the role of
  women
Settled agriculture
Shifting cultivation
Technical determinants of farming
  systems

LOOKING AHEAD

In this chapter, we briefly examined the nature and diversity of existing agricultural systems in developing countries. In the next section we consider means for improving those systems to increase agriculture's contribution to human welfare. We begin in the next chapter by providing an overview of agricultural development theories and strategies before exploring in detail the individual components of those theories and strategies.

QUESTIONS FOR DISCUSSION

1 What are the major technical determinants of farming systems?
2 Describe the major human determinants of farming systems. Be sure to distinguish exogenous from endogenous factors.

3 How might the political system affect the nature of the farming system?

4 What is shifting cultivation and why is it more commonly found in Africa and Latin America than in Asia?

5 What is pastoral nomadism and what problems might present themselves in this type of system?

6 Distinguish among the major types of settled agriculture.

7 What role do women and children play in agriculture?

8 In which region of the world is the role of women in agriculture the greatest?

9 What determines the role of women in agriculture?

10 What are some important implications of the role of women in agriculture?

11 Why might census statistics and other data undercount female participation in farming?

12 Why do women from near-landless and small-holder households participate more in agriculture relative to those from larger farms with more land ownership?

RECOMMENDED READINGS

Baker, Doyle C. with Hilary Sims Feldstein, "Botswana Farming Systems Research in a Drought Prone Environment, Central Regional Farming Systems Research Project," in Hilary Sims Feldstein, and Susan V. Poats, (eds.), *Working Together: Gender Analysis in Agriculture Volume I: Case Studies,* (West Hartford, Conn.: Kumarian Press, 1989), Chap. 3.

Boserup, Ester, *Women's Role in Economic Development* (London: Allen and Unwin, 1970).

Deere, Carmen D. "The Division of Labor by Sex in Agriculture: A Peruvian Case Study," *Economic Development and Cultural Change,* vol. 30, 1982, pp. 795–811.

Duckham, Alec N., and G. B. Masefield, *Farming Systems of the World* (London: Chatto and Windus, 1970).

Food and Agriculture Organization, "Women in African Food Production and Food Security," in J. Price Gittinger, Joanne Leslie, and Caroline Hoisington, (eds.), *Food Policy: Integrating Supply Distribution and Consumption* (Baltimore: Johns Hopkins University Press, 1987), Chap. 7.

Gladwin, Christine H. and Della McMillan, "Is a Turnaround in Africa Possible Without Helping African Women to Farm?" *Economic Development and Cultural Change,* vol. 37, 1989, pp. 305–344.

Jiggins, Janice, "Gender-Related Impacts and the Work of the International Agricultural Research Centers," Consultative Group for International Agricultural Research Study Paper Number 17, World Bank, Washington, D.C., 1985.

Loomis, Robert S., "Agricultural Systems," *Scientific American,* September 1976, pp. 98–105.

Ruthenberg, Hans, *Farming Systems in the Tropics* (Oxford: Oxford University Press, 1980).

United Nations, Centre for Social Development and Humanitarian Affairs, "Women, Food Systems and Agriculture," *1989 World Survey on the Role of Women in Development* (New York: United Nations, 1989), Chap. 3.

PART **FOUR**

GETTING AGRICULTURE MOVING

Agricultural instruction is an important component of the program at
Egerton University in Njoro, Kenya.

CHAPTER 10

AGRICULTURAL DEVELOPMENT THEORIES AND STRATEGIES

The process of agricultural growth itself has remained outside the concern of most development economists.

Hayami and Ruttan[1]

THIS CHAPTER

1 Describes how the sources of agricultural growth tend to change as development occurs, and examines alternative theories of agricultural development
2 Explains how the theory of *induced innovation* has been applied to agriculture and considers the implications for that theory of transactions costs, collective action, and enhanced information flows
3 Discusses the need for institutional and technical changes that recognize human behavior when designing workable agricultural development strategies

THEORIES OF AGRICULTURAL DEVELOPMENT

We have discussed the importance of agricultural development for solving the world food-income-population problem. We have considered the role of agriculture in economic development. We have examined the nature and diversity

---

[1] Yujiro Hayami and Vernon W. Ruttan, *Agricultural Development: An International Perspective* (Baltimore: Johns Hopkins University Press, 1985), p. 41.

of existing agricultural systems in developing nations. We are now ready to consider means for improving these systems to increase agriculture's contribution to human welfare. In this chapter we provide an overview of agricultural development theories and strategies. In subsequent chapters we will examine in more detail the individual components of the basic strategies outlined here. Our overriding concern is to find strategies that facilitate growth with equity. We explore why agricultural development has occurred in some countries and why it has not (or has proceeded very slowly) in others.

Many theories have been suggested to explain how the basic sources of growth (labor, natural resources, capital, increases in scale or specialization, improved efficiency, and technological progress) can be stimulated and combined to generate broad-based agricultural growth.[2] It is clear from historical experience that the relative importance of alternative sources of growth changes during the development process and has changed over time for the world as a whole. It is also clear that institutional arrangements such as marketing systems, price and credit policies, and property rights can play an important role in stimulating or hindering development. Let's examine agricultural development theories and evidence to see what lessons they provide for operational strategies.

Resource Exploitation and Conservation

One means of generating increased agricultural production is to expand the use of land and labor. The development of agriculture in North America, South America, Australia, and other areas of the world during colonization was based on using new lands. In some cases indigenous labor was also exploited. The opening up of forests and jungles by local populations in parts of Africa, Latin America, and Asia provide additional examples of expanded resource use.

In many of these cases, surplus lands and labor were used to produce commodities for both local consumption and export. Reductions in transportation costs facilitated exports. In Thailand, for example, rice production increased sharply in the latter half of the nineteenth century, and much of the increased production went to export markets.[3] In many colonies, exports of primary production were extracted for use in more developed countries.[4]

---

[2] Hayami and Ruttan, op. cit., have characterized previous agricultural development theories into six basic approaches: (1) resource exploitation, (2) resource conservation, (3) location, (4) diffusion, (5) high-payoff input, and (6) induced innovation. The first half of the chapter draws heavily on their ideas. Students interested in more detailed discussion of historical agricultural development theories are encouraged to read Chap. 3.

[3] See Hla Myint, "The Classical Theory of International Trade and the Underdeveloped Countries," *Economic Journal*, vol. 68, June, 1958, pp. 317–337, for a discussion of this phenomenon in the context of what Myint calls the "vent-for-surplus" model.

[4] In many cases, a large share of the benefits of these exports was not realized by the local countries but was transferred to the developed countries. In some cases, benefits flowed into the hands of a small indigenous elite.

Agriculture in Asia is intensive even in hilly regions.

Expansion of unutilized land resources provides *few* opportunities for sub-stantial growth in developing countries today. In areas of Latin America and Africa where additional land does exist, disease, insect, and soil problems prevent its use in agriculture. Abundant labor is available in many countries, and continued growth of the labor force will generate increases in total agri-cultural output. However, most growth in per capita agricultural output will have to come from more *intensive* use of existing resources.

There are many methods of achieving more intensive resource use. Early efforts in England, Germany, and other European countries included more intensive crop rotations, green manuring, forage-livestock systems, drainage, and irrigation. In many developing countries, these same factors increased land productivity. Terracing is an effective means of conserving soil productivity in hilly areas of Asia. In the mountainous regions of Central America, grass strips have been used to create terrace-like structures that conserve soil and enhance productivity. Hayami and Ruttan estimate that agricultural development based on similar types of "conservation" has been responsible for sustaining growth rates in agricultural production in the range of 1 percent per year in many countries, including developing countries, for long periods of time.[5]

While scientists are gaining additional knowledge of the technical and in-stitutional considerations that can lower the cost of conservation efforts, popu-lation pressures are creating a need for better ways of sustaining the natural

[5] Hayami and Ruttan, op. cit., p. 52.

resource base. Hence, conservation is likely to play an increasingly important role in maintaining if not expanding agricultural production in the future. Natural resource problems and potential conservation programs are discussed in more detail in Chap. 12.

Location and Diffusion

It has long been recognized that the pattern and intensity of agricultural production vary in relation to the proximity of urban-industrial centers and to the quantity and quality of transportation systems.[6] Theodore W. Schultz used a model of location to explain why agriculture in some areas grew more rapidly than in other areas.[7] Closeness to cities and transport matters because of differences in transportation and marketing costs, in effects on labor and capital markets, in the ease of obtaining new and more productive inputs, and in ease of information flows.

One implication of this "location" theory of agricultural development is that countries should encourage decentralized industrial development, particularly in the middle and late stages of development. During these stages, strong linkages between agriculture and markets for inputs (fertilizers and pesticides) and outputs can help stimulate the local economy. Developing nations should improve transportation infrastructure in rural areas. Issues related to infrastructure development are discussed in more detail in Chap. 14.

This location theory of agricultural development includes the notion that market linkages are important. A related theory, the *diffusion theory,* stresses the importance of linkages among farmers themselves. The basic idea is that transfer of existing technologies and economic knowledge from the more progressive to the lagging farmers could increase productivity. This idea has provided part of the rationale for agricultural extension systems, particularly in farm management. Unfortunately, in some cases diffusion theory has led to unrealistic expectations of the size of potential productivity gains under the existing level of technology.

Diffusion theory also has led to attempts to directly transfer knowledge and technologies from more-developed to less-developed countries. More success has been achieved with transferring knowledge than with transferring technologies. Adoption of transferred technologies has been limited except where efforts have been made to adapt the technologies to the new setting. We discuss the potential role for knowledge and technology transfer in Chap. 15.

---

[6] Modern day economists draw on theories proposed by Heinrick Von Thunen (1783–1850), who studied the optimal intensity of farm enterprises in relation to urban areas. See H. D. Dickinson, "Von-Thunen's Economics," *Economic Journal,* vol. 79, December, 1969, pp. 894–902; and David B. Grigg, *The Dynamics of Agricultural Change* (New York: St. Martin's Press, 1982), pp. 135–150.

[7] Theodore W. Schultz, *The Economic Organization of Agriculture* (New York: McGraw-Hill, 1953).

High-Payoff Inputs

In recent years, a theory of agricultural development has emerged that builds on the conservation, location, and diffusion approaches but adds the important dimension that the process of agricultural development can be accelerated through provision of new and improved inputs and technologies (particularly improved seeds, fertilizers, pesticides, and irrigation systems). This approach, articulated by Schultz in *Transforming Traditional Agriculture,* is based on the idea discussed in Chap. 8 that farmers in traditional agriculture are rational and efficient given their current resources and technologies.[8] What these farmers need are new high-payoff inputs and technologies to increase their productivity.[9]

The high-payoff input theory has been widely accepted because of the success achieved by modern wheat, corn, and rice varieties beginning in the 1950s and 1960s. These varieties are highly responsive to fertilizer, pesticides, and water management and have resulted in substantial growth in agricultural output in many developing countries. The distributional or equity effects of these inputs have been the subject of much debate and are discussed in more detail in Chap. 15.

Hayami and Ruttan argue that the high-payoff input theory is incomplete because it fails to incorporate the mechanism that induces these new inputs and technologies to be produced in a country. The theory also fails to explain how economic conditions stimulate the development of public agricultural experiment stations and educational systems. It does not attempt to identify the process by which farmers organize collectively to develop public infrastructure such as irrigation and drainage systems.[10] In the next section we explore the induced innovation theory proposed by Hayami and Ruttan to address these issues.

THEORY OF INDUCED INNOVATION

Induced innovation theory helps explain the mechanism by which a society chooses an optimal path of technical and institutional change in agriculture.[11] The theory says that technical change in agriculture represents a response to changes in resource endowments and to growth in product demand. Changes in

---

[8] Theodore W. Schultz, *Transforming Traditional Agriculture* (New Haven: Yale University Press, 1964).

[9] Hayami and Ruttan have labeled Schultz's approach the "high-payoff input" model.

[10] Hayami and Ruttan, op. cit., p. 62.

[11] Induced innovation theory was developed originally by John R. Hicks, *Theory of Wages* (London: MacMillan and Co., 1932). Hayami and Ruttan during the 1960s were the first to apply the theory to agricultural development. Their underlying assumption is that technological and institutional changes are vital to agricultural development.

institutions are induced by changes in relative resource endowments and by technical change.[12]

Induced Technical Innovation

Technical change in agriculture can follow different paths. Technologies can be developed that facilitate the substitution of relatively abundant and low cost factors of production for relatively scarce and high cost factors. A rise in the price of one factor relative to others will induce technical change that reduces the use of that factor relative to others. For example, if the price of land goes up relative to labor and fertilizer, indicating that land is becoming relatively scarce, technologies such as improved seeds will be developed that can be combined with labor and fertilizer to increase production per unit of land.

This process of induced technical change is illustrated graphically in Fig. 10-1. The range of possible technologies in time period 0 can be represented by what Hayami and Ruttan call the *innovation possibilities curve,* I_0^*. The specific technology employed in that time period is represented by the isoquant I_0. Production occurs at point A with N_0 units of land and L_0 units of labor, the least-cost combination of those resources given the price ratio P_0. Now, if over time labor becomes more abundant relative to land so that the price of labor is reduced relative to the price of land (the new price ratio is represented by P_1), incentives are created to adopt a more labor-intensive technology. If there were no technical change, production might occur at point B on isoquant I_1. However, the theory of induced innovation says that incentives are created not only to select a new technology from the current technology set (that is, move to point B on I_1), but also to develop new technologies to save scarce resources and use abundant resources. The new technology set is represented by the new innovation possibility curve I_1^*. As the innovation possibility curve moves toward the origin, the same quantity can be produced at lower cost. Following the generation of this new technology set, farmers can adopt the new least-cost technology I_1' and employ N_1 of land and L_1 of labor at point C.

Hayami and Ruttan compare the agricultural development histories of Japan and the United States to illustrate the validity of the theory. Japan experienced increasingly higher priced land compared to labor and stressed the development of biological technologies such as improved seeds and fertilizers. These technologies tend to save land and use labor more intensively. The United States, on the other hand, has approximately 100 times as much land per worker as does Japan. As the U.S. frontier was opened up, land became relatively abundant compared to labor, and the development of mechanical

---

[12] Hayami and Ruttan (op. cit., p. 94) define institutions as "the rules of society or of an organization that facilitate coordination among people by helping them form expectations which can reasonably hold in dealing with others. They reflect the conventions that have evolved in different societies regarding the behavior of individuals and groups relative to their own behavior and the behavior of others."

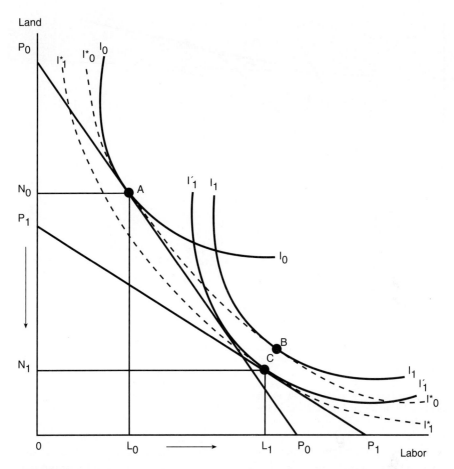

FIGURE 10-1
A model of induced technical change. If the ratio of the price of land to labor changes from P_0 to P_1, incentives are created not only to substitute labor for land and to move from technology I_0 at point A to technology I_1 at point B, but also to develop a new technology I_1' at point C.
Innovation possibility curves $I*_0$ and $I*_1$ represent the range of potential technologies that can be applied in period 0 and period 1. (*Source:* Yujiro Hayami and Vernon W. Ruttan, *Agricultural Development: An International Perspective,* Baltimore: Johns Hopkins University Press, 1985.)

technologies that saved labor was stressed. The result was successful agricultural development in both countries, but agricultural output per worker is 10.2 times greater in the United States than in Japan while output per hectare is 10.5 times greater in Japan than in the United States.[13]

Changes in output price relative to an input price also can induce technical change, as illustrated in Fig. 10-2. The curve *u* represents the range of current

---

[13] Hayami and Ruttan, op. cit. Many developing countries, particularly in Asia, are finding the Japanese path of technical change more appropriate than the U.S. path, given their relative resource endowments and the nature of changes in those endowments.

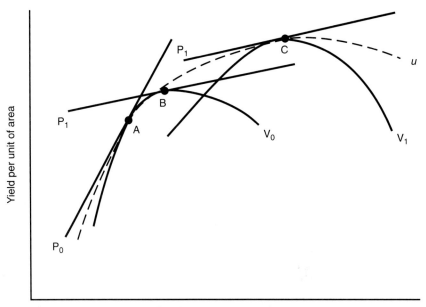

FIGURE 10-2
Shift in fertilizer response curve as price ratio changes. If the output/fertilizer price ratio changes
from P_0 to P_1, incentives are created not only to apply more fertilizer and increase output from A
to B using the traditional variety v_0, but to develop and adopt a new variety v_1 and to move to
point C. Curve u represents the "envelope" of a series of available and potential crop varieties.
(*Source:* Yujiro Hayami and Vernon W. Ruttan, *Agricultural Development: An International
Perspective,* Baltimore: Johns Hopkins University Press, 1985.)

and possible production technologies in a given time period. Hayami and
Ruttan call this the *meta production function*. Specific production technologies
are represented by v_0 and v_1. At the initial fertilizer-output price ratio (P_0),
producers use technology v_0 and produce at point A. If the price of fertilizer
falls relative to the price of output (P_1), then incentives are created to move to
point B on the existing technology. If the price ratio P_1 is expected to continue,
farmers press scientists to develop a more fertilizer responsive variety, v_1, if it
does not already exist. Farmers adopt the new variety and move to point C. In
the long run, the meta production function itself may shift as more basic
scientific advances are made.

Induced Institutional Change

Incentives are created for technical change, but where do these new technologies come from? How do farmers acquire them? What determines whether
technologies are developed that are suitable for all farmers or only for *some* of
the farmers? All of these questions are addressed by the theory of induced
institutional change.

Farmers demand new technologies not only from private input suppliers but from the public sector as well.[14] Hayami and Ruttan argue that public research scientists and administrators are guided by price signals and by pressures from farmers. The more highly decentralized the research system, the more effectively these pressures work. The development of the research systems themselves can be the result of pressures from farmers who are responding to market forces.

There are many other types of institutions (rules of society or organizations) that affect technical change and agricultural development. The rights to land, marketing systems, government pricing and credit policies, and laws governing contracts are just a few. The theory of induced institutional innovation recognizes that institutions can become obsolete and in need of adjustment over time. It says that new technologies and changes in relative resource endowments or price changes provide incentives for a society to demand new institutional arrangements (see Box 10-1 for an example).

Examples of institutional changes induced by technological change can be found in the shift from share tenure to more fixed-payment leases, which has occurred in several countries as new varieties and irrigation systems have increased yields while reducing risks.[15] An example of an institutional change due to a change in relative resource endowments is the switch from communally owned land to more restrictive property rights as population pressures increase the need for resource conservation.

In some countries we observe what appears to be socially desirable institutional changes, technical changes, and relatively rapid and broad-based agricultural development. However, in others we observe what seems to be perverse institutional change, agricultural stagnation, or agricultural growth with the benefits received by only a small segment of the population. Of course many countries fall between these extremes or may move from one group to the other over time. Why do we see these differences in institutional changes that influence agricultural performance, and how do they relate to the theory of induced innovation? The answer lies partly with transactions costs and with the incentives for and effects of collective action by groups of people with common interests.

Transactions Costs and Collective Action

The induced innovation theory presented above implicitly assumes perfectly functioning markets for all products and factors. Prices are assumed to convey all the relevant information to decision makers, and resources are allocated

---

[14] The determinants of private sector response to the demand for new technologies are discussed in Chap. 14.

[15] Share tenure is an arrangement whereby a farmer who is renting land pays the rent with a fixed percentage of the farmer's output. Masao Kikuchi and Yujiro Hayami "Inducements to Institutional Innovation in an Agrarian Community," *Economic Development and Cultural Change,* vol. 29, October, 1980, pp. 21–36, discuss a Philippine example of induced change in land tenure arrangements.

BOX 10-1

INDUCED INSTITUTIONAL INNOVATION IN JAVA

In Java, customary rules have governed both land rights and labor exchange for many centuries. With traditional technologies, these rules have helped allocate resources so that subsistence levels of foods have been available to all village members. These communal institutions have been put under stress by modern technologies that increase the productivity of labor and the returns to landowners. These changes induce changes in the institutions governing resource allocation.

An example of an institutional innovation is the disappearance of the *bawon* rice harvesting system. This traditional system allowed everyone, whether they were from a particular village or not, to participate in the harvest and share the output. As population grew with traditional technologies, this purely open *bawon* system gradually evolved into various forms, some of which limited harvest rights to village residents, while others limited harvest rights to a set number of participants, or to people who were invited by the farmer.

The widespread diffusion of fertilizer-responsive rice varieties created sharply higher returns to harvest labor, and induced a remarkable change in harvest-contract institutions. One such innovation was the introduction of the *tebasan* system, in which standing crops are sold to middlemen who hire contract labor for harvesting and thus reduce the harvester's share while increasing returns to the landowners. Another institution is the *ceblokan* system, which limits harvesting rights to those workers who perform extra services such as transplanting and weeding without pay. A study shows that in a village where *ceblokan* was first adopted in 1964 by seven farmers, by 1978, 96 out of 100 farmers had adopted the system.

These innovations in harvest-labor institutional arrangements were largely spurred by increased incomes and higher wages accompanying technological innovation. Increased incomes and wages created incentives for farmers to change their labor-contracting system. These changes are now widespread in Java.

Source: Masao Kikuchi, Anwar Mafid, and Yujiro Hayami, "Changes in Rice Harvesting Contracts and Wages in Java," Chap. 6, in Hans P. Binswanger and Mark R. Rosenzweig, (eds.), *Contractual Arrangements, Employment and Wages in Rural Labor Markets in Asia* (New Haven, Conn.: Yale University Press, 1984).

---

efficiently and independently of the distribution of assets (such as land) in society. Price responsive producers are assumed to possess knowledge about alternative technologies, and be able to lobby agricultural scientists to develop improved technologies to save scarce resources. Assuming no economies of scale in production, there is one optimal path for technological change and no room for collective action to influence that path.[16]

Unfortunately, transactions costs affect both factor and product markets, creating the possibility of differing optimal paths of technical change and of institutional change depending on farm size or other factors. Transactions costs refer to the costs of adjustment, of information, and of negotiating, monitoring,

---

[16] See Alain de Janvry, Elisabeth Sadoulet, and Marcel Fafchamps, "Agrarian Structure, Technological Innovations, and the State," Working Paper No. 442, Department of Agricultural and Resource Economics, University of California-Berkeley, July 1987, p. 9.

and enforcing contracts.[17] These costs arise because assets are fixed in certain uses in the short run, because there is a lack of perfect information, because there are differences in the ability to use information, and because people are willing to benefit at the expense of others.[18]

The presence of transactions costs may mean, for example, that the cost of credit decreases as farm size increases, that labor costs per hectare increase as farm size increases (because of supervision costs), and the cost of land transactions declines as farm size increases. Therefore, as farm size grows, labor use per hectare may decline while machinery use per hectare and the demand for capital-intensive technologies may increase. Owners of large farms also may be quicker to adopt new technologies because they have fewer credit constraints affecting input purchases.

The presence of transactions costs means that the distribution of assets matters for the direction of technical and institutional change. Because the demand for particular types of technical and institutional changes will vary by farm size, the potential is created for conflicting demands on the public sector. Politicians and other public servants respond to the demands of competing groups by considering their own personal gains and losses. Consequently, a change which would benefit society as a whole may not occur if a politician receives greater private gain from an interest group that does not want the change than from a group that does.

When producers of a commodity are few, economically powerful, and regionally concentrated, they may find it easier to influence public decisions in their favor than if these conditions do not hold.[19] Even if the conditions do not hold, if a commodity is very important in the diets of people in urban areas or if it earns substantial foreign exchange, the public sector still may act to help its producers. However, if producers are neither organized into a powerful collective lobby nor producing an important commodity for urban consumption or export, they will seldom receive public help such as new technologies. This fact may explain why peasant farmers with small land holdings are often neglected.

The implications of transactions costs and collective action for the induced innovation model presented earlier are illustrated in Fig. 10-3. Changes in the underlying resource base for the country as a whole might imply that the least-cost path of technical change would occur in the direction of arrow Z (i.e., a

[17] Discussions of transactions costs are found in Oliver E. Williamson, *The Economic Institutions of Capitalism* (New York: Free Press, 1985); Douglas C. North, "Institutions, Transactions Costs, and Economic Growth," *Economic Inquiry,* vol. 25, 1987, pp. 415–428; and de Janvry, Sadoulet, and Fafchamps, op. cit.

[18] William J. Baumol, "Williamson's The Economic Institutions of Capitalism," *Rand Journal of Economics,* vol. 17, 1986, p. 280, points out that if there were no fixed or sunk costs in land, capital, or people, resources could easily be transferred to optimal uses. If information were perfect or if people could always figure out how to design contracts to cover any contingency, fixed costs would not matter. If people did not try to profit at others' expense, contracts could be drawn loosely and adjustments made as conditions change.

[19] de Janvry, Sadoulet, and Fafchamps, op. cit., p. 15.

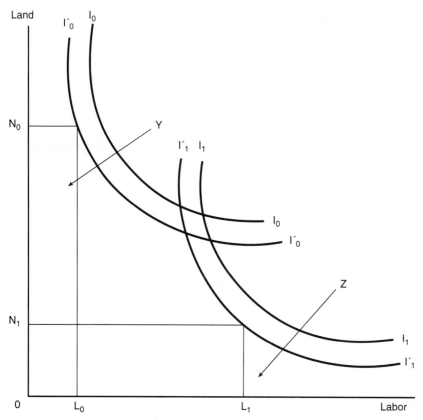

FIGURE 10-3
Induced technical innovation in the presence of transactions costs. The direction of technical change as dictated by changes in relative factor prices might call for cost-reducing path Z. However, transactions costs and collective action may create pressures to follow path Y, reducing the rate of overall economic growth.

path that would use relatively abundant labor and save relatively scarce land). Following path Z might be facilitated by the development of new labor-intensive, biologically-based technologies. However, if a few large-scale producers, due to the presence of transactions costs and collective action, were able to influence public officials so that technology I_0' were to be developed rather than I_1', then technical change might occur in the direction of arrow Y (perhaps through the development and adoption of capital-intensive, mechanically based technologies) rather than arrow Z. Benefits to the large farmers would be maximized but overall economic efficiency gains might be reduced (see Box 10-2).

The concern over the existence of transactions costs and collective action is not just a concern over the distribution of the benefits of agricultural develop-

---

BOX 10-2

THE RESULT OF INDUCED BUT DISTORTED TECHNICAL AND INSTITUTIONAL CHANGE

The northeast region of Brazil is poor and labor is abundant. Government money has been used to subsidize the development and adoption of capital-intensive technologies to build up California-like agribusinesses. Large landowners have benefited, but jobs have been cut at a time when farm laborers were already migrating to the Amazon in search of work.

In the education sector as well, roughly 60 percent of the Brazilian education budget is spent on public universities to provide an education for 500,000 mostly well-to-do students. The remaining 40 percent of the budget is spent on basic education for 30 million Brazilian children. Ninety times as much money is spent on each university student as each primary and secondary student because of the strong middle- and upper-class student lobby.

Source: The Economist, London, Vol. 321, number 7736, December 7, 1991.

---

ment. Rather, it is a concern that the rate of economic growth itself will be diminished as well. If, in the previous example, the farmers demanding path Y were few in numbers, and their total value of production compared to the farmers demanding path Z also was small, then the decision to develop technologies along path Y would mean a growth rate below the country's potential.

DESIGNING AN OPERATIONAL STRATEGY

The above discussion illustrates the multiplicity of forces (positive and negative) that influences the speed and breadth of agricultural development. An operational agricultural development strategy must incorporate means for reinforcing positive forces while neutralizing negative or distortionary forces. Interestingly, most previous development theories and strategies emphasize positive factors or bemoan negative factors, but seldom consider both. The reality that agricultural and overall economic development has proceeded rapidly in some countries while stagnating in others demonstrates that development is neither automatic nor hopeless. An operational agricultural development strategy should not contain the assumption that either conclusion is inevitable.

In the following sections, we distill the implications, positive and negative, from the above theories of agricultural development in the presence of transactions costs, collective action, and unequal asset distribution. The components required for a viable agricultural development strategy are identified. The resulting strategy must consider agricultural systems as they currently exist, the realities of human behavior, and the facts that agriculture is part of a larger economy, and that individual countries operate in an interdependent world.

Activities Specific to the Agricultural Sector

The sources of agricultural growth change over time; few countries today are able to achieve substantial production increases by expanding their land bases. In addition, land currently in production is being degraded in many countries due to population and other pressures on a fragile natural resource base. Ownership of land and other assets is highly unequal in many countries and fragmented in others. Hence one component of an operational agricultural development strategy is to reexamine the institutional arrangements governing land ownership and use and to make any needed adjustments.[20]

Improved transportation, marketing, and communications systems also become critical as development proceeds.[21] Lower transportation, marketing, and communications costs can reduce transactions costs and improve information flows, and thereby facilitate broad-based agricultural growth. Isolated regions tend to be poor regions.

The provision of high-payoff inputs and adequate financing for their purchase are additional components of a successful agricultural development strategy.[22] Farmers are rational and relatively efficient given their current resources. Consequently new inputs embodying improved technologies are needed to improve the productivity of farmers in developing countries. Pricing policies should be designed so as not to discourage the use nor encourage the abuse of these inputs. Otherwise, input use and technical change may diverge from the efficient path.

Agricultural research and extension are needed to generate and facilitate adoption of new technologies.[23] Educational levels of farmers also must be increased to improve their ability to recognize the benefits of and to use the technologies.[24] Education facilitates the inevitable structural transformation through which the employment base shifts from the agricultural to the non-agricultural sector as development proceeds. Education improves the capacity of people to assimilate and use information and thus can help reduce transactions costs.

The design of these institutions and technologies will be influenced by domestic prices (which are influenced by world prices) and by the current distribution of assets, transactions costs, and collective action. These costs and actions are influenced, in turn, by the existing political system, culture, ideologies, history, international forces, and ease of information flows. As a result, these technical and institutional changes may occur, as discussed earlier, in a direction that leads to widespread agricultural development, but they also may not, or at least part of them may not. They may reinforce existing inequality and social unrest. We suggest below some possible actions that

[20] See Chap. 11.
[21] See Chap. 14.
[22] See Chap. 13.
[23] See Chap. 15.
[24] See Chap. 15.

Improved transportation to reduce transactions costs becomes critical as development proceeds.

might lead to positive agricultural development rather than to stagnation or to growth accompanied by more unequal income distribution. First, however, we briefly mention macroeconomic and international factors to be considered when designing an operational agricultural development strategy.

Macroeconomic and International Actions

Agricultural development is affected to a significant extent by macroeconomic and trade policies that arise outside the agricultural sector. The levels and types of taxes, spending, and borrowing can dramatically influence farm prices and input costs. Exchange rates, or the value of the country's currency relative to currencies in other countries, can have major effects on agricultural prices and trade.

In some countries, foreign debt repayments significantly constrain growth and reduce domestic consumption. Internationally influenced interest rates and prices vary substantially over short periods of time, adding an additional measure of unpredictability to debt levels and national incomes. International labor markets for agricultural scientists mean that high salaries draw some of the brightest and most educated scientists to more developed countries and international agencies. Foreign aid is an important source of capital, land, and technical assistance for some countries, but is often unreliable and usually comes with strings attached.

In light of these and other factors, developing countries must carefully design macroeconomic and trade policies that do not discriminate against their agricultural sectors if they expect those sectors to grow and contribute to overall development. In addition, there is a need for more enlightened international institutional changes. We present suggestions for such policies and changes in Chaps. 16, 17, and 18.

Generating Enlightened Self-Interest

Any operational agricultural or economic development strategy must (1) treat people as individual economic agents irrespective of whether they are farmers, politicians, bureaucrats, military officers, scientists, or members of some other group; (2) recognize the realities of and motives for human behavior; (3) consider the lack of perfect information; (4) incorporate adjustment costs; and (5) design institutional arrangements to offset externalities and other market imperfections. Individuals will have to feel it is in their self-interest before necessary institutional changes will occur.

Groups Consist of Individuals   People belong to a variety of groups. These groups wield different types of power. For example, there are dozens of international agencies with financial and market power; hundreds of regional and national institutions with political and market power; thousands of scientists, planners, and other analysts with knowledge power; hundreds of thousands of military officers with military power; millions of villages and clans with cultural and social power; and hundreds of millions of families with labor and purchasing power.

While individuals may gain some measure of power by virtue of belonging to one of these groups, they are motivated to exercise that power by their individual desires and beliefs. Therefore we must consider the nature of human behavior if we are to design development strategies that encourage positive, but constrain negative activities, when groups of individuals exercise their collective power.

Human Behavior   People are basically self-interested, complex though their interests may be. Adam Smith recognized that individuals were self-interested, but felt that each individual, acting in his or her own behalf, would as if led by an "invisible hand" promote the welfare of society as a whole, even though unintentionally. Such is the implication of competitive markets.

However, Adam Smith's self-interest is a simple self-interest that ignores certain aspects of human behavior. When these aspects are combined with imperfect information, economies of scale, adjustment costs, externalities, imperfect markets, and political power, they can lead to economic outcomes that reflect an invisible foot stepping on the invisible hand.

What motivates people? People want to be content in their present situation and have some hope for the future. Most people are rational and try to maximize their well-being given their current situation. They are motivated by physical and emotional needs. Among many people we observe material greed, a thirst for power and social acceptance, and a willingness to sacrifice small losses for potentially larger gains. Most people gain pleasure from helping others and of course have desires for meeting their basic physical needs. They like to feel that their individual lives are significant. They are affected by their current situation: education, intelligence, skills, habits, family and cultural background, assets, and income. These factors constrain their activities and influence specific hopes and desires.

Many people's motivations lead to actions that benefit both the individual and society. Most current agricultural and economic development models recognize this fact, and rightly so. The model of induced innovation has this assumption embedded in it. However, certain motivations, particularly those derived from desires for money and power, can lead to behavior that hinders development. Some people will use their individual and group (collective) power to gain at the expense of others, even if their activities involve corrupt behavior.

Consequently an operational agricultural development strategy will need to consider means of raising the cost of engaging in behavior detrimental to society at whatever level (local, national, international). Several institutional changes centered around improving information and enacting and enforcing laws and regulations, could help accomplish the goal of raising this cost and could help create the environment that Adam Smith's invisible hand needs to function.

Imperfect Information Information is valuable, imperfect, and costly to acquire, and can exhibit economies of scale in acquisition. These attributes of information provide the incentives and the means for some people to use the advantage they have from asset ownership, military power, or their willingness to engage in unscrupulous behavior to acquire information before others.

In fact, even if all assets were initially distributed equally, unless information were available equally to all or unless enforceable rules were instituted to constrain dishonest behavior, the willingness of some to gain "unfair" advantage would eventually lead to unequal distributions of assets. In primitive societies, information is basically available to all and inappropriate activities are constrained by social and cultural norms. However, as societies become more complex concurrently with economic development, information becomes more imperfect and new institutions are needed to replace the rules that no longer constrain behavior.[25]

Standard neoclassical economics, as reflected in the induced innovation model, assumes that the lack of perfect information is of minor significance to

---

[25] These ideas are similar to those expressed by North, op. cit., pp. 420–425. North notes that impersonal exchange with third-party enforcement is essential for economic growth. Third-party enforcement implies that legal institutions exist.

economic development. As a result, the conclusions from this model tend to be overly optimistic. Other systems of economic analysis attack neoclassical economics for its overoptimism, but fail to provide an alternative analytical framework with prescriptive power.[26] In this book, we stress the importance of modifying the analytical framework of neoclassical economics to incorporate the presence of imperfect information and markets and factors that enhance information flows.

Adjustment Costs and Externalities Once physical and human assets are dedicated to certain activities, costs are incurred in moving them to alternative uses. Asset fixity creates incentives for people to protect their positions and therefore a need for compensation schemes to facilitate the transfer of resources to more productive uses. In addition, some activities will have unintended beneficial or negative effects on others or the environment. To the extent that individuals do not consider those benefits and costs when making decisions, they may engage in socially undesirable behavior or fail to produce enough of something that society needs.

The existence of adjustment costs and externalities creates a potential role for government actions to correct for those "market failures" to improve the welfare of society. However, because politicians, bureaucrats, the military, and other public servants have incentives to act in their own self-interest (as do all people), there is an inherent tendency for government intervention to exceed the socially desirable level. In addition, government actions use resources and can be distorted by collective actions of small groups. Therefore institutions also are needed to constrain government behavior.

Bringing About Needed Changes People must feel it is in their interest to design and enforce particular institutional changes. They need to know the implications of those changes. Institutional change involves costs because some people benefit from current arrangements and will fight any change.

The following six suggestions might help lower the cost of institutional change through enlightened self-interest: First, in those countries where asset ownership has become so unequal that inefficiencies in property rights are retarding agricultural development, asset redistributions (particularly land) are needed, usually with compensation arrangements (so that the changes will in fact occur).

Second, improvements in education, communications, and transportation can improve information flows and the ability of a large number of people in the country to act on information.

Third, decentralized industrial growth should lower labor adjustment costs (and facilitate employment), reduce externalities associated with urban crowd-

---

[26] These systems include the structuralist model, Marxist or radical political economics, or the other dependency theories mentioned in Chap. 6.

ing, improve market performances in rural areas, and help stimulate agricultural growth.

Fourth, social science research can be used to help lower the cost of designing and examining the implications of alternative institutional changes affecting agriculture.

Fifth, a government structure is needed that includes enforceable laws to protect citizens from each other and from the government itself. Government policies and regulations can also be used to reduce market failure.

Sixth, improved and enforceable international laws and other institutions are needed to reduce incentives for international abuses of power. We have discussed primarily domestic institutions, but rulers, politicians, military officers, and managers of international companies have incentives to satisfy their own self-interest by abusing the rights of people in less powerful circumstances in other countries. International institutional arrangements are needed to constrain economic and military action.

These suggestions may be wishful thinking unless domestic and international leaders become aware that it is in their own self-interest to undertake these changes. Otherwise, in those countries where existing institutions cause growing losses in efficiency or where frequent abuse of foreign power is being exercised, incentives are created for collective action that can lead to severe social unrest or revolution. Unfortunately, history has shown that transactions costs tend to be large enough that collective action through revolution is often the way that institutional changes are introduced. However, as events in eastern Europe and elsewhere have demonstrated in recent years, revolution is not the only way to obtain major institutional changes. As improvements in information flows reduce transactions costs, the potentially large gains from technological and institutional changes become clear to a broader spectrum of the population, and reforms can occur to stimulate agricultural and overall development. Thus, enhanced information flows must be at the heart of any development strategy.

SUMMARY

Several theories of agricultural development have been proposed over time. Expansion or conservation of resources, location, diffusion, high-payoff input, and induced innovation are some of the major ones. Technical and institutional changes are key components of an operational agricultural development strategy. These changes can be induced by relative price changes resulting from change in resource endowments and product demand. Because of transactions costs, collective action, and the realities of human behavior, agricultural sectors may not follow an economically efficient development path. The distribution of assets has important implications in the presence of transactions costs and collective action. If land is unequally distributed, then, because of transactions costs, the demands (for technologies, inputs, policies, etc.) of one group of producers are likely to be very different from those of others. Collective action can then pull the development process from its optimal path. Institutional changes to improve information flows and constrain exploitive behavior can become critical to agricultural development. Policymakers may become enlightened about the significance of transactions costs through social unrest.

IMPORTANT TERMS AND CONCEPTS

Agricultural research and
  extension
Asset distribution
Asset fixity and adjustment
  costs
Communications
Compensation schemes
Diffusion theory
Enlightened self-interest
Externalities
Government interventions
High-payoff inputs
Human motivation
Improved technologies
Induced institutional innovation

Induced technical innovation
Innovation possibilities curve
International factors
Invisible hand
Location theory
Macroeconomic factors
Market failure
Meta production functions
Perfect information
Resource conservation
Resource exploitation
Transactions costs
Transportation and marketing
  systems

LOOKING AHEAD

In this chapter we considered theories of agricultural development and suggested a broad framework for operational agricultural development strategies. In the following five chapters we consider sector-specific means of generating particular technical and institutional changes to stimulate agricultural growth. In later chapters we consider macroeconomic and international factors. We begin in Chap. 11 by focusing on land policies including land reform.

QUESTIONS FOR DISCUSSION

1 Contrast the resource exploitation, resource conservation, location, and diffusion theories of agricultural development.
2 Why is the resource exploitation theory of agricultural development less useful today than it was historically?
3 Why has the importance of resource conservation increased in recent years?
4 Describe two implications of the location theory of agricultural development.
5 What are the limitations of the diffusion theory of agricultural development?
6 Why has the high-payoff input theory become widely accepted?
7 What criticisms do Hayami and Ruttan make of the high-payoff input theory?

8 Describe the theory of induced technological innovation. Be sure to identify both the importance of relative input price changes and changes in the relative prices of inputs to outputs.

9 Describe the induced institutional innovation theory.

10 Contrast transactions costs and collective actions.

11 What are the implications of transactions costs and collective action for institutional innovation?

12 What do we mean by the term *enlightened self-interest?*

13 Why is it important to recognize the realities of human motivation, particularly greed, when designing an operational agricultural development strategy?

14 How might information be made more accessible to farmers?

15 Describe an example of a positive and of a negative externality.

16 What are the implications of a grossly unequal asset ownership pattern for economic growth?

17 Why are improved international institutions needed for agricultural development?

18 Why does Japanese agriculture have much higher output per hectare than U.S. agriculture, but much lower output per worker?

RECOMMENDED READINGS

Binswanger, Hans P., Vernon Ruttan, and others, *Induced Innovations: Technology, Institution, and Development* (Baltimore: Johns Hopkins University Press, 1978).

Boserup, Ester, *Population and Technological Change* (Chicago: University of Chicago Press, 1981).

Hayami, Yujiro, and Vernon W. Ruttan, *Agricultural Development: An International Perspective* (Baltimore: Johns Hopkins University Press, 1985), Chaps. 3 and 4.

North, Douglas, "Institutions, Transactions Costs, and Economic Growth," *Economic Inquiry,* vol. 25, 1987, pp. 415–418.

Schultz, Theodore, W., *Transforming Traditional Agricultural* (Chicago: University of Chicago Press, 1964).

Stevens, Robert D. and Cathy L. Jabara, *Agricultural Development Principles: Economic Theory and Empirical Evidence* (Baltimore: Johns Hopkins University Press, 1988).

Williamson, Oliver, *The Economic Institutions of Capitalism* (New York: Free Press, 1985).

CHAPTER 11

LAND TENURE AND REFORM

The distribution of rights in land relates to the distribution of power, income, social status, and incentives. A land reform that changes this distribution is by definition a change that shakes the roots and not the branches of a society.

Raup[1]

THIS CHAPTER

1 Discusses the meaning of land tenure and land reform
2 Explains why land reform is often necessary for agricultural development, why land reform is difficult to achieve, and what the requisites are for a successful land reform

MEANING OF LAND TENURE AND LAND REFORM

Land tenure refers to the rights and patterns of control over land. These rights include rights to use and to exclude use, rights to output from the land, and rights to transfer the land or its output to other users. Land rights determine social and political status as well as the economic power of a large proportion of the population in developing countries.

As population density increases, farming techniques change, and markets for agricultural products grow, pressures often develop to change existing land

---

[1] Philip M. Raup, "Land Reform Issues In Development," Staff Paper P75-27, Department of Agricultural and Applied Economics, University of Minnesota, St. Paul, 1975, p. 1.

tenure arrangements. In societies where land has been held in common, permanent and enforceable individual rights to land may evolve. In countries where ownership patterns are highly skewed with a few people owning much and many people owning little or no land, pressures often are exerted on the government to undertake a land reform. These pressures may arise from peasants who desire increased economic well-being or from those in power who hope that minimal concessions to the peasants will diffuse political unrest. A land reform, therefore, is an attempt to change the land tenure system through public policies. Land reform may change not only rights and patterns of control over the land resource, but also the mode of production (whether semifeudalistic, capitalistic, or socialist) and the agrarian class structure. Consequently, few subjects related to agricultural development are as controversial as land reform.

Land Ownership and Tenure Systems

A wide array of land ownership and tenure systems exists in the world. These systems reflect differences in historical influences, stage of development, culture, political systems, transaction costs, and many other factors. The systems vary in size and organization of land holdings, affect incentives to produce and invest, and influence the distribution of benefits from agricultural growth. Examples of average size of landholdings in Africa, Asia, and Latin America are presented in Table 11-1. The larger holdings in Latin America compared to Asia and Africa are particularly evident. A description of the impact of colonial rule on landholdings is provided in Box 11-1.

Family farms, corporate farms, state farms, and group farms are major types of farm ownership, but organization of farm enterprises within these types can vary substantially.[2] In many cases the owner of the farm is also the operator. In other cases, those who operate or work on the farm may earn a fixed wage or pay rent in cash or in a share of the farm output.

Small subsistence or semisubsistence family farms are common in developing countries. Families often provide most of the labor, and cultivation is labor-intensive. Much of the output is consumed on the farm where it is produced. However, not all small family farms are subsistence or semisubsistence farms; many are small commercial farms producing substantial surpluses for sale. Those farmers that do consume most of what they produce are usually very poor.

Large commercial family farms sell most of what they produce. While in developed countries these farms are highly mechanized and often involve only a small amount of nonfamily labor, in developing countries the operations are usually more labor-intensive and use a high proportion of hired labor. The

---

[2] See Sterling Wortman and Ralph W. Cummings, *To Feed This World: The Challenge and the Strategy* (Baltimore: Johns Hopkins University Press, 1978), p. 274.

TABLE 11-1
AVERAGE SIZE OF LANDHOLDINGS, SELECTED COUNTRIES, AROUND 1970

Region and country	Average size (in hectares)
Africa	
Cameroon	5.2
Ghana	3.2
Kenya	4.1
Malawi	1.5
Sierra Leone	1.8
Zambia	3.1
Asia	
India	2.3
Indonesia	1.1
Iraq	9.7
Korea, Republic of	0.9
Pakistan	5.3
Philippines	3.6
Latin America	
Brazil	59.7
Colombia	26.3
Costa Rica	38.1
El Salvador	4.1
Mexico	137.1

Source: Clive Bell, "Reforming Property Rights in Land and Tenancy," *World Bank Research Observer,* vol. 5, July 1990, pp. 143–166.

owner frequently does not live on the farm, but pays a manager to oversee the day-to-day operation.

Corporate farms often produce a limited number of commodities in large-scale units. These farms may have their own marketing (including processing) systems. This type of farm is more prevalent in developed than in developing countries, but there are numerous examples of large corporate farms in developing countries. The fruit plantations found in Central American countries, the banana plantations of the Philippines, and the cocoa plantations of West Africa are a few examples.

State farms are usually large, owned and operated by the government, and run by hired labor. The managers are responsible to a unit of a government planning agency that may set targets for production and direct the timing and method of key farming operations. Examples have existed recently in parts of China, the former Soviet Union, and Ethiopia. This type of farm usually suffers from inadequate incentives and ill-advised management decisions.

Group farms are communes, kibbutzim, collectives, or other types of farms that are operated by a group of people who work and manage the farm jointly. The joint income is then divided up among the members of the group. These group operations may also involve non-agricultural activities. Often, collec-

---

BOX 11-1

COLONIALISM AND LANDOWNERSHIP

Many of the landownership patterns found in developing countries are the vestiges of the colonial periods. The *latifundia* or extensive large-scale farms that currently exist in Central and South America alongside *minifundia* or very small farms are a direct descendent of colonialism. The Spanish and Portuguese colonizers allocated large tracts of land to elites who formed tropical plantations or large haciendas. Both types of landholding were made possible through the direct enslavement of indigenous populations, the importation of slaves from Africa, or the *encomienda* system that gave indirect control over local populations to certain elites.

Some of the richest agricultural lands in Africa have landownership patterns that were established during the periods of European colonization. Because European countries coveted exotic tropical products, such as cocoa, coffee, tea and various fruits, agricultural production in Africa was reorganized under colonial rule. Large landholdings were allocated to European settlers, such as the tea and coffee plantations in eastern Africa; rarely were the lands' original inhabitants compensated. Areas that had been self-sufficient in food production became exporters of large quantities of goods to Europe. An adequate labor supply was maintained sometimes through enslavement and sometimes through economic coercion.

In Asia, colonial rule led to similar forms of plantation agriculture. Japanese colonies in Korea and Taiwan produced for export to Japan; there was Dutch colonization in Indonesia, Spanish plantations in the Philippines, and European plantations in numerous countries.

Following the demise of colonial rule, many of these landownership patterns persisted, because of the political powers of the landed elite. Some of the antifeudal land reforms undertaken in various countries prior to 1970 were designed to remove the less desirable aspects of these landholding patterns. Implicit forms of enslavement of labor, such as through the maintenance of indebtedness, were prohibited. In many countries, the result of these reforms has been to reduce labor use, increase mechanization, and leave the distribution of land largely unchanged.

---

tivized farms are characterized by overinvestment in labor-saving capital-intensive technologies, since individuals do not receive the full returns from their labor. Special arrangements may be devised (for example a point system) to provide incentives for individual members to work harder. Small individual private plots also may be allowed. The kibbutzim of Israel, the Mennonites in the Paraguayan Chueo, and the Ujamaa villages of Tanzania are examples of group farm systems.

Not only do many types of land ownership and organization exist, but also many types of tenancy or leasing arrangements. Farm families may lease all or a part of their land for cash or for a share of the production from the land. A farmer may be allowed to farm a piece of land in exchange for his or her labor on another part of the owner's land. In some (or parts of some) countries, the village, tribe, or national government may own the land and grant use rights to part of the land to individual families. This system is common in Africa where social groups allocate land to individuals who maintain control over it and its output as long as they cultivate it.

Combine harvesters at a state farm in China.

The type of tenancy arrangement affects the risk and transactions costs borne by tenants and landlords and influences incentives to work or apply inputs. A share lease, for example, spreads the production risk between the landlord and tenant, while a cash lease concentrates the risk on the tenant. A cash lease implies lower transactions costs for the landlord than a share lease, since the amount received under the share lease has to be measured, and production has to be monitored. A tenant may have less incentive to apply additional fertilizer under a share lease than under a cash lease unless the landlord also shares the cost of the fertilizer. Thus, the use of a particular land or labor contracting mechanism may be a response to the presence of risk or transactions costs (see Box 11-2).

Types of Land Reform

Because there are many types of land ownership systems, there are many types of land reform. Prior to the 1970s, many if not most land reforms involved a movement away from feudalistic and semifeudalistic land tenure arrangements toward capitalist or socialist ownership modes.[3] Feudalism involved estates controlled by the traditional landed-elite with labor bonded to the estates through peonage or extra-economic forms of coercion.

---

[3] See Alain de Janvry, "The Role of Land Reform in Economic Development: Policies and Politics," *American Journal of Agricultural Economics,* vol. 63, May 1981, pp. 384–392.

BOX 11-2

TENANCY, RISK, AND TRANSACTIONS COSTS: THE CASE OF SHARECROPPING

Sharecropping is a widely practiced form of tenancy whose existence can be attributed to risk sharing and transactions costs. Because production is risky, and both tenants and land-owners desire to share risks, sharecropping represents a compromise between fixed-rent contracts, where the renter bears all the risk, and wage employment, where the landowner bears all the risk. Sharecropping also represents a response to the costly supervision of workers. Since under a wage system the worker receives wages based on hours worked rather than effort expanded, there is a tendency to shirk. Supervision is necessary, yet costly. Sharecropping returns some of these incentives to the tenant, yet also allows risk sharing.

Antifuedal land reforms have eliminated fuedalism in most of the world. In place of feudalism we see the existence of small subsistence or semisubsistence family farms, small and large commercial farms, corporate farms, state farms, and socialist or group farms. In many countries, however, this postfeudal order has resulted in some large capitalist farms or estates controlled by an elite well-to-do class and a coexisting small-farm sector. In a few countries (for example, South Korea and Taiwan), the postreform agricultural sector consists primarily of small family farms. And, in a few, such as Cuba, socialist farms predomi-nate. The form of the postreform agrarian structure depends largely on the motivation and political ideology behind the reforms.

Land reform today generally does not refer to the types of antifeudal reforms instituted in many countries prior to the 1970s. In those reforms, prohibition of bonded labor and reductions in labor exploitation were achieved, but in many cases a significant redistribution of land was not. As de Janvry notes, countries like Colombia, Ecuador, and India had successful antifeudal land reforms but very little redistribution of land.[4] Land reform as a policy issue today usually relates to seeking a shift in the dominant rural class from an elite-landowning class to medium-size and smaller peasant landowners.

In countries where socialist- or group-farms predominate (as opposed to capitalist farms of whatever type), future land reforms may involve a transition to increased capitalism as these countries struggle with the incentive problems that have plagued many types of group farms (see Box 11-3). Land reforms in socialist countries are difficult to achieve without a fundamental restructuring of the political system. The change in China from the socialized agricultural system to the market-based Household Responsibility System in 1979 was accompanied by political and economic upheaval.

---

[4] Ibid.

BOX 11-3

LAND REFORM IN EASTERN EUROPE

Following the collapse of Soviet-style models of central economic planning and control and the movement toward democracy in the late 1980s, governments in Eastern Europe were faced with the problem of how to reform their agricultural sectors. The organization of the agricultural sectors in these countries was rather similar; approximately one-third of the farms were state farms, and two-thirds were collectives (cooperatives). Most farm employees managed a household plot of about one-half hectare, while the state farms and collectives were large, about 2000 to 3000 hectares. Two paths of reform are illustrative of general trends in the region: Romania and Bulgaria.

In both countries, the rights of landowners prior to collectivization were recognized by parliamentary decree in February 1991. These decrees also established procedures for reclaiming these property rights. In Romania, land redistribution proceeded quickly. Local land commissions were established to hear household claims for up to 10 hectares. Some proof of the claim was needed. Whenever possible, claimants were given back the land actually owned, and when not, an alternative of equal size and quality was returned. Once in possession, the owner could sell it immediately, or purchase more land. Thus, a market for titled land, with very few institutional restrictions, was established. There was not an attempt to create farms of optimal size.

The Bulgarian redistribution proceeded much more slowly. Administrative delay hindered progress, and local commissions were very slow in forming. The laws implementing the distribution were very rigid and the construction of "appropriate size holdings" through administration was attempted. The local commissions adjudicated claims, but a planning team reassigned plots. The law prohibited the purchase and sale of land for three years, which hindered development of a land market.

In both cases, most of the new landowners remained integrated into the collective management system. In Romania, the formation of a land market opened a period of holdings consolidation and resale, but actual exit from the collective was delayed until the infrastructure for individual managment was developed. The slowness of the redistribution in Bulgaria guaranteed the existence of collective systems for many years.

Source: Karen Brooks, J. Luis Guasch, Avishay Braverman, and Csaba Csaki, "Agriculture and the Transition to Market," *Journal of Economic Perspectives,* vol. 5(4), Fall 1991, pp. 149–162.

Transactions Costs and the Agrarian Structure

No form of land tenure is universally efficient.[5] Differences in natural resource endowments, in the availability of new technologies, and in institutional arrangements all influence risk, transactions costs, and the farmer's opportunity to exploit his or her managerial ability. If there were well-defined private property rights and a reasonably equitable distribution of land, perfect information, and zero transactions costs (especially the cost of enforcing contracts), markets would work perfectly and it would not matter as much what type of agrarian structure prevailed. Bargaining would occur among landowners,

[5] See Yujiro Hayami and Vernon W. Ruttan, *Agricultural Development: An International Perspective* (Baltimore: Johns Hopkins University Press, 1985), p. 398, for additional discussion.

Plowing on a state farm in Bulgaria.

renters, and laborers and neither the returns to labor nor the overall economic efficiency of the agricultural system would depend on the type of agrarian structure.

In the real world, however, risk varies from country to country. Markets are not perfect. The cost of information and of negotiating, monitoring, and enforcing contracts can be quite high. People are willing to exploit others, labor hired on a time-rate basis may shirk (increasing the cost of supervision), the price of land may decline as farm size grows (due to the fixed cost associated with land transactions), and larger landowners may have better access to markets and information.

Many of these risk and transactions cost factors confer an economic advantage to large farms. Larger landowners can gain additional political advantage through collective action and can reinforce their advantage through the tax laws and pressures on the types of new technologies produced by the public research system. The result can be additional gains for an elite, but reduced economic efficiency for the agricultural sector and the country as a whole. Land reform is needed in these cases.

ACHIEVING SUCCESSFUL LAND REFORM

A country can desire land reform for a variety of economic, social, and political reasons. Yet land reforms, whether they involve changes in land tenancy or ownership, are usually difficult to achieve. And, it frequently is difficult for a society to even agree on whether a land reform, once implemented, has in fact succeeded. Let's examine briefly why land reform may be needed, why it may be difficult to achieve, how a country can measure whether a land reform has succeeded, and what factors improve the chances of achieving successful land reform.

Need for Land Reform

The broad economic and development goals of most societies include desires for improved income growth (efficiency), equity (income distribution), and security (political and economic stability). Land reform is needed in many countries because of its potential contribution to all three of these goals.

A skewed distribution of landholdings can hamper economic efficiency gains for several reasons. First, large land holdings often are not farmed intensively even in countries that are very densely populated. Some land owners hold land for speculative reasons. Others are absentee landlords who provide little supervision of those working on the farm. If the farm is owned by the government, planning and management may be centrally and poorly controlled, and individual incentives may be stifled since farms are forced to respond to output and input quotas. Large farms may substitute machinery for labor, exacerbating an unemployment problem. Large farmers facing labor supervision or other management problems often demand capital-intensive innovations from the agricultural research system in the country. Thus, new technologies are generated that do not reflect the true scarcity values of land, labor, and capital in the country.

Countries with large landholdings often have a coexisting sector of farms that are too small to provide an adequate living. These extremely small holdings of one or two hectares or less may have labor employed to the point at which its marginal product is close to zero. Thus, reducing the size of large farms and increasing the size of very small farms may be the only way to raise the marginal product of labor in agriculture. The marginal product must go up if income per worker is to increase.

As discussed earlier, other land tenure problems, including the need for tenancy reform, may have to be solved to improve entrepreneurial incentives and to reduce risks facing farmers. For example, as population density increases, property rights for land pastured in common may need to be redefined to avoid overgrazing. Or, share or cash rents may need to be changed as new technologies become available. Or, lease lengths may need to be more securely established to encourage capital investment.

Apart from growth or efficiency concerns, land reform often is needed for equity reasons. The number of landless laborers is growing rapidly in many countries, along with associated poverty and malnutrition. The only resource that these people control is their labor, whose value is depressed by the underuse of labor on large farms. Providing land resources to these people can be an effective means of raising incomes. As large farms are broken up, even those poor who do not receive land can benefit due to increased demands for labor. Large farms convey political power to a small group. This group may distort economic policies in a direction that hinders overall economic growth and creates severe hardship on the poorest segments of society. Thus, to achieve development as defined in Chap. 1, land reform is usually necessary.

In addition to growth and equity concerns, land reform is needed for political and economic security or stability in a country. In fact, exappropriations of land and partial land reforms experienced in many countries in the past have probably occurred primarily for purposes of political stabilization. This stabilization can have positive and negative impacts on economic growth and equity. To the extent that land reform appeases political unrest and reduces the chances of revolution, it reduces the chances of a country's experiencing the extremes of death and suffering that accompany a revolution. However, to the extent that a partial land reform achieves political stability without redistributing enough land or economic power to generate widespread growth and fundamentally reduce economic hardship and hunger, it may only perpetuate a status quo of chronic suffering.

Economic and political stability facilitate economic development. With little land, peasants are forced to live very close to the margin of survival. Drought, floods, or other natural disasters can quickly push the landless or small farmers below the margin.

Why Land Reform Is Difficult to Achieve

Because of the political and economic power that accompanies landownership in many countries, it is frequently difficult to conduct a significant land reform. Historically, land reforms have most often been made possible only after significant social upheaval caused by revolution, the overthrow of colonial powers, or war. In the former Soviet Union and China, social revolutions destroyed the power of the landed elite prior to the institution of collectivizing land reforms. An army of occupation enforced the socialist reforms in Eastern Europe following World War II. The extreme economic, political, and social turmoil of the 1970s in China and of the 1980s and 1990s in the Soviet Union and Eastern Europe, once again created the conditions for land reforms in those countries. In capitalist countries such as Japan, the Republic of Korea, and Taiwan, defeats in war or occupation were followed by redistributive reforms.[6]

In countries with capitalist forms of social and economic relationships, land reforms are difficult to achieve because those holding the land rights also have strong political power. Urban consumers often align with landowners. Because large farms tend to have large marketed surpluses, consumers fear that steep food price increases may follow a dramatic reform. Small changes may be supported as a means of political stabilization, but large-scale restructuring of property rights is difficult. Occasionally, governments support redistributive land reforms in response to strong revolutionary pressures, such as in Mexico

---

[6] See Clive Bell, "Reforming Property Rights in Land and Tenancy," *World Bank Research Observer,* vol. 5, July 1990, pp. 143–166.

(1940 to 1977) or the Philippines (1972 to 1975). Or, land reforms result following military overthrows of the government, such as in Peru (1969 to 1975). However, usually land reforms within capitalist agriculture are slow to occur because compensation is required if they are to be accepted by those losing land. Unless there is a large fiscal surplus in the government's budget, which is rare in developing countries, or substantial foreign aid, gainers cannot compensate the losers sufficiently for the land reform to be politically viable.

In countries with a socialist economic system and group farming, land reforms also may involve increased privatization of land or the rights to plan and to market output from the land. These reforms are difficult to achieve because they may imply movement toward a more market-driven economy and freer-political system. However, because the potential economic efficiency gains may be larger from this type of reform than from a redistributive reform within capitalist agriculture, the chances for a successful land reform may even be greater when the initial agrarian structure is socialist. The Chinese reform begun in 1979 had the wide support of the rural peasantry and urban consumers.

Measures of Successful Land Reform

Many countries have had land reforms in the sense that changes in the land tenure system have occurred. The mere fact that a change has taken place does not necessarily imply that a *successful* land reform has transpired. Many national leaders are interested in land reform because the reform may lead to increased political stability. However, unless there is evidence that incentives have been created for farmers to undertake hard work and increase their capital investment and unless poverty has been reduced and social status improved for the rural poor, a successful land reform has not occurred.

A successful land reform should alter the incentive structure in rural areas. Whether this structure has been altered is perhaps best measured by evidence of increased and continuous capital accumulation by small farmers in the form of livestock, farm buildings, equipment, and other improvements in land resources. Because these investments may be small in any one year, it usually takes a generation, perhaps 25 to 30 years, to truly evaluate the success of land reform.[7]

Agricultural productivity also should increase in the long run. However, in the first five years following a land reform, productivity may stagnate for a couple of reasons. First, the mix of commodities produced may shift a little more toward food crops and away from as heavy a reliance on cash crops. This shift and other disruptions to the normal input and output marketing channels, credit flows, changes in technologies needed from the agricultural research system and so forth, can hinder productivity growth in the short run.

[7] See Philip M. Raup, "Land Reform Issues in Development," Staff Paper P75-27, Department of Agricultural and Applied Economics, University of Minnesota, St. Paul, November 1975, for additional discussion.

Marketable surpluses may decrease because the poorer segments of the rural population, who benefit from the land reform, have a very high income elasticity of demand for food. As their incomes increase through more access to land, they consume more, and the aggregate marketed surplus may decline. Thus, short-term increases in agricultural productivity or marketable surpluses are not good measures of the success of land reform.

A land reform also can affect capital formation in the public sector. Countries with land tenure systems in need of reform often have poor rural schools and other public infrastructure. Large landowners typically hesitate to tax themselves to support schools, roads, and so on. Countries in need of land reform usually find it easier to collect public revenues by taxing export crops or by placing tariffs on imports. Governments implementing land reform have an opportunity to restructure the tax system. The new owners of small plots have increased ability to pay taxes and may do so willingly if they see that the tax system is honest and the proceeds will be used for schools, roads, and other local infrastructure.

Peasant associations and other farm groups also are likely to be formed after a successful land reform. These associations can play an important role in promoting the development and adoption of new technologies for agriculture, improving marketing channels and so forth. The formation of these associations therefore is another test of a successful land reform.

Evaluation of the success of a land reform is a dynamic process that should be undertaken for many years following its inception. An additional indicator of success is the changing pattern of landholdings. If the reform has any prospect for success, incentives should be in place to make agriculture in the reform sector profitable. If it is not, then farm failures will occur, and, under capitalist reforms, consolidation into larger units will follow. Thus, quickly growing farm size can be an indication of failure of a reform.

Requisites for a Successful Land Reform

Government commitment, government power, and administrative organization are essential for any successful land reform.[8] No land reform occurs without strong government resolve and power. If transactions costs can be reduced, particularly those related to the cost of information, people may find it easier to express their views, which may help strengthen government resolve. However, in countries with corrupt leaders and little sincere desire for effective land reform, no change is likely unless peasants take land reform into their own hands. Even in countries with sincere leaders who have a strong commitment to land reform, the government must possess sufficient power to prevent those opposed to land reform from sabotaging it or overthrowing the government (see Box 11-4).

---

[8] See Wortman and Cummings, op. cit.

BOX 11-4

REFORM OF CAPITALIST AGRICULTURE IN COLOMBIA

Colombia presents an example of some of the pitfalls associated with land reforms in many countries. In the 1930s, there was public outcry, mostly by urban consumers who desired cheaper foods, over the lack of productivity on the large landholdings of the rural elite. In 1936, Law 200 was passed that said that potentially productive but poorly cultivated or abandoned large holdings were to be expropriated by the government. This threat caused land productivity to rise for a short time, and virtually no land was confiscated. During the 1950s, there was a long period of civil conflict known as "La Violencia" that hastened the destruction of traditional social relations and weakened the political powers of the old agrarian oligarchy.

Following a peace pact, a new phase of land reform began. Law 135 of 1961 set forth an ambitious reform package that included full compensation to existing landholders. The gradualist approach doomed the package from the start. Political pressure from landed groups allied with urban consumer interests successfully diverted inputs, often with substantial subsidies, to large-scale farms. Land values on favored farms increased dramatically, making compensation financially impossible. By 1972, only 1.5 percent of all land in large farms had been redistributed.

Law 4 in 1973 declared an end to this redistributive reform and returned the country to the principles of Law 200. At the same time, a political coalition between large-scale farmers, a small but substantial family-farm sector and urban consumers formed and created pressure for a rural development program that favored the first two groups. Landless and marginal farmers were politically and economically excluded.

The conditions for a successful land reform never really existed in Colombia. Shifting alliances between urban and rural power groups diminished the political will. A lack of clear conviction for redistribution, combined with the slow pace of reform, further inhibited the efforts. Policies favoring large farms, largely intended to diffuse political opposition, had the effect of destroying any prospects for real reform.

Source: Clive Bell, "Reforming Property Rights in Land and Tenancy," *World Bank Research Observer,* vol. 5, July 1990, pp. 152–153.

Political opposition to land reforms can be diffused by reforming policies that benefit owners of larger holding. These policies, such as tax exemptions, credit policies, and input subsidies that favor larger farms, have the effect of increasing land prices, thus making compensation more expensive, and providing economic advantages to the privileged class. Policies favoring large farms create incentives for opposition to land reforms and lower the probability of successful reform.

An administrative organization that coordinates national and local decision making and implementation of the reform program is essential. This organization must implement a series of critical steps decisively and quickly. Speed is particularly important because if a reform is announced but not implemented quickly, capital will be removed from farms and productivity will suffer. For example, in Peru in the late 1960s a land reform was announced long before it was implemented. Landowners sold as many capital items as they could and halted any new investment.

Central authorities must act quickly to assemble land records that clearly identify the targeted land and its productivity. Criteria for acquiring land must be clear and simple, and rules for compensating former owners must be established. Former owners must not be allowed to reacquire the land after the reform.

Payments by new owners must be modest and should be integrated into a system of land taxes. One of the best ways for a country to raise revenues for local development is to tax owners of small landholdings. A land reform is incomplete if it is not associated with a tax reform that increases the tax burden on those who receive the land.[9] Land reform increases the capacity of farmers to pay taxes, and the new landowners can identify the payment of taxes with the benefits they receive.

Land reform disrupts the institutions providing services such as credit, inputs, marketing, and technical information. Unless these systems are adjusted concurrently with the land reform, the reform will almost certainly fail. A marketing system that effectively serves small farms may be substantially different than the one that functioned before the land reform. New methods for distributing technical information may be needed, as the previous landowners may have been able to deal directly with the scientists in the agricultural research system. Group action such as cooperatives may be needed to coordinate services in a manner that is responsive to requirements of numerous owners of small farms.

SUMMARY

Land tenure refers to the rights and patterns of control over the land resource. Land rights determine social and political status as well as the economic power of a large proportion of the population in developing countries. A land reform is an attempt to change the land tenure system through public policies. Land tenure systems vary in farm size and organization, affect incentives to produce and invest, and influence the distribution of benefits from agricultural growth. Family farms, corporate farms, state farms, and group farms are major types of farm ownership. Many types of tenancy or leasing arrangements also exist.

The postfeudal order has resulted in some large capitalist farms and a coexisting small farm sector in many countries. Socialist farms predominate in some countries. No form of land tenure is universally efficient. Land reform is difficult to achieve because those holding the land rights have political power. Land reform is needed for improved economic efficiency, equity, and political and economic stability. Unless there is evidence that incentives have been created for farmers to undertake hard work and increase their capital invest-

[9] See Raup, op. cit., p. 8.

ment, and, unless poverty has been reduced and social status improved for the rural poor, a successful land reform has not occurred. Government commitment, government power, and administrative organization are needed for a successful land reform. Land reform must take place quickly and must be accompanied by credit, marketing and other services, and new land owners should be taxed to support development.

IMPORTANT TERMS AND CONCEPTS

Capitalistic agriculture
Compensation
Corporate farms
Entrepreneurial incentives
Family farms
Group farms
Land reform
Land tenure
Marketable surplus

Political stabilization
Property rights
Public capital formation
Semifeudal land tenure
Socialist agriculture
State farms
Successful land reform
Tenancy reform
Transactions costs

LOOKING AHEAD

In this chapter, we considered institutional changes related to land tenure. In the next chapter, we consider additional institutional changes related to land, but also to water and air. We focus on environmental problems, their nature, their causes, and potential solutions to them. As countries develop, as populations grow, and as incomes change, stresses are created on the environment and/or natural resource base. The implications are felt locally, regionally, nationally, and internationally.

QUESTIONS FOR DISCUSSION

1 What is land tenure?
2 What are the major ways farms are organized?
3 What are the major types of tenancy arrangements?
4 What is land reform?
5 How does an antifeudal land reform differ from land reforms within a capitalist or socialist agrarian structure?
6 Why is a land reform often necessary?
7 Why is a land reform difficult to achieve?
8 How do you judge if a land reform has been successful?
9 Why are large land holdings in a densely populated country bad?
10 What are the requisites of a successful land reform?
11 What pressures might population growth or new technologies place on existing land tenure arrangements?
12 Why is it important for a land reform to take place quickly?
13 What services must accompany a land reform?

RECOMMENDED READINGS

Bell, Clive, "Reforming Property Rights in Land and Tenancy," *World Bank Research Observer,* vol. 5(2), July 1990, pp. 143–166.

Berry, Albert, and William Cline, *Agrarian Structure and Productivity in Developing Countries* (Baltimore: Johns Hopkins University Press, 1979).

de Janvry, Alain, "The Role of Land Reforms in Economic Development: Policies and Politics," *American Journal of Agricultural Economics,* vol. 63, 1981, pp. 384–392.

Dorner, Peter, and Don Kanel, "The Economic Case for Land Reform: Employment, Income Distribution, and Productivity," in P. Dorner, (ed.), *Land Reform in Latin America,* Land Economics Monograph No. 3, University of Wisconsin, Madison, 1971.

Hayami, Yujiro, and Vernon W. Ruttan, *Agricultural Development: An International Perspective* (Baltimore: Johns Hopkins University Press, 1985), pp. 389–398.

Ip, P. C. and C. W. Stahl, "Systems of Land Tenure, Allocative Efficiency, and Economic Development," *American Journal of Agricultural Economics,* vol. 60, 1978, pp. 19–28.

Raup, Philip M., "Land Reform and Agricultural Development," in Herman M. Southworth and Bruce F. Johnston, (eds.), *Agricultural Development and Economic Growth,* (Ithaca, N.Y.: Cornell University Press, 1967).

Raup, Philip M., "Land Reform Issues in Development," Staff Paper P75-27, Department of Agricultural and Applied Economics, University of Minnesota, St. Paul, 1975.

Wortman, Sterling and Ralph W. Cummings, Jr., *To Feed This World: The Challenge and the Strategy* (Baltimore: Johns Hopkins University Press, 1978), pp. 271–288.

CHAPTER 12

ENVIRONMENTAL PROBLEMS AND POLICIES

. . . poverty compels people to extract from the ever shrinking remaining natural resource base, destroying it in the process. In fact, the major characteristic of the environmental problem in developing countries is that land degradation in its many forms presents a clear and immediate threat to the productivity of agricultural and forest resources and therefore to the economic growth of countries that largely depend on them.

Schramm and Warford[1]

THIS CHAPTER

1 Examines the nature of environmental or natural resource problems that influence the sustainability of agricultural development in developing countries

2 Identifies the principal causes of environmental problems in developing countries

3 Discusses some potential solutions to environmental problems in developing countries

NATURE OF ENVIRONMENTAL PROBLEMS

Sound environmental management is generally recognized as essential for sustainable agricultural and economic development. Yet the effects of environmental degradation and poor natural resource management are increasingly

---

[1] Gunter Schramm and Jeremy J. Warford, (eds.), *Environmental Management and Economic Development* (Baltimore: Johns Hopkins University Press, 1989), p. 1.

evident throughout the world. The wide-ranging yet often interrelated problems of soil erosion, siltation of rivers and reservoirs, flooding, overgrazing, poor cropping practices, desertification, salinity, waterlogging, deforestation, energy depletion, possible climate change, loss of biodiversity, and chemical pollution of land, water, and air, appear to be increasing problems in developing countries. The poorest countries tend to be most dependent on their natural resource base and thus have the potential of being the most vulnerable to environmental degradation. These countries find environmental problems particularly difficult to solve because rapid population growth, outmoded institutional relationships, poverty, and a lack of financial resources conspire against solutions. The poorest people within these countries usually suffer the most as a result of environmental degradation.

As agricultural and economic development proceed, forces are set in motion, some reducing and others increasing the pressures on the environment. Changes in the rate of population growth, new technologies, social and institutional relationships, the increased value of human time, and shifts in the weight placed on future as opposed to current income, all influence the relationship between human activity and natural resource base. Economic and natural resource policies and other institutional changes can either alleviate or aggravate natural resource problems. The nature of particular types of environmental problems is discussed below, followed by a description of causes and potential solutions.

Soil Erosion, Siltation, and Flooding

Soil erosion is slowly undermining agricultural productivity in many parts of the world. The extent of the world erosion problem is very difficult to assess because few nations have systematically surveyed the condition of their soil resources.[2] Nevertheless, the amount of agricultural land now being retired due to soil erosion is estimated to be at least 20 million hectares per year.[3] An erosion rate of 50 tons per hectare is common in upland watersheds in many developing countries, whereas soil can regenerate somewhere between 0 and 25 tons per hectare.[4]

A loss of 50 tons per hectare represents a loss of only about 3 millimeters from the top of the soil, yet often the gullies and exposed bedrock from uneven erosion scar the landscape.[5] The effects on productivity are potentially serious.

---

[2] See Randall L. Kramer, "An International Overview of Soil Conservation Policy," in Allen Maunder and Ulf Renborg, (eds.), *Agriculture in a Turbulent World Economy*, (England: Gower Publishing Co., 1986), p. 307.

[3] See Norman Meyers, "The Environmental Basis of Sustainable Development," in Gunter Schramm and Jeremy J. Warford, (eds.), *Environmental Management and Economic Development*, (Baltimore: Johns Hopkins University Press, 1989), p. 59.

[4] See Alfredo Sfeir-Younis, "Soil Conservation in Developing Countries," Western Africa Projects Department, World Bank, Washington, D.C., 1986.

[5] Meyers, op. cit., p. 60.

Results of soil erosion in the Dominican Republic.

Eroded soils typically are at least twice as rich in nutrients and organic matter as the soil left behind.[6] Soil nutrient losses can be partially replaced by increased use of chemical fertilizers, but only up to a point, and fertilizer can be expensive. At any rate, the yields with fertilizers are lower than they would be in the absence of erosion, so that erosion reduces productivity below its potential. It is estimated that erosion of good soils in the tropics may be resulting in maize-yield reductions of 10 to 30 percent.[7] In Guatemala, 40 percent of the productive capacity of the land may have been lost through erosion.[8]

Watersheds are seriously deteriorating in the hills of the Himalayas, on the steep slopes of the Andes mountains, in the Yellow River basin in China, in the Central American highlands, in the Central Highlands of Ethiopia, and on densely populated Java. It appears that the worst erosion in terms of average

[6] See Robert Repetto, "Managing Natural Resources for Sustainability," in Ted J. Davis and Isabelle A. Schirmer, (eds.), *Sustainability Issues in Agricultural Development,* World Bank, Washington, D.C., 1987, p. 172.

[7] See Meyers, op. cit.

[8] See Repetto, op. cit.

soil loss per hectare may be in Asia, the second worst in Latin America, and the next worse in Africa. Differences are due to the intensity of cultivation on highly erodible soils.

The indirect or off-site effects of erosion through siltation of rivers and reservoirs are perhaps more serious than the on-site effects. When reservoirs fill with sediment, hydroelectric and irrigation storage capacity is lost, cutting short the useful lives of these expensive investments. When rivers silt up, flooding occurs during rainy seasons. Soil erosion in the hills of Nepal, for example, causes flooding in the plains of Nepal, India, and Bangladesh. Flooding in the Yellow River basin in China is another example. This flooding causes both direct human suffering and crop destruction.

While flooding is a serious periodic problem in certain countries, not all or even most flooding is due to siltation. Low-lying countries like Bangladesh and parts of Egypt, Indonesia, Thailand, Senegal, The Gambia, and Pakistan are particularly vulnerable to flooding due to high river levels during the rainy season and sea surges during storms. About 80 percent of Bangladesh, for example, is a coastal plain or river delta. In 1988, approximately two-thirds of this country of 115 million people was flooded. While a certain amount of normal flooding can have a positive effect on agricultural production, excessive flooding results in substantial loss of life from disease as well as drowning.

Desertification

Excluding real deserts, potentially productive drylands cover about one-third of the world's land surface.[9] About one-sixth of the world's population lives in dryland areas that produce cereals, fibers, and animal products. In the arid regions, averaging 200 to 300 mm of annual rainfall, vegetation is sparse and nomadic herding of animals like goats and cattle predominates. In the semi-arid regions, with 300 to 600 mm of rain, dryland farmers grow cereals such as wheat, sorghum, and millet in more settled agriculture. The semi-arid regions are smaller in area but more densely populated than are arid regions.

The term *desertification* applies to a process occuring in these arid and semi-arid regions. Desertification involves the depletion of vegetative cover, exposure of the soil surface to wind and water erosion, and reduction of the soil's organic matter, soil structure, and water-holding capacity. Intensive grazing, particularly during drought years, reduces vegetative cover; the loss of vegetation reduces organic matter in the soil and thus changes soil structure. After a rain, the earth dries out and becomes crusted, reducing the infiltration of future rains. Then, even more vegetation is lost for lack of water, the surface crust is washed or crumbles and blows away, leaving soil that is less fertile soil and unable to support much plant life.[10]

---

[9] See William W. Murdock, *The Poverty of Nations: The Political Economy of Hunger and Population* (Baltimore: Johns Hopkins University Press, 1980), pp. 284–289, for additional discussion.

[10] See Murdock, op. cit., p. 285.

The Yellow River in China is subject to frequent flooding due to siltation.

Cropping, particularly when very intensive and when combined with drought, is another major cause of desertification. If soil organic matter is depleted by intensive farming practices and not replaced, a process similar to that described above occurs. As supplies of firewood dwindle, people use dried manure for fuel rather than fertilizer. As the soil loses its fertility, crop yields fall and wind and water erosion accelerates. Eventually the land may be abandoned.

Moderate desertification may cause a 25 percent loss of productivity while severe desertification can reduce productivity by 50 percent or more. It is estimated that 65 million hectares of productive land in Africa have been abandoned to desert over the last 50 years. Desertification is particularly a problem in the Sahel region of Africa and in parts of the Near East, South Asia, and South America. In terms of people directly affected, approximately 50 to 100 million people are currently dependent on land threatened by desertification. This number is less than 2 percent of the world's population, making the problem globally less important than the more general problem of soil erosion, except of course to the 50 to 100 million affected people. Areas where desertification is a problem also tend to be areas with rainfall that is both low and unpredictable. The ensuing periodic droughts create short-term severe food crises in those areas.

Salinity and Waterlogging

Irrigation, one of the oldest technological advances in agriculture, has played a major role in increasing global food production. However, bringing land under irrigation is costly, and degradation of irrigated land through questionable water management practices is causing some land to lose productivity or be retired from production completely. The major culprits are waterlogging and salinity.

Seepage from unlined canals and heavy watering of fields in areas with inadequate drainage can raise the underlying water table. Almost all water contains some salts. High water tables concentrate salts in the root zones and also starve plants for oxygen, inhibiting growth. Evaporation of water leaves a layer of salt that accumulates and reduces crop yields. A typical irrigation rate leaves behind about 2 to 5 tons of salt per hectare annually, even if the water supply has a relatively low salt concentration. If not flushed out, salt can accumulate to enormous quantities in a couple of decades.[11]

No one knows for sure how large an area suffers from salinization, but the Food and Agriculture Organization of the United Nations (FAO) estimates that one-half the world's irrigated land is so badly salinized that yields are affected. Others put the figure closer to one-quarter of the world's irrigated land. Regardless, the figure is large. Some 20 to 25 million hectares are affected in India, 7 to 10 million hectares in China, and 3 to 6 million hectares in Pakistan. Other developing areas severely affected include Afghanistan, the Tigris and Euphrates river basins in Syria and Iraq, Turkey, Egypt, and parts of Mexico.

Deforestation, Energy Depletion, and Climate Change

Forests play a vital role in providing food, fuel, medicines, fodder for livestock, and building materials. They provide a home for innumerable and diverse plant and animal species. They protect the soil, recycle moisture, and reduce carbon dioxide in the atmosphere. But forests are being cleared at an alarming rate throughout the world. Every year more than 11 million hectares are cleared, and the rate of cutting is increasing. The earth's forested areas have declined by about one-half in this century. Deforestation exceeds 2 percent of the remaining forest annually in Côte d'Ivoire, Paraguay, Nigeria, Nepal, Costa Rica, Haiti, El Salvador, and Nicaragua. It is proceeding very rapidly in Brazil, Indonesia, and Colombia.

Deforestation creates environmental problems on land and in the air. Forest clearing can degrade soils and increase erosion in tropical watersheds. Soils in tropical forests tend to be fragile and unsuited for cultivation; their fertility is quickly depleted with ensuing erosion following tree clearing. In semi-arid areas, deforestation contributes to loss of organic matter, increases wind and water erosion, and speeds the rate of desertification.[12] As forests are burned to clear land, carbon dioxide and carbon monoxide are emitted into the atmo-

---

[11] See Sandra Postel, "Saving Water for Agriculture," *State of World 1990,* Lester Brown and others, (eds.), (New York: W. W. Norton and Co., 1990), p. 44.

[12] See Repetto, op. cit.

Deforestation has led to soil erosion in Nepal.

sphere, contributing to global warming. Brazil, for example, contributes some 336 million tons of carbon to the air each year through deforestation, more than six times as much as it does through burning fossil fuels.[13]

In developing countries, seven out of ten people depend on fuelwood for meeting their major energy (cooking and heating) needs. The FAO estimates that three out of four people who rely on fuelwood are cutting wood faster than it is growing back. When people cannot find fuelwood, they turn to other sources of organic matter such as dung for fuel, thereby depleting soil fertility and aggravating soil erosion and desertification.

Deforestation also threatens the world's biological diversity. Tropical forests cover only 7 percent of the world's landmass, yet they contain more than 50 percent of the plant and animal species.[14] In Madagascar, for example, there were, until recently, 9500 documented plant species and 190,000 animal species, most of them in the island's eastern forest. More than 90 percent of the forest has now been eliminated, along with an estimated 60,000 species.[15]

Global warming is an environmental problem affected by and felt by all countries. Much of the increased buildup of carbon dioxide and other gases is the result of fossil-fuel combustion in developed countries, but burning of forests is also a major cause. As carbon dioxide and other gases accumulate in the atmosphere, they may trap heat, creating the so-called greenhouse effect. If world temperatures rise, average sea level may rise, thus threatening coastal

[13] See Christopher Flavin, "Slowing Global Warming," in Lester Brown and others, (eds.), *State of the World 1990*, (New York: W. W. Norton and Co., 1990), p. 20.

[14] See E. O. Wilson, "The Current State of Biological Biodiversity," Chap. 1, in E. O. Wilson, (ed.), *Biodiversity*, (Washington, D.C.: National Academy Press, 1988), p. 8.

[15] See Repetto, op. cit., p. 174.

lands. Violent storms, monsoons, droughts, floods, and generally increased weather variability are likely. While a warmer world is not necessarily less favorable to agriculture, regional impacts are harder to predict. And global warming could be very hard on certain animal species because their ecosystem may shift while the property-line boundaries of their preserves do not.

Chemical Pollution

Misuse of chemical pesticides and fertilizers has contaminated the land and water in many developing countries, damaging the health of producers and consumers, stimulating the emergence of pests resistant to pesticides, destroying the natural enemies of pests, and reducing fish populations or rendering them unsafe for human consumption. Acute pesticide poisonings are common, and little is known about potential long-term health effects. Few developing countries have established meaningful pesticide regulatory and enforcement systems.

More than 400 pests have become resistant to one or more chemicals, and the number is growing rapidly.[16] World pest populations have increased as pesticides kill natural predators of pests. Fertilizer runoff increases nitrate levels in ponds and canals, reducing oxygen levels and killing fish. Fish in irrigated rice paddies often are destroyed by excessive pesticide levels.

Heavy use of pesticides and fertilizers tends not to hurt agricultural production in the short run. However, as resistance to pesticides builds up and predators are reduced, future production potentials are jeopardized. And society bears the cost of off-farm pollution.

CAUSES OF ENVIRONMENTAL PROBLEMS

Environmental degradation can result from physical, economic, and institutional factors. Many environmental problems are interrelated; for example, deforestation, erosion, and siltation of rivers and reservoirs are all linked. Natural resource degradation usually has both direct and indirect causes. For example, desertification can directly result from overgrazing and poor cropping practices, but indirectly result from poverty and population growth. Understanding the true causes of environmental degradation requires a searching for and analysis of complex direct and indirect physical, economic, and institutional linkages.

Physical Causes of Natural Resource Degradation

Physical or technical causes of natural resource degradation are often the most visible and direct, even though a series of complex linkages may be involved.

---

[16] See Michael J. Dover and Brian A. Croft, *Getting Tough: Public Policy and Management of Pesticide Resistance,* (Washington, D.C.: World Resources Institute, 1984).

Land clearing for timber, fuelwood, cattle ranching, or farming causes deforestation. Deforestation results in loss of biodiversity and soil erosion. If the forest is burned, carbon dioxide enters the atmosphere. If the area is semi-arid, loss of forests can contribute to desertification. Desertification can also result from overgrazing, which itself is caused by too many cattle eating grass in an area subject to dry spells or droughts. Intensive cropping in semi-arid areas contributes to desertification. Many other examples of physical causes of natural resource degradation can be cited. Salinity and waterlogging result from poorly constructed and poorly managed irrigation systems. Chemical pollution results from excessive fertilizer and pesticide use. Siltation of rivers and tidal surges during storms cause flooding.

It is important to identify physical causes of environmental problems. However, if solutions to these problems are to be found, it is even more important to identify the underlying economic and institutional causes including social, cultural, and policy-related causes.

Economic Causes of Natural Resource Degradation

Poverty and environmental degradation go hand in hand. Poverty drives people to farm marginal lands intensively, to seek fuelwood relentlessly, and to follow other agricultural practices that produce food at the potential sacrifice of future production. As discussed in Chap. 4, poverty reinforces population growth, which is a major cause of deforestation, overgrazing, and farming on steep slopes, drylands, and flood plains.

The concern of the poor for the present, implying heavy discounting of future costs and benefits (see Box 12-1), is matched by the needs of governments in developing countries to deal with internal and external debt problems. Indeed, the existence of debt problems in many LDCs reflects previous decisions to spend on current consumption rather than save for the future. Governments follow policies that encourage natural resource-based exports to pay off debts and import capital goods. They lack the financial resources to address environmental problems.

Countries implementing economic development programs usually find high rates of return to many types of capital investment. The high interest rates often characteristic of these cases encourage current consumption and may place demands on natural resources. Interest rates in developing countries are also influenced by interest rates in major developed countries. Therefore, factors such as the U.S. federal budget deficit, which places upward pressure on interest rates, encourages natural resource degradation in developing countries.

Market failures due to externalities and transactions costs are an additional cause of natural resource problems. Actions of farmers that influence soil erosion or pesticide pollution create social costs that are not borne by the farmers themselves. Thus, these external costs may not be considered by farmers when making decisions (see Box 12-2). Furthermore, a lack of informa-

---

BOX 12-1

THE DISCOUNT RATE AND THE ENVIRONMENT

Positive interest and discount rates are caused by two factors: a preference for benefits now rather than later, and the productivity of capital. If current consumption is sacrificed and invested, this capital investment will provide greater potential for consumption in the future. The effect of a positive discount rate is to place more value on present than on future consumption. While there is continual discussion about the ethics of using discount rates to gauge the environmental impact of projects, individuals, businesses, and governments all use discounting to make decisions.

Discount rates, along with the length of time in the future that a payoff or cost will be incurred, have a large influence on the current value of that payoff or cost. Most decision makers make their decisions based on the difference between the present value of benefits and the present value of costs. If this difference is positive, then the action will be undertaken, and if negative, it will not. Small holders who perceive current benefits, such as food production, from their actions and distant future costs, such as productivity losses from erosion, are unlikely to invest heavily in erosion control devices because they heavily discount these future costs. Similarly, governments deciding to promote policies that boost current incomes at the expense of future costs will be more likely to decide in favor of those policies if future costs are discounted. The higher the discount rate, the lower the value of future costs.

Interest rates do not, however, have an unambiguous effect on the environment. High interest rates clearly slow investments that will conserve natural resources for future use. Low interest rates, on the other hand, stimulate investments in industries, roads, irrigation systems, etc. Often, future environmental costs are not taken into account, either by private decision makers or governments, and the low cost of capital induced by low interest rates permits investments that degrade the environment.

Present Value of $100

Years in future	Discount rate (%)		
	5	10	12
10	61	38	32
20	38	15	10
30	23	6	3

*Note: PV = V/(1 + r)^t, where r = discount rate, t = years, V = value of item being considered—in this case, $100.

---

tion or concern about environmental damage creates transactions costs that facilitate environmentally destructive behavior. In summary, a variety of economic factors are responsible for natural resource problems.

Institutional Causes of Natural Resource Degradation

A major cause of environmental degradation is institutional failure, both private and public. Institutions are rules of behavior that affect private incentives. Existing social structures and local customs may not be adequate to preserve

BOX 12-2

EXTERNALITIES AND PRIVATE DECISIONS

One commonly cited cause of environmental degradation is the divergence between private and social costs of actions. This divergence is caused by external costs. An external cost exists when an activity by one agent causes loss of welfare to another agent *and* the loss of welfare is uncompensated. The effect of externalities on private decisionmaking is illustrated in the figure below.

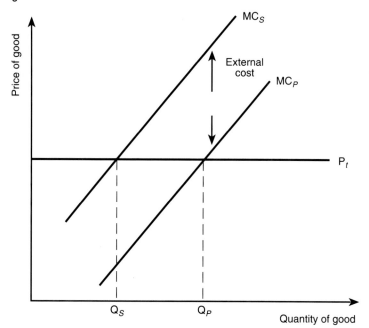

A farmer who cannot influence market prices will produce a good up until the point where the private marginal cost of its production (MC_p) equals the market price. In the figure, this point is shown where $MC_p = P_t$ and Q_p units are produced. An external cost is represented by the social marginal cost curve (MC_s) which exceeds the private cost curve. From society's point of view, the desirable production level is Q_s (where $MC_s = P_t$). Thus, the externality leads to more production of the good than is socially desirable.

the environment as population growth and economic development proceed. Or, environmentally constructive social structures and customs may be destroyed by national policies or by increased transactions costs and collective action. In some cases, inadequate institutions are the legacy of colonial interference or the result of more recent international influence.

Inadequate property rights in forests, pastures, and ground and surface waters can undermine private or local collective incentives to manage resources on a sustainable basis. In some areas the land or water resource was traditionally held in common. Under a common-property regime, people in the village or community had access to use the resources but did not own or rent them privately. When the local society could maintain authority over the resource, or when population pressures were such that the resource was in abundant supply, then this common property could be managed in a socially optimal manner. However, as population increases and as national policies usurp local authority, breaking down traditions and customs, incentives for resource preservation and traditional means of controlling access often are destroyed. If one person does not cut down the tree for fuelwood, another will. Or, if one person's goat does not eat the blade of grass, another person's goat will. Or, if one person does not use the water or catch the fish, another will. The result is that incentives exist for each individual to overexploit resources because otherwise someone else will.

Common-property regimes do not have to cause resource mismanagement if local institutions create incentives to efficiently manage the resource. In many areas of Africa, common-property institutions were said to cause overgrazing on rangelands. However, attempts by the government to replace these institutions with private-ownership schemes were largely counterproductive, contributing to more rapid degradation of resources and leading to increased economic inequality. As Southgate and Runge show, common-property institutions can be a viable means of managing resources.[17]

Public policies are another major institutional cause of natural resource degradation. Agricultural pricing policies, input subsidies, and land use policies often discourage sustainable resource use. Governments in developing countries intervene in agricultural markets to keep food prices artificially low. This discrimination against agriculture causes land to be undervalued, reducing incentives for conservation. And, low incomes make the investment required for sustainable output difficult.

Governments frequently subsidize fertilizer and pesticides, in part to compensate for keeping farm prices low. If there are externalities caused by pesticide or fertilizer use, then subsidies, because they increase input use will increase the level of externality. Subsidies may be indirect in the form of roads or export subsidies that encourage deforestation. Subsidized irrigation water can encourage its wasteful use.

Land tenure and land use policies may cause exploitation of agricultural and forest lands with little regard for future productivity effects. Short leases, for example, create incentives to mine the resource base for all it is worth in the short run. And, as just noted, it is an error to think that local incentive problems can be entirely corrected by national policies. Bromley and Chapagain point out that, in Nepal, national policies on forests have destroyed local

---

[17] Douglas Southgate and C. Ford Runge, "The Institutional Origins of Deforestation in Latin America," Staff Paper P90-5, Department of Agricultural and Applied Economics, University of Minnesota, St. Paul, January 1990.

conservation practices and incentives.[18] A common policy in Latin America is to require that land be developed, which usually means cleared of trees, prior to receiving title to the land. A large part of the deforestation in the Brazilian Amazon is associated with these types of titling rules.

Land use patterns are sometimes affected by colonial heritage or other international influences. In parts of Latin America and the Caribbean, large sugarcane, coffee, and banana plantations, or even cattle ranches are found in the fertile valleys and plains, while small peasant farms intensively producing food crops dot the eroding hillsides. The low labor intensity of production in the valleys depresses job opportunities and forces the poor to rely on fragile lands to earn incomes. These patterns are the legacy of Spanish and Portuguese colonists. Colonial powers in Africa changed cropping systems to cash-cropping in areas where cash-cropping could not be supported by the natural resource base. Peasants have been forced onto marginal lands, reducing lands for nomads. Traditional nomadic trading patterns were also disrupted.[19]

These and other institutional policies have contributed to natural resource problems as they exist today. Institutional change is therefore one of the potential solutions to these problems, as described below.

POTENTIAL SOLUTIONS TO NATURAL RESOURCE PROBLEMS

Solutions to environmental problems contain technical, economic, and institutional dimensions. Technical solutions are needed to provide the physical means of remedying natural resource degradation, while economic and institutional solutions provide the incentives for behavioral change.

Technical Solutions to Natural Resource Degradation

A variety of technical solutions are available to solve deforestation, erosion, desertification, flooding, salinity, chemical pollution, and other environmental problems. Where technical solutions are lacking, government-sponsored research and education can develop new natural-resource-conserving practices and facilitate their adoption.

Windbreaks, contour plowing, mulching, legume fallow crops, alley cropping, deferred grazing, rotational grazing, well-distributed watering places, and revegetation or reforestation are all examples of physical practices which could help reduce soil erosion, siltation, and desertification.[20] Solar pumps, biogas generators, and more efficient cooking stoves can provide or save energy,

---

[18] See Daniel W. Bromley and Devendra P. Chapagain, "The Village Against the Center: Resource Depletion in South Asia," *American Journnal of Agricultural Economics,* vol. 68, December 1984, pp. 868–873.

[19] See Murdock, op. cit., p. 304.

[20] Alley cropping is an agroforestry system in which food crops are grown in alleys formed by rows of trees or shrubs.

A brush fence in Kenya being used to facilitate rotational grazing.

thereby reducing fuelwood consumption, deforestation, and desertification. Embankments can provide protection from flooding for limited areas, and dams can be built on rivers to control water flows.

Irrigation canals can be better lined to reduce waterlogging and salinity. Integrated pest management techniques can be developed that involve increased biological and cultural control of pests to reduce pesticide pollution. Germplasm banks can be used and conservation reserves established to preserve endangered plant species.

These are just a few of the potential technical or physical solutions to environmental problems. In many cases these technical solutions are already known, but in others additional research is essential for success. In the pest management area, for example, much work still needs to be completed on biological controls for major pests in developing countries. New varieties of plants can be developed that are resistant to certain diseases and insects.

The availability of technical solutions to natural resource problems is essential for reducing environmental degradation. In almost all cases, however, these solutions must be combined with economic and institutional changes which create incentives for behavioral change. Without these incentives, it is unlikely that the technologies will be widely adopted, since they usually imply increased costs to their users.

Economic Solutions to Natural Resource Degradation

International and national agricultural research systems can generate new technologies that increase food production and incomes. As incomes grow, population pressures are reduced, and the demand for environmental protec-

Terraces with grass strips being used to control erosion in the Dominican Republic.

tion increases. New institutions may be formed (or existing institutions may evolve) in response to this demand, and incentives for resource conservation are created.

As countries develop, the major source of growth is not the natural resource base, but new knowledge. This knowledge can, to some extent, substitute for natural resources and is less subject to the diminishing returns associated with use of natural resources. Increases in agricultural productivity resulting from the new knowledge or technologies not only raise incomes, but also the value of human time. As the value of human time increases, population growth rates decline with favorable implications for natural resource problems.

Economic development means more resources for servicing external debts and addressing environmental problems. The poorer the country, the fewer the resources that tend to flow toward solving environmental problems.

Institutional Solutions to Natural Resource Degradation

Many of the economic solutions to environmental problems described above are long-term or indirect. A series of direct institutional changes may hold greater promise for more immediate improvements in the natural resource base. Changes in taxes, subsidies, regulations, and other policies can influence local incentives for conservation.

Reducing the discrimination against agriculture in pricing policies should help. Low returns to agriculture depress farmland prices and the returns to investments in land conservancy practices, as noted earlier. Low returns reduce the demand for labor and therefore labor income. If returns to agri-

culture were raised, subsidies on inputs such as agrichemicals could be eliminated.

Subsidies and taxes can be used as "carrots" or "sticks" to reduce externalities or off-site effects associated with agricultural and forestry use (see Box
12-3). An example of a conservation subsidy (i.e., a "carrot") might be a
program in which the government shares the cost of building terraces, windbreaks, and fences, or of planting trees. In some cases, local workers can be
paid in-kind with food from internationally supplied food aid. An example of a
"stick" is a sales tax on chemical pesticides.

Regulation is an alternative institutional mechanism for influencing environmental behavior. Although difficult to enforce, regulation can play a role when
combined with other economic incentives. For example, burning of crop stub-
ble, farming of particularly erosive lands, or logging in certain areas can be
prohibited in conjunction with a program that also provides other government
economic benefits to farmers or forest owners. Families can be restricted from
settling in flood-prone areas, perhaps with the provision of funds for resettlement. Experience shows that without incentives for changing behavior, regulations tend to be ineffective, since enforcement is costly and there are private
incentives to cheat.

Institutional change that creates secure property rights will help address
some problems of environmental degradation. Ownership of land titles increases the returns to long-term investments in land. On the other hand, the
removal of institutions that guarantee land titles only if forests are cleared will
help stop deforestation (see Box 12-4). The provision of property rights does
not necessarily imply privatization. There are numerous examples of common-
property regimes managed in environmentally sound fashions, and it is only
when population growth or other changes put pressure on group management
that the effectiveness of the management is diminished. Institutional changes
that reinforce these common-property management schemes may be more
effective than privatization.

Physical restrictions on grazing, land reform programs that distribute land to
small farmers, revised leasing arrangements, and many other government-
sponsored institutional changes can improve natural resource sustainability if
certain principles are followed. First, there is a need for careful assessment of
the economic benefits and costs, including externalities, resulting from the
policies. Second, local input is needed in the decision-making process. Third,
compensation often is required for any losers. That society as a whole will be
better off following these institutional changes is not enough.[21] Losers may
need to be compensated or they may oppose any change.

These three principles hold for institutional changes at various levels—local,
regional, national, and international—and they are not always easy to apply. If

[21] See Robert W. Fri, "Energy and the Environment a Coming Collision?" *Resources,* No. 98,
Resources for the Future, Washington, D.C., Winter 1990, pp. 3–4.

BOX 12-3

THE IMPACT OF AN EXTERNALITY ON CONSERVATION ACTIVITIES

Externalities also cause the private benefits of resource conservation activities to diverge from social benefits. These private benefits determine the demand for, or use of, conservation activities. In the figure below, the net private benefits (NPB), or the private marginal returns from conservation activities, are shown to be lower than the net social benefits (NSB). This divergence occurs because the benefits of conservation to society (such as the off-farm benefits of erosion reduction) are not considered by the private decision maker. Thus, the private decision maker may employ fewer conservation techniques than are socially optimal ($Q_P < Q_S$).

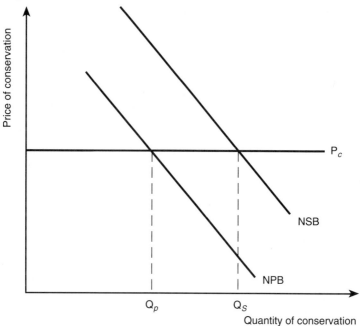

In the case of inputs that create external costs, such as pesticides, the reverse situation arises, and NPB exceeds NSB. In this case, Q_P will exceed Q_S, and more pesticides are applied than are socially optimal.

Price and incentive policies such as taxes and subsidies can be used to move the NPB curve so that it corresponds to NSB. In this case $Q_S = Q_P$ and the external costs or benefits are said to have been internalized.

developed countries want developing countries to reduce carbon-dioxide emissions associated with forest burning, developed countries must be willing to foot part of the bill. Both the Indian and Chinese governments have stated publicly that their vast coal reserves will provide energy needed for economic development; any international agreement to reduce carbon emissions must consider national development schemes. If national governments want de-

---

BOX 12-4

INSTITUTIONS AND DEFORESTATION IN THE BRAZILIAN AMAZON

Brazil contains 3.5 million square kilometers of tropical forests, some 30 percent of the world's total. Most of these forests are found in the Amazon Basin. Deforestation of this rich reserve of plant and animal species has increased in recent years, raising concerns for its effects on atmospheric carbon levels and on the maintenance of global biodiversity.

Between 1973, when there was little evidence of deforestation, and 1988, more than 10 percent of the Amazon was deforested. Government policies and institutions have been largely responsible for this outcome.

The Brazilian government made a conscious decision in the 1960s to develop the Amazon as a means of relieving population pressures, providing territorial security, and exploiting the region's wealth. Ambitious road-building programs, other infrastructure development, agricultural colonization projects, and policies providing tax and other incentives for agricultural and industrial development were begun. These projects had the effect of opening access to the Amazon, and promoting environmentally unsound development.

Tax exemptions and cheap credit spurred the creation of large-scale livestock projects, whose economic and environmental suitability to the region is questionable. The National Integration Program established a network of villages, towns, and cities and cleared lots for in-migrating settlers. The plans for these settlements were made without regard for soil fertility or agricultural potential, and the cleared forest lands were quickly eroded and otherwise degraded.

Environmentally destructive settlement practices are promoted throughout the Amazon by the Brazilian government's practice of awarding land titles only for deforested lands. A migrant in either an official settlement project or an invaded area can obtain title to the land simply by clearing the forest. Once the title is granted, the migrant can sell or transfer it to someone else, and proceed to clear additional lands. Calculations show that it is more profitable to clear land, plant subsistence crops for two years, and then sell and move than it is to remain as a permanent settler.

Clearly, the rate of deforestation in Amazonia is directly influenced by government policies and other institutional arrangements. It is just as clear that policy reform and institutional adjustments can slow, or even reverse, this process.

Source: Dennis J. Mahar, "Deforestation in Brazil's Amazon Region: Magnitude, Rate, and Causes," Chap. 7, in Gunter Schramm and Jeremy J. Warford, (eds.), *Environmental Management and Economic Development,* (Baltimore: Johns Hopkins University Press, 1989).

---

forestation reduced, they cannot just pass a national decree. They must involve local decision makers in designing an institutional solution that provides individual incentives for appropriate behavior. And someone may need to estimate the costs and benefits associated with alternative institutional mechanisms.

In many cases, the presence of transactions costs and collective action have created institutional environments that are destructive to the natural resource base. Imperfect information, corrupt government officials, and the absence of new institutional arrangements to replace previous social and cultural norms that constrained behavior harmful to the groups are serious problems. For example, in one country frequently subject to flooding, the highly competent and honest director of the national agricultural research system was fired because he gently questioned the seemingly inappropriate technological solution to the flooding problem proposed by the government. That technological solution would have resulted in massive construction projects for which government officials could receive sizable kickbacks. Thus, the officials would not tolerate opposition.

Improvements in information flows are essential if such corrupt behavior and reductions in other transactions costs are to be reduced. Education also becomes vitally important. Thus, focusing on communications infrastructure and human-capital development, as discussed in Chaps. 13 and 16, are two of the keys to environmental improvement.

SUMMARY

Sound environmental management is essential for sustained agricultural and economic development. Yet environmental degradation is evident throughout the developing world. Soil erosion, siltation of rivers and reservoirs, flooding, overgrazing, poor cropping practices, desertification, salinity and waterlogging, deforestation, energy depletion, loss of biodiversity, and chemical pollution have become major problems. Poverty, high rates of return to capital, debt problems, rapid population growth, and misguided public policies conspire against solutions. Environmental problems are interrelated, and understanding their causes requires sorting out complex physical, economic, and institutional linkages. Technical solutions are needed for each of these problems, but economic and institutional changes must provide the incentives for behavioral change. As incomes grow, population pressures are reduced, and the demand for environmental protection increases. Economic development means more resources in the long run for addressing environmental problems. Changes in taxes, subsidies, regulations, and other policies can influence local incentives for conservation. Balancing benefits with costs, obtaining local input in the decisionmaking process, and compensating losers are needed for effective solutions to local and global environmental problems. Because transactions costs must be reduced for natural resource conservation to occur, information flows must be improved and human capital must be developed.

IMPORTANT TERMS AND CONCEPTS

Biodiversity
Chemical pollution
Climate change
Common property
Deforestation
Desertification
Discounting of costs and
 benefits

Global warming
Greenhouse effect
Institutional change
Natural resource management
Overgrazing
Regulations
Salinity and waterlogging
Soil erosion

Environmental degradation

Externalities

Flooding

Subsidies and taxes

Sustainable resource use

LOOKING AHEAD

In this chapter, we examined the nature and causes of environmental problems in developing countries. Potential technical, economic, and institutional solutions were considered. In the next chapter, we consider additional institutional changes related to inputs and credit policies. Governments often intervene in input and credit markets. We will examine the nature and advisability of these interventions.

QUESTIONS FOR DISCUSSION

1 What are the major natural resource problems facing developing countries?
2 Are the poorest countries the most vulnerable to environmental degradation? Why, or why not?
3 How are flooding and soil erosion related?
4 What is desertification?
5 How are waterlogging and salinity problems interrelated?
6 How are deforestation and energy problems interrelated?
7 How are deforestation and global climate change interrelated?
8 What are the major technical or physical causes of natural resource degradation?
9 What are the major economic causes of environmental degradation?
10 What are the major institutional causes of environmental degradation?
11 What are some of the technological solutions to natural resource problems?
12 What are some of the economic and institutional solutions to natural resource problems?
13 What are three key principles that must hold if institutional changes are to successfully solve environmental problems?
14 Why are reductions in transactions costs important for sustainable natural resource use?

RECOMMENDED READINGS

Anderson, Jock R. and Jesuthason Thampapillai, "Soil Conservation in Developing Countries: Project and Policy Intervention," Policy and Research Series 8, World Bank, Washington, D.C., 1990.

Barbier, Edward B., *Economics, Natural Resource Scarcity, and Development* (London: Earthscan Publications Limited, 1989).

Bromley, Daniel W. and Devendra P. Chapagain, "The Village Against the Center: Resource Depletion in South Asia," *American Journal of Agricultural Economics*, vol. 66, 1984, pp. 868–873.

Brown, Lester R. and others, *State of the World 1990* (New York: W. W. Norton and Company, 1990).

Brown, Lester R. and Edward C. Wolf, *Soil Erosion: Quiet Crisis in the World Economy,* Worldwatch Institute Paper No. 60, September 1984.

Davis, Ted J. and Isabelle A. Schirmer, *Sustainability Issues in Agricultural Development,* World Bank, Washington, D.C., 1987. This edited proceedings of a conference contains several useful chapters on environmental degradation issues, especially the chapter by Robert Repetto on "Managing Natural Resources for Sustainability," and the chapter by G. Edward Schuh, "Some Thoughts on Economic Development, Sustainability, and Environment."

Kramer, Randall A., "An International Overview of Soil Conservation Policy," in A. Maunder and U. Renborg, (eds.), *Agriculture in a Turbulent World Economy,* (England: Gower Publishing Company, 1986).

Lal, Rattan, "Managing the Soils of Sub-Saharan Africa," *Science,* vol. 236, May 29, 1987, pp. 1069–1076.

Lipton, Michael, "New Strategies and Successful Examples for Sustainable Development in the Third World," International Food Policy Research Institute Reprint No. 170, Washington, D.C., 1989.

Murdock, William W., *The Poverty of Nations* (Baltimore: Johns Hopkins University Press, 1980). See Chap. 10, "Limits to Growth and the Structural Causes of Deteriorating Environments."

Norgaard, Richard B., "Traditional Agricultural Knowledge: Past Performance, Future Prospects, and Institutional Implications," *American Journal of Agricultural Economics,* vol. 66, 1984, pp. 874–878.

Pearce, David W. and R. Kerry Turner, *Economics of Natural Resources and the Environment* (Baltimore: Johns Hopkins University Press 1990), pp. 61–69, pp. 342–360.

Schramm, Gunter and Jeremy J. Warford, (eds.), *Environmental Management and Economic Development* (Baltimore: Johns Hopkins University Press, 1989).

Southgate, Douglas, Fred Hitzhusen, and Robert Macgregor, "Remedying Third World Soil Erosion Problems," *American Journal of Agricultural Economics,* vol. 66, 1984, pp. 879–884.

Tietenberg, T.H., "The Poverty Connection to Environmental Policy," *Challenge,* September-October 1990, pp. 26–32.

Veeman, Terrence S., "Sustainable Development: Its Economic Meaning and Policy Implications," *Canadian Journal of Agricultural Economics,* vol. 37, 1989, pp. 875–886.

Warford, Jeremy J., "Environmental, Growth, and Development," World Bank, Washington, D.C., 1987.

World Bank, "Striking a Balance: The Environmental Challenge," World Bank, Washington, D.C., 1989.

World Commission on Environment and Development, *Our Common Future,* (New York: Oxford University Press, 1987).

CHAPTER 13

INPUT AND CREDIT POLICIES

To take maximum advantage of technological advances in farming systems, farmers must have access to recommended production inputs at the specific times and in the quantities and qualities needed; (and) access, if necessary, to outside sources of finance to purchase these inputs . . .

Wortman and Cummings[1]

THIS CHAPTER

1 Explains why it is important for farmers to have access to particular production inputs and to credit
2 Describes the nature of rural money markets and the determinants of rural interest rates
3 Discusses why governments tend to subsidize credit and why these subsidies are generally inadvisable

IMPORTANCE OF NEW INPUTS

Successful agricultural development in most developing countries today requires increased output per hectare and per worker. This agricultural intensification depends in part on the availability and financing of new, often manufactured, inputs (see Box 13-1). Fertilizers and pesticides, new seeds, irrigation systems, mechanical power, and supplemental minerals and nutrients

[1] Sterling Wortman and Ralph W. Cummings, Jr., *To Feed This World: The Challenge and the Strategy* (Baltimore: Johns Hopkins University Press, 1978), p. 343.

BOX 13-1

INPUT USE AND AGRICULTURAL OUTPUT IN INDIA

The contributions of modern inputs to increases in agricultural output are visible throughout Asia. India provides an interesting illustration. Production of foodgrains in India grew consistently from 1949 to 1984, averaging roughly 2.6 percent annually. Prior to 1967, there were few modern inputs and output growth was evenly attributable to increases in areas planted and increases in yields (see table below). Following 1967, the growth rate of area planted fell dramatically, while growth in total output remained strong. Sustained output growth during this latter period was created by the widespread use of modern inputs, mostly irrigation water and fertilizer, and modern high-yielding varieties (HYVs). Yield-based growth contributed to more than 90 percent of the growth in production during the period from 1975/76 through 1983/84.

GROWTH RATES IN FOODGRAIN PRODUCTION AND INPUT USE IN INDIA, 1949/50–1983/84

	Annual growth rate (%)					
	Foodgrains			Inputs		
Period	Production	Acreage	Yield	Irrigation	Fertilizer	HYVs
1949/50–1964/65	2.84	1.41	1.41	—	—	—
1967/68–1975/76	1.91	.40	1.50	3.2	11.4	20.8
1975/76–1983/84	2.48	.19	2.28	2.8	12.3	6.5

Source: J. S. Sarma and Vasant P. Gandhi, "Production and Consumption of Foodgrains in India: Implications of Accelerated Economic Growth and Poverty Alleviation," International Food Policy Research Institute Report No. 91, Washington, D.C., July 1990.

---

for animals are examples of these inputs. Governments must address a series of issues related to production, distribution, pricing, financing, and regulation of inputs, and to the identification and encouragement of optimal on-farm input usage.

Role of Manufactured Inputs

Manufactured inputs have an important role to play in agricultural development because the potential for expanding the land resource is limited in most countries. This scarcity or inelastic supply of land means that its price tends to increase over time, both absolutely and relative to the price of labor. The induced-innovation theory described in Chap. 10 indicates that farmers will seek new agricultural technologies that will enable them to substitute lower cost inputs for those whose scarcity and price are rising. These inputs include new seeds, fertilizer, irrigation, and pesticides.

Seeds, fertilizer, irrigation, and pesticides tend to be highly complementary inputs. To be more productive than traditional varieties, new varieties of wheat, rice, corn, and other food crops require more fertilizer and better water control than would be used under traditional practices. Water and fertilizer tend to induce lush plant growth and an environment favorable to weeds and other pests, thus raising the profitability of pesticides as well. If this package of inputs is available to farmers together with the necessary financing and information on usage, the productivity of both land and labor can be raised. The result is an increase in output per hectare and per unit of labor applied, at least in those areas where the new inputs are suited and adopted. A description of these key inputs will help better define their potential and limitations:

Seed   Seed of high-yielding varieties is usually a relatively low-cost input. However, seed of superior varieties must be developed or identified, tested, produced and multiplied, monitored for quality, and distributed to farmers. The government often has a role to play in the development, testing, quality monitoring, and production of the basic seed. Private firms can be involved in the multiplication of seeds and their distribution to farmers. The exact roles of the public and private bodies in a particular country may change as the seed industry develops.

Fertilizer   Higher-producing varieties require additional fertilizer, particularly nitrogen, phosphate, and potash. These nutrients can be obtained from natural fertility in the soil, animal and plant wastes, and leguminous plants that can fix nitrogen from the air. These natural sources often, but not always, must be supplemented by chemical (commercial) fertilizers to provide the necessary quantities and precise mixtures required. In areas where the supply of natural fertilizers is relatively inelastic, as commercial fertilizers become less expensive and are available in relatively elastic supply, their use can be expected to increase.

Unfortunately, for many remote, particularly upland, areas of developing countries, suitable high-yielding grain varieties have not been developed. Or the remoteness and lack of infrastructure hinders the distribution of chemical fertilizer to farmers. In these areas, traditional varieties and practices may continue to dominate and incomes remain low or even decline as higher production in more-favored regions drive prices lower.

Water   Availability of irrigation water significantly influences the number of crops grown per hectare per year, the inputs used, and hence production. Higher levels of fertilizer application require more and better-timed water input. Drainage is also important because few crops can tolerate excessive standing water or salinization. Development and management of irrigation and drainage systems often require a combination of public and private initiatives. Governments can seek to expand and modernize irrigation and drainage facilities. They can design rules of water pricing to encourage economically sound water use. Farmers and villages themselves can develop smaller, often well-based, systems and the necessary canals for distribution on farms along with rules for water distribution.

Pesticides Farmers often find using pesticides (insecticides for insects, fungicides for diseases, and herbicides for weeds) highly profitable, as agricultural production intensifies through increased use of new seeds, fertilizer, and water. Sometimes these pesticides are applied as a preservative treatment and other times after a major pest problem develops.

Pesticides can have serious drawbacks, however. Some pesticides are toxic to humans and animals and result in poisonings in the short run or chronic health problems in the longer term. Applications with improper equipment or inadequate clothing for protection exacerbate health problems. Chemical pollution can spread beyond the area where the pesticide is applied, with particularly deleterious effects on fisheries. Some pesticides kill insects that are beneficial to agriculture. Often, when pesticides are applied over a period of time, the target insects, diseases, or weeds develop resistance to the chemicals, making increased pesticide amounts necessary to maintain the same level of effectiveness.

Pesticides, despite these problems, likely will be needed for some time until new pest-resistant varieties, biological and cultural practices, and other substitute methods for pest control can be developed. Several of these methods, called integrated pest management, have already been developed and are viable for certain pests on certain crops in certain locations. Much additional research is needed, however, to make these practices more widely available in developing countries. Weed control is especially important to intensified production in Africa where labor for weeding is less abundant than in other regions.

Animal Inputs As discussed in Chaps. 8 and 9, livestock play an important role in farming systems in LDCs. Animal productivity is often very low, and new inputs related to disease control, supplementary minerals and other feed supplements, improved shelter, and, in some cases, better breeds can make a difference. Inputs for controlling diseases and parasites are perhaps the most important; the significance of feed supplements, shelter, and new breeds varies from country to country and by type of livestock. Because indigenous livestock have been adapted to their specific environments, the transfer in of new breeds is particularly complex, except perhaps for poultry.

Mechanical Inputs Agricultural mechanization is frequently a controversial subject. Tilling, planting, cultivating, and harvesting are still done by hand in large parts of the developing world, particularly in Sub-Saharan Africa and in hilly regions on other continents. In many areas of Asia and Latin America, animals are an important source of power. Even in countries where farming is more mechanized, power tillers and tractors are often restricted to tillage and a

Treating cattle for parasites in Ethiopia.

few other operations.[2] The controversy arises because machinery usually substitutes for labor or animals. In many developing countries labor is abundant
and its cost is low. Alternative employment opportunities outside agriculture
are limited, so that labor displacement is undesirable. Therefore, mechanization is most profitable in countries where land is abundant, labor is scarce, and
capital is cheap; this situation would seem to exist in relatively few countries.

Does this mean that there is little role for agricultural mechanization? Not
necessarily, but the types of mechanization should be very different from what
tends to be observed in most western, developed countries. Highly productive
cropping systems, whether on small or large farms, can often benefit from more
precise planting depths and fertilizer placement, mechanically pumped irrigation water, mechanical threshing (but usually not harvesting unless labor is
scarce), transport, power spraying of pesticides, and tilling when timing is
critical for multiple cropping. Many of these mechanical devices, however,
may be hand held (e.g., sprayers) or stationary (e.g., pumps and threshers).
Even in areas where labor is usually abundant, shortages can occur in certain
seasons which, if relieved through mechanization, could increase the overall
demand for labor.

Individual farmers will consider the private profitability when deciding
whether to invest in a machine. If very large farms exist in countries with
surplus labor in agriculture, operators of these farms may prefer labor-saving
machinery because it allows them to deal with fewer employees, and, given the
transactions costs and capital subsidies that may exist, it may be more privately

---

[2] See Hans Binswanger, "Agricultural Mechanization: A Comparative Historical Perspective,"
World Book Research Observer, vol. 1, January 1986, pp. 27–56.

profitable to follow large-scale mechanization even if society as a whole would be better off without it. Such behavior is one of the reasons that land reform is so important to many developing countries (see Chap. 11).

Governments and foreign assistance agencies must be careful not to encourage nonoptimal mechanization (from society's viewpoint) through ill-advised subsidies or other means. Mechanization is inevitable over time, but the type of mechanization should be appropriate given the relative endowments of land, labor, and capital.

The Advisability of Input Subsidies

Developing countries often subsidize the purchase of seeds, fertilizers, irrigation water, pesticides, and occasionally mechanical inputs. Is this a good idea? Generally speaking, it is not. Such subsidies can lead to losses in economic efficiency for the country as a whole, can be very costly to the government, can discourage private-sector competition in the provision of these inputs, and, in the case of pesticides, may lead to environmental damages from overapplication.

Many governments become involved in multiplying and selling improved seeds to farmers at or below cost. In some cases, scarce research resources are diverted to multiplying seeds rather than developing new varieties. Private firms, unable to compete with the government treasury, do not take on the function of multiplying and selling seeds. Without development of these private firms, the government must continue to be responsible for this function.

BOX 13-2

MODERN INPUTS AND ECONOMIC GROWTH

New technologies and inputs are critical for achieving increases in agricultural output and income in rural areas. This income is spent by the households on goods and services, some of which are produced locally and others which are imported into the region. These expenditures induce income growth in the nonfarm economy, the so called *multiplier effects*. By far, the largest portion of these multipliers is caused by household expenditures on consumer goods and services, though the effects resulting from increased use of farm inputs and in processing, marketing, and transportation of farm output are substantial contributors to regional growth.

Linkages between farms and suppliers of inputs create spillovers into the local economy. Though seeds, agrichemicals, irrigation supplies, and farm machinery usually are not produced in agricultural regions, input supply services including technical advice, machinery repair, and a large proportion of irrigation construction and maintenance are produced locally. These activities create opportunities for non-farm employment and income that is in turn spent locally. The creation and deepening of backward linkages from agriculture are important contributions to rural economic development.

Fertilizer subsidies can be used in selected situations in which governments desire to increase the adoption of new inputs by groups of farmers that might not otherwise adopt them. Unfortunately, in many countries these subsidies are necessitated by the artificially low prices imposed on agricultural output for the purpose of keeping food prices down for urban consumers. Input subsidies help compensate farmers for income losses from these policies. While this combination of policies can have the desired effect, at least in the short run, high costs to the government and potential fiscal problems result in the long run, making the policies nonsustainable. Also, the economic efficiency losses associated with these policies can be substantial.

Efficiency losses are also a problem for water and pesticide subsidies. The latter also can create excessive use of toxic chemicals and can result in all the deleterious effects described earlier. In summary, input subsidies are generally inadvisable. The government can play a more constructive role by ensuring the availability of these inputs (including the improvement of rural roads), publishing price information to encourage competition, setting quality standards for seeds and fertilizers, requiring and enforcing labeling of input containers, and regulating use of toxic pesticides.

Role of Credit

Credit for purchase of seeds, fertilizers, chemicals, and other inputs becomes important as a developing country moves from traditional to more modern agriculture. Credit also helps households better manage their resources; it can be used for investment, for marketing, or for consumption. Without credit, even high-return investments, long- or short-term, would be infeasible for many farmers. Loans enable farmers to better manage risks since they can borrow during bad years and pay back the loans during good years.

Without widespread availability of credit, inputs associated with improved technologies can be purchased only by the larger, wealthier farmers. Capital formation and improvements on smaller farms are hampered. Fewer farmers are able to purchase, or even rent, land. In cases where produce marketing requires cash outlays, lack of credit can disrupt marketing activities. Well-functioning rural financial institutions are essential to improving economic efficiency, reducing income risk, and meeting income distribution goals.

NATURE OF RURAL MONEY-MARKETS AND DETERMINANTS OF RURAL INTEREST RATES

Credit facilitates the temporary transfer of purchasing power from one individual or organization to another. However, many types of lenders or *money-markets* exist, and credit institutions may or may not adequately serve the needs of a developing agriculture. Credit is often viewed as an oppressive or exploitive device in LDCs. We need to examine both the types of lending sources found in developing countries and the evidence of exploitive behavior associated with these money-markets.

Types of Money-Markets

Rural money-markets consist of two broadly defined lending sources: organized and informal. Private commercial banks, government-controlled banks, cooperative banks, and credit societies are called organized credit sources. Public or private, these lending sources usually are regulated by the government and are open to audit and inspection.[3]

Informal or unorganized credit sources consist of moneylenders, merchants, pawnbrokers, landlords, friends, and relatives. Some of these credit sources— e.g., landlords and merchants—combine other economic activities with lending. Except for absentee landlords, the relationship between borrower and informal lender is marked by personal contact, simple accounting, and low administrative costs.

Informal lenders are important sources of funds in rural areas of many developing countries. These lenders usually know the borrowers personally, require little collateral, make consumption as well as production loans, are accessible at all times, and usually are flexible in rescheduling loans. However, these informal lenders also tend to charge high rates of interest and are frequently accused of exploitive activities. In cases where lenders are landlords, merchants, or both, they have been accused of using their position to tie borrowers to themselves by forcing their clients to rent from, borrow from, buy from, and sell to them. Thus, these moneylenders/landlords/merchants are said to extract monopoly profits from their clients. Are borrowers consistently being exploited? It is important to examine this question because it has important implications for the role of more formal private and public credit institutions.

Do Informal Money-Markets Exploit Borrowers?

The issue of borrower exploitation revolves around the existence of usury or monopoly profits earned by the lenders. Hence we need to consider the factors that determine the interest rates charged by these lenders. The major components of rates of interest on loans are: (1) administrative costs, (2) the opportunity cost of lending, (3) a risk premium due to the probability of default in repayment, and (4) monopoly profit.[4]

The administrative cost should not be too high for moneylenders, given their simple contracting procedures and personal knowledge of their clients. A large

---

[3] See Subrata Ghatak and Ken Ingersent, *Agriculture and Economic Development* (Baltimore: Johns Hopkins University Press, 1984), p. 229, for additional discussion.

[4] Ibid, p. 231.

number of loans with small amounts of money per loan have the potential of creating excessive administrative costs, but these costs are probably not excessive. Opportunity costs of lending are low in rural areas because interest rates offered by organized money-markets tend to be low. Therefore, the critical factor in determining whether interest rates are generating monopoly profits in the informal money-market is the risk premium or the probability of default. The risk premium for loans to small, particularly tenant, farmers is quite high. These farmers are close to the margin of subsistence, and a streak of bad weather or a serious illness can spell disaster. Without formal collateral, the risk of default grows. At the same time, because weather tends to affect all farmers in a given area equally, a spell of bad weather can create the potential for simultaneous default of a large number of borrowers. Therefore one would expect relatively high interest rates just to cover the risk factor. Exploitive situations do exist in which moneylenders extract monopolist gains. However, careful empirical studies seem to indicate that monopoly profits may not be as prevalent or large in informal credit markets as is often believed.[5] The reason is competition. The amounts of the loans are often small, and start-up costs required to become a moneylender are low. This ease of entry serves to keep interest rates at an appropriate level given the level of risk, administrative costs, and the opportunity cost of capital. If profit margins become large, incentives are created for new moneylenders to enter the business and compete away those profits.

The high risk associated with loans to subsistence farmers, however, means that lenders have an incentive to maintain tight control over borrowers. Moneylenders who are also landlords or merchants have means of tying their clients to themselves through leases, consumer credit, and so forth. Other moneylenders may be hesitant to loan to someone who already owes substantial sums or who has defaulted to another. In summary, it appears that some exploitation by moneylenders does occur, particularly if the moneylenders control the land or the market. However, the magnitude of this exploitation may not be as great as is often believed. Evidence of high interest rates on rural loans is alone not sufficient to conclude that moneylenders are exploitive, since there are high costs associated with making these loans. Informal sources of credit serve a vital function in most developing countries because, without them, most small farmers would not have access to credit.

Organized Money-Markets and Transactions Costs

Why are small farmers in developing countries not served more frequently by organized money-markets? Both private and public credit institutions find that transactions costs are quite high. Loans are small, and the paperwork and time

---

[5] See, for example, P. Bardham and A. Rudra, "Interlinkage of Hand Labor and Capital Relations: An Analysis of Village Survey Data in East Asia," *Economic and Political Weekly*, 1978, pp., 367–384.

spent evaluating potential borrowers, collecting payments, and supervising loans in order to reduce risks of default are costly. In many cases, the government regulates the maximum interest allowed, and that rate will fail to cover the administrative costs and risk. Thus, where private and public sources of credit exist, they tend to loan to larger farmers to reduce both administrative costs and the chances of default (see Box 13-3).

The magnitude of these transactions costs is illustrated by an apparently successful bank that provides credit to the rural poor in Bangladesh. The Grameen Bank of Bangladesh targets households that own less than 0.5 acres of cultivable land.[6] The bank organizes the poor into groups and associations, provides credit without collateral, and supervises utilization of the loans. A maximum of 5000 Taka (about $160) is loaned to one individual; nearly three-fourths of the borrowers are women. The interest rate charged is 16 percent a year and the default rate is less than 2 percent. The bank is subsidized, however, by the State Bank of Bangladesh and by the International Fund for Agricultural Development (IFAD). The cost of the loans would be 26.5 percent rather than 16 percent if the bank had, to break even, to borrow at the same rate as the other financial institutions in the country.[7] Because both the default rate and the opportunity cost of capital are low, it is clear that most of the 26.5 percent is administrative cost. The bank could lower this cost with less supervision, but the default rate would likely rise and offset the cost saving.

The Grameen Bank also loans very little money for activities associated with crop production. In 1986, 46 percent of its loans were for livestock and poultry raising, 25 percent for processing and manufacturing, and 23 percent for trading and shopkeeping. These activities are less risky than crop production.

One can see that small agricultural loans are costly and, as a result, most commercial lenders loan to larger farmers where the risk and administrative

---

BOX 13-3

ADMINISTRATIVE COSTS AND LOAN SIZE

The costs of administering a loan are composed of fixed and variable costs. Fixed costs include processing the application and repayments, and bookkeeping. For a given loan length, these fixed costs tend to be constant. Thus the rate of interest ascribed to these costs is a decreasing function of the loan size. A lender with fixed costs of $10 must charge 10 percent of a loan of $100 to recover these costs and only 1 percent of a loan of $1000 because of these fixed and variable administrative costs, intermediaries will desire to lend larger amounts at lower rates.

---

[6] See Mahabub Hossain, "Credit for Alleviation of Rural Poverty: The Grameen Bank of Bangladesh," International Food Policy Research Institute Research, Report No. 65, Washington, D.C., February 1988, for an excellent discussion of the Grameen Bank.
[7] Ibid, p. 11.

Recipients of Grameen Bank loan in Bangladesh.

costs are lower. Government-supported credit programs often have subsidized interest rates in developing countries, but these rates tend to encourage loans to large farmers (the Grameen Bank is an exception).

Transactions costs for private or public loan transactions can also be high because of fraud, favoritism, or embezzlement of funds from within the system. This situation arises most frequently when loans are subsidized, creating excess demand for credit and incentives for bribery.

GOVERNMENT CREDIT PROGRAMS

Many governments use credit programs as part of their development program, and many international donors support these programs. Government-supported credit is based on the notions that (1) credit is critical to the adoption of new technologies, (2) moneylenders exploit farmers and public credit can provide them with competition, (3) credit can be combined with supervision and education to increase the capacity of farmers to use modern inputs, (4) subsidized credit can offset disincentives to production created by other policies that discriminate against agriculture, and (5) government-supported credit programs can lessen inequities in the rural sector.[8]

Subsidized credit provides an easy vehicle for transferring public funds to the rural sector. Examples of subsidized credit programs abound in every region of the developing world. Dale Adams points to a number of studies of

---

[8] See Yujiro Hayami and Vernon Ruttan, *Agricultural Development: An International Perspective* (Baltimore: Johns Hopkins University Press, 1985), pp. 398–403.

such programs in Honduras, Sudan, Jamaica, and elsewhere that demonstrate how ill-advised subsidized credit is from a development perspective.[9]

Adams finds that while evaluations of subsidized credit programs often find favorable impacts on the individual borrowers involved, a broader examination of the net effects of these programs usually finds few positive effects on economic development, or on the viability of the rural financial system.

Effects of Subsidized Credit

Subsidized credit tends to create excess demand for credit by lowering interest rates. In many cases, because interest rates are negative after controlling for inflation, the demand that is created for credit is infinite. Subsidized credit erodes the capital available in financial markets and undermines rural financial institutions. Private banks cannot cover expenses (administrative costs, defaults, etc.) at low interest rates, yet they are forced to lower interest rates in order to remain competitive with public credit sources, even if not required to lower them by law. Thus, the survival of these private institutions is threatened. If they fail, additional government involvement and additional budget outlays will be needed. An equally important effect of subsidized loan rates is that they lower all interest rates and, hence, discourage private savings. If agricultural development is to be able to generate capital, then viable rural financial institutions are needed to both provide loans and mobilize savings.

Because excess demand exists for subsidized credit, it is rationed and almost inevitably goes to the larger farms for which the administrative costs are less. The phenomenon of successful impacts of subsidized credit on individual borrowers yet negligible effects on overall development exists because rationed credit means that few people are touched by the programs. Seldom are more than 5 percent of the potential credit recipients reached. Because the subsidized loans are valuable, the credit system often becomes politicized as large landowners offer favors to bank managers to obtain loans or financially support politicians to encourage continuation of the program. In addition to these distributive effects, default rates on subsidized loans tend to be high. Public sector lenders may be less familiar with the borrowers than are the lenders in the private sector. Because there are pressures to lend to larger borrowers, the productive potential of the loan may not be considered, leading to high default rates.

Adams and his colleagues at Ohio State have conducted numerous studies of government credit programs and consistently find these programs to be counterproductive. Even the apparently highly successful Grameen Bank in Bangladesh mentioned earlier is struggling with the issue of whether it might be able to reach more areas of the country and thus have a greater impact if it

---

[9] See Dale W. Adams, "The Conundrum of Successful Credit Projects in Floundering Rural Financial Markets," *Economic Development and Cultural Change*, vol. 36, January 1988, pp. 355–367.

charged the market rate of interest. As long as it must rely on government subsidies, its expansion is limited by size of the transfer program that Bangladesh can afford or that international donors are willing to support.

Lessons for Credit Policies

Several lessons emerge from the applied research on rural credit. First, adoption of new technologies often requires purchase of modern inputs. Consequently, credit availability has been found to be more important to development than the interest rate charged, and there is a tradeoff between credit availability and subsidized interest rates. Second, the viability of rural financial institutions is jeopardized by subsidized credit. This weakening of rural financial markets can constrict both the supply of, and demand for, credit. The rural poor are penalized on their deposits as well as their loans.[10] Third, credit is *fungible*, or in other words, it may not be used for its intended purpose. It is easy for subsidized production credit to be used for consumption items or nonproductive assets. This fungibility is not necessarily bad unless it raises the default rate, but should at least be understood by policymakers. Fourth, a key to reducing market interest rates is to reduce agricultural risk (and hence defaults) and the transactions costs associated with lending and borrowing. Higher income levels associated with economic development may help reduce the risk of defaults as may certain crop insurance and other government policies discussed in Chap. 14. Improved roads and other means of communication, and in some cases, group borrowing and guarantee of loans, can help reduce transactions costs.

Because administrative costs per dollar loaned to small farms are higher than to large farms, banks either must charge higher interest rates (or other hidden charges) to small farms than large, or give loans mainly to large farms. Thus, many countries need a land reform or the credit system will also work against the poorest farmers.

SUMMARY

Successful agricultural development requires increased output per hectare and per worker. This agricultural intensification depends on the availability of new, often manufactured, inputs. Seed, fertilizer, pesticides, irrigation, mechanical power, and supplementary minerals and feeds are examples of these inputs. Manufactured inputs can substitute for inelastic supplies of land to increase production at a lower per unit cost. A variety of issues must be resolved by each country, however, with respect to externalities associated with certain inputs such as pesticides, the appropriate types of mechanization, and the role of the government in producing, distributing and financing inputs. Govern-

---

[10] See Adams, Ibid, p. 366.

ments often subsidize inputs. These subsidies can discourage private competition for input supply, can be costly to the government, and may encourage overuse of inputs such as pesticides that create externalities.

Credit is essential as a country moves from traditional to modern agriculture. Credit from informal sources such as moneylenders is often viewed as oppressive. However, risks and administrative costs of loans to small farms are high and, given the typical competition among moneylenders, monopoly profits may not be as prevalent or as high as often portrayed. When moneylenders are also landlords or merchants, the chances of exploitation are greater. Formal private and public lenders do not serve a high proportion of the farmers because risks and transactions costs are high. Because governments frequently subsidize interest rates, rationed credit tends to go to the larger farms. The subsidies erode the capital in the financial system and, thus, the number of farms served. Low interest rates also discourage deposits and reduce the ability of formal private banks to compete.

Important Terms and Concepts

Administrative costs	Informal credit sources
Exploitation	Input subsidies
Fertilizers and pesticides	Integrated pest management
Fungibility	Irrigation systems
Grameen bank	Mechanical power
Moneylenders	Organized credit sources
Money-markets	Purchased inputs
Monopoly power	Risk of default
New seeds	Subsidized credit
Opportunity costs of lending	Supervised credit

LOOKING AHEAD

Governments often intervene in agricultural markets to influence prices. In the next chapter we examine why governments intervene and the effects of those interventions. Efficient marketing systems are essential for agricultural development and we consider the role that governments can play in improving the marketing system.

QUESTIONS FOR DISCUSSION

1 Why are manufactured agricultural inputs usually necessary for agricultural development?
2 What are some of the key manufactured inputs needed?
3 In what manner are agricultural inputs complementary in nature?
4 What are the advantages and disadvantages of pesticides?
5 Why is mechanization a controversial issue?

6 Why do governments subsidize the purchase of manufactured inputs?
7 Why is agricultural credit important to agricultural development?
8 How do organized and informal sources of credit differ?
9 Why might bankers be biased against small farmer loans in developing countries?
10 What factors would you examine if you were trying to assess whether interest rates charged in informal money-markets were exploiting borrowers?
11 What are subsidized interest rates? Are they a good idea for getting agriculture moving?
12 What might be one problem associated with the fact that credit is fungible?
13 Why do governments support credit programs?
14 How might transactions costs associated with rural financial markets be reduced?

RECOMMENDED READINGS

Adams, Dale W., "The Conundrum of Successful Credit Projects in Floundering Rural Financial Markets," *Economic Development and Cultural Change*, vol. 36, January 1988, pp. 355–367.

Adams, Dale W., Douglas H. Graham, and J. D. Von Pischke, (eds.), *Undermining Rural Development with Cheap Credit* (Boulder, Colo.: Westview Press, 1984).

Binswanger, Hans, "Agricultural Mechanization: A Comparative Historical Analysis," *World Bank Research Observer*, vol. 1, January 1986, pp. 27–56.

Bouman, F. J. A. and R. Houtman, "Pawnbrokering as an Instrument of Rural Banking in the Third World," *Economic Development and Cultural Change*, vol. 37, October 1988, pp. 69–90.

Ghatak, Subrata and Ken Ingersent, *Agriculture and Economic Development* (Baltimore: Johns Hopkins University Press, 1984), pp. 227–237.

Hayami, Yujiro and Vernon W. Ruttan, *Agricultural Development: An International Perspective* (Baltimore: Johns Hopkins University Press, 1985), pp. 398–403.

Hossain, Mahabub, "Credit for Alleviation of Rural Poverty: The Grameen Bank in Bangladesh," International Food Policy Research Institute, Research Report No. 65, Washington, D.C., February 1988.

Long, Millard F., "Why Peasant Farmers Borrow," *American Journal of Agricultural Economics*, vol. 50, November 1968, pp. 991–1008.

Mellor, John W., *The Economics of Agricultural Development* (Ithaca, N.Y.: Cornell University Press, 1966), Chaps. 16 and 17.

Pingali, Prabhu, Yves Bigot, and Hans P. Binswanger, *Agricultural Mechanization and the Evolution of Farming Systems in Sub-Saharan Africa* (Baltimore: Johns Hopkins University Press, 1987).

Stevens, Robert D. and Cathy L. Jabara, *Agricultural Development Principles: Economic Theory and Empirical Evidence* (Baltimore: Johns Hopkins University Press, 1988), pp. 252–265.

Von Pischke, J. D., Dale W. Adams, and Gordon Donald, *Rural Financial Markets in Developing Countries: Their Use and Abuse* (Baltimore: Johns Hopkins University Press, 1983).

Wortman, Sterling and Ralph W. Cummings, Jr., *To Feed This World: The Challenge and the Strategy* (Baltimore: Johns Hopkins University Press, 1978).

CHAPTER **14**

PRICING POLICIES AND MARKETING SYSTEMS

The links between price policies and food marketing take the food policy analyst to the very core of an economy and the most basic issues concerning the consequences of market organization for economic efficiency and income distribution.

Timmer, p. 293 in Gittinger, Leslie, and Hoisington[1]

THIS CHAPTER

1 Discusses how and why governments tend to intervene in agricultural markets to influence prices and indicates the effects of those interventions
2 Explains the importance of efficient marketing systems and identifies deficiencies in marketing systems in less-developed countries
3 Considers the role that government can play in providing marketing infrastructure, market information, marketing services, and regulations

PRICING POLICIES

Food and agricultural prices are major determinants of producer incentives and of real incomes in developing countries. Governments in those countries often adopt pricing policies to reduce food prices for urban consumers even if farmers are forced to bear the costs. Ironically, in developed countries where

---

[1] J. Price Gittinger, Joanne Leslie, and Caroline Hoisington (eds.), *Food Policy: Integrating Supply, Distribution, and Consumption* (Baltimore: Johns Hopkins University Press, 1987), chapter by C. Peter Timmer, p. 293.

242

farmers are a much smaller proportion of the population, government price interventions tend to support agricultural prices, often at the expense of taxpayers and consumers. Why do we observe these policies? How are they implemented, and what are their short- and long-run effects? These questions are addressed below and linkages are drawn between pricing policies and agricultural marketing.

Reasons for Price Intervention

Governments intervene into agricultural price formation for two major reasons. First, political leaders generally favor policies that improve their chances of staying in power. As discussed below and throughout this book, food prices have a large influence on welfare in less-developed countries. Governments use price policies to effect changes in welfare to ensure continued political support. Sometimes the policies adopted for short-run political objectives also serve the broader objectives that society holds for its agricultural sector, other times not. Second, all governments must intervene in their economies with taxes to generate the revenue needed for roads, police, and other public services.

Regardless of the political structure, government leaders have a difficult time maintaining political stability unless they follow policies that (1) contribute to economic growth, (2) improve income distribution or at least meet minimum nutritional needs for all citizens, and (3) provide a certain measure of food security or stability for the country over time. However, alternative growth paths and distributional patterns can be pursued. The choice among these paths and patterns is influenced by key interest groups. Urban consumers want lower food prices, which are particularly important determinants of real income given the high proportion of income spent on food in developing countries. Concerns for food prices are especially strong during times of rapid inflation. Also, employers want to raise profit rates; cheap food helps them do so by permitting them to lower money wages. Agricultural producers want higher prices for their products, but for most commodities in developing countries the large number of and geographic dispersion of producers make it difficult to organize and place collective pressure on the government. Thus, political power with respect to food prices is centered in urban-industrial areas.

As development proceeds and incomes grow, several factors typically cause the political pressures to shift toward protection for agricultural commodities. First, food prices become less important in household budgets because the proportion of income spent on food declines with higher incomes. Second, the declining relative size of the agricultural sector makes it less costly for the government to succumb to pressures from farmers, while at the same time the reduced number and increased specialization of farms improves the ability of farmers to organize for collective action. Third, when densely populated countries lose their comparative advantage for certain agricultural products, the governments may support farmers by imposing import controls that do not require tax dollars.

The form of government interventions into agricultural commodity markets also shifts as development proceeds. There is usually a continued need to make food more accessible to the poor even as agricultural prices are supported. Governments often develop targeted food-price subsidy schemes or food-stamp programs for the poor, using funds from general tax revenues. These do not tax agricultural producers, but provide benefits for the poorest groups. Targeted price-subsidy schemes generally enjoy the support of farmers because the schemes increase the effective demand for foods.

During early stages of development, most governments must intervene in agricultural markets to raise revenues because the economic base is primarily agricultural. Because it is politically and bureaucratically difficult to tax land or incomes directly, food prices are manipulated through a variety of mechanisms that implicitly tax agriculture. As development proceeds, with its accompanying structural transformation of the economy, the need to tax agriculture diminishes.

Methods of Price Intervention

Governments intervene to influence agricultural prices in several ways. They set price ceilings or floors and enforce them with commodity subsidies or taxes, manipulation of foreign exchange rates, commodity storage programs, restrictions on quantities traded, and/or other policy instruments. Let's examine how a few of these instruments work.

Suppose the government wants to lower the price of rice, an important food in the diet. The supply of rice must therefore be increased in the market relative to demand. Additional supplies can be created by increasing imports or by inducing domestic production. In either case, government revenues must be used to bridge the gap between the initial price and the desired *price ceiling*. Figure 14-1 presents an illustration of how the price ceiling and subsidy might work.

The supply and demand schedules would intersect at price P_0 and quantity Q_0 if there were no trade in rice. However, the country in this example is assumed to be a rice importer, so the world price of rice, P_w, is below P_0. Initially, at P_w and without government intervention, quantity Q_1 is produced domestically, Q_2 is demanded by consumers, and the difference, $Q_2 - Q_1$, is met by imports. If the government desires to artificially create a domestic price for rice, P_d, below the world price, it must pay a subsidy per unit of rice equal to the difference between the world price and the desired domestic price ($P_w - P_d$). This subsidy could be paid on a per ton basis to commercial importers to cover their losses for importing rice at a price below what they pay on the world market, or it could be paid to a government agency that imports rice.[2] In either case, the direct cost to the government of the subsidy is ($P_w - P_d$) times (Q_4 —

---

[2] C. Peter Timmer, *Getting Prices Right: The Scope and Limits of Agricultural Price Policy* (Ithaca, N.Y.: Cornell University Press, 1986), p. 36.

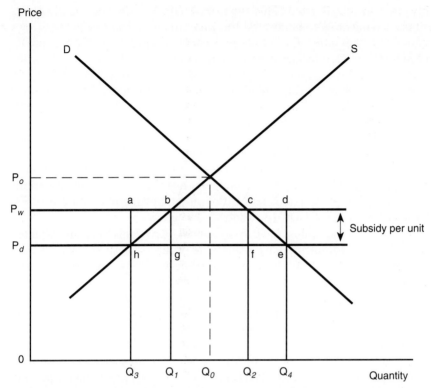

FIGURE 14-1
Economics of a price ceiling and consumer subsidy to lower agricultural prices.

Q_3), which equals area *adeh* in Fig. 14-1. This kind of price ceiling program is common in many African and Asian countries. Consumers benefit but rice producers are hurt by the lower price of rice.

Sometimes the government prefers not to allow scarce foreign exchange to be spent on increased imports. In this case, farmers may be legally forced to sell their commodity to the government at a low price. For example, the government might force farmers to deliver Q_3 units of rice at P_d. Although nothing is imported, the demand for rice (Q_4) exceeds its supply (Q_3). The government must then ration rice to consumers. The shortage in the market provides incentives for farmers to sell their crop illegally on the *black market* for a higher price. Even if the government allows adequate imports to meet the projected demand at the lower price, if the price of the product is higher across the border, farmers will (usually illegally) sell in a neighboring country, thus further reducing domestic supplies.

One means to avoid reducing domestic production and illegal sales while at the same time supporting farm incomes is for the government to administer a two-price scheme in which producers are paid the world price but consumers pay only the subsidized price. This type of system is illustrated in Fig. 14-1. Rather than paying *adeh* to importers, the government would pay $P_w bg P_d$, or a subsidy of $(P_w - P_d)$ times $(Q_1 - 0)$ to producers and a subsidy of bdeg, or $(P_w - P_d)$ times $(Q_4 - Q_1)$, to importers. Producers would still receive P_W, while consumers would face a price of P_d, thus the name two-price scheme. Of course an even higher subsidy could be paid to producers to further reduce imports and increase the producer price. The obvious difficulty with this scheme is its large impact on the government budget. The subsidy costs have to be paid for by some means. Because of this cost, very few major commodities are subsidized this way in developing countries, although related schemes are common in developed countries such as the United States and Japan, and in Europe. Two-price wheat programs have been operative, however, at various times in Brazil, Egypt, Mexico, and a few other low-income countries. Table 14-1 lists examples of LDC food subsidy programs.

Developing countries often have food subsidy programs that are targeted toward the poor or to nutritionally vulnerable groups. These subsidies sometimes are implemented through ration shops, ration cards, or food stamps. Usually only the very poor are eligible, to keep the cost down, but in some cases ration shops are located in poor neighborhoods under the theory that only the poor will frequent them. Alternatively, self-targeting can be achieved by subsidizing foods with very low income elasticities, such as starchy staples or maize. Substantial savings can result from targeting: in Sri Lanka, targeting and program modification reduced outlays for consumer food subsidies from 15 percent of total government expenditures in the late 1970s to less than 3 percent in 1985.[3] The impact of targeted subsidies on agricultural prices and incentives depends on how they are financed, but food subsidies need not have adverse effects on agricultural incentives.[4]

Another common price-policy instrument in developing countries is the export tax. The purpose of an export tax is to raise government revenues and/or reduce domestic commodity prices. The effects of the tax are illustrated in Fig. 14-2. Because the country exports the commodity, the world price, P_w, is shown above the price, P_0, that would have prevailed domestically if there were no trade. If exports were freely allowed, this world price would prevail in the domestic market, and a total quantity of Q_2 would be produced domestically; Q_1 would be demanded by domestic consumers, and the difference $(Q_2 - Q_1)$ would be exported. Then, if an export tax equal to $P_w - P_d$ were imposed, the domestic price would fall to P_d, consumers would increase consumption to Q_3, producers would reduce the quantity supplied to Q_4, exports would decline to $Q_4 - Q_3$, and the government would earn an export tax revenue of $(P_w - P_d)$ times $(Q_4 - Q_3)$ or the area bcfg in Fig. 14-2. Poor countries often impose export taxes because they lack an alternative source of

---

[3] Per Pinstrup-Andersen, "The Social and Economic Effects of Consumer-Oriented Food Subsidies: A Summary of Current Evidence," *Food Subsidies in Developing Countries* (Baltimore: Johns Hopkins University Press, 1988), Chap. 1, pp. 13–14.

[4] Pinstrup-Andersen, ibid, p. 16.

TABLE 14-1
SOME SELECTED CONSUMER PRICE SUBSIDY PROGRAMS IN DEVELOPING COUNTRIES

Country	Principal foods subsidized	Type of program	Food distribution	Actual coverage (implicit targeting)
Bangladesh	Wheat and rice	Price subsidy	Targeted and rationed	Mostly urban
Brazil	Wheat	Price subsidy	General	Total population
China	Rice	Price subsidy	General	Mostly urban
Colombia[a]	Selected processed food	Food stamps	Targeted and rationed	Poor households with preschoolers or women who are pregnant or lactating
Egypt	Wheat	Price subsidy	General	Total population
Egypt	Rice	Price subsidy	Rationed	Mostly urban
Egypt	Sugar, tea, frozen meats, fish, and certain other foods	Price subsidy	Rationed	Total population
India	Wheat and rice	Price subsidy	Rationed	Total population
Mexico	Maize and certain other foods	Price subsidy	General	Mostly urban
Morocco	Wheat	Price subsidy	General	Total population
Pakistan	Wheat	Price subsidy	Rationed	Mostly urban
Philippines	Rice and oil	Price subsidy	Targeted and rationed	All households in areas selected for high level of poverty
Sri Lanka (up to 1977)	Rice	Price subsidy	Rationed	Total population
Sri Lanka (from 1979)	Rice	Food stamps	Targeted and rationed	50 percent of population, biased toward the poor
Sudan	Wheat	Price subsidy	General	Mostly urban
Thailand	Rice	Price subsidy	General	Total population
Zambia	Maize	Price subsidy	General	Mostly urban

[a] Consumer price subsidy program discontinued.
Source: Per Pinstrup-Andersen, *Food Subsidies in Developing Countries* (Baltimore: Johns Hopkins University Press, 1988), p. 6.

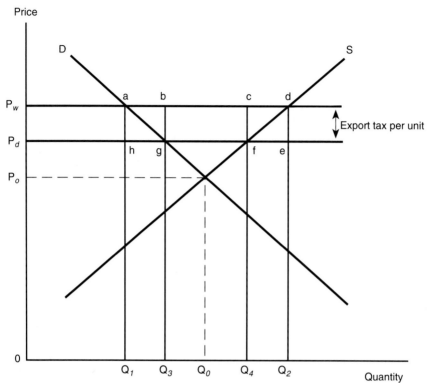

FIGURE 14-2
Economics of an export tax to raise government revenue.

revenue. In the Fig. 14-2 example, the country is unable to influence the world price P_w because it is a small producer in the world market for the commodity. Domestic producers pay the cost of the tax through lower prices. If the country is a large producer, such as Brazil in the coffee market, its exports and any export tax influence the world market price. Therefore, part of the burden of the export tax can be passed on to producers in other countries.

Governments follow many types of pricing policies; those described above are among the most common and direct pricing instruments employed in developing countries. Another common direct pricing policy is the attempt to stabilize commodity prices through a *buffer-stock* program. With such a program, supplies are purchased by the government if the price drops below a certain minimum floor level, and then dumped on the market if the price rises above a certain ceiling level. The purpose of the program is to stabilize rather than alter the long-run price.

Perhaps the most common indirect pricing policy in developing countries is to overvalue the foreign exchange rate. The foreign exchange rate is the value of the country's currency in relation to the value of foreign currency: for example, the number of Mexican pesos that equal one U.S. dollar. If the official foreign exchange rate implies that the local currency is worth more than it actually is, and if exports occur at the official rate, then this overvalued exchange rate acts as an implicit export tax. However, it does not provide tax revenue to the government. More discussion of the trade effects of direct and indirect pricing policies is found in Chap. 16.

Interventions to shift either the supply of, or demand for, agricultural products also affect prices. Income transfer and employment programs with population control activities are examples of policies to shift demands. Policies that steer investments into different sectors, credit programs, and land reforms all affect supplies. The net effect is to change equilibrium prices in markets. Governments tend to examine price trends and shifts and treat them as indicators of an underlying problem. For example, rapidly increasing food prices could be symptomatic of food demand increasing at a faster rate than food supply.

Using prices as indicators of sectoral performance is a legitimate activity. However, price policies that attack the symptom—in the above case, rapidly rising prices—by, perhaps, directly imposing price controls, can create long-run damage to economic growth. A preferred price intervention would be to address the causes of the problem by either investing in productivity enhancing technologies or making more imports available. If demand lags behind supplies, then programs to stimulate demands might be contemplated. In general, it is preferable to directly address the causes of undesirable price trends rather than to directly intervene in price formation for reasons discussed below.

Short- and Long-Run Effects of Pricing Policies

A few of the direct, short-run effects of food and agricultural pricing-policies are illustrated in Figs. 14-1 and 14-2. As producer and consumer prices are raised or lowered, changes in production and consumption occur. Producer incomes, foreign exchange earnings, price stability, and government revenues are also directly influenced by price policies. These and other direct and indirect, short- and long-run effects of pricing policies are summarized in Table 14-2 and illustrated in Box 14-1.

An important short-run effect of many LDC policies is to transfer income from producers to consumers. Within consumer groups, the poor tend to benefit most, since they spend proportionately more income on food.

A major feature of both direct and indirect effects of price policies is the influence of those policies on efficiency of resource allocation. In the short run, resources are diverted to less-productive uses because of the subsidy or tax. Additional indirect or long-run misallocation of resources can result as investments and structural changes occur that expand less efficient sectors of the economy at the expense of more efficient ones. In addition, efficiency losses occur due to the resource costs associated with collecting taxes or administering the policy.

TABLE 14-2
SUMMARY OF PRICE POLICY EFFECTS

Direct short-run effects of price policies

---

1. Changes in consumer and producer prices
2. Changes in quantities produced and consumed
3. Changes in exports, imports, and foreign exchange earnings
4. Income transfers between and among consumer and producer groups
5. Government budget effects
6. Price stability effects
7. Changes in marketing margins and their effects on efficiency of resource allocation

---

Indirect and long-run effects of price policies

---

1. Employment changes
2. Incentives for capital investment
3. Incentives for technical change
4. Changes in health and nutrition
5. Long-run changes in allocation of resources in production, storage, transportation, and processing.

BOX 14-1

FOOD PRICE POLICY IN EGYPT

The Egyptian government has, since before 1950, operated a complex set of policies that distort agricultural output and input prices. These policies initially were imposed to transfer resources out of agriculture for industrialization while maintaining low prices for consumers. These policies have slowly evolved so that currently the tax burden on agriculture, resulting from the policies, is no different from that on other productive sectors of the economy, while consumer price subsidies have been increased dramatically. This food subsidy bill accounted for more than 15 percent of total government expenditures in the early 1980s.

Consumer prices for numerous goods are subsidized below free-market levels. Every family receives a ration card entitling it to a certain quantity of goods at these fixed prices. Additional goods must be purchased at substantially higher prices in the black market. The government imports large quantities of goods to maintain these low prices. The government is also heavily involved in marketing both agricultural products and agricultural inputs. Input prices are highly subsidized, partly to compensate producers for the implicit tax of other policies. Livestock producers are protected and receive heavily subsidized feeds.

All of these policies have created substantial distortions in resource allocation. Important incentives for the production of livestock are created, while wheat, rice, and cotton production are discriminated against. The budgetary cost of the subsidies is enormous. It has been estimated that the distortions caused by the policies is the equivalent of 1.5 percent of national income.

Source: Joachim von Braun and Hartwig de Haen, "The Effects of Food Price and Subsidy Policies on Egyptian Agriculture," International Food Policy Research Institute, Research Report No. 42, Washington, D.C., November 1983.

Distortions in the normal price differences for a commodity across locations, between points in time, and at different levels of processing can influence storage, transportation, and processing of the commodity. For example, urban prices are normally expected to be higher than rural prices for the same food commodity because of transportation costs. If the government sets a ceiling price that is equal in both rural and urban areas, transporting the good from the rural to the urban area may no longer be profitable. In fact, in some cases governments have been known to set urban food prices lower than rural prices, with the result that food, supplied by imports, is transported from urban areas to rural areas.

Likewise, ceiling prices can discourage the normal seasonal storage of a crop if prices are not allowed to rise to cover storage costs. Also, if a government reduces the price margin allowed between farm and retail levels, processors and marketers can be forced out of business.

Pricing policies are often implemented through government procurement agencies with *monopsonistic* (single buyer) power. Thus, opportunities are created for illegal garnering of rents by government employees, and inefficiencies can arise that may force additional reductions in farm prices. These often unintended results of pricing policies can be particularly severe in countries with poor communications and underdeveloped legal systems.

Finally, other indirect effects of pricing policies include employment changes, incentives to develop and adopt new technologies, and changes in health and nutrition. If total revenues for one sector or commodity are raised through pricing policies, more people may be employed. Also, producer incentives to press private firms or public research agencies for new technologies as well as incentives to adopt technologies may be enhanced. Consumer price subsidies can have important impacts on health and nutrition. In cases where they are financed through government tax revenues and not by depressing producer prices, they can be an effective means of transferring income to targeted groups.

Once price policies are instituted, they are difficult to repeal. Urban consumers in numerous countries have reacted in negative and sometimes violent manners to government attempts to lower subsidies. In summary, price-policy effects are pervasive and influence the efficiency of the production and marketing systems.

MARKETING FUNCTIONS AND DEFICIENCIES

Marketing transforms products over time, space, and form through storage, transportation, and processing. Through marketing, goods are exchanged and prices are set. Markets communicate signals to producers, processors, input suppliers, and consumers about the costs of buying, selling, storing, processing, and transporting. These major marketing functions and their linkages to price policies are summarized in Fig. 14-3.

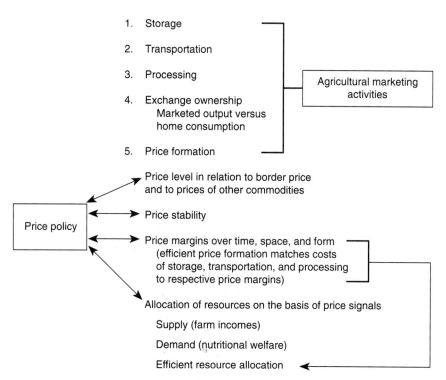

FUNCTIONS OF MARKETS AND MARKETING

1. Storage
2. Transportation
3. Processing
4. Exchange ownership
   Marketed output versus
   home consumption
5. Price formation

Agricultural marketing activities

Price policy

Price level in relation to border price and to prices of other commodities

Price stability

Price margins over time, space, and form (efficient price formation matches costs of storage, transportation, and processing to respective price margins)

Allocation of resources on the basis of price signals

Supply (farm incomes)

Demand (nutritional welfare)

Efficient resource allocation

FIGURE 14-3
Links between agricultural price policy and agricultural marketing. (*Source:* C. Peter Timmer, "The Relationship Between Price Policy and Food Marketing," in J. Price Gittinger, Joanne Leslie, and Caroline Hoisington, (eds.) *Food Policy: Integrating Supply, Distribution, and Consumption,* Baltimore: Johns Hopkins University Press, 1987, p. 294.)

In the earliest stages of development and in remote areas, a high proportion of the population lives on farms and is relatively self-sufficient. The demand for marketing services is limited. As development proceeds, with resulting increased living standards and urbanization, the size and efficiency of the marketing system become more important. Unless marketing services are improved concurrently with the development and spread of new technologies, improvements in education and credit, and the other factors discussed in this section of the book, economic development will be hindered. And, inefficient marketing systems can absorb substantial private and public resources and result in low farm-level and high retail-level prices.

Marketing System Deficiencies in Developing Countries

Private marketing systems in many developing countries operate relatively well, in that prices are influenced by underlying supply and demand conditions.

Products are stored, transported, processed, and exchanged in roughly the amounts expected given prevailing costs, except where governments have intervened with price policies. Price rigging by opportunistic marketing agents is generally not a serious problem. However, because marketing costs are frequently high and some price distortions do occur, marketing system deficiencies may retard the rate of agricultural growth and influence the distribution of the benefits of that growth. Let's consider the nature of these deficiencies before turning in the following section to the possible public role in solving them.

The principal weaknesses in marketing systems in developing countries are: (1) infrastructure deficiencies, (2) producers' lack of information, (3) the weak bargaining position of producers of certain commodities, and (4) government-induced market distortions. The magnitude of each of these deficiencies differs across regions and by country; perhaps the most severe problems are found in Sub-Saharan Africa. The most visible effect of these weaknesses is to create a large spread between the prices producers are paid for their products and the retail prices. Marketing system deficiencies also create wide variations in producer prices within countries. Examples of producer/retail price spreads and of intracountry price variations are presented in Table 14-3 for selected countries in Africa and Asia. The Sub-Saharan African countries have larger price spreads than the Asian countries, indicating more deficient marketing systems.

Good communications (roads, railroads, telephones, postal services, etc.) and storage infrastructure are crucial to a well-functioning marketing system. The availability and quality of rural roads, in particular, have a strong influence on marketing costs and on the willingness of farmers to adopt new technologies and sell any surplus production. A farmer who has only a few hectares may still have to market several tons of output to apply new seeds, fertilizers, and other modern inputs. Telephones, postal services, radio stations, etc., increase access to information. Modern storage facilities are important, to minimize rodent, insect, and water damage while commodities are being held. Most storage can occur on the farm or at facilities owned by private traders. Storage may also be provided by the government for buffer stocks and food distribution programs.

Producers require market information to improve market efficiency and reduce transactions costs, as discussed in Chap. 10. Unequal access to information can give a competitive advantage to particular groups of farmers or traders who have more information. When roads, basic telecommunications, and news services are lacking or are available only to a few, those with better information on market prices, crop prospects, prospective changes in international forces, etc., can earn higher profits, and, in some cases, gain political power as well. Thus, access to information is of fundamental importance for agricultural development.

The structure of agricultural markets is usually such that the number of middle agents is smaller than the number of producers. Economists hold

TABLE 14-3
PRODUCER/CONSUMER AND REGIONAL PRICE SPREADS,
SELECTED AFRICAN AND ASIAN COUNTRIES,
VARIOUS YEARS, 1975–1980

Country	Commodity	Producer/consumer[a] price spread	Regional[b] spread
Nigeria	Maize,	54.5	35.6
	rice, and	57.0	72.9
	sorghum	59.8	45.9
Malawi	Maize and	48.2	21.9
	rice	55.1	68.2
Tanzania	Maize,	38.2	25.7
	rice, and	56.6	61.3
	sorghum	48.1	35.5
Kenya	Maize	42.0	30.0
Sudan	Sorghum	61.2	48.2
	and wheat		52.1
Indonesia	Rice	84.0	71.9
India	Rice,	82.0	68.9
	wheat, and	79.5	65.9
	sorghum	80.0	63.5
Bangladesh	Rice	79.0	75.0
Philippines	Rice and	87.8	82.7
	maize	71.5	64.2

[a] Producer price/retail price × 100
[b] Lowest price/highest price × 100
Source: Raisuddin Ahmed, "Pricing Principles and Public Intervention in Domestic Markets," Chap. 4, in *Agricultural Price Policy for Developing Countries*, John W. Mellor and Raisuddin Adhmed (eds.), (Baltimore: Johns Hopkins University Press, 1988), p. 67.

differing views on whether relatively fewer such intermediaries result in monopsonistic power on the part of the intermediary and an unfair bargaining advantage.[5] One needs to be cautious in drawing conclusions. Because the more efficient traders and processors tend to deal in large volumes, there are naturally fewer of these people than there are producers. On the other hand, in most countries with private marketing systems, ease of entry is such that there are still enough processors and other middle agents to provide competition for each other. Examples of collusion and monopsonistic power, however, undoubtedly exist for certain products, particularly in isolated areas and where social and cultural factors play a contributing role.

Probably a more common marketing problem for producers in developing

[5] Subrata Ghatak and Ken Ingersent, *Agriculture and Economic Development* (Baltimore: Johns Hopkins University Press, 1984), p. 240.

Roadside market in Bangladesh.

countries is a situation in which government-controlled marketing organiza-tions (often called *parastatals*) are given monopsonistic power and legal au-thority to purchase all of a product while setting its price as well (Box 14-2). As discussed in the price-policy section, these tightly controlled markets can have negative effects on producer incentives and market efficiency. Agricultural economic systems are inherently complex. A large amount of information is transmitted through market signals, and decisions made by central marketing boards and parastatal agencies often create serious market distortions. If these types of government agencies are a cause of, rather than a solution to, market-ing problems in developing countries, how might the public sector improve marketing efficiency? This issue is addressed in the following section.

THE ROLE OF THE PUBLIC SECTOR IN AGRICULTURAL MARKETING

The primary role of the government is to provide the infrastructure required for an efficient marketing system, particularly roads; a market information system; a commodity grading system; and regulations to ensure the rights of all partici-pants. The underlying rationale for government involvement is the presence of public goods and market failures creating externalities. Public goods provide benefits to society as a whole but would be supplied in less than the socially desirable amounts by the private sector alone. Externalities involve often-unintended positive or negative effects of the actions of one person (firm) or persons (firms) on other people.

BOX 14-2

COMMODITY MARKETING BOARDS IN SUB-SAHARAN AFRICA

Sub-Saharan African states are distinguished from many others in the developing world in that most of them possess publicly sanctioned monopsonies for the purchase and export of agricultural goods. These marketing boards serve as the sole buyers of major exports, purchase crops at administratively determined prices, and sell them at prevailing world market prices. These state marketing agencies are vestiges of the colonial period, and their origins and histories vary considerably. Many were established during the Great Depression of the 1930s or World War II. Their official mandates were almost invariably to benefit producers by reinvesting revenues in agriculture and, especially, stabilizing producer prices. In Nigeria, for example, 70 percent of the trading surplus was consigned to price stabilization, with the remainder earmarked for agricultural development.

As the colonial governments were confronted with growing needs for revenues, they quickly found ways of diverting marketing board funds away from agricultural development and into general revenue coffers. Following independence, African governments continued to use the commodity marketing boards as extensions of their normal revenue-generating arms, and the initial purposes of the boards were ignored. Examples are found in Ghana and Nigeria immediately following independence. World prices of cocoa fell dramatically in 1959 to 1962, yet the boards, despite their mandate for stabilizing prices, allowed the full burden of the price drop to fall on the producers.

From colonial through current times, these boards have been used to transfer resources from agriculture into "modernizing" and mostly urban development. They have served political objectives by raising revenues, increasing employment of favored groups, and keeping primary commodity prices low to benefit urban and industrial concerns. The boards never really fulfilled their mandate to improve and stabilize conditions in agriculture. In combination with certain other policy distortions, they contributed to the stagnation and decline of agriculture during the 1970s and 1980s.

Source: Robert M. Bates, *Markets and States in Tropical Africa: The Political Basis of Agricultural Policies* (Berkeley, Calif.: University of California Press, 1981), pp. 11–62.

Provision of Infrastructure

The private sector can be expected to build many of the required storage facilities, processing plants, etc., but investments in roads, seaports, airports, and, in most cases, telecommunications, will require government involvement. One firm, or even a small group of firms, will lack the incentives to build sufficient roads, not just because of their high cost but because of the difficulty of excluding others from or charging for their use. Roads are a public good that serve all industries, consumers, and national defense.

Several studies have estimated the economic importance of roads to agriculture in developing countries. For example, Spriggs estimated a benefit/cost ratio of 8 for surfaced roads in the eastern rice regions of India.[6] Ahmed and

---

[6] John Spriggs, "Benefit-Cost Analysis of Surfaced Roads in the Eastern Rice Region of India," *American Journal of Agricultural Economics*, vol. 59, May 1977, pp. 375–379.

Driving cattle to market.

Hossain estimated that incomes were roughly one-third higher for villages with well-developed infrastructure, compared to those with poor infrastructure, in Bangladesh.[7] The evidence in numerous countries suggests that investments in infrastructure have greatly narrowed farm-retail margins.

Provision of Information

Provision of accurate crop and livestock reports requires investments in data collection and dissemination. Production and consumption data may be poor quality, but accurate data on marketing quantities, qualities, and prices can give essential information for formulating agricultural policies and for decisions by individual economic agents.

To ensure equal access to information, data need to be collected in all important markets and disseminated on a regular basis. Information on current market prices, crop prospects, and factors influencing demand can be spread through radio broadcasts and newspapers once the government reports are released. An efficient, competitive market requires widespread access to information. Otherwise, a small group of large farmers, traders, or processors can gain market power at the expense of small farmers, particularly those in remote areas. These large farmers can then use the resulting profits to influence political and economic policy to favor themselves. The result is both efficiency losses (reduced economic growth) and distributional inequities.

[7] Raisuddin Ahmed and Mahabub Hossain, "Developmental Impact of Rural Infrastructure in Bangladesh," International Food Policy Research Institute, Research Report No. 83, Washington, D.C., October 1990, p. 70.

Commodity Grading Systems

In economies highly oriented toward subsistence production, markets offer few premiums for higher-quality products. As interregional communication, and particularly as export trade develops, quality standards increase in importance because buyers need to compare the products of many different sellers, often without seeing the product before the sale. In markets using modern technology, purchases are often made electronically or over the phone, something that can only happen with a recognized system of grades and standards.

Threshing, drying, cleaning, storage, and processing practices for crops and feeding, slaughtering, storage, and other practices for livestock influence the quality of the final product. Unless grades and standards are established with corresponding price differentials, then producers and processors have little incentive to incur the costs of producing higher quality goods.

Regulations

Market regulations related to factors affecting health and safety, but also to weighing practices and other legal codes that influence the enforceability of contracts, are important to a well-functioning marketing system. The purposes of many of these regulations are to ensure basic honesty and reduce transactions costs in marketing. As discussed in Chap. 10, development brings with it a reduction in personal exchange and some associated social and cultural constraints on behavior. Increased impersonal exchange requires new institutional arrangements to substitute for the rules of behavior that had been imposed previously by a more personal society.

The importance of market regulations does not imply a need for heavy involvement of government marketing boards or other parastatal trading agencies. Banning private marketing activities does not improve the welfare of either farmers or consumers. While there is a role for the government in the activities discussed above and perhaps in implementing a price stabilization scheme, more extensive monopolization of domestic marketing functions tends to produce high marketing costs and large market distortions.

SUMMARY

Food and agricultural prices are major determinants of producer incentives and of real incomes in developing countries. Governments in those countries often adopt pricing policies to reduce food prices for urban consumers at the expense of producers. Political leaders devise policies to meet society's objectives and the demands of interest groups, to generate revenue, and, in some cases, to line their own pockets. Governments can influence agricultural prices by setting price ceilings or floors and enforcing them with subsidies, taxes, manipulation of exchange rates, storage programs, quantity restrictions, and other policy instruments. These interventions influence producer and consumer prices and incomes, production and consumption, foreign exchange earnings, price stability, government revenues, the efficiency of resource allocation, employment, capital investment, technical change, health and nutrition, and marketing margins.

Marketing refers to the process of changing products in time, space, and form through storage, transportation, and processing. Goods are exchanged and prices are determined in markets. The importance of these functions increases as markets become more commercialized. Developing countries often have marketing systems characterized by deficient infrastructure, inadequate information, weak bargaining position for producers for certain commodities, and government-induced distortions. The government can help solve certain marketing deficiencies, particularly the lack of roads and information. The public sector can provide a system of grades and standards as well as other regulations. These contributions can help reduce transactions costs that rise as markets become less personal. Governments should avoid the larger parastatal marketing agencies that tend to introduce marketing distortions.

IMPORTANT TERMS AND CONCEPTS

Buffer-stock programs
Competitive market
Export tax
Externalities
Foreign exchange rate
Grading system
Infrastructure
Interest groups
Market information
Market regulations
Marketing board
Marketing functions
Marketing margin

Middle agents
Monopsony
Parastatal
Price ceiling
Price distortions
Price floor
Price formation
Pricing policies
Public good
Resource allocation efficiency
Two-price programs
Time, space, and form

LOOKING AHEAD

Technical change and education are critical components of any agricultural development program. In the next chapter you will examine the role of public and private research and education in generating and facilitating adoption of improved technologies and institutions. You will consider how the benefits of technical and institutional changes are distributed.

QUESTIONS FOR DISCUSSION

1 Why do developing country governments frequently set agricultural prices below market levels?
2 Why do governments get involved in stabilizing prices?

3 What are the direct short-run effects of price policies in agriculture?

4 What are the indirect and long-run effects of price policies in agriculture?

5 Draw a graph to illustrate the effects on supply and demand of a price ceiling set below the market equilibrium price.

6 Draw a graph to illustrate the effect of a price support to farmers set above the market equilibrium price.

7 What are the major food marketing functions? Why are these functions necessary to get agriculture moving in developing countries?

8 What are the major deficiencies in agricultural marketing systems in developing countries?

9 What role might the government play in improving an agricultural marketing system?

10 Discuss the potential role of buffer stocks in an agricultural development program in a developing country.

11 Why might government marketing boards and parastatals create inefficiencies in resource use?

12 Why do governments in developing countries use export taxes on agricultural commodities more frequently than do governments in more developed countries?

13 Why does the increasing impersonal exchange that accompanies development imply a need for increased government regulation?

14 Why are marketing grades and standards important?

15 Why does increased market information improve marketing efficiency?

RECOMMENDED READINGS

Anderson, Kim and Yujiro Hayami, *The Political Economy of Agricultural Protection* (Sydney: Allen and Unwin, 1986).

Byerlee, Derek, and Gustavo Sain, "Food Pricing Policy in Developing Countries: Bias Against Agriculture or for Urban Consumers?" *American Journal of Agricultural Economics,* vol. 68, November 1986, pp. 961–969.

Ghatak, Subrata and Ken Ingersent, *Agriculture and Economic Development* (Baltimore: Johns Hopkins University Press, 1984), pp. 237–250.

Gittinger, J. Price, Joanne Leslie, and Caroline Hoisington (eds.), *Food Policy: Integrating Supply, Distribution, and Consumption* (Baltimore: Johns Hopkins University Press, 1987); see especially the two chapters by C. P. Timmer and the ones by P. Streeten and P. Pinstrup-Andersen.

Johnson, D. Gale and G. Edward Schuh (eds.), *The Role of Markets in the World Food Economy,* (Boulder, Colo.: Westview Press, 1983); see especially the chapters by L. Reca, Robert Bates, and Alain de Janvry.

Krueger, Anne O., Maurice Schiff, and Alberto Valdes, "Agricultural Incentives in Developing Countries: Measuring the Effects of Sectoral and Economywide Policies," *World Bank Economic Review,* vol. 2, September 1988, pp. 255–271.

Mellor, John W., "Food Price Policy and Income Distribution in Low-Income Countries," *Economic Development and Cultural Change,* vol. 27, October 1978, pp. 1–26.

Pinstrup-Andersen, Per (ed.), *Food Subsidies in Developing Countries* (Baltimore: Johns Hopkins University Press, 1988).

Stevens, Robert D. and Cathy L. Jabara, *Agricultural Development Principles* (Baltimore: Johns Hopkins University Press, 1988); see Chaps. 12 and 14.

Streeten, Paul, *What Price Food? Agricultural Price Policies in Developing Countries* (Ithaca, N.Y.: Cornell University Press, 1987).

Timmer, C. Peter, *Getting Prices Right: The Scope and Limits of Agricultural Price Policy* (Ithaca, N.Y.: Cornell University Press, 1986).

Timmer, C. Peter, Walter P. Falcon, and Scott R. Pearson, *Food Policy Analysis* (Baltimore: Johns Hopkins University Press, 1983), Chap. 4.

Webb, Alan J., Michael Lopez, and Renata Penn, "Estimates of Producer and Consumer Subsidy Equivalents," U.S. Department of Agriculture, Economic Research Service Statistical Bulletin No. 803, Washington, D.C., April 1990.

World Bank, *World Development Report 1986* (New York: Oxford University Press, 1986), see especially Chaps. 4 and 5!

Wortman, Sterling and Ralph W. Cummings, Jr., *To Feed This World: The Challenge and The Strategy* (Baltimore: Johns Hopkins University Press, 1978), Chap. 13, pp. 365–375.

CHAPTER **15**

RESEARCH, EXTENSION, AND EDUCATION

The man who farms as his forefathers did cannot produce much food no matter how rich the land or how hard he works.

Shultz[1]

THIS CHAPTER

1 Discusses the role of public and private agricultural research in generating improved technologies and institutions and the effects of those technologies on income growth and distribution and on food security
2 Describes the major types of agricultural research, alternative ways of organizing research, and factors influencing the transfer of research results from one country to another
3 Examines the role of education and the major types of education, including agricultural extension

THE ROLE OF AGRICULTURAL RESEARCH

A major determinant of whether the "stork outruns the harvest" is the effectiveness of agricultural research. Through research, the productivity of existing resources is increased, new higher-productivity inputs and ways of producing food are generated, and new or improved institutional arrangements are de-

[1] Theodore W. Schultz, *Transforming Traditional Agriculture* (Chicago: University of Chicago Press, 1964), Chap. 1, p. 3.

signed. Examples of research outputs include higher-yielding plant varieties, better methods for controlling insects and diseases, increased knowledge about methods for manipulating plant or animal genes, and designs for improved agricultural policies. Research creates the potential for increased agricultural production, moderated food prices, increased foreign exchange, reduced pressure on the natural resource base, and many other positive results. Let's consider in more detail the nature of these effects and the possibilities for negative as well as positive outcomes.

Agricultural Productivity

Productivity increases generated through agricultural research imply a shifting upward of agricultural production functions. The simple example of increasing the output per unit of an input, say fertilizer, is illustrated in Fig. 15-1. If a more responsive seed variety is made available through research, output produced per kilo of fertilizer may increase. The research that produced that higher quality seed may be either public or private or both. Public research is conducted in national research institutions, public universities, or government-sponsored research in private entities. Private research is financed by private companies.

FIGURE 15-1
The effect of research on input productivity. New technologies generated through research can shift the production response function upward.

Output

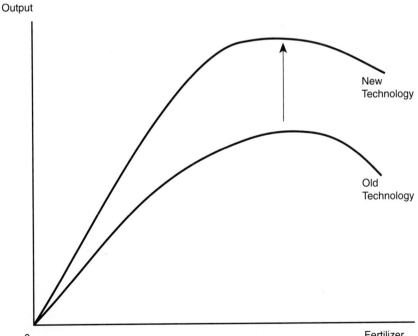

Fertilizer

0

Partial productivity ratios (i.e., crop production per hectare, output per agricultural worker) are shown in Table 15-1 for India, Indonesia, Nigeria, and Brazil, four of the more populous countries of the world. Despite rapid population growth, which might be expected to push production onto more marginal agricultural lands, agricultural output per hectare and per worker rose in each of these countries from 1980 to 1985. This same pattern is found in most other developing countries, although output per capita for the total population has declined in several Sub-Saharan Africa countries partly because of rapid population growth.

The productivity increases shown in Table 15-1 are largely the result of new technologies that are generated through agricultural research. The examples shown in Fig. 15-1 and Table 15-1 are oversimplified in the sense that seldom are levels of all other inputs held constant. Measurement of total productivity gains due to research requires netting out the cost of any additional inputs employed with the improved technologies. The resulting total net cost reduction per unit of output produced can then be used to summarize the total productivity effect. This total productivity effect is illustrated in Fig. 15-2. New or improved technology shifts the original supply curve (S_1) downward to S_2 because the supply curve is a marginal cost curve and the new technology has reduced the cost of production. The new lower cost of production per unit of output means that more output is produced at a lower price.

Many studies have been conducted to estimate the economic returns to society from public research investments aimed at achieving these productivity increases (see Box 15-1). The results of a sample of these studies are presented in Table 15-2. Most studies have found very high annual rates of return to agricultural research, often in the 20 to 60 percent range. National leaders have

TABLE 15-1
CHANGES IN AGRICULTURAL OUTPUT PER HECTARE AND PER WORKER, 1970–1985

Country	1970	1975	1980	1985
		Indices (1979–1980 = 100)		
India				
Crop production per hectare	85.7	93.3	98.1	120.1
Ag production per ag worker	87.2	93.7	98.4	119.4
Indonesia				
Crop production per hectare	73.7	76.6	100.4	116.4
Ag production per ag worker	73.5	80.8	100.6	122.8
Nigeria				
Crop production per hectare	101.6	96.8	104.0	119.3
Ag production per ag worker	107.0	96.9	103.4	116.2
Brazil				
Crop production per hectare	89.2	97.3	100.7	120.9
Ag production per ag worker	72.1	84.7	101.2	120.5

Source: U. S. Department of Agriculture, *World Agricultural Trends and Indicators, 1970–1988,* Economic Research Service, Statistical Bulletin No. 781, Washington, D.C., 1989.

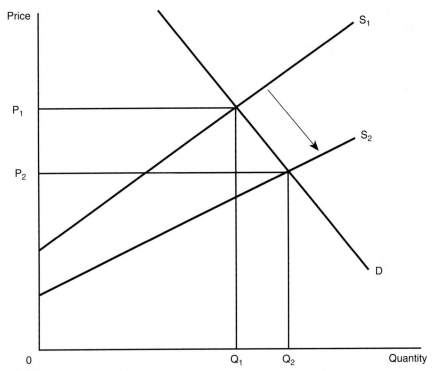

FIGURE 15-2
Effect of research on supply. Agricultural research reduces the cost per unit of output, thereby causing the supply curve to shift down to the right.

a responsibility to invest scarce public resources in activities that yield high returns. Agricultural research is a very high-return activity for many countries.

Increased agricultural productivity not only creates the potential for higher real incomes to producers through lower costs and to consumers through lower food prices, but also can help a country's agriculture become more competitive in world markets. Efficiency gained through higher agricultural productivity can be turned into foreign exchange earnings or savings as a result of additional exports or reduced imports.

The fact that agricultural research has yielded high returns in many countries in the past does not imply that these returns are guaranteed for all research systems or types of research. Each country must carefully consider the appropriate type of research organization and portfolio of activities, given its resource base and special needs (see Box 15-2 for an example of a research portfolio). This issue is discussed in more detail below.

Distributional and Nutritional Effects of Research

Agricultural producers at different income levels, with different farm sizes, in different locations, and with different land tenure arrangements can gain or lose

---

BOX 15-1

RATES OF RETURN ON INVESTMENTS

A widely used criterion for determining the value of a project or investment is the internal rate of return (IRR). The IRR is the discount rate that makes the net present worth of a project's stream of benefits minus its stream of costs equal to zero. It represents the maximum interest that could be paid for the resources if the investment is to recover costs and still break even. The *IRR* may be calculated by solving

$$\sum_{t=1}^{n} \frac{B_t - C_t}{(1 + IRR)^t} = 0$$

where B_t and C_t are the benefits and costs from each year of the project or investment, and n is the planning horizon. The higher the IRR relative to the interest rate on borrowed money, the more favorable is the investment.

Source: J. Price Gittinger, *Economic Analysis of Agricultural Projects*, 2nd ed. (Baltimore: Johns Hopkins University Press, 1982), especially pp. 329–342.

TABLE 15-2
INTERNAL RATES OF RETURN TO INVESTMENTS IN AGRICULTURAL RESEARCH FOR SELECTED COUNTRIES AND COMMODITIES

Commodity and country	Author(s)	Time period	Annual internal rate of return (%)
Brazil			
Cotton	Ayer (1970)	1924–1967	77
Mexico			
Wheat	Ardito-Barletta (1970)	1943–1963	90
Maize	Ardito-Barletta (1970)	1943–1963	35
India			
Aggregate	Evenson and Jha (1973)	1953–1971	40
Aggregate	Kahlon et al. (1977)	1960–1973	63
Japan			
Rice	Hayami and Akino (1977)	1930–1961	73–75
Malaysia			
Rubber	Pee (1977)	1932–1973	24
Colombia			
Rice	Hertford et al. (1977)	1957–1980	60–82
Philippines			
Rice	Flores et al. (1978)	1966–1975	46–75
Bangladesh			
Wheat and Rice	Pray (1980)	1961–1977	30–35
Pakistan			
Wheat	Nagy (1983)	1967–1981	58

Sources: See references at the end of this chapter.

BOX 15-2

MAJOR TYPES OF RESEARCH IN THE NATIONAL AGRICULTURAL RESEARCH INSTITUTION IN ECUADOR

The listing below of the major types of agricultural research activities in Ecuador provides an example of a typical applied research portfolio for a small developing country. Ecuador conducts research on more than 40 commodities. Given its limited research budget, the country must decide which commodities to concentrate on and how much to emphasize each type of research.

1 Plant breeding	development of new lines and varieties that yield more and are resistant to insects and diseases; maintenance of a germplasm collection
2 Cultural practices	determination of optimal planting densities, improved harvesting methods
3 Crop protection	improved methods for control of insects, diseases, weeds, nematodes, including integrated biological, cultural, and chemical methods
4 Soils and fertilizers	development of improved soil conservation methods, chemical analysis of soils including macro- and microelement analysis, toxicity studies, economic analysis of soil conservation and fertilization practices
5 Water management	studies of water needs, improved irrigation methods, salinity control
6 Mechanization	design of improved agricultural implements appropriate for Ecuador's resource base
7 Socioeconomics	diagnosis of constraints to technology adoption, monitoring and evaluation of research, analysis of farm management practices and opportunities
8 Technology validation	on-farm transferring, testing, and validating of new technologies
9 Seed production	basic and registered seed production, technologies for seed production, improved vegetative propagation
10 Post-harvest technologies	improved methods for storage, drying, cleaning, packaging, and transporting agricultural products
11 Agroforestry	improved systems of agroforestry and of pasturing forests
12 Animal improvement	animal breeding, introduction and selection of animals from outside the country, adaptation of animals to different climates
13 Animal health	prevention and cure of diseases and external and internal parasites
14 Animal nutrition	improved forages, analysis of concentrates and other supplementary feeding programs, evaluation of nutritional deficiencies, nutritive value of feeds

Source: Julio Palomino, Planning Director, National Agricultural Research Institution, Ecuador.

as a result of new technologies and institutional changes generated through research. Consumers are major beneficiaries of agricultural research, but the benefits they receive vary as well by income level and are influenced by the nature of the research portfolio. Returns to land versus labor also are influenced by research. Nutritional implications follow from these differential producer, consumer, and factor-income effects.

Farm Size and Tenure The issue of whether improved agricultural technologies benefit large farms more than small farms has been the subject of substantial debate. Evidence suggests that farm size has not been a major impediment to adoption of new biological technologies, the major focus of developing country agricultural research.[2] However, large farms do tend to adopt new technologies first, probably because it pays large farms more to invest in obtaining information about the technologies. Owners of large farms may have more formal education that helps them process the information, and a greater ability to absorb risk. Large farms sometimes have better access to credit needed to purchase modern inputs. Most small farms in the same region as large farms do eventually adopt the technologies, but larger farms frequently adopt first and thereby receive greater income gains than small farms. In addition, late adopters often are faced with lower producer prices because supplies shift outward as early adopters increase output. Of course even if all producers in a given region adopted a scale-neutral technology at the same time, absolute income differences would widen because the increased returns per hectare are spread over more hectares on larger farms.

As noted in Chap. 10, not all technologies and institutional changes are scale-neutral. For example, certain types of mechanical technologies can be used on large but not small farms. With differences in transactions costs, large farmers may press research systems for research results suitable for them even if the country's resource base on average would dictate a different type of technology. Also, while many technologies are scale-neutral and some are biased toward large farms, it may be difficult to generate technologies biased toward small farms. All this implies that reducing transactions costs through improved information is important, but it also implies that research may not be the best policy tool for achieving distributional objectives.

Tenant farmers represent an important producer group in many countries. It is difficult to generalize about the effects of research on the incomes of tenants versus landlords. One might expect that improved biological technologies would make land more productive and thus help tenants, but the distribution of income gains is influenced by other factors as well. If each landlord has several tenants, so that the average size of landlord holdings is greater than the average size of tenants' farms, then the average landlord would gain relative to the average tenant if each received equal shares of income gains per hectare.

[2] See Grant M. Scobie, "Investment in International Agricultural Research: Some Economic Dimensions," World Bank Staff Working Paper No. 361, Washington, D.C., October 1979.

Contractual arrangements influence the distribution of research benefits, and the arrangements may change as well as a result of new technologies.[3] If the tenant pays the landlord a fixed share of the output, the division of any income gains after adopting the new technology depends on the relative sharing of both output and production costs. But if the tenant pays a fixed amount to the landlord, the tenant can keep the income gains until the landlord raises the rent. Often, increases in land productivity are bid into land rents, and landowners are able to capture these rents by changing tenancy agreements. In the Philippines case covered in Chap. 8, the rent from increased productivity created by the irrigation system and higher-yielding rice varieties was captured by the landowners who were able to change land-leasing and labor-contracting arrangements to benefit themselves.

Regional Disparities Regional differences in resource endowments and basic infrastructure can influence the distribution of research gains among producers. In fact, interregional disparities in the net benefits from research tend to be larger than intraregional disparities. Data from India indicate that the new rice and wheat varieties that increased production so dramatically in that country in the late 1960s benefitted primarily the more productive wheat and rice states. Productivity increased dramatically in the country's northern region. At the same time, during 1967 to 1976, the central and eastern regions actually had decreasing rice yields. These interregional yield differentials have diminished over time, but the technologies clearly have benefitted certain regions more than others.[4] The introduction of modern crop varieties has exacerbated interregional disparities in many countries because those technologies have often required irrigation and greater use of farm chemicals. Producers in dryland areas and regions with poor infrastructure for transporting fertilizer have been disadvantaged. Broadening the scope of agricultural research and decentralizing the research structure should help reduce regional disparities, although rates of return on research aimed at more productive regions are consistently higher than those for marginal areas.

Producers and Consumers The impacts of technological change on the distribution of income between producers and consumers depend to a large extent on the degree to which quantity demanded responds to price changes. If producers face an elastic demand for their output, increased supplies will place little downward pressure on prices so producers rather than consumers capture most of the benefits. Export crops, for example, tend to have relatively elastic demands, and thus new technologies for the production of these commodities

---

[3] See George W. Norton, Philip G. Pardey, and Julian Alston, *Science Under Scarcity: Theory and Practice for Agricultural Research Evaluation and Priority Setting* (Ithaca, N.Y.: Cornell University Press, 1993), Chap. 3.

[4] J. S. Sarma and Vasant P. Gandhi, "Production and Consumption of Foodgrains in India: Implications of Accelerated Economic Growth and Poverty Alleviation," International Food Policy Research Institute Research Report No. 81, Washington, D.C., 1990, pp. 17–34.

tend to favor producers. Many commodities that are basic staples in the diet have relatively inelastic demands, as discussed in Chap. 3. The benefits of research on these commodities flow largely to consumers through lower prices.

Within consuming groups, low-income consumers spend a higher proportion of their current incomes, and any increases in incomes, on food than do wealthier consumers. The poorest groups may spend 80 percent of any additional income on food. Thus, a decline in food prices due to research-induced increases in food supplies confers a disproportionate benefit on the poor. This benefit is received by both the urban and the rural poor. The rural poor are often landless laborers, who purchase food, or small owner-operators or tenants, who retain a large part of their output for home consumption. Scobie and Posada found in Colombia, for example, that while the lower 50 percent of Colombian households received about 15 percent of total national household income, they captured nearly 70 percent of the net benefits of the rice research program.[5] These benefits to consumers flow across regions, especially where adequate transportation exists, and dampen the interregional disparities to producers mentioned above.

Land, Labor, and Capital   New technologies allow the same output to be produced with fewer resources, thus freeing up those resources to be used elsewhere in the economy. The dual-economy model described in Chap. 6 illustrated the potential for labor released from agriculture to become a fundamental source of industrial growth. However, the effect of technical change on the demand for resources is influenced by the inherent nature of the technology and by the nature of product demand.

Some new technologies result in proportionate savings of all inputs, while others save labor and use land or vice versa. For example, a new machine to cultivate the land may save labor and require a farmer to use more land to justify the cost. A higher-yielding rice variety may require more labor but produce more per unit of land. If a technology is neutral with respect to its effect on land and labor use, and if the demand for the product is elastic, the demand for both land and labor may grow proportionately. The reason is that, with elastic demand, total revenue increases with a shift out in the supply curve, providing increased returns to all resources. On the other hand, if product demand is inelastic, a neutral technical change can reduce the demand for all inputs proportionately.

Most new technologies are biased toward the use of one resource or another. In countries where markets are highly competitive and input prices reflect true input scarcity, the induced-innovation model presented in Chap. 10 predicts that new technologies will be developed to save the relatively scarce resources. However, if input prices are distorted, externalities exist, or transactions costs

[5] Grant M. Scobie and Rafael Posada T., "The Impact of Technical Change on Income Distribution: The Case of Rice in Colombia," *American Journal of Agricultural Economics*, vol. 60, No. 1, February 1978, pp. 85–92.

are high, technical change will not necessarily be biased in a direction that saves the scarcest resources; this "inappropriate" bias will thus reduce the rate of overall agricultural growth below its potential.

Because so many factors influence the effect of new technologies on resource use, it is difficult to generalize about the effect of research on employment, on the long-run returns to land, etc. One implication is that agricultural research is a blunt instrument for implementing a policy of distributing income to particular resources.

Nutritional Implications   Agricultural research can influence human nutrition through several mechanisms. First, if new technologies are aimed at poor farmers, a high proportion of the resulting income streams will be spent on improving the diet. If the technologies are aimed at commodities produced and consumed at home, the effect will be direct. If the technologies affect export crops produced by small farms, the extra income may be substantial as the price farmers receive may decline very little with the increased supply. Even if the new technologies are suitable only for large farms producing export crops, the influence on nutrition of the poor may be positive if the demand for labor increases. However, this employment effect is not at all certain and depends on the factor biases discussed above.

An important nutritional effect of research comes from the increased availability of food at lower prices. As supply shifts out against a downward sloping demand curve, all consumers benefit from lower food prices that improve their real wages.

Research can be used to reduce fluctuations in food supply, prices, and income and thereby alter nutrition. Some of the severest malnutrition occurs in rural areas during years of low rural incomes due to lower than normal production and prices.

It is difficult to draw conclusions about the nutritional implications of a particular portfolio of research activities because the sources of nutritional impacts identified above can act counter to one another. For example, a labor-saving technology used to produce export crops might lower wages and not induce changes in food supply, thus making landless laborers worse off. Some concern has been voiced about the nutrition effects of research devoted to export-crop production. If numerous producers switch from food crops to export crops, then there is potential for domestic food prices to rise, and such a rise would hurt the urban and landless poor. However, there is little empirical evidence of this switch, and nutritional levels are perhaps most influenced by research that generates the largest income gains, particularly if those gains are realized by low-income producers. Therefore, focusing research disproportionately on commodities with high nutritional content may result in less income than if the research were focused on other commodities. For example, improving the productivity of a small farm's coffee crop in the coffee zone of Colombia may improve the family's nutrition more than improving the productivity of its maize crop, because the former will lead to a greater increase in farm income and therefore the family's ability to buy food.

Environmental Effects of Research

The concern over environmental degradation in developing countries was considered in Chap. 12. Deforestation, soil erosion, desertification, pesticide pollution, etc., have become serious problems in many countries, and research can play a significant role in their solution.

First, new technologies for mitigating soil erosion, providing alternative energy sources, and substituting for chemical pesticides can be generated through research. Second, research can be used to design improved government policies that provide increased incentives to adopt management practices and help sustain the integrity of the natural resource base. Third, the higher incomes generated through research-induced productivity increases will put downward pressure on population growth in the long run. Fourth, higher income streams will also reduce the pressures to abuse the environment in the short run just to obtain food and fuel. Finally, income growth will create more demand for environmental quality. Thus agricultural research is critically important for encouraging environmentally sound and sustainable agricultural growth.

Research organizations have been criticized in the past for devoting too many resources to research related to modern inputs such as fertilizer, pesticides, and irrigation. Improper use of these inputs can cause environmental damage. An additional criticism has been that too little research is aimed at resource-conserving technologies, such as integrated pest management and methods for reducing soil erosion. There is some truth in these claims, although research on sustainable farming practices has accelerated (see Box 15-3). Also, market failures tend to cause an undervaluation of environmental services, as discussed in Chap. 12. Because of this undervaluation, producers and consumers often do not demand resource-conserving technologies. In the long-run, one of the best ways to combat forces leading to environmental degradation is to raise incomes and reduce poverty. Research is an effective means of raising incomes, though in the short-run, more research should, perhaps, be aimed at conserving environmental resources.

Institutional Change

Much of agricultural research results in new or improved technologies that are embodied in inputs or methods of production. However, agricultural research can be directed toward the design of new or improved policies or institutional changes. In other words, agricultural research can help lower the cost of adjusting institutions to the changing physical, natural resource, economic, and biological environments. A static or distorted institutional environment can be as great a hinderance to agricultural development as can a static technology base.

Credit policies, marketing and pricing policies, land tenure rules, and natural resource policies are examples of institutional arrangements that can be improved through research. Institutional changes that improve the flow of market information and reduce externalities are particularly important.

BOX 15-3

RESEARCH AND THE ENVIRONMENT: THE CASE OF THE CASSAVA MEALYBUG

The cassava mealybug was accidentally introduced from Latin America into Africa in the early 1970s, and soon began causing severe damage to cassava crops. Because some 200 million Africans depend on cassava as a staple food, this damage became a deep concern.

Researchers at the International Institute of Tropical Agriculture (IITA) in Africa, in collaboration with those at the International Center for Tropical Agriculture (CIAT) in Latin America found a means of biological control. Importation and distribution of the parasitic wasp *Epidinocasis lopez*, a natural enemy of the mealybug from Latin America, has led to dramatic reductions in African mealybug populations with biological methods. No extensive pesticides are required, and the small-scale African farmers are freed from a damaging pest by nature itself.

Source: John Walsh, "Preserving the Options: Food Productivity and Sustainability," *Issues in Agriculture*, No. 2, Consultative Group on International Agricultural Research, Washington, D.C., 1991, pp. 7–8.

Public versus Private Sector Research

Just because agricultural research is important to development does not imply that the public sector must carry it out. Yet, typically, the public sector is heavily involved in agricultural research in both developed and developing countries. Why does the private sector not provide all the needed research? There are three basic reasons. First, individual farms are too small to do all their own research, although they often cooperate with public research institutions and certainly do a great deal of experimenting. Second, and most important, for many types of research it is difficult for one firm to exclude other firms from capturing the benefits from the research. In other words, a firm may incur substantial costs in conducting research but, once the research is completed, other firms can make use of the results without incurring much cost. Thus, the firm has little incentive to do the research in the first place. Third, many types of research are highly risky, so that many firms are hesitant to take the risk for fear of incurring a substantial loss.

Certain types of research, particularly applied research related to mechanical and chemical innovations, are less risky and potentially patentable and thus attract sizable private research activity. Many types of biological and soils research, on the other hand, are difficult to patent and are primarily conducted in the public sector. As a country develops, the research role of the private sector typically increases in developing and marketing hybrid seeds as well as in mechanical and chemical innovations. However, there is often a time lag between the development of public sector research and the establishment of substantial private sector research activity. One action that a country can take to promote private research is to establish enforceable property rights (licenses, patents, etc.) over research results.

NATURE, ORGANIZATION, AND TRANSFER OF RESEARCH

Some research is very "applied" and yields immediate practical results. Other research is more "basic" or fundamental and may not yield results for many years. Research systems themselves are organized in a variety of different ways. Let's consider the major categories of agricultural research and organizational arrangements.

Categories of Agricultural Research

Agricultural research can be categorized into basic research, applied research, adaptive research, and testing. *Basic* research develops knowledge with little or no specific use in mind. Studies of evolution, genetics, biochemical processes, etc., may discover fundamental principles of substantial significance to more applied researchers, but the specific end use of the research results are often difficult to identify prior to the research. Most basic research is carried out in developed countries or in the largest of the developing countries.

Applied agricultural research is aimed at solving particular biological, chemical, physical, or social science problems affecting one or more countries or areas in a state or region. Development of new plant varieties, methods for controlling specific insects and diseases in plants or animals, and animal nutrition research are examples of applied research. Applied research may take place at international research centers or in national research systems.

Adaptive research takes the results of applied research and modifies or adapts them to local conditions within a country or region. A plant variety developed for a broad area may need to be modified for a specific microclimate. Fertilizer recommendations, methods for controlling soil erosion, and many

Swine nutrition research in China.

other technologies require adaptation to the local setting. Most of this research takes place on local experiment stations or on farms.

Much applied and adaptive agricultural research involves what has been called *biotechnology* research. *Traditional biotechnology* research includes well-established techniques in plant breeding, biological control of pests, conventional animal vaccine development, and many other types of research. *Modern biotechnology research* includes use of recombinant DNA, monoclonal antibodies, and novel bioprocessing techniques (see Box 15-4 for a discussion of these technologies).

Testing research is conducted on local experiment stations or on farms to assess whether research results from other locations are suitable for solving

---

BOX 15-4

MODERN BIOTECHNOLOGY RESEARCH

Modern biotechnology provides new tools and strategies for increasing agricultural production. The tools for improving agricultural output range from novel approaches to cell and tissue culture to the genetic manipulation of biological material. Modern biotechnology is based on three new technologies. The first, recombinant DNA, enables the essential genetic material in cells, DNA, to be manipulated. It offers the possibility of transferring genetic material from one species to another, thereby transferring a useful genetic trait. The second, monoclonal antibodies, is used to detect individual proteins produced by cells. Thus it provides improved methods for rapid and specific diagnosis of animal and plant diseases. The third, novel bioprocessing techniques, involves new cell and tissue culture technologies that enable rapid propagation of living cells. These techniques provide improved methods for large-scale production of useful compounds by the microbial or enzymatic degradation of various substrates.

The types of products that modern biotechnology can potentially produce include new plant varieties, new animal breeds, plant and animal growth hormones, biopesticides, biofertilizers, diagnostic reagents for plant and animal diseases, and enzymes and food additives. They may improve the tolerance of both plants and animals to particular stresses and pests, and increase the efficiency with which plants and livestock utilize nutrients. They may reduce the need for agrichemicals.

It is likely to take several years before modern biotechnologies can be developed to an effective level for use with the crops of economic importance in the developing countries: perhaps 5 years for potato, rapeseed, and rice; 5 to 10 years for bananas/plantain, cassava, and coffee; and 10 or more years for cocoa, coconut, oil palm, and wheat. Developing countries that are successful in developing their own modern biotechnologies will need scientists trained in microbiology and biochemistry. These countries will need to integrate modern biotechnology into traditional biotechnology research programs. Support for biotechnology research in developing country agricultural research systems will be provided by the International Agricultural Research Centers described later in this chapter.

Sources: Gabrielle Persley, "The Application of Biotechnology to Agriculture in Developing Countries: Background Paper," International Service for National Agricultural Research, Biotechnology Study Project Paper No. 1, The Hague, Netherlands, October 1988; World Bank, "Agricultural Biotechnology: The Next Green Revolution?", Technical Paper No. 133, Washington, D.C., January 1991.

local problems. Improved pesticides, management practices, or plant varieties are examples of research results that may be tested. All countries conduct some testing research, but for very small countries with limited resources, testing may represent a large portion of total research. Much testing is conducted by farmers themselves.

These categories of research are linked and dependent on each other. A research center may be involved in several categories. The expanding linkages among research institutions in developed countries, international agricultural research centers, and national research systems in developing countries has increased the efficiency of agricultural research in all categories.

Organization of Agricultural Research

Public agricultural research systems in developing countries have a variety of organizational structures. Often there is a central station and several substations located in different geoclimatic zones. Research may be conducted at universities, but the proportion of agricultural research conducted at colleges and universities tends to be much less than in developed countries such as the United States.

The structure of the research system is influenced by historical forces including, among others, colonial history and major foreign assistance projects. A large portion of research in many developing countries is organized along commodity program lines: for example, a maize program, a rice program, a wheat program, or a sheep and goats program. Other cross-cutting research areas such as soil fertility, socioeconomics, and even plant or livestock protection, may have separate programs.

Some agricultural research systems have a mandate for extension or other programs designed to reach out to farmers. Even if extension is not included in the mandate of the national research institution, that institution still must contain a mechanism for obtaining information on the current problems facing farmers and for testing new technologies under actual farm conditions. This mechanism may involve *farming systems research*, a major part of which involves on-farm research (see Box 15-5).

International Agricultural Research Centers   The 1960s saw the emergence of a set of international agricultural research centers (IARCs) that by 1991 had grown to 16 centers located primarily in Africa, Asia, Latin America, and the Middle East. The location, mandates, and budgets for these centers are presented in Table 15-3. Although the first center, The International Rice Research Institute (IRRI), was founded in 1960, the international center model drew on the historical experiences of the colonial agricultural research institutes that were effective in increasing the production of export crops such as rubber, sugar, and tea. The model also drew on the experiences in the 1940s and 1950s of the Rockefeller Foundation's wheat and maize programs in Mexico and the Ford and Rockefeller foundations' rice program in the Philippines. The results

---

BOX 15-5

THE NEED FOR FARMING SYSTEMS RESEARCH[a]

In recent years, a number of countries have added a component to their agricultural research system called *farming systems research* (FSR) to facilitate the necessary interaction between farmers and scientists. While the term *farming systems research* has been applied to a wide variety of activities, in its broadest sense FSR is research that treats the farm in a holistic manner and considers the various interactions in the system.

Each research system must determine the appropriate mix of on-farm and experiment station research. Experiment station research is needed so that experiments can be run under controlled conditions that enable particular components of new technologies to be developed and tested without the confounding of numerous and possibly extraneous factors. However, the real-world robustness, profitability, and cultural acceptability of new technologies cannot be assessed without testing under actual farm conditions. Frequent contact between scientists and farmers increases the likelihood that constraints and problems facing farmers will be included in the development and evaluation of new technologies. Because extensive on-farm interaction is expensive and scientific resources are scarce in developing countries, each research system must decide at the margin whether additional funds should be spent on-farm or on-station to receive the greatest return from the funds expended.

[a] For discussion of farming systems research see: Robert Tripp, Ponniah Anandajayesekeram, Derek Byerlee, and Larry Harrington, "Farming System Research Revisited," in Carl K. Eicher and John M. Staatz (eds.), *Agricultural Development in the Third World* (Baltimore: Johns Hopkins University Press, 1990), Chap. 23; and Willis W. Shaner, Perry F. Philipp, and W. R. Schmehl, *Farming Systems Research and Development: Guidelines for Developing Countries* (Boulder, Colo.: Westview Press, 1982).

---

of the research and training programs of the centers are aimed not just at the country where the center is located, but at the neighboring region or even the world.

The first IARCs, IRRI and CIMMYT, produced new varieties of rice and wheat that resulted in substantial yield increases, particularly for rice in Asia. The first of several rice varieties (IR-8), released by IRRI and cooperating national programs, responded to high rates of fertilizer and water application by producing more grain and less straw. Subsequent research has focused as well on improving grain quality, incorporating disease and insect resistance, and developing varieties for drier upland areas. The substantial yield boosts experienced in parts of Asia in the late 1960s resulting from these new technologies was termed the *green revolution* (see Box 15-6).

The success of the green revolution in increasing yields and incomes in many areas led to the expansion of the internationl agricultural research center concept to the other commodities and regions identified in Table 15-3. Maize, millets, tropical legumes, cassava, livestock, potatoes, and many other commodities have received emphasis. The research results from these newer centers have not been as spectacular as the early gains in rice and wheat, but these centers too have made significant contributions. For example, disease-resistant beans, cassava, and millet varieties are now being grown in several countries.

TABLE 15-3
THE INTERNATIONAL AGRICULTURAL RESEARCH CENTERS

Center	Headquarters, location and year established	Research	Coverage	Core funding for 1990 ($000,000)
IRRI (International Rice Research Institute)	Los Baños, Philippines (1960)	Rice under irrigation, multiple cropping systems; upland rice	Worldwide, special emphasis on Asia	29.8
CIMMYT (International Center for the Improvement of Maize and Wheat)	El Batan, Mexico (1966)	Wheat (also triticale, barley); maize (also high-altitude sorghum)	Worldwide	27.1
ITTA (International Institute of Tropical Agriculture)	Ibadan, Nigeria (1967)	Farming systems; cereals (rice and maize as regional relay stations for IRRI and CIMMYT); grain legume (cowpeas, soybean, lima beans); root and tuber crops (cassava, sweet potatoes, yams)	Worldwide in lowland tropics; special emphasis on Africa	22.5
CIAT (International Center for Tropical Agriculture)	Palmira, Colombia (1968)	Phaseolus bean, cassava, rice, tropical pastures	Worldwide in lowland tropics	27.7
WARDA (West Africa Rice Development Association)	Monrovia, Liberia (1971)	Rice, rice-based cropping systems	West Africa	6.2
CIP (International Potato Center)	Lima, Peru (1971)	Potato, sweet potato, other root crops	Worldwide, including linkages with developed countries	16.9
ICRISAT (International Crops Research Institute for the Semi-Arid Tropics)	Hyderabad, India (1972)	Sorghum; pearl millet; pigeon peas; chickpeas; farming systems; groundnuts	Worldwide, special emphasis on dry semi-arid tropics, nonirrigated farming.	31.5
ILRAD (International Laboratory for Research on Animal Diseases)	Nairobi, Kenya (1973)	Trypanosomiasis; theileriasis; other diseases	Mainly Africa	13.6

Center	Headquarters, location and year established	Research	Coverage	Core funding for 1990 ($000,000)
IBPGR (International Board for Plant Genetic Resources)	FAO, Rome, Italy (1974)	Conservation of plant genetic material with special reference to crops of economic importance	Worldwide	7.0
ILCA (International Livestock Center for Africa)	Addis Ababa, Ethiopia (1974)	Livestock production systems	Major ecological regions in tropical zones of Africa	20.2
IFPRI (International Food Policy Research Institute)	Washington, D.C., United States (1975)	Food policy	Worldwide	9.1
ICARDA (International Center for Agricultural Research in Dry Areas)	Lebanon, Syria (1976)	Crop and mixed farming systems research, with focus on sheep, barley, wheat, broad beans, and lentils	West Asia and North Africa, emphasis on the semi-arid winter precipitation zone	18.7
ISNAR (International Service for National Agricultural Research)	The Hague, Netherlands (1980)	Strengthening the capacity of national agricultural research programs	Worldwide	7.0
ICRAF (International Council for Research in Agro-Forestry)	Nairobi, Kenya (1978)[a]	Agroforestry	Worldwide	9.6
IIMI (International Institute for Irrigation Management)	Colombo, Sri Lanka (1984)[a]	Irrigation	Worldwide, special emphasis on Asia	5.8
INIBAP (International Network for the Improvement in Banana and Plantain)	Montpellier, France (1984)[a]	Bananas and plantain	Worldwide	1.6

[a] CGIAR membership began in 1991.

Sources: Anne O. Krueger, Constantine Michalopoulos, and Vernon W. Ruttan, *Aid and Development* (Baltimore: Johns Hopkins University Press, 1989), pp. 146–147; Consultative Group for International Agricultural Research, "1992 Funding Requirements of the CGIAR Centers," CGIAR Secretariat, Washington, D.C., September 1991, pp. 1–131.

Research plots at the International Rice Research Institute in the Philippines.

To some extent, the dramatic breakthroughs in yields in the early years of the green revolution created unfair expectations that these gains would be repeated with regularity. Agricultural research is, in fact, a continuous process that generally produces small gains from year to year.

The overall program and core funding for all 16 centers is managed by an organization called the Consultative Group for International Agricultural Research (CGIAR) whose members include the World Bank, the Food and Agricultural Organization of the United Nations (FAO), the United Nations Development Program (UNDP), and several national governments, regional banks, and foundations. These institutions provide the funds for the centers. The CGIAR, founded in 1971, is centered at the World Bank. The total budget for the 16 centers is now more than $300 million when all funding sources are considered.

The last three centers joined the CGIAR system in 1991, although each began its operations a few years earlier. A completely new center, with a focus on forest management and the social and biological factors that lead to deforestation, is scheduled to open in 1992. Several other centers have been considered for membership in the CGIAR system, particularly one working on aquaculture and another working on vegetables.

Transfer of Research Results

The discussions of research categories, of national and regional experiment stations and on-farm research, and of international agricultural research centers all imply that research results may be transferred from one location to another. These transfers can occur internally in a country or across national

---

BOX 15-6

THE GREEN REVOLUTION

The term *green revolution* was coined in 1968 by William S. Gaud, former Administrator of the U. S. Agency for International Development, to describe the dramatic wheat harvests that had been achieved in 1966 to 1968 in India and Pakistan. The term gained further publicity in 1970 when Norman Borlaug was awarded the Nobel Peace Prize for his research that produced the high-yielding, semidwarf Mexican wheats that had performed so well in Asia and Latin America. At the same time that the semidwarf wheats were making their dramatic entry, IRRI released new semidwarf rice with the same dramatic effect.

The big innovation of the green revolution was developing varieties of wheat and rice that would not fall down (lodge) when nitrogen fertilizers were applied. These new lines of plants also tended to be earlier maturing, to produce many shoots (tillers), and to be less sensitive to daylength.

Source: Donald L. Plucknett, "Saving Lives Through Agricultural Research," Consultative Group on International Agricultural Research, Issues in Agriculture Paper No. 1, Washington, D.C., May 1991, pp. 9–10.

---

boundaries. Let's examine the possibility and advisability of transferring new technologies or institutions.

Prior to the 1960s, little attention was focused on the importance of indigenous agricultural research in developing countries. It was thought that the possibilities for transferring technologies from developed countries were substantial and that, therefore, extension programs were needed to assist in this transfer. The relative lack of success with direct transfer of machinery, plant varieties, and other materials from developed to developing countries led to the realization that improved developing-country research capacity was essential. The desire to improve location-specific research was one of the driving forces behind the development of the IARCs mentioned above. However, many research results are regularly transferred from one country to another. What types of research results are transferrable and what determines their transferability?

Materials such as improved seeds, plants, and animals; scientific methods, formulas, and designs; and basic research output are all potentially transferable to some extent.[6] Each country must decide whether to simply screen these items and attempt to directly transfer them, to screen them and then modify and adapt them to their own environment, or to undertake a research program that is comprehensive enough to produce its own technologies.[7]

---

[6] See Yujiro Hayami and Vernon W. Ruttan, *Agricultural Development: An International Perspective* (Baltimore: Johns Hopkins University Press, 1985), pp. 260–262.

[7] See Robert E. Evenson and Hans P. Binswanger, "Technology Transfer and Research Resource Allocation," in Hans P. Binswanger and Vernon W. Ruttan (eds.), *Induced Innovation: Technology, Institutions, and Development*, (Baltimore: Johns Hopkins University Press, 1978), Chap. 6. This section draws heavily on the ideas in Evenson and Binswanger.

The choice among these transfer and research options will depend first on the relative costs of direct transfer of technology and of adaptive and comprehensive research. Transfer of research results involves costs of information and screening or testing. There may also be license costs or fees for patented items. Most of these transfer costs increase with the physical size and environmental diversity of the country. A country's own research costs are somewhat independent of size; for that reason, it may be more cost effective for larger countries to conduct their own research than for smaller countries.

Second, the complementarity between screening transferred technologies and conducting in-country research can come into play. It takes some scientific capacity just to bring in and screen research results from outside the country. Therefore, it may be cost-effective to have these scientists do some of their own adaptive research.

Third, if the natural resource base in one developing country is similar to that in another country where the new technology is produced, then the chances of transfer will increase. New wheat varieties, for example, are often transferred from Argentina to Uruguay because those countries have similar wheat-growing regions. These similarities tend to reduce the cost of transfer and to increase the likelihood that the transferred technology will be physically and economically viable.

Fourth, some technologies are more environmentally sensitive than others. For example, new plant and animal materials may be more environmentally sensitive than more basic research results, formulas, designs, etc. The International Agricultural Research Centers attempt to produce plant and animal materials that have broad environmental suitability. In many cases, it is necessary for the receiving country to then adapt these materials more specifically to its microclimates. Relatively basic advances in modern biotechnology have the potential for widespread applicability if the scientific capacities are created in developing countries to enable them to effectively utilize the research results.

Fifth, the availability of research results to transfer in is also important. For example, if a country has low labor costs and high capital and land costs, yet the technologies available to transfer in are large machines suitable for a resource environment with high labor costs and abundant land, then the country will not find the outside technology suitable.

In summary, a developing country must assess several factors in deciding whether to transfer in research results from another country or from an international center. Agricultural research is a long-term investment. Research takes time, adoption of new technologies takes time, and research results eventually depreciate as insects and diseases evolve, the economic environment changes, etc. Developing countries often attempt to bring in research results from other countries during the early stages of development in order to shorten this process and meet critical needs. Perhaps a 1 percent productivity growth rate can be accomplished through a relatively simple transfer process, though such productivity will depend on the conditions previously mentioned.[8] However,

---

[8] Hayami and Ruttan, op. cit., p. 260.

the requirements of modern rates of growth in food demand, often in the 3 to 6 percentage range, require the coexistence of at least some indigenous agricultural research capacity.

Agricultural development today requires a research system with internal and external linkages that bring in appropriate technologies; screen, adapt, and produce new technologies and institutions; and perform both on-station and on-farm testing. The major components of such a research system are illustrated diagrammatically in Fig. 15-3. National and local experiment stations must interact with on-farm research and extension. This national research system also must maintain ties with the international research centers. Research in the larger national systems feeds into both the international centers and the smaller national research systems. If any of these linkages is weak or missing, agricultural productivity growth will be slowed.

ROLE OF EDUCATION AND EXTENSION

The underutilization of human resources is a serious problem facing agriculture in most developing countries today. Countries unable to develop the skills and knowledge of their farmers and their families find it difficult to develop anything else. The development and utilization of new technologies and institutions are critically dependent on an educated workforce.

Objectives and Benefits of Education and Extension

Rural education is an investment in people that has as its objectives: (1) improving agricultural productivity and efficiency, and (2) preparing children

FIGURE 15-3
Components of a well-linked agricultural research system for developing countries.

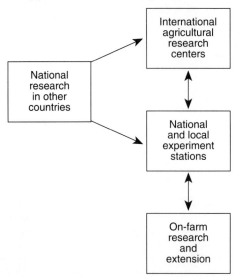

for nonfarm occupations if they have to leave farming. Education may help motivate farmers toward change, teach farmers improved decision-making methods, and provide farmers with technical and practical information. Agricultural extension is complementary to other sources of information because it speeds up the transfer of knowledge about new technologies and other research results.

A country with a literate people in rural areas will have better information flows than one without, due simply to better written communications. Better communications help reduce the transactions costs that hold back development. Education helps farmers to acquire, understand, and sort technical, institutional, and market information.

The result is a return on investment not just for the farmer, but for society as a whole. Because rural education results in a more productive and efficient agriculture and in a more productive labor force for nonfarm employment, and because of its public good characteristics, most countries—both developed and developing—finance education, particularly at the primary and secondary levels. As countries develop, the social benefit from education becomes so great that the scope of rural education grows. Schultz has argued that education helps people to deal with economic disequilibria.[9] Thus, as agriculture in a country shifts from a traditional to a more dynamic, science-based mode, the value of education increases.

Education is important not just for the farmer and for children who will continue farming, but for those who leave agriculture. Education for nonfarm jobs is particularly important for agricultural development if children of farmers acquire jobs as agricultural extension agents, managers of cooperatives and other business firms supplying inputs to farmers or marketing their products, agricultural scientists, or government officials who administer agricultural programs.

Major Types of Education

There are three basic types of education: (1) primary and secondary education, (2) higher education, and (3) adult education. Most countries have a goal of almost universal primary education and eventually secondary education as well. Primary education provides the basic literary and computational skills. Secondary education provides training for students going on to higher education, but also technical education for those who seek immediate employment.

The need for higher education related to agriculture depends in part on the growth of agricultural research, extension, agribusiness, and government employment. Undergraduate agricultural programs have expanded in many African, Asian, and Latin American countries in recent years. Some of these colleges, such as the Panamerican Agricultural School in Zamorano, Hon-

---

[9] See Theodore W. Schultz, "The Value of the Ability to Deal with Disequilibria," *Journal of Economic Literature*, vol. 8, September 1975, pp. 827–846.

School children in rural Colombia.

duras, require a mix of academic and practical training and draw students from several countries.

Postgraduate programs also have expanded in several larger developing countries such as India, the Philippines, Brazil, and Mexico. The quality of these programs is variable, but the programs have a better track record of their students returning home after completing their degrees than do graduate programs in developed countries. Foreign academic training in developed countries also has the disadvantage that the training and research may be less relevant to the home country of the student.

In adult education, often called *extension* education in agriculture, farmers are the primary clientele and the programs are mostly oriented toward production problems facing farmers. Extension accelerates the dissemination of research results to farmers and, in some cases, helps transmit farmers' problems back to researchers. Extension workers provide training for farmers on a variety of subjects and must have technical competence, economic competence, farming competence, and communication skills. Thus extension workers require extensive training and retraining to maintain their credibility with farmers.

Organization of Extension Education

Many types of organizational structures for and approaches to extension exist in developing countries. For example, a highly structured approach that has been advocated by the World Bank and applied in numerous countries over the past 15 years is called the *training and visit (T&V) system.* The T&V system includes a single line of command, a set schedule of visits to farmers' groups,

Extension field day in Peru.

regular and continuous training of extension officers and workers by subject-matter specialists, and no nonextension responsibilities.[10] The T&V system facilitates discipline, accountability, and research linkages and has had apparent success in some countries, particularly Asia.

Another model with a slightly different structure that also has worked well is illustrated by the extension service of the Colombian Coffee Federation. That service has extension workers that operate on a fixed schedule of visits to farmers' groups, but the extension worker spends one day a week in an office receiving farmers and scheduling individual farm visits that coincide with days when the worker is visiting a particular location. Village extension workers (agents) are supported by regional subject matter specialists who also spend most of their time visiting farmers' groups and individual farms. Village extension workers are all drawn from coffee farms and receive three years of intensive training after high school. Extension programs are planned six months ahead and are developed jointly between the farmers' group and the agent.

A third model is the Farming Systems Research and Extension (FSR&E) approach mentioned earlier (Box 15-5). FSR&E integrates a multidisciplinary team of scientists with the extension workers and involves team diagnosis of farmers' problems and extensive on-farm trials. This approach can be effective in small areas, but also can be relatively expensive.

---

[10] See Daniel Benor, James A. Harrison, and Michael Baxter, "Agricultural Extension: The Training and Visit System," World Bank, Washington, D.C., 1989 for more details.

Colombian extension agent illustrates how to disinfect a coffee seedbed.

Each of these approaches is relatively structured and attempts to overcome the perennial problems of poorly trained and little-motivated extension workers who visit relatively few farms and become diverted into nonextension activities. Often extension services become highly politicized, corrupt, and unconnected to research. There is a need to add clear lines of authority, adequate training, and financial rewards for personnel. It is not necessary to follow one of the models mentioned above, but some structure and discipline are essential for an effective extension service. Research and extension linkages are essential and tend to be facilitated if research and extension are housed in the same institution.

SUMMARY

Agricultural research generates new or improved technologies and institutions that increase agricultural productivity, moderate food prices, generate foreign exchange, and reduce pressures on the natural resource base. Most studies have found the economic returns on public agricultural research investments to be high. Agricultural research can have distributional effects by farm size and tenure, by region, by income level, by factor of production, and so forth. Consumers, particularly low-income consumers, are major beneficiaries of agricultural research, as the poor may spend 80 percent of any income increases on food and food prices tend to fall as productivity increases. Agricultural research can influence nutrition by raising farm incomes, lowering food prices, and reducing the variability in food production. Agricultural research can generate technologies, institutional changes, and higher incomes that lead to reduced pressures on the environment. The public sector has a role to play in agricultural research because the private sector has inadequate incentives to conduct a sufficient amount of socially beneficial research, in part because often private firms conducting research cannot capture enough of the benefits.

Agricultural research can be classified into basic, applied, adaptive, and testing research. These categories are linked and dependent on each other. Research is conducted on national and local experiment stations and, to be effective, must contain an on-farm component. Farming systems research has been developed to treat the farm in a holistic manner and strengthen on-farm interactions in the research system. Since 1960, a system of International Agricultural Research Centers (IARCs) has provided new technologies and institutional changes suitable to several developing countries. Research can be transferred across national borders, but the ease of transfer depends on the type of research, the relative cost of transfer and indigenous research, the natural resource base, and other factors.

Rural education is an investment aimed at improving agricultural productivity and preparing children for nonfarm occupations. Education can enhance information flows and reduce transactions costs. Primary and secondary education, higher education, and adult education are all important. Many types of extension systems exist, some more structured than others. Training for extension workers, incentives, clear lines of authority, and strong linkages to research are each critical for an effective extension service.

IMPORTANT TERMS AND CONCEPTS

Adaptive research
Agricultural education
Agricultural extension
Agricultural productivity
Agricultural research
Applied research
Basic research
Biotechnology
Experiment stations

Farming systems research
Green revolution
International agricultural research
  centers
Scale-neutral technology
Technology transfer
Testing research
Training and visit system

LOOKING AHEAD

This chapter concludes the discussion of technical and institutional factors that can influence development of the agricultural sector. The following set of chapters moves beyond the agricultural sector and considers international trade, foreign aid, and macroeconomic forces and policies that feed back on agricultural development. We begin in the next chapter by considering the importance of trade. Problems faced by developing countries with respect to agricultural trade, and potential solutions to those problems, are explored.

QUESTIONS FOR DISCUSSION

1 What is the purpose of agricultural research in developing countries?
2 How does research influence agricultural productivity and food prices?
3 Under what conditions might research on a nonfood export crop have as much or greater positive effect on nutrition than research on a food crop?
4 Why might agricultural research tend to benefit large farms more than small farms?
5 Why might the type of lease influence the proportion of the benefits of technical change that go to the tenant compared to the landlord?
6 Why might agricultural research increase the regional disparity in income in a developing country?
7 Why are consumers, especially poor consumers, often the major beneficiaries of agricultural research?
8 What factors influence the returns to particular factors of production following research?
9 How might agricultural research help improve the environment?
10 How might research result in institutional change?
11 Why should the public sector get involved in research? Why not leave it to the private sector?
12 Distinguish among basic, applied, adaptive, and testing research.
13 What is Farming Systems Research?
14 What are the International Agricultural Research Centers and how does their work tie into the agricultural research systems of developing countries?
15 What is the "green revolution," when did it occur, and where?
16 What is the purpose of education for the farmer and his or her family?
17 What are the major types of education?
18 What role does extension play in agricultural development?
19 What are the characteristics required of successful extension workers? Successful extension systems?
20 How might research, education, and extension be complementary activities?

RECOMMENDED READINGS

Benor, Daniel, James Q. Harrison, and Michael Baxter, "Agricultural Extension: The Training and Visit System," World Bank, Washington, D.C., 1989.

Binswanger, Hans P., Vernon W. Ruttan, and others, *Induced Innovation: Technology, Institutions, and Development* (Baltimore: Johns Hopkins University Press, 1978).

Harbison, Frederick H., *Human Resources As the Wealth of Nations* (New York: Oxford University Press, 1973).

Hayami, Yujiro and Vernon W. Ruttan, *Agricultural Development: An International Perspective* (Baltimore: Johns Hopkins University Press, 1985), Chaps. 5 to 10.

Norton, George W., Philip G. Pardey, and Julian Alston, *Science Under Scarcity: Theory and Practice for Agricultural Research Evaluation and Priority Setting* (Ithaca, N.Y.: Cornell University Press, 1993).

Ruttan, Vernon W., *Agricultural Research Policy* (Minneapolis: University of Minnesota Press, 1982).

Schultz, Theodore W. "The Value of the Ability to Deal with Disequilibria," *Journal of Economic Literature*, vol. 8, September 1975, pp. 827–846.

Schultz, Theodore W., *Investment in Human Capital: The Role of Education and of Research* (New York: Free Press, 1971).

Scobie, Grant M. "Investment in International Agricultural Research: Some Economic Dimensions," World Bank Staff Working Paper No. 361, Washington, D.C., October 1979.

Scobie, Grant M. and Rafael Posada T., "The Impact of Technical Change on Income Distribution: The Case of Rice in Colombia," *American Journal of Agricultural Economics,* vol. 60, February 1978, pp. 85–92.

Wortman, Sterling and Ralph W. Cummings, Jr., *To Feed This World: The Challenge and the Strategy* (Baltimore: Johns Hopkins University Press, 1978), Chaps. 7, 12, and 14.

REFERENCES FOR TABLE 15-2.

Ardito-Barletta, N., "Costs and Social Benefits of Agricultural Research in Mexico," Ph.D. Dissertation, University of Chicago, Chicago, Illinois, 1970.

Ayer, H., "The Costs, Returns, and Effects of Agricultural Research in Sao Paulo Brazil," Ph.D. Dissertation, Purdue University, West Lafayette, Ind., 1970.

Evenson, R. E. and D. Jha, "The Contribution of Agricultural Research Systems to Agricultural Production in India," *Indian Journal of Agricultural Economics,* vol. 28, 1973, pp. 212–230.

Flores, P., R. E. Evenson, and Y. Hayami, "Social Returns to Rice Research in the Philippines: Domestic Benefits and Foreign Spillover," *Economic Development and Cultural Change,* vol. 26, 1978, pp. 591–607.

Hayami, Y. and M. Akino, "Organization and Productivity of Agricultural Research Systems in Japan," in T. M. Arndt, D. G. Dalrymple, and V. W. Ruttan (eds.), *Resource Allocation and Productivity in National and International Agricultural Research* (Minneapolis: University of Minnesota Press, 1977).

Hertford, R., J. Ardito, A. Rocha, and G. Trujillo, "Productivity of Agricultural Research in Colombia," in T. M. Arndt, D. G. Dalrymple, and V. W. Ruttan (eds.), *Resource Allocation and Productivity in National and International Agricultural Research* (Minneapolis: University of Minnesota Press, Minneapolis, 1977).

Kahlon, A. S., H. K. Bal, P. N. Saxena, and D. Jha, "Returns to Investment in Research in India," in T. M. Arndt, D. G. Dalrymple, and V. W. Ruttan (eds.), *Resource Allocation and Productivity in National and International Research,* (Minneapolis: University of Minnesota Press, 1977).

Nagy, J. G., "Estimating the Yield Advantage of High Yielding Maize and Wheat: The Case of Pakistan On-Farm Yield Constraints Data," *Pakistan Development Review,* vol. 93, 1983.

Pee, T. Y., "Social Returns to Rubber Research on Peninsular Malaysia," Ph.D. Dissertation, Michigan State University, East Lansing, Michigan, 1977.

Pray, C., "The Economics of Agricultural Research in Bangladesh," *Bangladesh Journal of Agricultural Economics,* vol. 2, 1980, pp. 1–36.

PART FIVE

AGRICULTURAL DEVELOPMENT IN AN INTERDEPENDENT WORLD

Wheat being loaded on a ship for export.

CHAPTER 16

TRADE AND AGRICULTURAL DEVELOPMENT

Trade contributes to food security mainly by facilitating faster agricultural and economic development, thereby increasing per capita food production and incomes.

Thompson[1]

THIS CHAPTER

1 Explains why countries trade
2 Describes recent trade experiences of some less-developed countries and indicates why trade patterns change as economic development occurs
3 Discusses problems that impede less-developed countries from realizing their trade potential and presents some possible solutions

WHY COUNTRIES TRADE

The role of international trade in economic development has attracted the attention of economists and policymakers for more than 100 years (Box 16-1). Discussions about the desirability of trade often involve two opposing positions: (1) that trade, particularly exports, causes many of the problems facing

[1] Robert L. Thompson, "The Role of Trade in Food Security and Agricultural Development," in D. Gale Johnson and G. Edward Schuh (eds.), *The Role of Markets in the World Food Economy*, (Boulder, Colo.: Westview Press, 1983), p. 251.

BOX 16-1

HISTORICAL ROOTS OF INTERNATIONAL TRADE DEBATE

Trade among countries has existed for thousands of years, most of that time in a very loosely structured system. By the sixteenth and seventeenth centuries, money, goods, and credit markets had developed to facilitate trade and colonial expansion. An economic doctrine known as *mercantilism* encouraged exports but discouraged imports. The preferred form of payment was gold rather than goods. A wide range of restrictive trade policies was implemented including tariffs, licenses, export subsidies, and general state control of international commerce. As the Industrial Revolution spread in the late 1700s, mercantilist ideas were increasingly questioned. Raw materials for expanding factory output were imported and markets for the output were sought abroad. Technological advances in transportation and communications further stimulated trade.

A strong movement toward economic liberalization began in the early 1800s. Perhaps the most important factor in the movement was the unilateral removal of trade restrictions in the United Kingdom. The world's leading economic power at the time, the United Kingdom, repealed its Corn Laws in 1846, ending the world's first major price-support program for agricultural commodities. Britain then sought worldwide trade liberalization, with some success. World trade was relatively free until World War I, although several countries, including the United States and Germany, followed selective protectionist policies. World War I changed the trading environment. Industries, including agriculture, that expanded during the war, suffered slack demand and falling prices afterward. Governments attempted to protect these industries by introducing protectionist policies during the 1920s and 1930s that the world is still struggling to remove today. Persistent protectionist policies for agricultural products are especially evident.

---

developing countries and (2) that a relatively open-trade orientation is necessary for successful economic development. This difference in views was mentioned in Chap. 6 in the discussion of dependency versus neoclassical theories of development.

Proponents of the negative view of trade argue that as countries become more integrated into the world economy, they open themselves up to increased exploitation by the more-developed countries and by the wealthy elites within their own countries. Past exploitation has meant that export sectors in LDCs are more capital-intensive than the underlying resource base would dictate. Hence, export expansion has had limited effects on employment and overall economic development. In addition, it is argued that the terms of trade, or the prices received for exports from developing countries compared to the prices paid for imports, tend to decline over time. This decline results in part from the relatively slow growth in demand for primary products, the major exports of developing countries, compared to the demand for manufactured products.[2] It

---

[2] It is argued that relatively slow growth in demand results from low price and income elasticities of demand for primary products compared to manufactured products and from protectionist measures in more-developed countries. Prices for developed-country products are also said to be high because of monopolistic elements in the production of developed-country products that are imported by developing countries, and protectionist measures in the more-developed countries.

is also argued that dependence on international markets for food endangers national security since international markets are volatile and unpredictable. Finally, it is argued that at very early stages of development domestic industries need to be protected from international competition in order to survive. The solutions prescribed are import-substitution policies. Examples of these policies are direct import restrictions, setting of foreign exchange rates above the market equilibrium, and export taxes that discourage exports and stimulate substitution of domestically produced, often industrial, goods for imports.[3]

Proponents of the more positive view of trade argue that trade facilitates development because it permits more efficient use of resources. A country can benefit if it exports what it can produce more cheaply than others, and imports items that others can produce more cheaply. For example, some inputs needed for development such as minerals or specific capital items cannot be obtained or can only be obtained at a very high cost within a particular country. However, the rationale for trade extends beyond this simple notion of *absolute* cost differences between countries. It includes *relative* cost differences within a country as well. The principle of *comparative advantage*, first articulated by David Ricardo in 1817, states that it is best for each country to produce those goods for which it has the greatest relative cost advantage and to trade for others. This principle implies that one country could produce all goods at lower cost than other countries, yet it would still pay the country to trade. The reason is that if the country specializes in what it produces relatively best, and trades part of that production for goods and services it produces at a relatively high cost, its total income and consumption would be higher than if the country tried to produce everything itself (Box 16-2). Holders of this positive view argue that the distortions and inefficiencies induced by policies designed to insulate countries from international markets have been detrimental to development.

Many of the differences in the two viewpoints on the role of trade in economic development stem from different judgments about (1) the degree to which any gains from trade will, in fact, be retained in the developing country and be relatively broadly distributed and (2) the magnitude of the efficiency losses resulting from attempts to become relatively self-sufficient through import-substitution policies. Few dispute the *potential* for gains from trade and most desire that any gains be broadly distributed.

Most less-developed countries do, in fact, trade and most of these countries also follow some restrictive trade policies. And, many LDC exports come initially from agriculture because agriculture is the largest sector. The preponderance of empirical evidence over the past 40 years supports the view that a relatively open-trading environment is more conducive to economic development than a highly restrictive one. However, we find a wide variety of strategies for managing agricultural trade in developing countries. In the next

---

[3] The higher the value of the country's currency compared to another currency, the harder it is to export because the higher value makes the prices of the country's goods seem more expensive to other countries.

BOX 16-2

ILLUSTRATION OF THE PRINCIPLE OF COMPARATIVE ADVANTAGE

To illustrate the principle of comparative advantage, we will consider two countries, each of which produces two outputs: manufacturing (MFG) and agriculture (AGR). Assuming factors of production are mobile within each country, we can specify a production possibility frontier (PPF) for manufacturing and agriculture for each country. The PPF shows the maximum (or total) amount of MFG and AGR that the resources in each country can produce. For example, suppose we have the linear PPF for each country shown below. Country A can produce 30 units of MFG and no AGR, 30 units of AGR and no MFG, or a combination in between such as 15 MFG and 15 AGR.

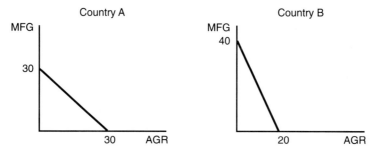

For country A, the internal terms of trade equals 1. It must give up 1 unit of AGR to produce 1 additional unit of MFG and vice versa. For country B, the internal terms of trade between MFG and AGR is 2. It must give 1 unit of AGR to produce 2 units of MFG or 2 units of MFG to produce 1 unit of AGR.

If country A gave up 4 units of AGR, it could increase production of MFG by 4 units. But if it could sell 2 units of AGR to country B, country B could exchange those for 4 units of MFG (i.e., 1 unit of AGR costs 2 MFG in country B). Therefore, country A now has 2 units of MFG more than it would have without trade. Likewise, country B could give up 4 units of MFG to country A and receive up to 4 units of AGR (i.e., 1 unit of MFG costs 1 unit of AGR in country A). Trade would leave country B better off by 2 units of AGR than before. Country A will specialize in AGR and country B in MFG, and the international terms of trade (price of AGR in terms of MFG) will be somewhere between the slopes of the two PPFs (perhaps 1.5 to 1). Exactly where will depend on the demands for MFG and AGR within each country.

section we review the trade experiences of these countries and consider the lessons that experience provides.

DEVELOPING COUNTRY EXPERIENCE WITH TRADE

During the 1950s and 1960s import-substitution policies predominated in many developing countries. These inward-oriented policies helped produce a decline in the ratio of exports to GDP in many LDCs until the early 1970s.[4] Since that

[4] Thomas Vollrath, "Development Consequences of Unrestricted Trade," Foreign Agricultural Economic Report No. 213, Economic Research Service, U.S. Department of Agriculture, Washington, D.C., May 1985.

time, the ratio of exports to GDP has generally increased, paralleling an overall expansion in world trade.[5] However, many developing countries still pursue import-substitution policies. Countries that followed these policies for several years, for example Argentina, India, and Egypt, tended to grow more slowly than those that have followed more open-trading regimes, for example Malaysia, South Korea, and Botswana. While it is difficult to make generalizations based on a few cases, studies that have examined the overall statistical significance of trade restrictions have generally found a negative impact on economic growth.

It is often difficult to classify a country as relatively open or relatively restricted because policies change over time. Brazil, for example, followed an import-substitution policy from 1955 to 1965 but a more open-trading regime from 1966 to 1976.[6] The Mexican economy was quite closed until 1985, but has been relatively open since then. Even South Korea, which is often cited as an example of a successful export-oriented economy, has imposed substantial restrictions on trade from time to time. Trade intervention is usually a matter of degree.

Changing Structure of Trade

Total trade has grown for developing countries over the past 30 years. But the share of agricultural exports in LDC trade has declined steadily from about 60 percent of total exports in 1955 to about 20 percent in the 1990s. This lower share reflects partly the import-substitution policies mentioned above. It also reflects the shifts in comparative advantage of less-developed countries from agricultural to industrial products, demand changes in the more-developed countries, increased domestic demand for food in less-developed countries, and the increased importance of fuels in LDC exports and imports. Nevertheless, several low-income countries—for example Honduras (bananas and coffee), Burundi (coffee), and Ghana (cocoa)—still depend on a few agricultural exports for a large share of their foreign exchange earnings.

The change in comparative advantage is best illustrated by several Southeast Asian countries such as Singapore, South Korea, Taiwan, the Philippines, Malaysia, and Indonesia. As these countries invested in human and physical capital, their comparative advantage shifted from natural resource-based and low-skilled, labor-based production activities to more skill-intensive and, for some countries, capital-intensive products. Their export mix reflects in part this changing comparative advantage (Table 16-1). Agricultural trade is often

---

[5] By 1989, exports of goods and services made up about 14 percent of the GDP of low-income countries and 25 percent of GDP of middle-income countries, compared to 7 and 17 percent, respectively, in 1965. Exports from high-income countries also increased over this period, from 13 to 23 percent of GDP. See the World Bank, *World Development Report 1991* (New York: Oxford University Press, 1991).

[6] See Anne O. Krueger, *Trade and Employment in Developing Countries* (Chicago: University of Chicago Press, 1983), p. 44.

TABLE 16-1
STRUCTURE OF EXPORTS FOR SOUTHEAST ASIAN COUNTRIES, 1965 AND 1989

	Percentage share of total exports			
	Primary commodities		Manufacturing	
Country	1965	1989	1965	1989
Indonesia	96	68	4	32
Malaysia	94	56	6	44
Philippines	95	38	6	62
Singapore	65	27	34	73
South Korea	40	7	59	93
Taiwan	30	8	69	93

Note: Numbers may not add to 100 because of rounding.
Source: World Bank, *World Development Report 1991* (New York: Oxford University Press, 1991).

important in early stages of development, but other, nonagricultural products assume more importance as development proceeds due to changing comparative advantage.

Less-developed countries have had, and will continue to have, a comparative advantage in several tropical or sub-tropical commodities such as coffee, cocoa, tea, rubber, bananas, and sugar. It appears that their comparative advantages in citrus and soybeans have increased over time as well.

Increases in demand by more-developed countries for many of the agricultural exports of less-developed countries are limited due to relatively small income elasticities of demand for those commodities, and, in some cases, to the development of synthetic substitutes (e.g. for rubber, jute, sisal, cotton). On the other hand, domestic demand for food within the developing countries often increases rapidly with development. Not only are populations growing, but a high proportion of any income increases are spent on food. Also, the mix of foods demanded shifts toward more expensive foods (often meats and vegetables, wheat, and certain other grains rather than roots) as incomes grow. As a result, the more rapidly growing, middle-income countries have actually become less self-sufficient in food production over the past two decades, even as their agricultural production and incomes have risen.

Some countries have reacted to the increased domestic demand for food by setting artificially low prices for food commodities and overvaluing their exchange rates to tax exports and subsidize inputs. These policies tend to be counterproductive, as they discourage production. The effects of exchange rate manipulation are discussed in more detail in Chap. 17.

Trade, Employment, and Capital Interactions

Employment growth is crucial for economic development. While few people are totally idle, there is clearly underemployment in most developing countries. By underemployment we mean people working only part-time or in very low-

---

BOX 16-3

FACTOR ENDOWMENT THEORY OF TRADE[a]

The Factor Endowment Theory of Trade (often called the Heckscher-Ohlin-Samuelson Theory because it is derived from their work) argues that because countries have different factor endowments, they adopt different production techniques, and the result is profitable trade. A country with relatively abundant labor (compared to land and capital), will have a low wage rate relative to land prices, rents, and interest on capital-borrowing. Such a country will find it optimal to adopt labor-intensive rather than capital-intensive technologies. The opposite would be true for capital-abundant countries. Without trade, the price ratio of labor-intensive goods to capital-intensive goods will be lower in the labor-abundant country than in the capital-abundant country. Opening the country up to trade would mean that the labor-abundant country would export labor-intensive goods in exchange for capital-intensive goods. Trade will have the effect of increasing the demand for the abundant factor, thus bidding up its price, and increasing the supply of the scarce factor (in the form of imported goods) thereby reducing its price. Trade is expected to reduce factor price differences between countries.

[a] This discussion is drawn from David Colman and Trevor Young, *Principles of Agricultural Economics: Markets and Prices in Less Developed Countries* (Cambridge: Cambridge University Press, 1989), pp. 232–234.

---

productivity jobs. Several possible linkages exist between trade and employment.[7] One such linkage is the effect of trade on overall growth through more efficient resource allocation, assuming faster growth entails more employment. A second linkage, explored empirically in a set of studies summarized by Krueger, is that export industries in countries in early stages of development tend to be labor-intensive, consistent with the Factor Endowment Theory of Trade (Box 16-3). Thus, increased exports might lead to greater employment. A third possible linkage is that trade policies might influence the degree of labor intensity in all industries. For example, trade policies might encourage capital-intensive industries through subsidized capital-goods imports.   .

Empirical evidence suggests that increased exports from developing countries, including agricultural exports, have positive employment implications. Those countries that have followed import-substitution policies (e.g. India) have suffered greater employment problems than more open economies. Research in several countries by the International Food Policy Research Institute (IFPRI) indicates that an export-oriented agriculture increases the demand for hired labor, raises family incomes, and benefits both landowners and landless laborers.[8] Small farmers who produce sugarcane, rice, coffee, and other cash

---

[7] David Colman and Trevor Young, *Principles of Agricultural Economics: Markets and Prices in Less Developed Countries* (Cambridge: Cambridge University Press, 1989), pp. 232–234.

[8] Several studies conducted by Joachim Von Braun and others at the International Food Policy Research Institute involved farm and household surveys in Guatemala, The Gambia, Rwanda, and elsewhere.

crops for export usually maintain some production of subsistence crops as insurance against market and production risk, but these farmers also benefit from the additional income from the cash crops.

The Role of Trade in Agricultural Development[9]

As discussed in Chap. 7, agriculture has many roles to play in economic development, and trade can affect the relative importance of different roles. In fact, an outward-looking trade orientation helps solidify the role of agriculture in development, especially if the outward orientation is accompanied by an agriculture- and employment-based growth strategy.[10] Removal of impediments to trade will facilitate exports, and thus will enhance the foreign exchange contribution of agriculture. An open-trading regime helps provide accurate signals of relative resource scarcity to producers and to investors; the abundance of labor usually found in most developing countries signals the need for employment-intensive investment. With no bias in favor of capital-intensive industries, demands for capital-intensive manufacturing processes can be met through imports, increasing the importance of agriculture's labor contribution.

The food and fiber contribution of agriculture under an outward-looking strategy is usually of most concern to policymakers. Fear of excessive reliance on imports to meet domestic food needs often leads to protectionist policies. However, if agricultural production and employment are stressed, it is unlikely that imports will displace domestic food production. Comparative advantage would dictate that labor-intensive food products be produced. Of course, if growth in demand exceeds domestic food production, then imports may be needed to fill the gap, but these imports should be viewed as evidence of success in employment and income growth.

TRADE IMPEDIMENTS: PROBLEMS AND SOLUTIONS

The variety of agricultural trade strategies that exists in developing countries reflects differences in resource endowments, history, food security, sources of government revenues, balance of payments, etc. This variety also indicates differences in perceptions about the ability of markets to generate prices consistent with desired income distributions. Virtually no country in the world operates with a completely free-trade regime. Most developing countries employ trade policies that discriminate against the agricultural sector, as discussed in Chap. 14. Domestic trade policies, however, are just one of the impediments to agricultural trade. In this section we discuss the major constraints to trade and suggest potential solutions to trade problems. Impedi-

---

[9] See John W. Mellor, "Agriculture on the Road to Industrialization," Chap. 3, in Carl I. Eicher and John M. Staatz, (eds.), *Agricultural Development in the Third World, Second Edition*, (Baltimore: Johns Hopkins University Press, 1990).

[10] See Chap. 6 for a discussion of inward- versus outward-looking orientation.

ments to agricultural trade for developing countries can be classified into three major categories: (1) external demand constraints, (2) market instability, and (3) internal direct and indirect restrictions.

External Demand Constraints

Developing countries have long been concerned that producers of primary products face relatively inelastic demands in more-developed countries. With inelastic demands, additional exports may result in a fall in world prices for the commodities. While individual countries face relatively elastic export demands, if several countries export the same products (e.g. cocoa, coffee, bananas, etc.), prices might fall by a higher percentage than export quantities increase. Thus, export revenues could decline, even as export quantities grow. And the products that developing countries import have more elastic demands, thus creating the terms-of-trade problem mentioned earlier. Historical evidence suggests that the terms of trade for commodities traded by developing countries may have declined over time.[11]

The demand for certain LDC agricultural exports is affected by trade restrictions in more-developed countries (MDCs). The MDCs are more protectionist of their agricultural than of their industrial products. Whereas LDCs tend to discriminate against agriculture, MDCs tend to support farm prices above market equilibrium levels in hope of supporting farm incomes (see Chap. 14). Thus, MDCs have to restrict imports to avoid supporting the whole world price structure.[12] Restrictions particularly affect exports from temperate and subtropical areas of LDCs that compete with MDC agricultural products: commodities such as beef, certain fruits and vegetables, and sugar. Raw tropical products such as cocoa and coffee face few restrictions because they do not compete with more-developed country production. However, semiprocessed products, cocoa and certain fibers being prime examples, do face restrictions. Developing countries would like to export more processed commodities because those products have a higher unit value and provide more employment.

Subsidized agricultural prices in MDCs encourage increased production in those countries while high prices discourage consumption. If production exceeds consumption, stocks accumulate unless they are exported at subsidized prices. The additional volume of exports can depress world prices, making it difficult for LDCs to compete. Dairy products, wheat, and sugar are examples of subsidized exports of high-income countries. Urban consumers in LDCs can

---

[11] *Gross* terms of trade do not take into account differences in costs of production between the products. However, it is difficult to draw a firm conclusion about the *net* terms of trade because improved technologies have reduced the cost of producing the exports as well. It is possible for the *gross* terms of trade to decline but the *net* terms of trade and comparative advantage for agricultural products to improve.

[12] See Robert L. Thompson, "The Role of Trade in Food Security and Agriculture," in D. Gale Johnson and G. Edward Schuh (eds.), *The Role of Markets in the World Food Economy*, Chap. 7, (Boulder, Colo.: Westview Press, 1983).

Sugarcane. Many developing countries restrict imports of sugar
to protect domestic producers.

benefit from these policies, at least in the short run, due to lower prices, but
LDC farmers are faced with production disincentives and lower incomes.
These price distortions, though benefitting MDC farmers, are globally ineffi-
cient. They create conditions for lower growth worldwide.

Market Instability

Government officials in developing countries often perceive food insecurity
and national income risks to be associated with a relatively open agricultural
trade orientation. Price instability in international commodity markets contributes to these risks. The result is a set of policies to restrict food exports to
promote domestic food production and diversify into nonfood agricultural
exports. The concern over food security arises due to both production and
price risks. Agricultural production is sensitive to weather and pest risks
(droughts, floods, typhoons, locusts, etc.). Because world prices for agricultural products are highly variable, countries worry that they may not be able
to afford imports in years of poor production.

Why are agricultural prices so variable? First, world demand for most
primary commodities is relatively inelastic. Therefore as supply shifts back and
forth against an inelastic demand curve, prices vary substantially for small
changes in quantity supplied (Fig. 16-1). If the demand curve in Fig. 16-1 were
elastic (flatter), then the price changes would be much less pronounced. Second, many MDCs cut the linkage between their domestic prices of food commodities and world prices. They do this through import quotas, variable levies,
and other methods of price fixing. Because producers and consumers in the

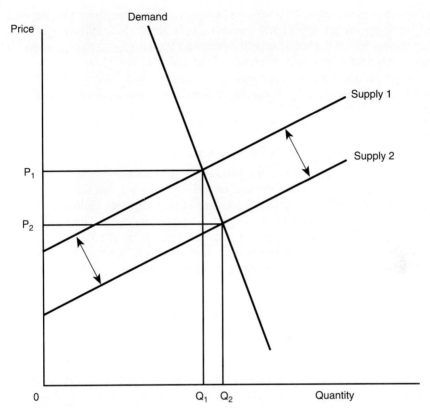

FIGURE 16-1
Small changes in the supply of agricultural products can result in large changes in price.

MDCs bear less of the price risks as a result of these policies, the price variability is greater in the rest of the word.[13] World grain price variability may be as much as 40 to 50 percent higher as a result of government policies, mostly in more-developed countries.[14]

The concern over national income risk is especially acute in those countries that rely on one or very few export commodities for a large portion of their foreign exchange earnings and national income. Prices of agricultural commodities often fluctuate more than 10 percent per year. Hence national income,

---

[13] See Shun-Yi Shei and Robert L. Thompson, "The Impact of Trade Restrictions on Price Stability in the World Wheat Market," *American Journal of Agricultural Economics*, vol. 59, 1977, pp. 628–638.

[14] See D. Gale Johnson, "World Agriculture, Commodity Policy, and Price Variability," *American Journal of Agricultural Economics*, vol. 57, 1975, pp. 823–828. Recent work by Kym Anderson and Rodney Tyers, "Welfare Gains to Developing Countries from Food Trade Liberalization Following the Uruguay Round," Department of Agricultural Economics and Centre for International Economic Studies, University of Adelaide, Australia, July 1990, indicates that if all countries liberalized their trade, that variation in international agricultural prices would be reduced by about two-thirds.

foreign exchange earnings, inflation, and employment in countries that depend on only a few exports are highly volatile. To reduce this volatility, and to insulate themselves from variability of prices and food imports, many countries attempt to become more self-sufficient in food and diversify their exports even if they have to sacrifice average income gains. Risk is like a cost. If policymakers are averse to risk, it can be optimal for them to raise the price of imports and to export less.[15]

Internal Direct and Indirect Policy Restrictions

Many developing countries proclaim food self-sufficiency as an objective, but employ direct and indirect policies that, on net, tax farmers, subsidize consumers, and increase their dependence on food imports. Examples of direct policies that influence agricultural trade are export taxes and subsidies, import tariffs, export and import quotas, import or export licenses, and government-controlled marketing margins. Multiple and overvalued exchange rates and high rates of industrial protection are the principal indirect means of discriminating against agriculture.

Agricultural export taxes are one of the oldest and most common trade interventions in developing countries. Export taxes tend to raise the prices of the products to foreign buyers and reduce the prices received by domestic producers. Producers of cocoa in Ghana, cotton in Mali, coffee in Togo, tobacco in Tanzania, and tea in India, to name just a few products and countries, typically receive less than half the border prices for their products.[16] Some of this difference is due to marketing system inadequacies (see Chap. 14), but a large portion is caused by export taxes.

Some taxation of export crops involves direct taxation of products as they move through ports. Alternatively, public marketing agencies are established that control marketing margins or set farm prices lower than market equilibrium. These agencies, often called marketing boards or parastatal marketing agencies, were discussed in Chap. 14. They are granted monopoly power for buying and selling the commodity, and they may set quotas for exports or imports.

Export taxes are particularly prevalent in the least-developed countries because they are a relatively easy tax to institute and collect compared to alternatives such as income or land taxes. Export taxes generate government revenues and, in some cases, reduce exports and encourage the shifting of production from exports to domestic food crops.

Occasionally, developing countries impose export taxes in attempts to exploit monopoly power that they believe they hold in world markets. If a country

[15] Catherine L. Jabara and Robert L. Thompson, "The Optimum Tariff for a Small Country Under International Price Uncertainty," *Oxford Economic Papers*, vol. 34, 1982, pp. 326–331.

[16] This price difference is measured at the official exchange rate after adjusting for differences in transport and marketing margins. Source: World Bank, *World Development Report 1986* (New York: Oxford University Press, 1986).

is a large enough exporter in the world market to affect the world price, it can use a tax to raise the world price. Although the volume of trade would be lower following the imposition of the tax, the hope is that additional income is earned at the expense of other countries because the price is higher. Ghana has used this rationale for its export tax on cocoa, Brazil for a tax on coffee, and Bangladesh for a tax on jute. Although theoretically valid, the ability of individual developing countries to exploit monopoly power for particular commodities is quite limited. Higher prices create incentives for increased production in other countries as well as for the development of substitute products. Even if the government in the country imposing the tax is able to raise revenues, producers are still discouraged by the lower prices they receive.

Developing countries sometimes use export quotas to partially or totally restrict exports. These restrictions force the sale of the products in domestic markets, thereby reducing prices to consumers. The result, however, is to discourage domestic production and to generate profits for those holding the quota rights.

Import tariffs and quotas are used relatively infrequently on agricultural products in developing countries, but are commonly employed on industrial products. When an import tariff or quota is imposed on industrial goods, the prices of industrial goods are raised relative to those of agricultural goods, creating an *indirect* tax on agriculture. Another significant source of indirect taxation is exchange rate misalignments that result from both macroeconomic policies and direct industrial protection policies. When fiscal and monetary policies (see Chap. 17) lead to higher inflation at home than that prevailing abroad, the value of the local currency falls. If governments fail to adjust the official exchange rate downward, the currency becomes *overvalued*. An overvalued currency makes exports from a country more expensive and imports into it cheaper. Thus, fewer goods are exported and more imported. The additional supply of agricultural products on the domestic market reduces farm and consumer prices. Exchange rate overvaluation is common in developing countries and has been particularly severe in several African countries; for example, Nigeria, Ghana, and Tanzania.[17]

Countries sometimes establish a *multiple exchange rate system*. With this system different commodities are traded at different rates. For example, the government allows one rate of exchange for a commodity it wants to keep inexpensive in the country and another for a commodity it wants to make expensive. Multiple exchange rate systems often discriminate against the agricultural sector.

Recent evidence indicates that indirect taxation of agriculture in developing countries is more than twice as large as direct taxation.[18] Examples for several countries are provided in Table 16-2. Ghana, for example, experienced a

[17] Ibid, p. 67.
[18] See Anne O. Krueger, Maurice Schiff, and Alberto Valdes, "Agricultural Incentives in Developing Countries: Measuring the Effect of Sectoral and Economywide Policies," *World Bank Economic Review*, vol. 2, September, 1988, p. 262.

TABLE 16-2
**DIRECT, INDIRECT, AND TOTAL NOMINAL PROTECTION RATES FOR AGRICULTURE
(AVERAGE, PERCENT)[a]**

Country	Period	Indirect nominal protection rate	Direct nominal protection rate — Importable commodities	Exportable commodities	All commodities	Total nominal protection rate
Cote d'Ivoire	1960–1982	−23.3	26.2	−28.7	−25.7	−49.0
Ghana	1958–1976	−32.6	42.9	−29.8	−26.9	−59.5
Zambia	1966–1984	−29.9	−16.4	−3.1	−16.1	−46.2
Egypt	1964–1984	−19.6	−5.1	−32.8	−24.8	−44.4
Morocco	1963–1984	−17.4	−8.2	−18.5	−15.0	−32.4
Pakistan	1960–1986	−33.1	−6.9	−5.6	−6.4	−39.5
Sri Lanka	1960–1985	−31.1	39.0	−18.4	−9.0	−40.1
Malaysia	1960–1983	−8.2	23.6	−12.7	−9.4	−17.6
Philippines	1960–1986	−23.3	17.9	−11.2	−4.1	−27.4
Thailand	1962–1984	−15.0	n.a.	−25.1	−25.1	−40.1
Argentina	1960–1984	−21.3	n.a.	−17.8	−17.8	−39.1
Brazil	1969–1983	−18.4	20.2	5.4	10.1	−8.3
Chile	1960–1983	−20.4	−1.2	13.5	−1.2	−21.6
Colombia	1960–1983	−25.2	14.5	−8.5	−4.8	−30.0
Dominican Republic	1966–1985	−21.3	19.0	−24.8	−18.6	−39.9
Total Average		−22.5	14.4	−12.6	−7.9	−30.3

n.a. = not available
[a] The direct nominal protection rate reflects the degree of price support, on a percentage basis, compared to a situation with no direct price interventions. A negative value indicates taxation, or negative protection. The indirect nominal protection rate reflects the degree of price support (taxation), on a percentage basis, that results from indirect government intervention. The total nominal protection rate is the sum of the direct and indirect interventions.
Source: Alberto Valdes, "Agricultural Trade and Pricing Policies in Developing Countries: Implications for Trade," invited paper presented at the XXI Conference of the International Association of Agricultural Economists, Tokyo, August 1991.

taxation rate for agriculture of 59.5 percent from 1958 to 1976, more than half of which was indirect. The Philippines had a 27.4 percent rate of taxation on exportables from 1960 to 1986, most of which was indirect.

The differences between direct protection of importable commodities and of exportable commodities in Table 16-2 indicate a strong antitrade bias. Importables generally receive positive protection—that is, imports are taxed either directly or indirectly. This taxation reflects a desire to achieve a certain level of self-sufficiency in food production. Exportables are taxed, reflecting policies designed to raise government revenues. Direct price intervention in agriculture often accounts for 5 to 10 percent or more of total government revenue in developing countries.

Domestic trade restrictions affect agricultural production, consumption of agricultural products, and trade flows. These restrictions reduce economic efficiency and influence the government budget revenues and expenditures.

They affect the distribution of income across rural and urban households. Urban households benefit when food prices are held low, while rural households suffer because of depressed incomes and decreased employment.

Farmers in developing countries respond strongly to prices. The output responses to price changes for different commodities in Africa and the rest of the world are indicated in Table 16-3. Production of individual crops tends to be very responsive to changes in price. Total agricultural output is less responsive to changes in the average price of agricultural products, but substantial shifts occur among commodities produced as prices change. The types and amounts of commodities produced and the technologies adopted depend on the prices farmers receive. Thus, government policies that affect these prices influence production and resource allocation. In a study of 18 developing countries over the period 1960 to 1989, Schiff and Valdes found that removal of taxation on agriculture would have increased the annual rate of agricultural growth in these countries from 2.5 to 3.1 percent.[19]

Not only is agricultural growth retarded by trade restrictions, but real incomes in agriculture are substantially reduced. Lower real incomes hasten the exodus of people from rural areas, creating social costs in urban areas as sewer, water, health systems, and other infrastructure are stretched to the limit. Just as important, lower incomes in agriculture reduce farmers' incentives to invest in land improvements such as irrigation and farm buildings, to adopt new technologies, and to support rural schools with local resources.

TABLE 16-3
SUMMARY OF OUTPUT RESPONSES TO PRICE CHANGES

Crop	Percentage change in output with a 10% increase in price[a]	
	African	Other developing countries
Wheat	3.1–6.5	1.0–10.0
Maize	2.3–24.3	1.0–3.0
Sorghum	1.0–7.0	1.0–3.0
Groundnuts	2.4–16.2	1.0–40.5
Cotton	2.3–6.7	1.0–16.2
Tobacco	4.8–8.2	0.5–10.0
Cocoa	1.5–18.0	1.2–9.5
Coffee	1.4–15.5	0.8–10.0
Rubber	1.4–9.4	0.4–4.0
Palm Oil	2.0–8.1	

[a] The lower end of the range shows short-term supply responses, and the upper end shows long-term responses.
Source: World Bank, *World Development Report 1986* (New York: Oxford University Press, 1986), p. 68.

[19] See Maurice Schiff and Alberto Valdes, *A Synthesis of the Economics of Price Interventions in Developing Countries* (Baltimore: Johns Hopkins University Press, 1991).

Arguments against a relatively free trade regime often are based on anticipated effects of trade on income distribution. The basic concern is that the benefits of trade may accrue to the wealthiest segments of society. While there is reason for concern that a disproportionate amount of economic gains from trade might go to the wealthiest, historical evidence suggests that a high proportion of the benefits from trade *restrictions* also accrues to them. Trade restrictions provide a fertile environment for powerful domestic interest groups to pressure for advantages. The benefits of quota rights, export and import licenses, and subsidized inputs provide economic incentives for people to lobby for these privileges. Visible corruption often emerges as well. It is naive to assume that governments are simply selfless protectors of social welfare. They are politicians and civil servants who respond to pressures from private individuals and interest groups.

While many government employees act with the overall public good in mind, most are just as concerned with their own self-interest as people are in the private sector. Self-interest can encompass monetary gain, reelection, promotion, or other rewards.[20] And, even when there are no conflicts of public and private interests, administrative complexities associated with trade restrictions can lead to waste, costly time delays in marketing, and other types of inefficiency.

What are possible solutions to these problems of external trade constraints, instability, and internal policy restrictions? We consider below several potential solutions that have been attempted or suggested and assess their relative merits.

Solutions to External Constraints

The primary methods that have been suggested as potential solutions to external trade constraints include trade negotiations and preferences, product diversification, and regional cooperation among LDCs. Countervailing trade restrictions to offset the external constraints also have been suggested, but they can generate the problems discussed above.

Trade Negotiations and Special Preferences   Bilateral and multilateral negotiations have provided opportunities for liberalizing external restrictions on LDC trade. Bilateral negotiations occur when one country negotiates preferential trade arrangements with a second country either for specific goods or for whole categories of goods and services. For example, nation A might grant nation B preferential access to its sugar market—that is, reduce or remove restrictions to sugar imports from nation B—in exchange for special access to nation B's wheat market. Or, nation A, a more-developed country, might

---

[20] See Anne O. Krueger, "Government Failures in Development," *Journal of Economic Perspectives*, vol. 4, Summer 1990, pp. 9–23.

simply grant a special preference to nation B, a less-developed country. Numerous variations of bilateral trade negotiations and special preferences are found.

Since World War II, the primary focus for trade negotiations has been multilateral rather than bilateral under the auspices of the General Agreement on Tariffs and Trade (GATT). The GATT, signed in 1947, replaced a series of bilateral agreements that segmented world trade before the war.[21] Currently more than 100 countries are signatories to the GATT. The GATT has attempted to foster adherence to the principle that countries should not discriminate in the application of tariffs.[22] Nondiscrimination implies that bilateral preferential agreements are not allowed. The agreement allows for exceptions for LDCs. Several developed countries maintain preferential trading arrangements with particular groups of LDCs for certain categories of products. For example, a few years ago the United States instituted the Caribbean Basin Initiative that eliminated tariffs and quantitative restrictions for many agricultural products from Caribbean countries. LDCs have called for more generalized preferences to be granted to countries with incomes below a particular level.

The GATT currently contains several provisions related to consultation and negotiation to avoid disparities, rules concerning non-tariff as well as tariff barriers, and agreements to periodic multilateral negotiations to lower trade barriers. Over time, success in reducing tariff barriers has increased the importance of nontariff barriers. Nontariff influences on trade include, but are not limited to, certain types of health and safety regulations (see Box 16-4), domestic content restrictions, and complex customs formalities and reporting requirements.

Eight rounds of multilateral trade negotiations have taken place under the GATT. Most of the early rounds involved negotiations on tariffs and on rules for trading blocs such as the European Community (EC). The middle rounds increasingly focused on non-tariff issues. Agricultural trade restrictions received relatively little attention until the Uruguay Round in the late 1980s and early 1990s.[23]

Developing countries have felt that GATT negotiations have focused far too little on MDC trade restrictions affecting LDCs. As a result, since 1964, they have met periodically under the auspices of the United Nations Conference on Trade and Development (UNCTAD), a permanent organization within the United Nations, to develop proposals for trade arrangements more favorable to LDCs. These discussions led to calls for a *new international economic order* (NIEO). The NIEO contains provisions for improved access to MDC markets

---

[21] See Martin K. Christiansen, (ed.), "Speaking of Trade: Its Effect on Agriculture," University of Minnesota, Agricultural Extension Service, Special Report No. 72, 1978, for more details.

[22] Nondiscrimination has been called the *most-favored nation principle*, that a country should apply to other countries the same tariff levels that it applies to its most-favored nations.

[23] Tariff rounds are frequently named after individuals or after locations where the initial discussions in the round take place. The Uruguay Round began with a meeting in Punta del Este, Uruguay, in 1986.

BOX 16-4

ENVIRONMENTAL, HEALTH AND SAFETY REGULATIONS

Environmental or health and safety regulations can have a significant effect on trade. The United States prohibits the importation of products that have certain pesticide residues. Fresh or frozen beef is prohibited from countries that have a history of foot-and-mouth disease. Clearly, governments are wise to regulate trade in products potentially injurious to public health. More-developed countries usually have tighter environmental and food-safety regulations than less-developed countries. These regulations raise the cost of production so that without corresponding restrictions on trade, not only might there be environmental or health threats, but MDC producers might be placed at a competitive disadvantage. This issue has been a point of discussion with respect to a possible free trade agreement between Mexico and the United States. However, the environmental or health and safety argument sometimes is used arbitrarily to protect the economic health of some industry when the true human health hazard is seriously in doubt.

---

through a generalized system of trade preferences and for a set of mechanisms aimed at reducing price and foreign exchange earnings instability.

Aside from some compensatory financing schemes for stabilizing foreign exchange (discussed below), some specific trade preferences, and a few other measures, UNCTAD proposals for a NIEO have gone largely unheeded. The Uruguay Round of the GATT produced the first serious attempt to address agricultural trade restrictions, including those of particular concern to LDCs. The reason for finally considering agricultural restrictions had little to do with agricultural development problems per se. By the mid-1980s, budget costs, shrinking foreign demand, and world surpluses that threatened a global trade war forced agricultural issues to the top of the GATT agenda.[24]

These latest GATT negotiations highlighted the divisions among more-developed countries and between more-developed and less-developed countries with respect to trade policy, but also illustrated the diversity of interests among less developed countries.[25] Net exporting LDCs were very concerned about access to markets in MDCs and effects of MDC export subsidies. Net importing LDCs, while concerned about market access, were just as concerned about possible rising prices in world markets, particularly for food grains, if MDCs reduced export subsidies and made internal reforms.

Numerous studies have attempted to measure the size and distribution of benefits that would result from the liberalization of agricultural trade. Runge summarizes the results from these studies, each of which evaluated the benefit to LDCs of (1) improved market access through reduced tariffs, quotas, and so

---

[24] See C. Ford Runge, "The Developing Countries and the Uruguay Round," University of Minnesota, Department of Agricultural and Applied Economics, Staff Paper SP91-9, February 1991, for an excellent assessment of agricultural trade issues and developing countries in the Uruguay Round.

[25] Ibid.

forth, (2) reduced export subsidies, and (3) internal policy reforms in MDCs that impact on trade.[26] Each of these three types of reform has been the subject of the recent GATT negotiations. Runge concludes that, of the three elements, market access emerges as having overriding importance to developing countries. Also, the gains to exporting countries such as Argentina and Brazil from reduced export subsidies on commodities such as wheat and soybeans would be substantial.

Product Diversification   Many countries that receive a high proportion of their export earnings from one or two commodities could likely moderate the effects of external trade restrictions by some diversification of exports. The terms of trade can turn against any single product as substitutes are developed (e.g. for jute and sisal) or new technologies shift supply out against a relatively inelastic and slowly shifting world demand (e.g. peanuts). Also, even if progress is made through negotiations in opening up market access for commodities such as sugar or reducing explicit or implicit export subsidies for commodities such as peanuts, total removal of MDC policy distortions is unlikely.

The difficulty for developing countries is in deciding how much to diversify away from a commodity for which it has a strong comparative advantage. Diversification out of agriculture is a natural consequence of economic development that may eventually increase exchange-earnings stability, but too much diversification within agriculture can be a costly means of achieving stability.

Regional Cooperation   International trading relations are increasingly influenced by regional organizations and trading blocs. A common market such as the European Community is an example, but so too are the more loosely integrated free trade areas that have been established from time to time in Latin America, the Caribbean, Southern Africa, and elsewhere. *Free trade areas* are trading blocs whose member nations agree to lower or eliminate tariffs and perhaps other trade barriers among themselves, but each country maintains its own independent trade policy toward nonmember nations. Free movement of factors of production, e.g. labor, are usually not included.[27]

One of the recommendations in the NIEO proposed by UNCTAD is for increased *collective self-reliance* among LDCs. Reduced trade restrictions among a group of LDC countries can allow for increased specialization, economies of scale (particularly for manufacturers), and competition that reduces

[26] Examples of these studies include: Kym Anderson and Rodney Tyers, "Welfare Gains to Developing Countries from Food Trade Liberalization Following the Uruguay Round," Department of Economics and Centre for International Economic Studies, University of Adelaide, Australia, July 1990; and UNCTAD, "Agricultural Trade Liberalization in the Uruguay Round: Implications for Developing Countries," UNDP/UNCTAD Projects of Technical Assistance to Developing Countries for Multilateral Trade Negotiations. UNCTAD/ITP/48, New York, 1990.

[27] Free movement of factors is allowed in a tighter form of economic integration such as a Common Market or an Economic Federation or Economic Union. One type of regional economic integration that is tighter than a free trade area but looser than a Common Market is a "Customs Union," in which member countries agree to a common trade policy against all outside countries.

costs of production and improves economic efficiency. Occasionally a group of countries can gain some market power through closer economic integration. However, exercise of that power usually creates incentives for one member country to undercut another in terms of production or prices. The power is then eroded and the cohesion of the group jeopardized. Regional economic groupings can be helpful to LDCs, but their usefulness is constrained somewhat by the fact that gains from trade among themselves often are constrained by the similarity of products produced among different countries in a region.

Solutions to Instability Problems

The primary solutions suggested for instability in prices of traded goods and of foreign exchange earnings include: diversification, commodity agreements, compensatory financing, and enhanced use of market information.

Product Diversification Diversifying the production of export and food crops can help not only to reduce the terms-of-trade problems arising from external constraints, but may reduce risks associated with price, production, and foreign exchange variability. However, as mentioned above, diversification can come at the cost of reduced overall production efficiency. For many developing countries, some diversification may be called for anyway as consumption patterns shift with income growth.

Commodity Agreements One possible solution for reducing price variability for individual traded commodities is to develop international commodity agreements. Several of these agreements have been concluded over the past 30 years for commodities such as wheat, sugar, coffee, and cocoa. However, few of these agreements have lasted very long. Some, like the international wheat agreement, have attempted to balance interests of producers and consumers, setting no limits on production. Others, such as the coffee and sugar agreements, have attempted not only to stabilize prices but also to prevent competitive price-cutting by setting export and import quotas. However, when production varies, these quotas can actually serve to destabilize world prices.

A third type of commodity agreement involves *buffer stocks*. With a buffer-stock scheme, when supplies are high, the commodity is bought up and stored. These buffer stocks provide protection against a time when supply of the commodity drops for some reason. If there is a shortage, stocks are released on the market to keep prices down. The agreement might specify a minimum and a maximum price, a buffer stock of say 15 percent of world production, a tax on imports or exports to build up the stocks, and perhaps some quotas for producing countries. The NIEO called for increased use of buffer-stock schemes and for a *common fund* that would be financed initially by MDCs to buy up the commodities.

With most commodity agreements, exporters and importers have had diffi-

An international agreement was in effect for coffee for several years.

culty agreeing on an appropriate target price range. The agreements also have proven expensive to administer, especially buffer-stock programs with their high costs of storage.

Compensatory Financing Schemes aimed at stabilizing foreign exchange earnings rather than directly intervening in commodity markets have met with some success. The basic idea behind compensatory financing schemes (CFS) is illustrated in Fig. 16-2. A reference line is set for each country for its total export earnings or earnings from particular commodities. Upper and lower acceptable bounds are set around the reference line. When earnings go below the lower bound, the CFS fills in the shortfall by providing cash or credit to the particular country. When earnings are in excess of the upper bound, LDCs may pay back what was previously taken out.

Two CFSs currently operate. The first, the International Monetary Fund's (IMF) Compensatory Financing Facility (CFF), was established in 1963 to provide financial assistance to member countries experiencing temporary export shortfalls. To use the CFF, the IMF must be convinced that the country will seek means to correct its balance of payments problem in the case that export earnings shortfalls are caused by structural problems. Countries also can borrow against the CFF when adverse weather and other circumstances beyond their control result in high cereal import costs. This component of the CFF, called the *cereal import facility*, was set up in 1981, but has been relatively little used.

The second compensatory finance scheme is run by the European Community (EC) and is called the STABEX. The STABEX was established in 1975

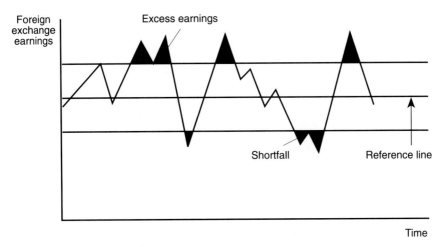

FIGURE 16-2
Example of a compensatory finance scheme.

under the Lomé Convention.[28] This scheme is restricted to African, Caribbean, and Pacific countries and is aimed at stabilizing export earnings for 48 agricultural products. Usually only exports to the EC are covered. A reference line is set for each commodity based on the average value of exports for the products in the preceding four years. To qualify for compensation, export earnings must fall at least 6.5 percent below the reference line. All loans are interest free and the least-developed countries repay nothing. The major commodities supported have been cotton, sisal, coffee, cocoa, and peanuts. Major beneficiaries have been Senegal, Sudan, Côte d'Ivoire, Mauritania, and Tanzania.[29] The CFF and the STABEX compensatory financing schemes have been more successful than international commodity agreements in part because money is cheaper to store than commodities.

Enhanced Use of Market Information   A country can attempt to minimize the negative effects of commodity price fluctuations through use of market information. Futures markets exist in London, New York, Sydney, and elsewhere; the largest futures market "exchange" is in Chicago. With futures markets, commodities can be bought and sold for delivery at a future date. Farmers or exporters can fix a price for goods to be sold later, thus reducing the risk. This activity is called *hedging*. Alternatively, sellers can insure against

[28] The EC's economic arrangements with African, Caribbean, and Pacific countries, which replaced former colonial preference schemes, are spelled out in the Lomé Convention. Other arrangements include free access for many African, Caribbean, and Pacific products to EC markets and the European Development Fund, which administers foreign aid to these countries. See World Bank, *World Development Report 1986* (New York: Oxford University Press, 1986) for additional details.
[29] Ibid.

extremely low prices and buyers against extremely high prices by trading in *options* on futures contracts. Farmers or exporters can insure against low prices by purchasing an option to sell if prices fall to a specified level. If prices fall below that level, they can exercise their option to sell at that price. If prices rise above it, they lose what was paid for the option, but they can sell the products for the higher price.

The usefulness of international futures and options markets is limited for developing countries because internal commodity prices may not follow the same pattern as commodity prices in Chicago, New York, etc. However, if trade becomes more liberalized in the future, these markets may become more useful.

Solutions to Internal Restrictions

Direct and indirect trade restrictions are imposed for several reasons in developing countries, the primary ones being to generate government revenues, to distribute benefits to particular groups, and to offset economic instability and food insecurity. Removal of these restrictions requires alternative revenue sources, enhanced information to reduce transactions costs, and institutional arrangements that offset short-term losses associated with long-term gains.

Alternative Revenue Sources Export taxes and overvalued exchange rates (implicit export taxes) are among the easiest mechanisms for raising government revenues in developing countries. Improved information systems are essential if less-distorting income taxes are to replace export taxes. Some form of property tax may be possible in a few countries. Converting quantitative restrictions (quotas) to export taxes as an intermediate step to their removal, while not removing the distortion, would at least provide more revenues to the government rather than to private individuals.

Foreign debt reduction would reduce the pressure on LDC governments to generate revenues. The nature of LDC debt problems and potential solutions are discussed in Chap. 17. Most of these solutions require action on the part of both more- and less-developed countries. Several LDCs are realigning their exchange rates to encourage more exports, but this solution will be insufficient for most countries without additional assistance from MDCs.

Enhanced Information to Reduce Transactions Costs Transactions costs (particularly unequal access to information) when combined with collective action (particularly informal lobbying and protesting) enable particular groups to pressure the government for trade or other policies that distribute income streams in their favor at the expense of others. Collective action is not necessarily undesirable. It may help focus government behavior to remedy market failures. However, many internal trade restrictions in LDCs merely enhance the already favored positions of wealthy individuals and reduce economic efficiency. Collective action and political power can present important obstacles for reform of these policies. Experience shows that a concerted and sustained effort by governments is needed to reform policies benefitting powerful groups.

The development of basic infrastructure, communications systems, education, and other factors that enhance information flows is essential for reducing transactions costs. Information is needed if institutions are to be designed to constrain unscrupulous behavior. In essence, the same policy prescriptions mentioned in earlier chapters with respect to land tenure, environmental policy, price policy, and research policy are relevant for trade policy.

One external means of encouraging internal policy reforms is for an organization such as the IMF to require certain policy changes as conditions for loans. This type of IMF activity is viewed by many as meddling in the internal affairs of LDCs. Sometimes, however, it provides an excuse for an LDC government to undertake reforms it feels are necessary but could not otherwise accomplish because of political opposition.

Institutional Changes to Reduce Short-term Losses   Developing countries often find it difficult to undertake necessary long-term policy reform because the short-term consequences are so severe. Devaluation of an overvalued exchange rate raises the cost of imports and reduces the cost of exports. While these cost changes improve the foreign-exchange balance and may improve economic efficiency, they also mean that fewer goods are in the domestic market and that there may be severe price increases in the short run. Food prices may rise, real incomes fall, and a disproportionate burden may be placed on the poorest members of society.

International organizations can play a role in providing financial assistance to help offset short-term *cost-of-adjustment* problems associated with policies or structural adjustment programs. The hurt from policy reform is very real in developing countries.

SUMMARY

Proponents of a negative view of trade have argued that as countries become more integrated into the world economy, they open themselves up for exploitation by more-developed countries. Proponents of the more positive view of trade argue that trade facilitates development because it permits more efficient use of resources. It gives countries access to goods and services that otherwise would be unavailable or more expensive. Well-motivated efforts to restrict trade often serve merely to benefit the wealthy. Most less-developed countries do trade and also follow some restrictive trade policies. Many LDC exports come from agriculture. The preponderance of evidence supports the view that a relatively open-trading environment is more conducive to economic development than a highly restrictive one.

Developing countries have a comparative advantage in several agricultural products, particularly tropical ones. They often become less self-sufficient in food in the middle stages of development. Trade tends to have favorable employment implications.

External demand constraints, market instability, and internal direct and indirect trade restrictions all impede exports from and imports into LDCs. Lack of access to MDC markets is probably the most severe external problem. Governments impose internal trade restrictions to raise revenue, to distribute income to particular groups in response to pressures from interest groups, to exploit monopoly power for certain export crops, and for reasons of food security. Indirect restrictions such as overvalued exchange rates are often more significant sources of discrimination against agriculture than are direct restrictions such as export taxes and quotas.

Trade negotiations have been undertaken under the GATT since 1947 but have only recently addressed in any substantial way the restrictions on agricultural products that are so important to developing countries. Nontariff barriers to trade have assumed more importance as tariffs have fallen. International commodity agreements, compensatory financing, product diversification, and enhanced use of market information may help LDCs deal with economic instability. Alternative revenue sources, external help with foreign debt reduction, enhanced information to reduce transactions costs, and institutional changes to reduce short-term cost-of-adjustment problems would facilitate internal trade-policy reforms.

IMPORTANT TERMS AND CONCEPTS

Buffer stocks
Comparative advantage
Compensatory finance scheme
Export taxes
Foreign exchange rates
Free trade
Free trade area
GATT
Import substitution
International commodity
 agreement
International trade
Multilateral trade negotiations

Mercantilism
Multiple exchange rates
New international economic
 order
Options on futures contracts
Overvalued exchange rate
Product diversification
Protectionism
Quotas
Tariffs
Terms of trade
Trade preferences
UNCTAD

LOOKING AHEAD

The macroeconomic environment strongly influences agricultural production incentives, agricultural trade, and employment. Domestic macroeconomic policies affect key prices in the economy, including exchange rates, interest rates, wages, food prices, and land prices. Government revenues, taxation, borrowing, and inflation all influence agriculture. In the next chapter we will consider the effects of both domestic macroeconomic policies and the world macroeconomic relationships. Particular attention is devoted to world capital markets and the debt crisis facing many LDCs today.

QUESTIONS FOR DISCUSSION

1 Why do countries trade?
2 Why do some argue that the terms of trade turn against developing countries over time?
3 What is comparative advantage?
4 Has agriculture as a percent of total export earnings increased or declined for developing countries over the past 30 to 40 years?
5 Why might a country's comparative advantage for particular products change over time?
6 Identify the possible linkages between trade and employment.
7 What are the major external trade impediments facing LDCs?
8 Why is world price instability a problem for LDCs?
9 What are the major direct and indirect agricultural trade restrictions employed by LDCs?
10 Why do developing countries impose trade restrictions?
11 What is the GATT and why have developing countries felt that it has focused too little on their problems?
12 What are some key components of the new international economic order (NIEO) called for by LDCs under UNCTAD?
13 What is the purpose of a compensatory finance scheme and how might one work?
14 Why might product diversification be helpful to LDCs?
15 What is a free trade area?
16 How do buffer stocks relate in international commodity agreements?
17 How might enhanced information help reduce internal trade restrictions in LDCs?
18 Why does an overvalued exchange rate hurt agricultural exports from a country?

RECOMMENDED READINGS

Anderson, Kym and Yujiro Hayami, *The Political Economy of Agricultural Protection* (Sydney: Allen and Unwin, 1986).
Colman, David and Trevor Young, *Principles of Agricultural Economics: Markets and Prices in Less Developed Countries* (Cambridge: Cambridge University Press, 1989), Chap. 11.
Dornbusch, Rudiger, "The Case for Trade Liberalization in Developing Countries," *Journal of Economic Perspectives*, vol. 6, Winter, 1992, pp. 69–85.
Dornbusch, Rudiger and F. Leslie C. H. Helmers, *The Open Economy: Tools for Policymakers in Developing Countries* (New York: Oxford University Press, 1988), especially Chap. 5.
Houck, James P., *Elements of Agricultural Trade Policies* (New York: MacMillan, 1986).
Johnson, D. Gale, *World Agriculture in Disarray*, 2nd ed., (New York: St. Martin's Press, 1991).

Krueger, Anne O., *Trade and Employment in Developing Countries: Part 3, Synthesis* (Chicago: University of Chicago Press, 1983), Chaps. 1 to 3.

Runge, Ford C., "The Developing Countries and the Uruguay Round," University of Minnesota, Department of Agricultural and Applied Economics, Staff Paper SP91-9, February 1991.

Singer, Hans and Javed Ansari, *Rich and Poor Countries* (London: Allen and Unwin, 1982), Chaps. 4 to 6.

Stevens, Robert D. and Cathy L. Jabara, *Agricultural Development Principles: Economic Theory and Empirical Evidence* (Baltimore: Johns Hopkins University Press, 1988), Chap. 13.

Thompson, Robert L., "The Role of Trade in Food Security and Agricultural Development," in D. Gale Johnson and G. Edward Schuh (eds.), *The Role of Markets in The World Food Economy*, Chap. 7, (Boulder, Colo.: Westview Press, 1983); also see Chaps. 5, 6, and 8 in that volume.

Todaro, Michael P., *Economic Development in the Third World*, 4th ed. (New York: Longman, 1989), Chaps. 12 and 14.

Valdes, Alberto, "The Role of Agricultural Exports in Development," in C. Peter Timmer (ed.), "Agriculture and the State: Growth, Employment, and Poverty in Developing Countries," Chap. 3, (Ithaca, N.Y.: Cornell University Press, 1991).

Vollrath, Thomas, "Developmental Consequences of Unrestricted Trade," Foreign Agricultural Economic Report No. 213, International Economics Division, Economic Research Service, U.S. Department of Agriculture, Washington, D.C., May 1985.

World Bank, *World Development Report 1986* (New York: Oxford University Press, 1986), pp. 61–153.

CHAPTER 17

MACROECONOMIC POLICIES AND AGRICULTURAL DEVELOPMENT

In the long run, macroeconomic forces are too pervasive and too powerful for microsectoral strategies to overcome. When they work at cross-purposes, as they do in many developing countries, an unfavorable macroeconomic environment will ultimately erode even the best plans for consumption, production, or marketing.

Timmer, Falcon, and Pearson[1]

THIS CHAPTER

1 Discusses the importance of government policies associated with taxation, spending, borrowing, interest rates, wage rates, the money supply, and exchange rates in influencing the performance of the agricultural sector
2 Explains why governments in less-developed countries tend to pursue particular macroeconomic policies
3 Describes the significance of the interrelationships among (a) macroeconomic policies in other countries; (b) international capital, labor, and product markets; and (c) domestic agricultural markets in developing countries

MACROECONOMIC POLICIES AND AGRICULTURE[2]

Macroeconomic policies have a strong influence on output prices, factor prices, marketing margins, and, hence, on incentives for agricultural producers, consumers, and marketing agents. Foreign exchange rates, for exam-

[1] C. Peter Timmer, Walter P. Falcon, and Scott R. Pearson, *Food Policy Analysis* (Baltimore: Johns Hopkins University Press, 1983), p. 215.
[2] The material in this section draws heavily on C. Peter Timmer, Walter P. Falcon, and Scott R. Pearson, op. cit.

ple, affect export and import prices and quantities and, thus, output and input prices. Interest rates determine the cost of investments in machinery and equipment and, when combined with wage rates, the capital intensity of production. Interest rates also influence the cost of storage.

The macroeconomic environment conditions the rate and structure of agricultural and urban-industrial growth. Job creation and income growth and distribution are as much a function of macroeconomic policies as are policies and projects targeted at specific sectors. The short-run effects of macro policies on employment and income distribution can be quite different from their long-term effects. Real incomes of urban consumers can be sharply reduced in the wake of macroeconomic policy adjustments aimed at reducing public debt or controlling inflation. Policymakers often must seek means of softening short-run income and nutritional consequences of needed long-term policy changes.

Understanding the effects of macroeconomic variables on agriculture and on food prices is important for designing economically and politically viable short- and long-run policies. When macro policies create distortions such as overvalued exchange rates, heavily subsidized interest rates, and inflationary fiscal and monetary policies, agriculture is usually discriminated against and long-term prospects for development are compromised. Pressures build for major macropolicy reforms that, even if unintentionally, usually help the rural sector by increasing farm incomes and rural employment. Price increases and lower subsidies, however, necessitate painful adjustments by urban consumers. The pervasive nature of these macropolicy effects makes it imperative for those interested in agricultural development to understand how the macroeconomy works.

Describing a Macroeconomy

A macroeconomy can be described in terms of demand, supply, or income (see Fig. 17-1). A country's gross domestic product (GDP), a measure of its domestically produced national income, will be identical regardless of whether it is calculated by summing demands, supplies, or incomes. Macroeconomic policies in more-developed countries often focus on managing the demand side of the economy. Governments in these countries implement policies to stimulate private consumption or investment, use public expenditures to create demand, and closely manage trade. Policies in less-developed countries frequently are more concerned with managing aggregate supply. Governments in LDCs tend to use the types of policies described in Chap. 14 to manage agricultural supply; similar policies affect the other productive sectors. Numerous LDCs have attempted to stimulate supply by involving the government directly in the production of goods and services.

Demand equals supply when the components in Fig. 17-1 are expressed in real terms (inflation is netted out). The basic factors of production (land, labor, and capital) together with management, earn incomes when they produce goods and services. These incomes are spent on the components of aggregate

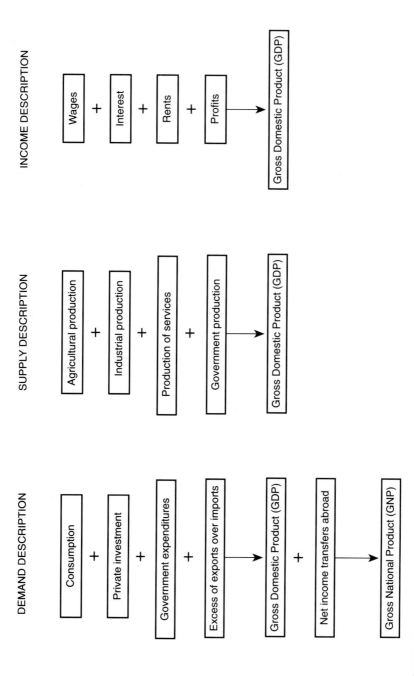

FIGURE 17-1
Three descriptions of a macroeconomy.

demand; hence total income equals GDP. Developing countries are often very concerned about the distribution of total income among wages, interest, rents, and profits, and undertake policies to manage this distribution.

The prices of goods and services are generally expressed in the country's currency units. The monetary value of a good or service can change due to inflation even when its real value has not changed. Policies that create inflation can change real values as well, though often indirectly. The causes of inflation are discussed below, but many of inflation's effects are, in a sense, unintended results of fiscal and monetary policies. We turn our attention to these policies first, highlighting their effects on agriculture. Then we consider the effects of macroprice policies, particularly those policies related to exchange rates, interest rates, and wage rates. Finally, we consider the effects of macro policies on rural-urban terms of trade and land prices. The major macroeconomic and agricultural policy connections are summarized in Fig. 17-2; these connections are described below.

Fiscal and Monetary Policy

Fiscal policy is the conscious attempt by government to meet employment, income growth and distribution, and other objectives through its powers to tax and spend. *Monetary policy* is the deliberate action of the government to manage the money supply or the interest rate to achieve employment and income growth and distribution objectives. Both fiscal and monetary policies influence inflation, intentionally or otherwise. They also influence the country's budget and determine whether fiscal surpluses or deficits will prevail. Governments differ substantially in their ability to tax the domestic economy to produce revenue and in their willingness to run and finance large budget deficits.

Governments in developing countries often go into debt because of their many pressing needs and limited tax revenues. Tax collection, particularly income tax collection, is difficult and costly, and taxes are easy to evade in countries with poor information systems. Consequently, developing countries raise large proportions of their tax revenues from export taxes, import tariffs, and sales taxes, as these taxes tend to be easier to collect than others.

Because agriculture is usually the largest sector in the economy, it generally provides more revenue to the government than it receives in return in the form of government programs. However, there are usually substantial budget allocations to the agricultural sector. Programs for producers include items such as irrigation systems, roads, agricultural research and extension, market information, and certain output or input subsidies. Programs for consumers include items such as targeted and nontargeted food price subsidies. Many of the investments in agricultural research and extension, irrigation, roads, etc., also benefit consumers.

Foreign aid can ease some of these revenue needs, as discussed Chap. 18. A few countries have petroleum and other mineral resources that they can export

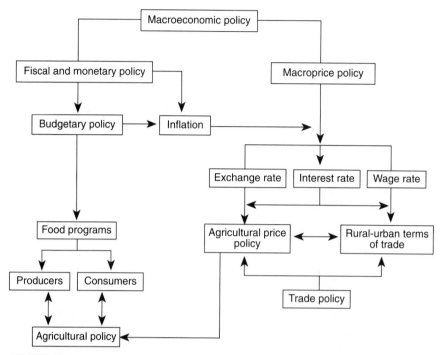

FIGURE 17-2
Major connections between macroeconomic policy and food policy. (*Source:* Based on Fig. 5-1 in C. Peter Timmer, Walter P. Falcon, and Scott R. Pearson, *Food Policy Analysis,* Baltimore: Johns Hopkins University Press, 1983, p. 223.)

so that foreign consumers help provide revenues for government spending. However, given the limitations to raising taxes, obtaining foreign aid, or exporting petroleum or minerals, most developing countries incur sizable budget deficits. They meet these deficits by borrowing, often from abroad, or by increasing the money supply (that is by printing more money).

Currently, many developing countries are heavily burdened by debts incurred through previous borrowing abroad. This *debt crisis*, its causes, effects, and potential solutions to it, are discussed later in the chapter. The debt incurred in previous borrowing currently constrains the ability of many LDCs to take on additional debt. Consequently, domestic money supply and budget finance policies become that much more important. The size of the money supply must match the needs for operating capital in the productive sectors of the economy. However, when a country prints money to finance a large budget deficit, inflation is the usual result (see Box 17-1).

Inflation can also result from price increases in other countries if a developing country fixes its exchange rate against that of a country whose prices are rising. When the LDC imports goods from the country with rising prices, it must continually pay more for those goods; hence inflation is transmitted from one country to another.

BOX 17-1

EFFECT ON INFLATION OF A GOVERNMENT BUDGET DEFICIT FINANCED
BY EXPANDING THE MONEY SUPPLY

Inflation is a sustained rise in the general price level for a country's goods and services. It is usually measured by a price index. The following example illustrates why expansion of the money supply to finance government budget deficits creates inflation. The aggregate supply of goods and services produced must equal the aggregate demand from total expenditures or, $Y = P \times Q = C + I + G + X - M$, where:

Y = monetary value of national output or income
P = price index for all goods and services produced
Q = quantity index for all goods and services produced
C = national consumption expenditures in private sector
I = national investment expenditures in private sector
G = government expenditures on consumption and investment
X = total value of exports
M = total value of imports

   If government demand for goods and services (G) increases because the government prints money to pay for a budget deficit, either the quantity produced of goods and services (Q) must increase, imports (M) must increase, or prices (P) will rise. Most developing countries do not have enough idle resources to meet this demand with enough Q. Changes in imports require foreign exchange. Thus the usual result is an increase in prices.

   Source: C. Peter Timmer, Walter P. Falcon, and Scott R. Pearson, *Food Policy Analysis* (Baltimore: Johns Hopkins University Press, 1983), pp. 227–228

Inflation often hurts agriculture because it increases the prices of inputs, usually by more than the rate of increase in output price. When inflation occurs, the foreign exchange rate should change to reflect the reduced value of the currency. Many developing countries do not allow this adjustment to take place completely. The resulting overvalued exchange rate increases the price of agricultural exports (thus reducing export demand) and makes food imports cheaper. The resulting increased supply of agricultural products on the domestic market reduces farm product prices. The foreign exchange rate policy is just one of the macroprice policies that has significant impacts on agriculture.

Macro Prices and Agriculture

Governments use macroeconomic policies to influence inflation, provide incentives, and distribute income. Three prices—foreign exchange rates, interest rates, and wage rates—have major effects on the macroeconomy and can be manipulated by the government. Timmer et al. call them macro prices.[3] These prices are all, in fact, determined by supply and demand conditions in their

---

[3] Ibid.

respective markets, so that if the government decides to set them by fiat, conditions of excess supply or demand can result. Two of these prices, interest rates and wage rates, signal the scarcity of basic factors of production, capital and labor. Governments often are tempted to set wage rates artificially high to directly raise incomes. They are tempted to set interest rates low to encourage borrowing and investment. Wages set above the free market, equilibrium value determined by supply and demand conditions will lead to excess supply of labor and, hence, unemployment. Interest rates set below equilibrium values will create excess demand for credit which will then have to be rationed. Government policy can be used to affect those macro prices indirectly by intervening to change the underlying supply and/or demand conditions. Public works projects, for example, stimulate demand for labor and could be used to raise wages.

The foreign exchange rate is relatively easy to control, and governments often do control it. Two other prices with major effects on the macroeconomy, food prices and land prices, are influenced indirectly through exchange rate manipulations, as mentioned in Chap. 16. These prices can also be affected directly by imposing tariffs, or by government interventions in their respective markets.

Exchange Rates An exchange rate is the number of units of one currency that it takes to buy a unit of another currency, or the price of one currency in terms of another. For many relatively developed countries, the foreign exchange rate is determined in international money markets by the supply of and demand for a country's currency. For example, there is a demand for U.S. dollars in Japan in order to pay for agricultural products imported from the United States. Similarly, there is a supply of dollars in Japan coming from the purchase of Japanese cars by U.S. consumers. The supply of, and demand for, dollars also are affected by international capital flows for investment or other purposes.

These same supply and demand factors exist in developing countries, but the exchange rates in these countries frequently are set by governments rather than determined in currency markets. A developing country typically fixes or "pegs" the value of its currency to that of a major trading partner such as the United States. For example, Honduras for several years fixed its currency, the Lempira, to the dollar at a rate of 2 Lempira equals 1 dollar. The Lempira then followed the fate of the dollar in foreign exchange markets. It declined in value when the dollar declined against third countries, and rose when the dollar rose.

A government can set a new official exchange rate to raise or lower the value of its currency. For example, Honduras eventually devalued its currency relative to the dollar and set it at a ratio of 4 to 1. This devaluation made imports into Honduras more expensive and its exports cheaper.

Many countries overvalue their exchange rates for long periods of time. Overvalued exchange rates usually result from differences in inflation rates between a country and its major trading partners. Domestic inflation in the presence of fixed exchange rates means that imports seem cheaper relative to domestically produced goods. At the same time, exports from the country become more expensive abroad. But the market for foreign exchange in the country will not balance unless capital flows in; thus the value of the currency is driven up. Any policy that creates inflationary pressures, such as government budget deficits or expansion of the money supply, will, when combined with fixed exchange rates, lead to overvaluation. Countries maintain overvalued exchange rates by controlling the movement of foreign exchange and foreign investment (see Box 17-2).

Countries overvalue exchange rates in part to keep domestic prices down. More imports and fewer exports mean more goods in the domestic market. The greater the domestic supply of goods relative to demand, the lower the price. The result of an overvaluation is that the prices of traded goods produced in the country, such as many agricultural goods, are depressed relative to those of nontraded goods and services. Thus rural incomes tend to be lowered compared to urban incomes.

A devaluation can correct the problem, at least temporarily, but unless fiscal and monetary policies are changed to reduce either government expenditures or aggregate demand, inflation will rather quickly result in a reoccurrence of the overvalued exchange rate. Devaluation can also cause hardship on those who produce nontradeable goods and services and consume tradeable goods; for example, civil servants and certain groups of factory workers. Food prices generally rise in response to a currency devaluation, helping farmers and hurting urban consumers. Policies are often needed to protect the welfare of the very poor when a devaluation occurs, especially if the currency has been allowed to become substantially overvalued and a large adjustment is needed.

Interest Rates   The price of capital investment is represented by the interest rate. The interest rate reflects, in part, the productivity of capital or the opportunity cost of using capital for one purpose rather than another. Interest

---

BOX 17-2

HOW A GOVERNMENT MAINTAINS AN OVERVALUED EXCHANGE RATE

Since supply and demand factors determine exchange rates, if a government wishes to fix the official rate at a level other than its equilibrium, then it must intervene in the foreign exchange market. It can support an overvalued rate by selling foreign exchange reserves (dollars or some other currency) and purchasing its own currency, thus supporting its value. Overvaluation thus diminishes foreign reserves and cannot be sustained for long periods of time. In the absence of significant reserves, a government can restrict access to foreign currency at the official rate, and thus effectively ration the commodity (foreign exchange) for which excess demand exists. This rationing is usually implemented by imposing direct currency controls, by controlled allocations of foreign exchange to preferred importers, and by tariffs and other barriers to imports.

rates also reflect risk and the value of current as opposed to future consumption. Interest rates are determined by the interaction of the supply of investment funds, basically household savings, and the demand for these funds.

Governments can influence interest rates by setting them for public credit sources and by imposing regulations such as reserve requirements on private financial sources. In addition, the method by which the government finances a fiscal deficit affects interest rates. If a deficit is financed by domestic borrowing, then interest rates will rise in response to the increased demand for funds. The alternative means of financing deficits is to print money, a policy which is inflationary. Thus, higher interest rates in the presence of budget deficits can help keep inflation down. Macroeconomic policy with respect to interest rates often represents an attempt to balance the value of capital in increasing production with the valuation of future, relative to current, consumption.

Governments may set a maximum interest rate that can be charged by lenders in the country. If the rate is set too low, excess demand for credit is created because demand for credit will exceed its supply. Under these circumstances, credit has to be rationed to privileged borrowers, and private lenders will have incentives not to lend or to circumvent the regulations. Formal lending institutions may be forced out of business. Moneylenders and other informal credit sources not under the control of the government find it easier to charge higher rates.

When interest rates are controlled, they may even be set below the inflation rate. When this happens, the *real* interest rate is, in fact, negative.[4] Negative real interest rates create credit crises since there is no incentive to save or lend. Low official interest rates encourage use of government credit for those who can obtain it and drive out private credit institutions.

Wage Rates   The primary source of income for most people in the world is returns to their labor. Hence creating jobs at decent wages is essential to reductions in poverty and hunger. Governments recognize the importance of labor remuneration and often set minimum wages in an attempt to raise people out of poverty. Unfortunately, minimum-wage legislation is a relatively impotent tool for raising returns to labor and can have unintended effects that hurt labor.

Labor markets are complex because they are segmented by skill levels, occupations, and locations. In rural areas, labor arrangements may include payment in kind (e.g. food or other goods), may involve conditional access to a piece of land, or may depend on other special relationships between employers and workers that are determined by local customs or institutions. Wages for unskilled workers in these areas may be close to the average product of labor rather than the marginal product (Chap. 5). This level in turn is close to a basic

---

[4] The *real* interest rate is equal to the nominal interest rate minus the rate of inflation.

subsistence level. Minimum-wage legislation is virtually unenforceable in rural areas in developing countries.

In urban areas, minimum wage legislation has been successful in large industries and government organizations. People who are able to obtain jobs at or above the minimum wage clearly benefit. Unfortunately, by raising the price of labor, minimum wage legislation reduces the demand for labor by these industries and organizations. Thus unemployment (or excess supply of labor) may result in the short run. In the long run, the industries may adapt more capital-intensive technologies, further displacing labor. The result is more people left in the informal urban sector described in Chap. 4. Also, the possibility of higher wages in the formal sector may attract more migrants to the urban area, even if jobs are scarce. This influx of migrants will also swell the informal sector. Consequently, minimum-wage legislation in the formal sector may, over time, depress wages in the informal sector. In summary, wages are an important macroprice, especially to the poor, but governments have little ability to raise people out of poverty by legislating wage levels.

Prices of Agricultural Products and Land   Agricultural prices are influenced by government interventions in output and input markets, as discussed in Chaps. 14 and 16. Price supports, input subsidies, export taxes, etc., directly influence the terms of trade between the agricultural and nonagricultural sectors. Fiscal and monetary policies and macroprices, however, usually have even larger effects on the terms of trade between the sectors than do the more direct price policies. For example, the agricultural sector produces a high proportion of tradeable commodities. Thus, an overvalued exchange rate that encourages imports and discourages exports typically has a strong negative effect on the agricultural sector.

When macropolicies and prices discriminate against the agricultural sector so that agricultural prices are depressed, downward pressures are placed on land prices as well. Incentives are reduced for improving the land base or for developing technologies to utilize land more efficiently.

In summary, macroprices reflect basic economic conditions in an economy. Unless agricultural productivity is increased, simply distorting these prices through government policies is likely to hinder the development process and create distributional effects that hurt the rural poor.

WHY GOVERNMENTS PURSUE PARTICULAR MACROECONOMIC POLICIES

Why do governments in developing countries commonly follow macroeconomic policies that discriminate against rural producers in favor of urban consumers? Why do they sometimes change course and introduce structural adjustment programs that may partially reverse this discrimination? Let's examine the motivation for these public interventions and the reasons that governments often use indirect macropolicy and macroprice interventions as much as, or more than, policies targeted directly at particular sectors.

At the simplest level, governments follow policies to distribute income in particular ways to stimulate economic growth, to correct past problems such as external debts, to reduce inflation, and to react to changing world conditions. Because food is a wage good (i.e., food is a high proportion of consumer budgets in LDCs), the interests of urban consumers coincide with owners of industrial firms. Consumers view lower-priced food as higher real wages, while industrialists see it as serving to decrease upward pressure on nominal wages. Thus, an overvalued exchange rate, for example, is seen as a quick fix for stimulating industrial growth, distributing income toward politically influential urban consumers and industrialists, and reducing inflationary pressures.

The growth stimulus of macroeconomic intervention is often short-lived. Discrimination against agriculture reduces agricultural growth and investment and foreign exchange earnings from agricultural exports. A severely over-valued exchange rate can turn a food exporter into a food importer. Rural opposition to the macropolicies increases over time, inflation worsens due to higher food prices, and unemployment grows. Then, because pressures from urban groups continue, governments may subsidize agricultural inputs, raise output prices through subsidized market margins for food staples, and under-take other measures to reduce prices to consumers. In other words, they pursue partially offsetting policies.

Why do governments institute such complex sets of policies? The basic reason is political expediency. Urban consumers and industrialists are potent pressure groups that demand low food prices and relatively more public goods for urban compared to rural areas.

Transactions Costs and Collective Action

Macropolicy interventions and more direct sectoral policies both influence the allocation of monetary and political benefits (often called political rents). Mac-ropolicy interventions are less obvious to society as a whole than are more specific taxes and subsidies. Thus, governments may provide direct subsidies to agriculture that are more than offset by overvalued exchange rates and still appear to be helping farmers. Food prices are kept low in urban areas, at least in the short run, and urban industrialists and civil servants, with better informa-tion than most farmers, press for the continuation of exchange rate distortions and other forms of protection that benefit the urban sector.

Both rural and urban households can form coalitions and lobby collectively for rural or urban interests. The policy preferences of politicians and other government officials are affected by the relative strength of these rural and urban lobby groups. The urban lobby is often quite strong because it may represent a coalition of households, students, civil servants, military factions, labor unions, and industrialists.

It is not the sheer size of the urban lobby that gives it power to influence policy. The rural lobby is even larger in many developing countries. However, the urban lobby is much more concentrated geographically, and this concentration facilitates its ability to organize. Students are concentrated near universities, civil servants in government offices, and labor unions and industrialists in a relatively small, concentrated formal sector. The military is highly organized. If people decide to protest rising food prices, the costs of organizing and coming together for this purpose are relatively small in the urban sector.

Because the urban lobby is made up of several relatively small but homogeneous groups, members of these groups see the benefits of organizing collectively to press for their interests. Rural interest groups, particularly small farmers, are so dispersed that individual members often see few benefits to themselves. Communication is difficult so that even if collective benefits are perceived, the costs of organization and action are prohibitively high. Interestingly, as development proceeds and the agricultural sector declines in relative and absolute size, its ability to organize and lobby often increases. Also, the cost to the government of subsidizing a small agricultural sector is lower than a larger sector. Therefore, once a country is relatively well-developed, it usually reduces its discrimination against agriculture.

Sometimes government policies are motivated by corruption among politicians and other officials. Policy distortion create gains for certain groups, and some of these gains are appropriated by individuals in public service as payment for instituting the policies.

Historical Factors, Structural Adjustment, and External Forces

A government at any particular point in time is constrained by the accumulated effects of past policy choices. It is natural for developing countries to go into debt to some degree as they invest in the future. However, several countries, particularly in Latin America and Africa, have accumulated internal and external debts well in excess of what their economies can service without imposing extreme hardship on people. In addition, previous distortionary macroeconomic and sectoral policies have caused inefficiencies in the economy that have reduced the potential for economic growth and limited foreign exchange earnings.

As a result of these historical public policy choices, governments may be forced to introduce a major *structural adjustment program*. The term structural adjustment is defined as government action aimed at adjusting the economy to reduce imbalances between aggregate supply and demand. Structural adjustment programs usually involve the following types of actions: devaluation of the foreign exchange rate to increase exports and reduce imports, reduced government spending almost across the board, more efficient tax collections, and removal of many distortionary policies. The devaluation and other types of trade liberalization are important because external debts can not be reduced without earning or saving foreign exchange. Reduced government spending and increased efficiency in tax collection are needed to bring spending more in line with revenues. The removal of policy distortions is needed to stimulate economic growth.

The economic growth effects of structural adjustment programs can take several years. Inflation may be sharply reduced relatively quickly after an initial increase in prices caused by the devaluation, but at a cost of increased unemployment in urban areas. Food prices will usually rise, hurting the urban poor. Public sector employees can be laid off, and standard services curtailed. Higher agricultural prices help farmers and, in the long run, increase employment and output in agriculture.

Governments undertake structural adjustment programs because the economy has deteriorated to the extent that existing policies are unable to control inflation, the country is shut off from additional borrowing, and political support has deteriorated, even from urban sources. Frequently, external sources of funding such as the International Monetary Fund (IMF) of the World Bank require structural adjustment as a precondition for additional assistance. Thus, external pressures become another source of policy change. There is no question, however, that structural adjustment programs are painful. In Latin America, the net capital transfer out of the region to repay previous debts was approximately $30 billion per year during the 1980s. Imports were slashed by about one-third. Sharp cutbacks were realized in public services such as water and sewage systems, schools and hospitals.

Some policy changes are made necessary by changing world economic conditions. A recession in the industrialized countries, for example, can reduce the demand for products from developing countries. High interest rates elsewhere in the world can exacerbate debt problems for developing countries. A shock to the oil market can severely strain exchange reserves for countries without petroleum. Consequently, some policy changes are necessitated just to react to these external forces. In the next section we examine how these world macroeconomic linkages occur and how they affect developing countries.

WORLD MACROECONOMIC RELATIONSHIPS[5]

Starting from the end of World War II when there was virtually no international capital market, the international monetary system has grown to the point that transfers of capital between countries dwarf the values of international trade in goods. In the mid-1980s, roughly $40 trillion in international financial flows occurred per year compared to $2 trillion in trade. These flows affect exchange rates, trade, and the extent to which fiscal and monetary policies influence national economies.

[5] Parts of this section draw heavily on G. Edward Schuh, "The Changing Context of Food and Agricultural Development Policy," in J. Price Gittinger, Joanne Leslie, and Caroline Hoisington, (eds.), *Food Policy: Integrating Supply, Distribution, and Consumption* (Baltimore: Johns Hopkins University Press, 1987), pp. 78–87.

A second major change in the structure of the international economy was the shift beginning in 1973 from a system of fixed exchange rates to one of bloc-floating exchange rates. With the fixed system, currencies around the world were fixed for long periods of time against the dollar.[6] With the bloc-floating system, the values of major currencies are allowed to change rapidly against each other in response to market conditions. Several developing-country currencies, however, remain fixed to the major floating currencies such as the U.S. dollar.

Implications of Well-Integrated Capital Markets and Bloc-Floating Exchange Rates

The emergence of a well-integrated international capital market and bloc-floating exchange rates means that interest rates, capital movements, exchange rates, and trade are interconnected. It means that fiscal and monetary policies in one country can affect the economic performance of another, especially of its trade sectors. For example, if the United States issues bonds at higher interest rates to attract capital to pay for its government budget deficit, capital can come from foreign as well as domestic sources. This foreign demand for U.S. bonds increases the demand for dollars, driving up the value of the dollar. Several international as well as domestic repercussions are felt. First, the higher interest rate in the United States places upward pressure on interest rates in U.S. banks and in developing countries that have sizable loans with U.S. banks at variable interest. Also, banks in other countries may need to raise their interest rates to compete with U.S. banks for savings. The higher interest rate makes it harder for developing countries to pay off their debt and forces them to reduce domestic spending or increase their trade balance by increasing exports or reducing imports.

Second, the higher value of the dollar makes U.S. exports more expensive abroad and encourages imports into the United States. Developing countries with currencies that are pegged to the dollar, will also find it harder to export and easier to import. Then, tradeable goods sectors, such as agriculture, in those countries suffer from downward pressure on prices. Economic growth is reduced as exports fall and imports rise.

If governments can partially isolate their domestic agricultural sectors from international markets, the effects of world macroeconomic forces may be reduced. However, such isolation would mean loss of gains from trade and from access to foreign capital to facilitate development. Consequently, developing countries usually choose to absorb a certain amount of instability in interest rates, exchange rates, etc., caused by world macroeconomic forces in order to benefit from international goods and capital markets. These countries

---

[6] The fixed exchange-rate system had been established at the Bretton-Woods Conference in 1944. Trade expanded rapidly under this system, but the system eventually became unworkable when certain currencies, particularly the U.S. dollar, became seriously overvalued and others, particularly the German deutschemark and Japanese yen, became severely undervalued.

however, may need to: (1) protect the poorest of the poor through targeted food subsidies or other means of ensuring basic food security and (2) take full advantage of international schemes aimed at stabilizing foreign exchange such as the compensatory finance arrangements discussed in Chap. 16. The IMF could play a significant stabilizing role for LDCs if it were given the resources to act more like an international central bank. The present system in which so many countries tie their currencies to the dollar leaves those countries vulnerable to U.S. economic policies.

Changes in International Comparative and Competitive Advantage

Comparative advantage increasingly is less influenced by physical resource endowments and more by human capital endowments. Government spending on education and agricultural research and the rapid international diffusion of certain technologies, particularly biotechnology, has the potential to influence human capital accumulation in many LDCs by improving education, nutrition, and incomes. These changes may eventually lead to restructured trade patterns.

Government macroeconomic and sectoral protectionist policies, however, can suppress underlying comparative advantage and distort a national economy away from what the physical and human resource base would seem to dictate. As exchange rates swing, so too does competitive advantage, in directions discussed previously. For example, the long decline in the value of the dollar in the 1970s misled U.S. producers and producers in other countries about their long-term ability to compete. The sustained rise in the value of the dollar in the

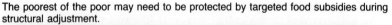
The poorest of the poor may need to be protected by targeted food subsidies during structural adjustment.

first half of the 1980s sent opposite but still misleading signals. These movements were induced by U.S. and foreign government macroeconomic policies, and did not reflect any changes in fundamental comparative advantage.

The Debt Crisis: Causes, Effects, and Potential Solutions

It is natural for the governments of developing countries to borrow to finance productive investment. As long as a country has investment opportunities in the public or private sector that yield returns comfortably above the cost of funds in the world market, then such investments should be made even if external borrowing is required. The country will grow more rapidly and can export to repay the loan in the future. A country may also borrow at times to finance consumption, a policy that would be appropriate, for example, if a natural disaster or a short-run economic shock such as a sharp oil-price change makes it reasonable to sustain consumption even though current income is lower.

Borrowing is imprudent, however, when the debt is increased to cover longer-run consumption, questionable investments, large government deficits, or capital flight out of the country.[7] Imprudent, large-scale borrowing by the government occurred in many LDCs during the 1970s, particularly in Latin America and Sub-Saharan Africa. The result was a *debt crisis* that began in the early 1980s and continues today. When a country has a debt crisis, it lacks the foreign exchange needed to make payment of interest and principal on its loans. Why did the crisis occur in so many countries, what were its effects, and how might it be solved? The answers to these questions are important for understanding why several developing countries experienced a "lost decade" during the 1980s and how these countries can be extricated from their economic predicaments in the 1990s.

Causes of the Debt Crisis   When a country makes more payments to the rest of the world than it receives in payments, it has a *current account deficit* (see Box 17-3). It has to sell off assets or borrow to finance the deficit. Developing countries began running abnormally large current account deficits beginning in 1973 with the first OPEC oil shock. Prior to that time, the total accumulated external debt for all developing countries was less than $100 billion. During the 1970s, commercial banks received a flood of dollars from the oil-producing countries. The banks recycled these petro-dollars to developing countries to finance their current account deficits. Banks were happy to invest in LDCs because they received high interest rates and the loans appeared to be guaranteed by governments. Several Latin American and Asian countries seemed to

---

[7] Capital flight occurs when capital leaves a country due to perceived risk at home. Capital flight, however, is difficult to distinguish from normal capital flows. It often occurs when the government borrows foreign exchange and makes it available to residents at a subsidized price. People acquire this foreign exchange, if they can, and move it to banks or other investments abroad.

BOX 17-3

CURRENT ACCOUNT DEFICIT

The current account deficit represents the excess of spending on imports and interest payments on the external debt over export revenues. In other words, it equals the trade deficit plus interest payments. The current account deficit in a particular year also represents the increase in the net debt for a country. Unless the trade surplus is large enough, the mere existence of an external debt means that interest on that debt will cause the debt to keep growing.

---

be good risks because they had grown rapidly for several years. In Africa, growth had, for the most part, not occurred, but countries there borrowed from official sources for development purposes or to meet consumption shortfalls caused by production problems.

By 1980, many developing countries were in trouble. A second oil shock in 1979 had made a mounting debt problem more severe. Interest rates on past loans rose in the early 1980s due to tight monetary policy in the United States Many of the commercial loans to LDCs had been made at adjustable interest rates and now increased sharply. LDC debts reached $400 billion by 1980 and rose to $660 billion by 1982.

In 1982, a world recession struck, depressing demands for LDC exports. Even the demand for oil declined, resulting in a drying up of petro-dollars for new loans. The first reaction of countries seriously in debt was to refinance the loans and spread them out over a longer period of time. Several LDCs, however, found it extremely difficult to service their debts (make scheduled interest and principal payments) or to acquire new funds. For Latin America, debt servicing exceeded 50 percent of the value of the region's exports during the early 1980s, and much of the debt was owed on short-term loans at variable interest rates that were rising.

The first of the large debtors to announce it could no longer service its debts was Mexico in 1982. Mexico was a net oil exporter, but it had borrowed heavily against anticipated future oil revenues. These oil revenues declined with the worldwide recession, and Mexico was left with a debt of more than $80 billion with few exports to make repayments. Banks and the U.S. government provided Mexico with new loans to forestall the repayment problem, but it was then clear that the world community had a major financial crisis on its hands that would have to be solved. As Mexico renegotiated its loans, the crisis came to a head in many other countries. By 1986, more than 40 countries in Latin America, Africa, and elsewhere had encountered severe financial problems. Except for the Philippines, countries in Asia largely escaped severe debt problems.

Comparisons of the external debt situation between 1970 and 1989 for low-income, middle-income, and several individual countries are presented in Table 17-1. For developing countries as a whole, external debts as a percent of GNP were almost three times as great in 1983–1989 as they were in 1970–1975. By 1989, developing countries owed more than $1.3 trillion. Debt service was running more than $100 billion per year. Twelve of the 17 countries identified by the World Bank as *heavily indebted* were in Latin America and the Caribbean. Africa's debt of more than $110 billion was three times the value of all its annual exports. Côte d'Ivoire (Ivory Coast) provides an example of the severity of the debt problem: with a population of 11.7 million in 1989, it owed $15.4 billion or $1300 per citizen in a country with an annual per capita income of $790. Forty-one percent of the country's export receipts were needed just to service the debt.

Effects of the Debt Crisis   When a country attempts to reduce its external debt, domestic consumption must be cut to free up resources to produce goods that can be exported to earn foreign currency for debt service. Reductions in import demand also are needed to save foreign exchange. Not all of the reduced spending affects traded goods. Some of it falls on nontraded goods and services when labor and capital shift to the production of traded goods for export.

Within the country, prices of traded goods must rise relative to wages and other prices to encourage the production of traded goods and to discourage domestic consumption. Exchange rate devaluation is the typical means of bringing about these adjustments in relative prices. Devaluation, however, takes time to have the desired effect. Thus, policymakers typically find ways to reduce their imports in the short term by other means, such as imposing tariffs or import quotas. Because some of the imports are raw materials or producer inputs, economic growth often is slowed as well.

Spending cuts and devaluations are painful since they inherently involve reductions in real income for the country. The cuts usually include reductions in basic social services that help the poor. The devaluations effectively cut real wages. As the currency is devalued, the country has to give up more in terms of domestic resources to earn each unit of foreign currency. The country is essentially selling its labor and other resources more cheaply on world markets.

TABLE 17-1
INDICATORS OF EXTERNAL DEBT FOR DEVELOPING COUNTRIES

Country or country group	Total external debt as a percentage of GNP		
	1970–1975	1976–1982	1983–1989
Low income	10.2	14.8	28.5
Middle income	18.6	34.6	54.9
Argentina	20.1	46.1	80.3
Brazil	16.3	28.2	42.0
Morocco	18.6	55.1	109.5
Philippines	20.7	45.8	79.2

Source: World Bank, *World Development Report 1991*, (New York: Oxford University Press, 1991) p. 125.

Many developing countries had overvalued exchange rates prior to the debt crisis; thus, adjustments were needed irrespective of the crisis. The devaluations raise the prices of many agricultural exportables and importables, thus helping the farm sector. However, the resulting higher food prices hurt the poor particularly. The magnitude of this debt-induced hurt is difficult to judge, because several of these countries would have had to adjust their economies even without the debt crisis. But there is little doubt that the poor in LDCs have shouldered a large portion of the burden of adjusting to the crisis.

There is another way in which the debt crisis has affected the macro-economic performance of debtor countries. Cuts in government spending have induced recessions that reduced government revenues. Because countries can no longer borrow enough abroad to meet these shortfalls, they often print money. Printing money usually results in high inflation. Devaluation and import restrictions contribute to these inflationary tendencies.

The result of economic restructuring or structural adjustment in several indebted countries has been trade surpluses (primarily achieved through reduced imports), a net transfer of capital from developing to developed countries, and declines in domestic investment. Markets in developing countries for exports from developed countries have therefore shrunk. U.S. agriculture, for example, has been particularly hurt by the debt crisis. Many countries that had been major markets for U.S. commodities are now unable to import these food products.

At the time the debt crisis first hit the news in 1982, there was a major concern over the impending peril to the world financial system. The fear was that countries like Mexico, Brazil, and Argentina could default on their loans, causing large commercial banks to go bankrupt. Today, however, the threat to the banking community has for the most part receded. Partly, the threatened banks have reduced their outstanding claims on LDCs, but mainly they have increased the revenues they set aside to guard against disruptions in debt service.[8]

The threat to the poor in developing countries has not receded. In the Latin American and Caribbean region, for all but three countries, real wages were lower in 1989 than in 1980. In Sub-Saharan Africa, per capita incomes were 15 percent lower in 1989 than in 1980. Governments in many developing countries cut their education and health budgets. Not all of these declines were due to debt problems, but many were, particularly in Latin America. The rise in poverty and the reduction in social services have led to increased hunger and malnutrition. Environmental problems have increased as well, as countries exploit resources to meet current food and foreign exchange needs. A closer look at effects on the poor of adjustment programs designed to solve debt and other structural economic problems is provided later in this chapter.

---

[8] See Benjamin J. Cohen, "What Ever Happened to the LDC Debt Crisis?" *Challenge*, vol. 34, May–June 1991, p. 49.

Potential Solutions to Debt Problems   External debt problems of developing countries impose major costs on both debtors and creditors. Risk of a commercial banking crash as a result of the debt crisis is now virtually nonexistent, but many heavily indebted, developing-country economies continue to stagnate or deteriorate. How can these external debts be reduced, and who should bear the burden of adjustment? Several debt-reduction plans have been proposed and, thus far, the burden of adjustment to debt reduction has fallen largely on the poor in debtor countries themselves. We consider below the pros and cons of potential solutions to the debt crisis.

The first potential solution to LDC debts is for the countries to default on the loans. Total default would have the advantage of relieving pressures to cut government spending and to export more to service the debt. The disadvantages are first that the creditors could seize debtor's overseas assets.[9] Second, the creditors might seize payments to firms that attempt to export to the debtor and payments made by firms that attempt to import from it. Thus, the country would lose its potential gains from trade. Third, default might leave a country unable to borrow again for several years. This combination of disadvantages has meant that no countries have totally defaulted on their loans during the current debt crisis, even though some countries have stopped payments or only made partial payments for a period of time (e.g., Peru, Brazil).

When considering solutions to debt problems, it is important to separate the two very different groups of countries whose governments have large debt problems. One group consists primarily of low-income African countries that owe money largely to governments or to multilateral lending agencies. The second group is composed of the heavily indebted countries (HICs), primarily in Latin America, that owe money mainly to commercial banks.

Both groups have high levels of debt, and income growth rates in each have been near zero or negative since 1982. Otherwise their circumstances are quite different. The low-income African countries possess limited domestic resources such as oil or minerals, do not own much abroad, have had slow income growth for reasons primarily unrelated to debt, and have continued to receive new loans in excess of debt service. The HICs by contrast own more resources (for example, Mexico, Venezuela, Nigeria, and Ecuador have oil reserves), have a great deal of wealth abroad in many cases, have had economic growth rates substantially reduced by their overhanging debt, and have been paying substantially more to creditors since 1982 than they have received back in new loans.

Because the low-income debtors owe mostly to governments, the creditor countries can mandate debt relief or restructuring without interfering in private international capital markets. Creditors can respond to the debt crisis in ways consistent with their humanitarian beliefs or, more likely, their overall foreign

---

[9] See Jonathan Eaton, "Debt Relief and the International Enforcement of Loan Contracts," *Journal of Economic Perspectives*, vol. 4, Winter 1990, pp. 43–56 for more details.

policy objectives. Low-income debtor countries can turn to the Paris Club for help in resolving debt issues (see Box 17-4). Because many loans to African countries are at below-market interest rates (subsidized), rescheduling these loans by extending the repayment period can significantly reduce the burden to the debtor.

The solutions to debt problems for the HICs are more difficult. Whatever solution is arrived at must operate within the context of international capital markets that include commercial banks. Any solution will affect the distribution of the debt burden among debtors, private creditors, and the public in creditor countries.[10]

Several potential solutions to the HIC debt problem have been proposed and, in some cases, partially implemented. Most proposals involve a combination of debt rescheduling and restructuring of economic policies within the debtor nations. Other proposals include debt-for-equity swaps, cash buybacks of debt, and debt-for-conservation swaps.

Debt rescheduling involves extending the repayment period for the loans, altering interest rates, forgiving part of the principal, or some combination of the three. Efforts to restructure economic policies (structural adjustment programs) involve reducing exchange rates to discourage imports and to encourage exports, cutting government spending and otherwise liberalizing the economy through reduced government intervention in markets and marketing.

In the 1980s there was debate over whether the debt problem could be solved by structural adjustment combined with stretching out the repayment period, or whether outright forgiveness of principal and interest was needed as well. Whatever path was chosen, there was agreement that debt repayment had

---

BOX 17-4

THE PARIS CLUB

The Paris Club is a forum for negotiations on countries' debts to government creditors. The Club, formed in 1956 in response to Argentine debt difficulties, has no set membership. The participants in any Paris Club negotiation are the debtor government and its creditors, who traditionally meet under the chairmanship of a senior French treasury official.

All creditors are treated equally in Paris Club rescheduling negotiations. Debtor countries approaching the Paris Club are usually required to conclude an agreement with the IMF for an IMF loan and an IMF-approved program for restructuring economic policies. An example of IMF conditions for a structural adjustment program would be reductions in government spending and fewer restrictions on exports.

Source: P. Krugman and M. Obstfeld, *International Economics* (Cambridge: Massachusetts Institute of Technology Press, 1988), p. 596.

---

[10] Ibid.

to be reduced to a level that would permit renewed economic growth in the debtor countries.

In October 1985, the U.S. Treasury Secretary, James Baker, developed a plan aimed at the 17 most highly indebted countries. The Baker Plan was centered on: (1) debt renegotiation to convert short-term loans into long-term loans, (2) structural economic changes by debtor countries under IMF supervision, and (3) as much as $7 billion a year in new loans from commercial banks. The plan worked fairly well at shifting debt from short to long term—by moving some of it to international agencies and governments—but commercial banks failed to respond with new capital.

In March 1989, the new U.S. Treasury Secretary, Nicholas Brady, developed a new plan that continued the Baker Plan but added provisions for commercial banks to reduce principal and interest for selected borrowers in return for various forms of financial guarantees by the IMF, World Bank, and creditor governments (see Box 17-5). Japan committed several billion dollars to the plan. By 1991, agreements for debt reduction had been reached with Mexico, Bolivia, Uruguay, Venezuela, Costa Rica, and the Philippines. The amounts of debt reduction involved were relatively modest.

Most countries' debt sells at a discount on a secondary market in which the debt can be shifted from bank to bank or to other institutions. The debt sells at a discount because creditors believe they will not be repaid in full. For example, each dollar of Peru's debt sold for about 5 cents on the secondary market in 1991. Debtor countries can sometimes buy back part of their debt with cash or by swapping government-owned assets (such as stock in publicly owned companies). Buying back the debt seems to make sense because the value of the debts on the secondary market are only a fraction of the face value of the loan. There have been few buybacks and swaps, however, because countries lack the cash for buybacks, and many countries are uneasy about foreign ownership of their assets. In a few cases, for example in Costa Rica, outside groups have agreed to buy up and eliminate part of the debt in exchange for government assurances of protecting rainforests or other natural resources. This type of activity has been called a debt-for-conservation (nature) swap.

The major failing of previous proposals for LDC debt reduction has been the lack of incentive for the commercial banks to undertake them on a large enough

---

BOX 17-5

THE MAIN FEATURES OF THE BRADY PLAN

The Brady Plan called for the IMF and the World Bank to provide financial support for two types of debt reduction transactions—conversion of bank loans into new bonds with reduced (but guaranteed) principal and interest rates, and debt buybacks for cash. The debtor countries had to undertake more growth-oriented economic policies, promote the return of the flight capital from abroad, and maintain viable debt-for-equity swap programs.

scale. Rescheduling debts over a longer period of time at a fixed but below market interest rate would eventually solve the debt problem. Commercial banks would be better off if loans were rescheduled because they have little hope of fully collecting their loans under current loan schedules. The debtor countries would clearly be better off. Why have so few loans been rescheduled at lower interest rates? The reasons are three. First, banks are not under great pressure to reduce the debt burden of LDCs now that the banks' reserves have increased to the point that they are no longer in danger of insolvency as a result of LDC defaults on loans.

Second, and more important, no single bank has an incentive to act alone. Debt reduction, like domestic bankruptcy, needs an institutional setting to bring it about. Even when it is in the collective interests of the banks to reduce the debt, each bank has an incentive to insist on full payment of its own loans. If one bank does grant a concession to lower the interest rate or principal, it becomes more likely that other banks will collect their loans. Hence each bank waits around for other banks to voluntarily reduce the interest rate or principal owed so they can get what is known as a "free ride." This free-rider problem exists for debt-equity swaps, cash buybacks, and other proposed solutions as well.

A third explanation for the lack of debt rescheduling is that developed countries have been reluctant to play too large a role in debt relief for fear of large budget expenditures. While there are strong humanitarian grounds for debt relief through Paris Club negotiations for the poorest countries, the arguments carry less weight for debt relief in Latin America if that relief comes at the expense of foreign assistance to even poorer countries in Africa and Asia.

What is the answer? An international debt facility (IDF) could be set up to coordinate a comprehensive debt reduction through reduction of interest rates to submarket levels on existing debt.[11] The debt facility would organize a comprehensive package for each country, requiring appropriate policy reforms in the debtor country. The facility would be housed in the IMF and the World Bank. It would guarantee interest payments for those banks that provide sufficient interest rate relief that the financial integrity of the debtor could be restored (see Box 17-6 for more details of how such a facility would work).

The advantage of an IDF is that it would remove the free rider problem that currently constrains individual banks from sufficient participation in initiatives like the Brady Plan. Such a plan would likely impose few if any more costs on creditor taxpayers than current plans.

Regardless of the plan used to reduce LDC debts, the viability of the plan would be enhanced by lowering of MDC trade barriers to LDC exports. These trade barriers make it difficult for LDC countries to acquire foreign exchange for debt service. For this reason, the GATT negotiations also have an important part to play in solving the debt problem.

---

[11] See Jeffrey D. Sachs, "A Strategy for Efficient Debt Reduction," *Journal of Economic Perspectives*, vol. 4, Winter 1990, pp. 19–29 for a more detailed discussion of how such a debt facility would operate.

17-6

HOW AN INTERNATIONAL DEBT FACILITY MIGHT WORK

The International Debt Facility (IDF) would "indicate a range of acceptable debt reduction, to be achieved mainly through a permanent cut in interest rates to submarket levels. It would call for universal participation of all banks in the agreement. Pending the completion of the debt reduction negotiations, the debtor country would pay only a fraction of the interest due on the existing debt, in line with IMF estimates of ability to pay. The IDF would give de facto protection to the debtor for the partial nonpayment of interest, since the IMF and the World Bank would continue to lend to the debtor country despite the presence of growing arrears to the banks. The IDF could probably also give de jure protection to the debtor, under an arrangement in which the IMF would formally approve the nonpayment of interest as an "exchange control" that is necessary to protect the economy of the debtor country.

Once a critical mass of banks (perhaps 80 percent of banks, by amount of loans) agrees to necessary debt reduction, the interest rate would be cut to those banks, and the IDF would then provide full guarantees on the reduced flow of interest payments. Thus, the banks would give up their claim to full repayments, but would instead get a guaranteed but smaller stream of interest repayments. Principal would be rescheduled (say, for 30 years), and would be fully repayable without a discount. For banks that do not agree to the debt reduction, the country would remain in arrears under the protection of the IDF."

Source: Jeffrey D. Sachs, "A Strategy for Efficient Debt Reduction," *Journal of Economic Perspectives*, vol. 4, Winter 1990, p. 25.

Effects of Structural Adjustment Programs on the Poor

Virtually all of the debt-reduction plans include provisions for structural adjustment programs in the debtor countries. Even countries without serious debt problems have been forced to undertake adjustment programs either as a condition for new loans or grants or because of independent financial crises. A key question is the extent to which these programs have hurt the nutritional status and overall health of the poor. A second question is whether the programs can be structured in a way that allows them to achieve their objective of stimulating economic growth without harming the poor.

Structural adjustment programs, which typically involve currency devaluation and reduced government involvement in markets, have direct effects on prices, employment, income, and government spending. Unfortunately, empirical measurement of the magnitude of program effects on the poor are hampered by lack of information about what would have occurred without the programs. Mexico, for example, undertook a substantial structural adjustment program in the 1980s. Incomes dropped substantially, but eventually inflation did as well. Subsequent economic growth has allowed the government to target new social programs at the poor. In Costa Rica, real wages declined by 40 percent from 1977 to 1982. After the country undertook a structural adjustment program, real wages rose back to the previous level by 1985. Peru, on the other hand, had sharply deteriorating economic conditions in the 1980s and did not undertake a structural adjustment program. Its economy continued to sharply decline into the 1990s. Do these experiences indicate that structural adjustment programs do not hurt the poor? Certainly not.

Adjustments to lower incomes and to higher food prices during these programs almost inevitably hurt the poor. In most cases, the adjustment period is too long to ignore the pain even if the pain is only temporary. Those hurt the most tend to be the urban poor and the rural landless. Farmers may benefit even in the short run due to higher agricultural prices. However, targeted food and health programs are needed as a safety net even if social services in general are temporarily reduced. In countries where social spending targeted toward the poor remained high, such as Costa Rica, Bolivia, and Chile, indicators of health and nutritional status were affected very little by the adjustment.

Structural adjustment programs can certainly help the poor in the long run. Many existing distortions in LDCs benefit the wealthy and hurt the poor. Unfortunately, poorly designed, structural adjustment programs may further hurt the poor by removing certain social programs or distortions that had been put in place to offset other distortions that favor the rich.

SUMMARY

Macroeconomic policies have a strong influence on prices, marketing margins, and hence on incentives for economic agents. A macroeconomy can be described in terms of aggregate demand, supply, or income. Polices in LDCs are frequently aimed at the supply side of the economy. Both fiscal and monetary policies influence inflation. Developing countries often go into debt because of many pressing needs and limited tax revenues.

Governments use foreign exchange rates, interest rates, and wage rates to influence trade, investment, and incomes. Many developing countries overvalue their exchange rates, a policy which discourages exports and encourages imports. They do so in part to keep prices down. They often subsidize interest rates and set minimum wages for the urban formal sector. Agricultural and land prices are influenced by macroeconomic policies.

Governments pursue particular macroeconomic policies to stimulate economic growth, distribute income, correct debt problems, reduce inflation, etc. Policies are influenced to a large extent by urban lobbies. Forces external to the country also come into play. Well-integrated capital markets and bloc-floating exchange rates tie economic policies of LDCs to MDCs more so than was the case in the 1950s and 1960s.

While it is natural for governments in developing countries to borrow to finance investment, massive borrowing during the 1970s, followed by high interest rates and tight money in the early 1980s, led to a severe debt crisis. In 1991, developing countries owed more than $1.3 trillion. Many of the loans in Latin America were from commercial banks, and many of the loans in Sub-Sahara Africa were from official sources. Countries are being forced to adjust their economies by exporting more, importing less, and reducing government spending in order to pay off debts. Proposed solutions to the debt crisis have done little to reduce LDC debts. Repayment of many loans has been re-scheduled over a longer period of time, and bank loan reserves have been increased, reducing the threat to world financial markets. The burden of adjust-ment continues to fall on the LDCs themselves. Banks are hesitant to reduce principal or interest rates because there is no coordinating body to exact a comprehensive reduction that would eliminate the free rider problem. Cash buybacks, debt-for-equity swaps, and debt-for-conservation swaps have been tried but are unlikely to be widespread or large enough to solve the problem. Structural adjustment programs have often hurt the poor in the short run, suggesting a need for safety-net programs.

IMPORTANT TERMS AND CONCEPTS

Balance of payments
Bloc-floating exchange rate
Capital flight
Cash buybacks
Current account deficit
Debt crisis
Debt-for-conservation swaps
Debt-for-equity swaps
Debt relief
Debt rescheduling
External debt
Fiscal policy

Free rider
International capital market
International debt facility
Macroprices
Minimum wage
Monetary policy
Money supply
Paris Club
Secondary market
Structural adjustment program
Urban lobby

LOOKING AHEAD

International relations between more-developed and less-developed countries are influenced in major ways by foreign assistance programs. In the following chapter we discuss the various types of foreign assistance, motivations for the aid, and effects on the less- and more-developed countries.

QUESTIONS FOR DISCUSSION

1 What are the three ways a macroeconomy can be described so as to arrive at gross domestic product (GDP)?
2 What do we mean by a country's "fiscal policy"?
3 What are the two primary monetary policies that can be used to finance a govern-ment deficit, and what are their effects?
4 What are the major macroprices that governments often try to set?
5 Why do countries overvalue their currencies, and what is the effect of overvalua-tion?
6 What are the advantages of high versus low interest rates?

7 How are wage rates determined, and what are the advantages and disadvantages of minimum wage laws?
8 How are land prices affected by macroeconomic policies?
9 Why do governments pursue particular macroeconomic policies?
10 What is a structural adjustment program, and what are its effects?
11 How does a bloc-floating exchange rate system differ from a fixed exchange-rate system?
12 How are interest rates, capital movements, exchange rates, and trade interconnected?
13 How might a macroeconomic policy suppress the comparative advantage of a country in producing a particular good?
14 Why is it natural for LDCs to borrow from MDCs?
15 Describe the major causes of the debt crisis.
16 Why have many heavily indebted countries devalued their currencies?
17 Why are commercial banks less concerned about LDC debt today than they were in 1982?
18 Why have voluntary reschedulings of debt servicing by commercial banks not resolved the debt crisis?
19 Why may it be more difficult to resolve the debt crisis in Latin America than in Africa?
20 What are the advantages and disadvantages of cash buybacks of debt? Of debt-for-equity swaps? Of debt-for-conservation swaps?
21 Why are the urban poor often hurt more by structural adjustment programs than are semisubsistence farmers?
22 What are the pros and cons of an LDC defaulting entirely on its debts?

RECOMMENDED READINGS

Cohen, Benjamin J. "What Ever Happened to the LDC Debt Crisis?" *Challenge,* vol. 34, May–June 1991, pp. 47–51.
Dornbusch, Rudiger and Stanley Fischer, "Third World Debt," *Science,* vol. 234, November 14, 1986, pp. 836–841.
Islam, Shafiqul, "Going Beyond the Brady Plan," *Challenge,* vol. 32, July–August 1989, pp. 39–46.
Journal of Economic Perspectives, vol. 4, Winter 1990, pp. 3–56, articles by Kenneth Rogoff, Peter Kenen, Jeffrey D. Sachs, Jeremy Rulow, and Jonathan Eaton on new institutional arrangements for solving the debt crisis.
Krugman, Paul and Maurice Obstfeld, *International Economics* (Cambridge: Massachusetts Institute of Technology Press, 1988), pp. 581–621.
Schuh, G. Edward, "The Changing Context of Food and Agricultural Development Policy," in J. P. Gittinger, J. Leslie, and C. Hoisington, (eds.), *Food Policy: Integrating Supply, Distribution, and Consumption,* (Baltimore: Johns Hopkins University Press, 1987), pp. 78–87.
Timmer, C. Peter, Walter P. Falcon, and Scott R. Pearson, *Food Policy Analysis* (Baltimore: Johns Hopkins University Press, 1983), Chap. 5.

CHAPTER 18

FOREIGN DEVELOPMENT ASSISTANCE

As we move into the post-cold war era, the process of assistance policy formation and resource allocation is increasingly troubling. Each assistance constituency, within the government and outside, is attempting to carve out for its favored area a larger share of a declining assistance budget. The lack of a central policy focus leaves the assistance budget particularly vulnerable to such efforts.

Ruttan[1]

THIS CHAPTER

1 Examines the rationale for and major types of foreign assistance to agriculture in less-developed countries
2 Discusses the types, the objectives, and the positive and negative effects of food aid programs in less-developed countries
3 Identifies means for improving the effectiveness of foreign assistance

DEVELOPMENT ASSISTANCE FOR AGRICULTURE

Foreign development assistance (aid) in support of agriculture in developing countries has been substantial, it has taken many forms, and the nature and magnitude of its effects have generated considerable debate. Multiple objectives drive all foreign aid programs, with the result that the distribution of aid among different countries often bears little relation to need as manifested by

[1] Vernon W. Ruttan, "Solving the Foreign Aid Vision Thing," *Challenge,* vol. 34, May–June 1991, p. 46.

hunger and poverty. Hence, we begin this chapter by examining the rationale for foreign assistance.

Rationale for Foreign Assistance

The rationale for foreign aid in general, as well as for aid to agriculture, rests on humanitarian (moral or ethical), political (strategic), and economic (commercial) self-interest grounds.[2] Several variants of the humanitarian argument have been made based on compensation for past injustices, uneven distribution of global natural resources, and a moral obligation to help the least-advantaged members of society.[3] The premise is that the emergence of international economic and political interdependencies has extended the moral basis for distributive justice from the national to the international sphere. Foreign assistance to agriculture can benefit one of the largest and poorest sectors in most developing countries.

The political self-interest rationale is based on the notion that aid will strengthen the political commitment of the recipient to the donor(s). A quick examination of the distribution of U.S. foreign assistance by country makes it clear that strategic political considerations have been a major motivation for aid, regardless of whether the intended results have been achieved (see Table 18-1). For example, in recent years roughly one-fourth of all U.S. development assistance has gone to Israel and Egypt. And, a small country like El Salvador receives more U.S. development assistance than a large country like India.

The argument that aid serves a country's economic self-interest is based on the notion that aid increases exports from and employment in the donor country. For example, producers of foodgrains in the United States might benefit from food aid because less grain is placed on the commercial market and, hence, prices rise. Food aid can open markets to a country's exports by initiating commercial contacts. Foreign aid to agriculture may increase agricultural growth in developing countries and that growth may increase incomes that, in turn, stimulate demand for agricultural imports and, by extension, donor exports. Much foreign assistance is tied to the purchase of goods such as food or equipment from the donor. These purchases directly benefit producers in the donor countries.

This complex set of reasons for foreign assistance means that aid to agriculture does not always go to where the need is greatest. The fact that aid is given in part for donor self-interest purposes would seem to impose on donors some obligation to ensure that the distribution and types of foreign assistance

---

[2] See Anne O. Krueger, "Aid in the Development Process," *World Bank Research Observer,* vol. 1, January 1986, pp. 57–58; and Vernon W. Ruttan, "Why Foreign Assistance?" *Economic Development and Cultural Change,* vol. 37, January 1989, p. 415.

[3] Ruttan, op. cit.

TABLE 18-1
U.S. OFFICIAL DEVELOPMENT ASSISTANCE (ODA) TO TOP 12 RECIPIENTS
(MILLIONS OF CURRENT U.S. DOLLARS)

1970–1971		1980–1981		1988–1989	
Country	ODA	Country	ODA	Country	ODA
India	462.6	Egypt	878.6	Israel	1207.4
Vietnam	349.4	Israel	801.9	Egypt	917.6
Indonesia	259.6	India	230.1	Pakistan	376.7
Pakistan	166.4	Turkey	195.2	El Salvador	318.7
Korea	149.8	Bangladesh	153.4	India	183.5
Brazil	119.8	Indonesia	146.4	Philippines	173.9
Turkey	119.8	Pacific Islands	118.5	Pacific Islands	154.5
Colombia	99.8	Pakistan	96.6	Guatemala	144.9
Israel	56.6	El Salvador	69.7	Bangladesh	135.2
Laos	53.2	Peru	62.8	Honduras	135.2
Pacific Islands	49.9	Portugal	62.8	Costa Rica	135.2
Morocco	46.6	Sudan	62.8	Sudan	106.2
Total above	1933.5	Total above	2878.8	Total above	3989.0
Multilateral ODA	379.4	Multilateral ODA	2119.8	Multilateral ODA	2096.0
Total ODA	3328	Total ODA	6973	Total ODA	9659

Source: Joseph C. Wheeler, *Development Co-Operation: Efforts and Policies of the Members of the Development Assistance Committee, 1990 Report,* Organization for Economic Cooperation and Development, Paris, December 1990.

provided do not harm the recipients. We return to this issue below after examining the types and amounts of foreign development assistance.

Types and Amounts of Foreign Development Assistance

Total foreign assistance encompasses economic development assistance plus military assistance and export credits. Often private funds from voluntary agencies also are included. Foreign development assistance, as the term is used in this chapter, excludes the military-related component and export credits, while the term *official development assistance* excludes private fund transfers as well. To qualify as any type of foreign assistance, the resources transferred must be sent from donor(s) to a recipient without a commensurate return flow of resources. There may be good will, political support, etc., but direct payments are not made in return.

At one extreme, foreign development assistance can occur as loans at near-market interest rates. At the other, this assistance can be an outright grant. In the middle, the assistance can be a loan at a concessional (below-market) interest rate or with a maturity period longer than that commercially available.[4] Foreign development assistance also can come in the form of food aid or as technical assistance to provide needed expertise. To be classified as official

[4] See Krueger, op. cit.

development assistance (ODA) by the Development Assistance Committee of the Organization for Economic Cooperation and Development (OECD), the assistance must have at least a 25 percent grant element.[5] The grant element is defined as the excess of the loan or grant's value over the (present) value of repayments calculated with a 10 percent interest rate.

The amount of U.S. and world ODA in recent years is presented in Table 18-2. The growth and decline of assistance flows has been influenced strongly by the intensity of the cold war. The recent declines in ODA illustrate this influence as well as the effects of budgetary constraints.

Foreign assistance to agriculture is a portion of total ODA and includes such diverse components as aid used for agricultural research and extension, irrigation projects, rural roads, agricultural education and training, flood control projects, health improvement programs, integrated rural development projects, and agricultural policy assistance. It is difficult and perhaps not appropriate to separate out agricultural from nonagricultural aid. Foreign exchange and budget support directed at a country as a whole can indirectly benefit agriculture, as can food aid funneled through food-for-work programs to improve rural infrastructure. Support for infrastructure and for education benefits all sectors of the economy.

Development Assistance Programs Since World War II, the number of development assistance programs has risen greatly. Initially the United States was the major provider of economic aid. The relief and recovery efforts in Western Europe and East Asia shortly after the war were followed by a U.S. development assistance program for developing countries, called the Point Four Program. That program grew out of the fourth point in President Harry S Truman's inaugural address of January 20, 1949. Truman called for a "bold new program for making the benefits of scientific advances and industrial progress available for the improvement and growth of underdeveloped areas."[6] The program provided technical assistance to Taiwan, South Korea, and other countries in Southeast Asia, the Middle East, and the less-developed countries of Europe. Point Four effectively marked a shift in focus of U.S. foreign assistance from Europe to developing countries. This program was followed by the Development Loan Fund in 1957. This fund was combined with a technical assistance program called the International Cooperation Administration in 1961 to form the U.S. Agency for International Development (AID).[7] AID is currently the major development assistance agency of the United States.

---

[5] OECD is an organization of western industrialized nations designed to promote economic growth and stability in member countries and to contribute to the development of the world economy. Member countries are Australia, Austria, Belgium, Canada, Denmark, Finland, France, Germany, Greece, Iceland, Ireland, Italy, Japan, Luxembourg, the Netherlands, New Zealand, Norway, Portugal, Spain, Sweden, Switzerland, Turkey, the United Kingdom, and the United States.

[6] Harry S Truman, "Inaugural Address of the President," Department of State Bulletin 33, Washington, D.C., January 1949, p. 125.

[7] See Elizabeth Morrison and Randall B. Purcell, *Players and Issues in U. S. Foreign Aid* (West Hartford, Conn.: Kumarian Press, 1988) for additional historical details.

TABLE 18-2
UNITED STATES AND WORLD OFFICIAL DEVELOPMENT ASSISTANCE (ODA), 1975–1989
(MILLIONS OF CURRENT U.S. DOLLARS)

Year	Total ODA	U.S. ODA	U.S. as % of total ODA
1975	13,585	4,007	29.5
1976	13,953	4,360	31.2
1977	15,733	4,682	29.8
1978	19,992	5,663	28.3
1979	22,820	4,684	20.5
1980	27,296	7,138	26.1
1981	25,568	5,782	22.6
1982	27,777	8,202	29.5
1983	27,590	8,081	29.3
1984	28,738	8,711	30.3
1985	29,429	9,403	32.0
1986	36,663	9,564	26.1
1987	41,595	9,115	21.9
1988	48,114	10,141	21.1
1989	46,679	7,659	16.4

Source: Joseph C. Wheeler, *Development Co-Operation: Efforts and Policies of the Members of the Development Assistance Committee, 1990 Report,* Organization for Economic Cooperation and Development, Paris, December 1990, and reports for earlier years.

During the 1950s, assistance was increasingly extended by the United Kingdom, France, the Netherlands, and Belgium to their former colonies. The list of donors grew during the 1960s and now includes most members of OECD and many members of the Organization of Petroleum Exporting Countries (OPEC).[8] While the United States provided almost 60 percent of total ODA in the early 1960s, it provided less than 20 percent by 1990. By 1989, Japan was providing more ODA than the United States, and France was providing almost as much (Table 18-3). In 1989, the United States had the lowest ratio of ODA to GNP of any OECD country, at 0.15 percent. The average for all OECD countries was 0.51 percent.[9]

Each donor country has its own internal agency for administering its bilateral (country-to-country) assistance programs. Some of the money and technical assistance is funneled through specific projects and other assistance through broader programs. Much of the direct assistance to agriculture comes through specific projects. While the agricultural component of total aid is large, support for agricultural assistance appears to have declined recently for several countries, particularly in Latin America.

[8] OPEC is a group of countries devoted to seeking agreement among themselves regarding selling prices and other issues related to oil exports. OPEC members include Algeria, Ecuador, Gabon, Indonesia, Iran, Iraq, Kuwait, Libya, Nigeria, Qatar, Saudi Arabia, the United Arab Emirates, and Venezuela.

[9] World Bank, *World Development Report 1991* (New York: Oxford University Press, 1991), p. 240.

TABLE 18-3
OFFICIAL DEVELOPMENT ASSISTANCE BY COUNTRY OF ORIGIN
(MILLIONS OF CURRENT U.S. DOLLARS)

Country	1960	1970	1980	1989
Australia	58.9	202.4	667	1,020
Austria	−0.1	19.1	178	283
Belgium	101.0	119.7	595	703
Canada	75.2	346.3	1,075	2,320
Denmark	5.5	59.1	481	937
Finland	—	—	110	706
France	848.3	911.0	4,162	7,450
Germany	351.0	599.0	3,567	4,949
Ireland	—	—	30	49
Italy	105.4	147.2	683	3,613
Japan	109.4	458.0	3,353	8,949
Netherlands	35.3	196.4	1,630	2,094
New Zealand	—	—	72	87
Norway	10.1	36.7	486	917
Portugal	36.9	41.1	—	—
Sweden	6.7	117.0	962	1,799
Switzerland	3.5	30.2	253	558
United Kingdom	407.0	446.9	1,854	2,587
United States	2,776.0	3,050.0	7,138	7,659
Total DAC Countries	4,930.1	6,840.1	27,296	46,679

Note: DAC is the Development Assistance Committee of OECD, whose members are shown above.
Source: Joseph C. Wheeler, *Development Co-Operation: Efforts and Policies of the Members of the Development Assistance Committee, 1990 Report,* Organization for Economic Cooperation and Development, Paris, December 1990, and reports for earlier years.

Not all development assistance is publicly funded or administered. Nongovernmental organizations (NGOs) are becoming increasingly significant sources of development assistance. Examples of NGOs are CARE, the Red Cross, Lutheran Relief Service, Catholic Relief, Oxfam, Save the Children, and a whole host of others. There is a wide range of types and sizes of NGO institutions. Many, but not all, are focused on community or microeconomic development. NGO projects tend to be small and designed to benefit the poorest of the poor. Some of the efforts are long-term and development-oriented while others provide short-term relief in crisis situations.

All NGOs are nonprofit, privately run institutions. While many, such as CARE, receive substantial public support, most depend heavily on private voluntary financial contributions. NGOs are based primarily in developed countries, but carry out their activities in developing countries. Several NGOs have religious affiliations.

In addition to publicly supported bilateral aid and assistance from NGOs, a variety of multilateral (multicountry) organizations provide significant financial and/or technical support to developing countries (see Table 18-4). The World Bank was created in 1944, followed shortly afterward by several other United Nations-supported agencies. A brief description of the major U.N. financial and technical assistance agencies is presented in Box 18-1.

TABLE 18-4
MAJOR DEVELOPMENT ASSISTANCE PROGRAMS

Multilateral financial network
 1 World Bank
 2 InterAmerican Development Bank
 3 African Development Bank
 4 Asian Development Bank
 5 European Development Fund
 6 United Nations Development Program (UNDP)
 7 World Food Programme (WFP)
 8 United Nations Children's Fund (UNICEF)
 9 International Fund for Agriculture and Development (IFAD)
10 Organization of Petroleum Exporting Countries (OPEC) Fund
11 Caribbean Development Bank

Bilateral financial assistance
 1 U.S. Agency for International Development (AID)
 2 Japanese Overseas Economic Cooperation Fund (OECF)
 3 Agencies in Germany, France, United Kingdom, and many other countries
 4. Nongovernmental Organizations (NGOs)
    (a) Foundations (Ford, Rockefeller, etc.)
    (b) Cooperative for American Relief Everywhere (CARE)
    (c) Catholic Relief
    (d) Many others

Technical assistance network
 1 United Nations Development Program
 2 Food and Agriculture Organization of the United Nations (FAO)
 3 Bilateral assistance programs listed above
 4 Private Assistance
 5 International Agricultural Research Centers (IARCs)
 6 Many others

The World Bank contains three major arms that together represent the single largest source of long-term multilateral economic development assistance. The first arm, the International Bank for Reconstruction and Development (IBRD), established in 1945, makes long-term loans at interest rates related to its own cost of borrowing, mostly for large-scale projects. The second arm, the International Development Association (IDA), established in 1960, makes loans only to the poorest LDCs (see Box 18-2 for an example of IDA lending). More than 90 percent of IDA lending goes to countries with an annual per capita income under $500. Loans from IDA have long repayment periods and concessional interest rates. The third arm, the International Finance Corporation (IFC), is a profit-making enterprise and is funded by capital from its 130 member countries. It makes loans to the private sector, to mixed (public/private) enterprises, and to government-owned agencies that channel financial assistance to the private sector. Since the late 1950s, regional development banks have been formed for Latin America, the Caribbean, Asia, and Africa. These banks make both concessional and nonconcessional loans.

The net financial receipts of developing countries for selected years between 1960 and 1987 are presented in Table 18-5. Total ODA has doubled in real terms

---

BOX 18-1

MAJOR UNITED NATIONS AGENCIES FOR FINANCIAL AND TECHNICAL
ASSISTANCE TO DEVELOPING COUNTRIES

The United Nations Development Programme (UNDP) is the central funding and coordinat-
ing mechanism within the United Nations for technical assistance to developing countries.
The United Nations Fund for Population Activities (UNFPA) helps countries gather demographic information, undertake family planning projects, and formulate population policies
and programs. The United Nations Children's Fund (UNICEF) provides technical and financial assistance to developing countries for programs that benefit children and for emergency
relief for mothers and children. The purpose of the Food and Agriculture Organization (FAO)
is to raise nutrition levels and standards of living by improving the production and distribution
of food and other commodities derived from farms, fisheries, and forests. It also helps
countries with food emergencies. The World Food Programme's (WFP) purpose is to
stimulate economic and social development through the use of food aid and to provide
emergency food relief. The World Health Organization (WHO) conducts immunization cam-
paigns, promotes and administers research, and provides technical assistance to improve
health systems in developing countries. The United Nations Education, Scientific, and
Cultural Organization promotes international intellectual cooperation in education, science,
culture, and communications. The UNDP, UNFPA, WFP and UNICEF are funded through
voluntary contributions, public and private, while FAO, WHO, and UNESCO are funded
primarily through assessments on member nations with some additional voluntary contributions and other sources of funds.

Source: Elizabeth Morrison and Randall B. Purcell, *Players and Issues in U.S. Foreign Aid* (West
Hartford, Conn.: Kumarian Press, 1988), pp. 41–45.

BOX 18-2

AN EXAMPLE OF IDA ASSISTANCE TO INDIA

In November 1987, the World Bank and its concessionary lending affiliate, the International
Development Association, approved a loan of $350 million to help India overcome the effects
of one of its worst droughts this century. The government's relief program included efforts to
minimize crop losses and provide emergency relief for those severely affected by the
drought. Estimates at the time of the drought indicated that about 93 million people had either
lost their jobs or had their incomes seriously affected.

The IDA loan was used specifically to finance imports of agro-industrial inputs (such as
oilseeds, veterinary medicines, and animal feed), petroleum and petroleum products, and
industrial equipment. The Bank advanced the Indian government an additional $100 million
to help farmers prepare the land for India's 1988 summer crop. The IDA program also
included a long-term food-supply strategy to help the country better prepare for future
droughts.

Source: World Bank News, vol. 6, no. 45, November 25, 1987 as reported in Elizabeth Morrison and
Randall B. Purcell, *Players and Issues in U. S. Foreign Aid* (West Hartford, Conn.: Kumarian Press, 1988),
p. 28.

TABLE 18-5
TOTAL NET RESOURCE RECEIPTS OF DEVELOPING COUNTRIES FROM ALL SOURCES,
1960–1987 (CONSTANT 1983 $ U.S. BILLIONS)

	1960	1970	1980	1987
Official development assistance	20.3	24.0	40.6	42.2
Concessional	19.5	22.2	36.1	37.0
Bilateral ODA	18.6	19.4	28.8	29.3
Multilateral ODA	0.9	2.8	7.3	7.7
Multilateral nonconcessional	0.8	1.9	4.6	5.2
Private voluntary contributions	—	2.3	2.2	2.7
Private lending	2.2	8.6	47.3	4.2
Private direct investment	6.5	9.7	9.9	15.4
Export credits	4.8	7.0	12.7	−0.5
Other	0.7	1.5	5.4	4.5
Total	34.8	53.1	118.1	68.5

Source: Anne O. Krueger, Constantine Michalopoulos, and Vernon W. Ruttan, *Aid and Development*
(Baltimore: Johns Hopkins University Press, 1989), p. 36.

(after taking into account inflation and exchange rate differences); most of the growth occurred in the 1970s. Multilateral aid and private direct investment have increased substantially in percentage terms, though bilateral ODA continues to be the largest means of transferring resources. Private lending increased dramatically during the 1970s and virtually dried up in the 1980s, causing total financial flows to decrease during the 1980s. This dramatic change in private lending behavior was discussed in the previous chapter in the context of the debt crisis.

In 1983 the ODA portion of total financial flows to developing countries was 87 percent for the least-developed countries, 66 percent for all low-income countries, 29 percent for lower-middle-income countries, and 14 percent for upper-middle-income countries.[10] ODA accounted for only about 1 to 5 percent of GNP in the low-income countries.

Effects of Foreign Assistance

The economic effects of development assistance on recipients can be assessed at the project, the sectoral, or the national levels. At the project level, rates of return have been calculated for individual projects such as in irrigation, flood control, roads, and agricultural research. For example, the World Bank has estimated that the rate of return on its IBRD loans from 1960 to 1980 was 17 percent and on its IDA loans, 18 percent.[11]

Given these high rates of return, questions are raised about why private lending has not been forthcoming, or why concessional loans are needed. Many

[10] Anne O. Krueger, Constantine Michalopoulos, and Vernon W. Ruttan, *Aid and Development* (Baltimore: Johns Hopkins University Press, 1989), p. 37.
[11] Ibid.

developing countries are unable to borrow at commercial terms due to imperfections in international capital markets. If the gestation period for the investment is very long or the investor cannot capture the stream of benefits (for example, for investments in roads, ports, and utilities), socially profitable investments may not be undertaken by private individuals. Poor countries often cannot borrow from private commercial sources for infrastructure investment despite high projected rates of return. This inability to borrow is particularly a problem for countries with a large overhang of previous debt. Thus, development assistance would seem to have an important role to play.

At the sectoral or national levels, development assistance theoretically can augment domestic savings, help provide foreign exchange, and minimize the adverse impacts of needed policy reforms. These effects can stimulate growth. Several studies have attempted to assess the impact of development assistance at the national level as it affects savings, investment, or growth. Generally, the results have been positive but, in many cases, inconclusive.[12] For example, Willis Peterson found a positive impact of development assistance to low-income countries, using data for 73 countries.[13] However, he found nonsignificant impacts for middle-income and centrally-planned economies.

The small size of aid relative to other capital sources, as described above, undoubtedly has contributed to many of the inconclusive findings about the effects of aid on growth. It is also difficult to measure the effects of aid without breaking aid down into its different types. For example, aid for infrastructure may have different impacts than aid for policy reform, or for emergency food relief.

Few studies have attempted to evaluate the effects of development assistance to the agricultural sector. One study for 98 countries did find a positive effect of foreign assistance to agriculture from 1975 to 1985, particularly in Asia. However, the effects of aid to agriculture in Latin America and the Middle East were nonsignificant.[14]

Effects on Donors Many donor countries believe that development assistance is effective in stimulating growth in developing countries, but ask whether the effects on their own countries are negative. In other words, they question whether their economic self-interest is served by aid. For example, farm groups and the farm press in the United States frequently express concern that foreign aid may be generating foreign competition.[15] Several studies have

[12] For more details, see Constantine Michalopoulos and Vasant Sukhatme, "The Impact of Development Assistance: Review of Quantitative Evidence," in Anne O. Krueger, Constantine Michalopoulos, and Vernon W. Ruttan (eds.), op. cit., Chap. 7.

[13] Willis L. Peterson, "Rates of Return on Capital: An International Comparison," *KYLOS,* vol. 42, 1989, pp. 203–217.

[14] See George W. Norton, Jaime Ortiz, and Philip G. Pardey, "The Impact of Foreign Assistance on Agricultural Growth," *Economic Development and Cultural Change,* vol. 40, July, 1992, pp. 775–786.

[15] See, for example, Joe Williamson, "American Farmers . . . First," *Southeast Farm Press,* April 2, 1986, p. 2.

been conducted to assess whether foreign aid to agriculture does indeed hurt U.S. farmers. These studies have found that for particular commodities in particular countries at particular stages of development, foreign competition is increased as a result of aid. However, they also have found that agriculture as a whole in donor countries is helped by foreign aid to agriculture in developing countries.[16]

The reason farmers in donor countries often benefit from aid to agriculture in developing countries is that agricultural growth in LDCs increases incomes, and these incomes, in turn, stimulate food demand. Middle-income countries, particularly, still have relatively high population growth rates and income elasticities of demand for food. Demands shift toward higher-quality grains and livestock products as incomes rise. Consequently, when agricultural production rises in these countries, if domestic economic policies permit that production growth to stimulate other sectors of the economy, the result is an expansion in food demand that must be met partially through food imports (see Box 18-3). Of course when countries eventually reach higher income status, their growth in food demand slows. If and when most of the currently developing countries reach that status, trade will be governed by comparative advantage and trade-distorting policies. Development assistance to agriculture will no longer be an issue.

In summary, while empirical evidence is not entirely conclusive about the effects of development assistance in general or to agriculture in particular, it appears that positive but modest gains are likely for both recipients and donors. It is unlikely that large gains will be realized except in a few small countries because aid usually represents a small portion of GDP.

FOOD AID

Food aid to developing countries has been an important dimension of foreign assistance since the mid-1950s. With a value of more than $3 billion per year, food aid constitutes nearly 10 percent of total ODA. About 45 percent of food aid is used to provide emergency relief in times of severe food shortages, 30 percent supports specific development projects, and the remaining 25 percent is program or nonproject food aid. The latter is given as hard currency assistance to buy imports of food, usually cereals, most often from the donor country.

The role and effects of food aid have been controversial because of food aid's many purposes. While food aid fulfulls a humanitarian and development mission, it also provides a means for donor countries to dispose of surplus commodities and to develop new markets. As with any foreign aid, food aid serves the foreign policy objectives of donors. While this multiplicity of objec-

[16] See, for example, Alain de Janvry, Elisabeth Sadoulet, and T. Kelley White, "Foreign Aid's Effect on U.S. Farm Exports," U.S. Department of Agriculture, Economic Research Service, Foreign Agricultural Economic Report Number 238, Washington, D.C., November 1989; and James P. Houck, "Link Between Agricultural Assistance and Agricultural Trade," *Agricultural Economics,* vol. 2, October 1988, pp. 158–166.

BOX 18-3

COUNTRIES WITH SUCCESS IN AGRICULTURE OFTEN INCREASE FOOD IMPORTS

The World Bank's *World Development Report 1991* lists 12 countries whose agricultural sectors grew at an annual rate of 4.3 percent or higher from 1980 to 1989. The report also lists cereal imports for those countries in 1974 and in 1989. In every case, cereal imports increased despite the relative success in agriculture.

| Country | Average annual growth rate (percentage 1980–1989) | | Cereal imports (thousands of metric tons) | | Total percentage increase in cereal imports |
	Agriculture	Overall GDP	1974	1989	1974 to 1989
Nepal	4.5	4.6	18	26	44
Burkina Faso	5.8	5.0	99	120	21
China	6.3	9.7	6033	14000	132
Pakistan	4.4	6.4	1274	2171	70
Togo	5.7	1.4	6	111	1750
Bhutan	5.8	8.1	3	20	567
Morocco	6.7	4.1	891	1329	49
Ecuador	4.3	1.9	152	536	253
Algeria	5.3	3.5	1816	7461	311
Iran	5.7	3.4	2076	6500	213
Oman	5.1	12.8	52	200	285

Source: World Bank, *World Development Report 1991* (New York: Oxford University Press, 1991), pp. 206 and 210.

---

tives has added instability over time to food aid allocations, it also has strengthened the political support for maintaining food-aid programs within the donor countries.

Critics of food aid have argued, among other things, that unrestricted cash donations would be preferable to food. While it is clear that recipients would prefer cash, many donors treat food aid as an addition to, rather than a component of, their economic assistance. It is highly unlikely that donor budgets would be expanded by the value of food aid if the latter were eliminated.

Food aid is provided both bilaterally and multilaterally. The United States has been the largest source of food aid since the enactment of the Agricultural Trade Development and Assistance Act of 1954, commonly referred to as Public Law (P.L.) 480. The U.S. share of total food assistance has been about 60 percent in recent years with the European Community contributing about

Food aid helped alleviate hunger in Ethiopia during the 1980s.

15 percent, Canada 10 percent, and other countries the rest.[17] About one-fourth of food aid is funneled through multilateral organizations, primarily the World Food Programme of the United Nations.

History of Food Aid

The history of food aid to developing countries is marked by shifting emphases on its multiple objectives. During the period of 1959 to 1965, the United States and Canada were particularly concerned about disposal of farm surpluses, developing markets for farm products, and providing emergency food relief. Most of the aid provided during this period was in grain, but several other products were given, including tobacco. In 1961, an amendment was added to P.L. 480 to permit food to be used for economic development instead of being restricted to emergency relief. Improved export markets, led by demand growth in developing countries, reinforced the objective that food aid helps develop markets.

In 1966, the name of P.L. 480 was changed to Food for Peace. The era from 1966 to 1972 was a period of heavy use of food aid for emergency relief, particularly in drought-struck areas of South Asia. Self-help of recipients also was promoted during this period. The European Community and Canada

---

[17] Food aid once represented about one-half of U.S. grain exports, but in recent years it has declined to less than 10 percent.

increased their shipments of food aid for emergency relief in this period. This expansion followed the Food Aid Convention in 1967 which significantly broadened the developed country base of support for food aid.[18] The 1966 to 1972 period might be called the idealistic era of food aid.

Unfortunately, any idealism with respect to food aid programs was pretty much destroyed by the cutbacks in food aid that followed the food price increases in 1972 to 1975. The United States had depleted its grain surplus by exporting commercially to the Soviet Union and other countries. From 1972 to 1973, U.S. commercial grain exports doubled and the volume of food aid fell in 1974 to its lowest level since the enactment of P.L. 480. Furthermore, during this period half of all U. S. food aid went to South Vietnam and Cambodia as a result of U.S. involvement in those countries and restrictions on other types of economic assistance.

In 1975, the U.S. Congress instituted more humanitarian and development criteria for receiving food aid by passing the International Development and Food Assistance Act (see Box 18-4). This legislation called for increased food aid to the poorest countries. The remainder of the 1970s also saw increasing food aid quantities from EC countries. However, the use of food aid for political purposes also increased after 1975. For example, U.S. food aid to Bangladesh declined from 1.15 million tons in 1975 to 0.34 million tons in 1985, while food aid to Egypt increased from 0.58 million tons to 2.00 million. This increase to Egypt was directly linked to the Camp David Peace Agreement signed with Israel in 1979. Food aid quantities increased in the mid-1980s in response to severe drought problems in Ethiopia, the Sudan, and other Sub-Saharan African countries. In the 1960s, most food aid went to Asia and Latin America. By the mid-1980s Sub-Saharan Africa was absorbing as much food aid as the much more populous Asia.

Types of Food Aid Programs Today

Emergency food aid grabs most of the headlines as it relieves crises associated with droughts in Ethiopia and the Sudan, flooding in Bangladesh, and, recently, political upheaval in the former Soviet Union. Emergency food aid has also played a significant role in feeding refugees from Afghanistan, Iraq, and other countries in recent years. This short-term food aid is essential for reducing acute hunger problems. The possibilities of using food aid to foster long-term development, however, are more closely linked to program or project food aid.

Program food aid is, in many respects, similar to more general financial assistance, as it provides currency to buy imports, in this case food, that can be sold or otherwise distributed in the domestic market. This aid fosters the development of marketing linkages with the donors, it helps the recipients save

---

[18] Shahla Shapouri and Margaret Missinen, "Food Aid: Motivation and Allocation Criteria," U.S. Department of Agriculture, Economic Research Service, Foreign Agricultural Economic Report No. 240, Washington, D.C., February 1990.

BOX 18-4

THE UNITED STATES P.L. 480 FOOD-AID PROGRAM

Since 1954, most U.S. food aid activities have been coordinated under P.L. 480. Numerous amendments and extensions have been added to the original act, but currently the major provisions fall under the three following titles:

Title I is the largest title, accounting for roughly 60 percent of food aid. Recipient governments buy grain on credit with interest rates of 3 percent or less over 20 to 40 years, repayable in local currency. These governments can sell the grain internally and use the profits for development. The low interest rates and long repayment period means that almost 70 percent of the food aid loan is a grant.

Title II involves gifts of food for emergency relief and to combat hunger. The food is given to and distributed by private agencies such as CARE who use the food for infant feeding programs and for mother and child health programs in addition to emergency distribution. In a recent year about 70 percent of CARE's budget was P.L. 480. Shipping and labor are paid for by the U.S. government. Food given under Title II also is used in food-for-work programs.

Title III was added in 1975 and involves using food aid to meet specific development goals. Countries eligible for Title I aid can enter into a Title III agreement. This agreement says that the proceeds from the sales of the commodities will be used for development purposes. As long as the funds are used in this way, the commodity loans are forgiven. Title III thus becomes a grant. The recipient country, however, still must pay the transportation costs.

In addition to these three titles, Section 401 of the P.L. 480 Act requires that the Secretary of Agriculture determine that there are adequate U.S. supplies of these commodities.

---

foreign exchange, and the funds generated by the sales can be used for development. Some donors participate in determining how the funds generated by commodity sales are used. Donors may insist that funds be used for investments in the agricultural sector or to support specific policy changes affecting agriculture. Some of the recent food aid shipments to the former Soviet Union and to Sub-Saharan African countries were intended to soften the adjustments to structural changes in those economies.

Project food aid is aimed at meeting specific development objectives. Projects tend to be multiyear, to be targeted at nutritionally vulnerable individuals or groups, and may involve food in exchange for work on the project. Donor and recipient countries agree on who will be targeted by the project, the amount of food each individual receives, the delivery system for the food, and the design, implementation, and monitoring of the project activities.[19] Most of the projects involve the rural sector and can vary in size from a few hundred thousand dollars to $100 million or more. Food aid projects often involve forestry development, soil conservation and watershed management, resettlement projects, training, development of irrigation works, and construction and maintenance of rural roads.

---

[19] See Robert Chase, ''Commodity Aid for Agricultural Development,'' in *Trade, Aid, and Policy Reform*, Colleen Roberts (ed.), World Bank, Washington, D.C., 1988, pp. 199–204.

In most of these projects, food aid is one component of a larger activity, and the food can be used in a variety of ways. The food may partially or fully pay the wages of those working on the project; it may be used as an incentive to encourage participation in training, visiting a health clinic, or undertaking a community development activity; or it may be used to support the budget of an institution. The food aid received usually can be sold. Evaluations of food aid projects have been mixed. These projects require technical support and extensive and careful administration.

Effects of Food Aid

The positive and negative effects of food aid on recipient countries have been studied and debated for many years. On the positive side, food provides real resources that can be used to expand investment and employment. Food aid can have a disproportionate but positive effect on disadvantaged groups, notably by supporting specific nutrition or food-for-work projects or by providing food to the poor for free or at concessional prices. Food also can be used to help recipient governments support storage and stabilization schemes to provide a small buffer against poor production years.

Food aid also can have adverse effects on the recipients. These potential adverse effects of food aid can occur in a number of ways: (1) disincentive effects on local agricultural production through reduced prices because of greater supply, (2) dependency effects because the government can substitute food aid for agricultural development programs, and (3) the uncertainty of food aid quantities from year to year.

Food aid is used in Kenya to help pay labor for road construction.

The disincentive issue has been examined empirically in several studies.[20] In theory, additional supplies could depress food prices and discourage production. Some empirical studies have found this to be the case, but many other studies have not. The disincentive effect is minimized if food aid is given or sold to those who otherwise could not afford the food. Transferring food is like transferring income. The quantity of the aid compared to the country's overall food production is important. For example, it appears that there has been a disincentive effect in Egypt due to the large quantities of aid shipped, but it is extremely difficult to sort out the impact of food aid from the many policy-induced distortions.

The idea that food aid creates dependency has not been examined as frequently. Food aid is no different from other aid in that, by providing resources, it may lead to less effort to raise revenues domestically or to promote agricultural development. Conditions are usually placed by donors on program aid that minimize this possibility. A second part of the dependency argument is that over the long run, food aid leads to more food imports and changes in preferences away from domestically produced foods. There is some evidence that this preference effect may be occurring, although it is difficult to separate changes induced by food aid from those that occur because of income growth.

Uncertainty in food aid deliveries has been criticized. Many donors have moved to longer-term, programmed food aid, a policy which improves its development impact and removes some of the year-to-year uncertainty.

Food aid can be used in a positive way by recipients to further both agricultural and overall economic development. And, of course it can play a major life saving role during short-term emergencies. It appears that the potential positive development role of food aid has not been fully exploited, though some efforts are under way to improve its development contribution. Efforts made by the U.S. government to maximize the development impact of P.L. 480 commodities are described in Box 18-5.

Most donor countries find public opinion is generally supportive of food aid. And, food aid is not as costly as it may seem because it reduces the costs associated with price-support programs in developed countries. However, stronger multi-year commitments are needed if food aid is to be a more effective development tool.

ADMINISTRATION OF FOREIGN ASSISTANCE

Foreign assistance is administered through a wide array of bilateral and multilateral public agencies and through private organizations (Table 18-4). Once the aid reaches the recipient country, the government usually plays an important role in implementing the program or project for which the aid is intended. If

---

[20] See S. T. Maxwell and H. W. Singer, "Food Aid to Developing Countries: A Survey," *World Development*, vol. 7, 1979, pp. 223–247, for a summary of the results of 21 studies.

BOX 18-5

EFFORTS TO IMPROVE DEVELOPMENT IMPACT OF P.L. 480 TITLE III

The U.S. Agricultural Development and Trade Act of 1990, an amendment to P.L. 480, focuses on the use of Title III commodities as an integral part of the recipient country's development plan. Multiyear commitments are encouraged, along with maximum integration into other development assistance programs. This aid must be used to meet one of the following objectives: food security, the privatization of food systems, support of nutrition improvement or child survival initiatives, or other activities to promote broad-based, equitable, and sustainable economic development.

The guidelines for negotiation of new Title III agreements emphasize close evaluation of country needs combined with analysis of how the development plan will meet those needs and how the Title III proceeds fit into the development plan. Maximum involvement of both domestic and international NGOs is encouraged. The law thus attempts to enhance the development impact of P.L. 480.

---

basic infrastructure is missing, incentive structures are severely distorted, or the government bureaucracy is highly inefficient, effective administration of economic assistance programs can be extremely difficult.

How Aid Is Administered

Most of the bilateral assistance agencies such as AID maintain offices in the recipient countries staffed with people who provide the link between the home office (and the policies of the donor government) and the local officials. Operating with a budget established for that country by the donor, programs and projects are designed, implemented, and evaluated by personnel in that office, by people sent from the donor country, and by local counterparts in the recipient country.

Bilateral foreign assistance often comes with strings attached. These strings can involve policy changes by the recipient country or simply a requirement that goods and services procured with the aid money be obtained from the donor country. For example, 75 percent of U.S. Title I shipments must go on American ships. In other cases, the donor government might make the provision of aid contingent on policy reforms or political changes.

Multilateral aid is administered by the appropriate international organization, which usually maintains an office in the recipient country. Assistance often is earmarked for specific purposes, and projects are designed and evaluated by teams of experts. Multilateral donors such as the World Bank often have more leverage in policy discussions than bilateral donors both because of the greater resources typically involved and because they are "owned" in part by the recipient countries that are also bank members. Also, multilateral donors may be regarded as having less political bias than bilateral donors.

Foreign assistance, especially food aid, may be channeled through non-governmental organizations. These NGOs generally have to spend an enormous amount of time and resources raising money. NGOs based in the United States receive about one-fourth of their resources from the government, but the remainder comes as donations from private donors.

Improving Aid Effectiveness

The effectiveness of foreign assistance in promoting development in LDCs could be improved by several changes on the part of both donors and recipients. Bilateral assistance would be more effective with reduced tying of aid to procurement of donor goods and services, by longer-term commitments, by reduced bureaucracy in many cases, by increased coordination with other donors, and by increased attention to the development and poverty alleviation goals and less to narrow political self-interest goals. For example, the total U.S. foreign assistance budget was recently held hostage to the issue of whether U.N. supported family planning activities might provide information on abortion.

Multilateral organizations need increased flexibility in many of their programs that support technical assistance. There is a need to improve recruitment and promotion practices in many of these organizations so as to reduce the importance of political influence. Many of the U.N. agencies need better evaluation and budgeting procedures.

Many NGOs need to improve their relations with local governments. They need to refine their ability to monitor and evaluate projects. Interactions with official development agencies also can be improved in many cases. Coordination of the activities of various bilateral, multilateral, and NGO aid sources could help increase aid effectiveness. This coordination would probably have to be provided by a multilateral agency working with the local government.

Many recipient countries could make more effective use of foreign assistance with more enlightened macroeconomic and sectoral economic policies. The differences in the relative effectiveness of aid to Côte d'Ivoire and Ghana in the 1960s and 1970s helps make this point. Ghana was significantly ahead of Côte d'Ivoire by most development measures in the late 1950s. Côte d'Ivoire followed policies that guided rather than controlled the private sector. Ghana pursued policies of import substitution and intervened strongly in almost every sector of the economy. The two countries received similar levels of aid, but by the early 1980s, Côte d'Ivoire had surpassed Ghana in most indicators of development.[21]

Streamlining the bureaucracies in many developing countries could significantly improve the effectiveness of foreign aid. In many cases bureaucracies

---

[21] Vernon W. Ruttan, "Solving the Foreign Aid Vision Thing," *Challenge,* vol. 34, May–June 1991, p. 43.

are a colonial legacy designed to improve accountability. However, they often merely reduce government efficiency and provide opportunities for corruption.

Foreign assistance can play a significant role in agricultural and overall economic development. With a stronger multiyear commitment on the part of donors, and policy and bureaucratic reform on the part of recipients, greater returns can be realized by both groups from foreign assistance programs. There are several examples of aid being used successfully to soften the adverse impacts of macroeconomic and policy reforms. Using aid to create safety nets for needed reforms can satisfy humanitarian, economic, and political goals.

SUMMARY

Foreign development assistance in support of agriculture in developing countries has been substantial, taken many forms, and generated considerable debate. The rationale for foreign aid rests on humanitarian, political, and economic self-interest grounds. As a result, aid does not always go to where the need is greatest. Economic aid may come in the form of financial assistance, food aid, or technical assistance. Some foreign aid comes as loans at below-market interest rates. To be classified as official development assistance by the Development Assistance Committee of OECD, the assistance must have at least a 25 percent grant element. Foreign aid to agriculture includes aid for agricultural research and extension, irrigation projects, rural roads, agricultural policy assistance, and many other items.

The United States used to be by far the largest bilateral donor, but the share of total ODA coming from the United States has steadily declined. Japan is now the largest bilateral donor and the United States gives the smallest percentage of its GNP of any OECD donor. Aid is also funneled through multilateral agencies and NGOs.

Food aid to developing countries has been an important dimension of foreign assistance since the mid-1950s. It constitutes about 10 percent of total ODA, provides emergency relief in times of severe food shortages, and supports specific development projects and programs. Food aid provides a means for donor countries to dispose of surpluses, develop new markets, and pursue foreign policy objectives.

Most U.S. food aid is provided through P.L. 480. The effects of food aid programs on recipients can be both positive and negative. Food aid provides real resources, helps meet the nutritional needs of the poor, and can be used to stabilize food availability. However, food aid can also create a disincentive to produce if not properly administered. Recipient countries also may become dependent on food aid. Aid effectiveness could be improved if fewer strings were attached, there were increased coordination among donors, and more attention were paid to needs than to politics. Developing countries could improve aid effectiveness by improving the policy environment and standardizing their currencies.

IMPORTANT TERMS AND CONCEPTS

Bilateral aid
Concessional interest rates
Dependency effect of aid
Disincentive effect of aid
Economic self-interest
Food aid
Foreign development assistance
International Bank for
  Reconstruction and Development
International Development
  Association

International Finance Corporation
Multilateral aid
Nongovernmental organization
Official development assistance
Point Four Program
Public Law 480
World Bank
U. S. Agency for International
  Development
World Food Programme

LOOKING AHEAD

This chapter concludes the section of the book concerned with macroeconomic and international issues affecting development. The book concludes in the next chapter with a discussion of how the various components required for agricultural development can be combined in an overall strategy. An assessment of future development prospects is provided, and suggestions are made for how you as individuals can contribute to solving the world food-poverty-population problem.

QUESTIONS FOR DISCUSSION

1 What is the rationale for foreign development assistance?
2 What are the major types of foreign development assistance?
3 What are some of the major effects of foreign development assistance on recipients and donors?
4 Distinguish between bilateral and multilateral aid.
5 Give several examples of foreign aid to agriculture.
6 How do NGOs differ from official sources of foreign development assistance?
7 What are the three major arms of the World Bank and how do they differ?
8 Which country is currently the largest bilateral donor of foreign aid?
9 Which OECD donor country gives the smallest amount of foreign aid as a percentage of GNP?
10 Why might foreign development assistance help U.S. farmers?
11 What are the objectives of food aid?
12 What is the case for and against food aid?
13 How have food aid programs changed over time?
14 What is the difference between program and project food aid?
15 How do the three Titles of P.L. 480 differ?
16 How might the effectiveness of foreign development assistance be improved?

RECOMMENDED READINGS

de Janvry, Alain, Elisabeth Sadoulet, and T. Kelley White, "Foreign Aid's Effect on U.S. Farm Exports," U.S. Department of Agriculture, Economic Research Service, Foreign Agriculture Economic Report Number 238, Washington, D.C., November 1989.

Houck, James P., "Link Between Agricultural Assistance and Agricultural Trade," *Agricultural Economics,* vol. 2, October 1988, pp. 158–166.

Krueger, Anne O., "Aid in the Development Process," *World Bank Research Observer,* vol. 1, January 1986, pp. 57–78.

Krueger, Anne O., Constantine Michalopoulos, and Vernon W. Ruttan, *Aid and Development* (Baltimore: Johns Hopkins University Press, 1989).

Maxwell, S. J. and H. W. Singer, "Food Aid to Developing Countries: A Survey," *World Development,* vol. 7, 1979, pp. 225–247.

Mellor, John W., "Food Aid and Nutrition," *American Journal of Agricultural Economics,* vol. 62, December 1980, pp. 979–983.

Morrison, Elizabeth and Randall B. Purcell, *Players and Issues in U.S. Foreign Aid* (West Hartford, Conn.: Kumarian Press, 1988).

Ruttan, Vernon W., "Why Foreign Assistance," *Economic Development and Cultural Change,* vol. 37, January 1989, pp. 411–424.

Ruttan, Vernon W., "Solving the Foreign Aid Vision Thing," *Challenge,* vol. 34, May–June 1991, pp. 41–46.

Shapouri, Shahla and Margaret Missinen, "Food Aid: Motivation and Allocation Criteria," U.S. Department of Agriculture, Economic Research Service, Agricultural Economic Report Number 240, Washington, D.C., February 1990.

CHAPTER 19

LESSONS AND PERSPECTIVES

Yes the numbers and needs are appalling. No, there are no simple and instant solutions . . . however, there still remains . . . some room for a "bias for hope" . . . because what individual people choose to do about development does make a difference.

Johnston and Clark[1]

THIS CHAPTER

1 Summarizes how the various components required for agricultural development can be combined to increase agricultural productivity, and how those productivity gains must in turn be combined with an employment-oriented industrial policy for broad-based economic development
2 Discusses how to use principles discussed in this book to assess future prospects for agricultural development in less-developed countries
3 Suggests ways that individuals can help solve the food-poverty-population problem in the world

AN INTEGRATED APPROACH TO AGRICULTURAL DEVELOPMENT

It is easy to be pessimistic about prospects for solving the widespread poverty and hunger problems in developing countries. Most countries in Sub-Saharan Africa have stagnated or declined for almost 30 years. Latin American coun-

---

[1] Bruce F. Johnston and William C. Clark, *Redesigning Rural Development: A Strategic Perspective* (Baltimore: Johns Hopkins University Press, 1982), p. 270.

tries suffered severe setbacks on the path to development during the 1980s. Population growth remains rapid in many already densely populated Asian countries. Concerns for the global environment have focused attention on the growing problem of resource degradation in all developing regions. Over the past 40 years numerous policy prescriptions have been suggested, yet none has been universally successful. Import substitution policies, land reform, foreign aid, education, privatization, investment in large-scale industries, rural development projects, farming-systems research, and many other solutions have been offered. Some of these suggestions have contributed to the development process; others have not. Blame for slow progress often is laid at the doorstep of more-developed countries, sometimes with justification.

While economic development has been painfully slow and uneven, there is certainly room for guarded optimism. Several lessons have been learned about what it takes to stimulate agricultural and overall economic development. One of these lessons is that there are no panaceas. Development requires a mix of technical and institutional changes that work only in combination. The exact mix varies between countries, and policies appropriate for one environment may not necessarily be so for another. A second lesson is that developing countries are primarily responsible for their own development, but interdependence in trade and capital flows means that developed-country policies can assist or retard that development.

In *Introduction to Economics of Agricultural Development,* you have examined the dimensions of world food-income population problems (see top of Fig. 19-1). You have considered the interconnections among these problems and their linkages to health, nutrition, literacy, and the environment. There is enough total food in the world at the moment, but hunger is caused by distributional problems that are, in many cases, related to poverty. There are short-term food crises and long-term or chronic malnutrition. You have considered economic development theories, the role of agriculture in those theories, and the nature of existing agricultural systems. You have learned that developing-country farmers tend to be relatively efficient at what they do, but have low productivity because of their limited access to resources and their existing technological and institutional environments. Having learned something about the dimensions of the problem, the role of agriculture in economic development theories, and the nature of agriculture in LDCs, you then examined several components of the development process. Let's review below the interrelationships among those components, and assess where the need is greatest for additional insights with respect to the development process.

Technical and Institutional Change in Agriculture

In the 1950s, many development experts felt that the keys to agricultural development were capital investment and the transfer of technologies from more-developed countries. By the 1960s and 1970s, it was clear that technology transfers and capital investment had a role to play, but that many other factors

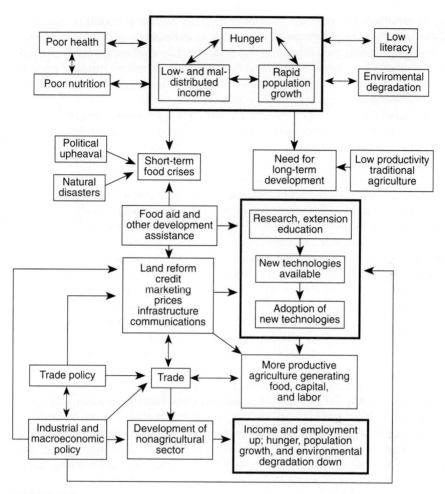

FIGURE 19-1
The hunger problem and the solution process.

were equally or more important. Differences in resource bases across countries meant that indigenous research and extension were vitally important. Education was required if countries were to domestically produce, adapt, transfer, and receive new technologies. By the 1990s, countries that were successful in agricultural development had put in place a research and technology transfer system that included: (1) indigenous agricultural research stations and educational institutions, (2) a mechanism for linking those stations to on-farm research and testing, and (3) ties between the national research system and the international agricultural research and training network.

As important as indigenous capacity for agricultural research and extension is, the last 30 years have also demonstrated the need for a whole series of institutional reforms related to the agricultural sector. These reforms have been proven important not only because of their influence on production incentives and the distribution of economic gains, but also because of their influence on the types of technologies produced and adopted. Land reform, improved credit policies, marketing system development, nondiscriminatory pricing policies, and incentive systems to reduce environmental externalities are examples of the institutional changes that may be required.

New technologies are not gifts of nature, and institutional changes do not magically appear. New technologies require research investments, and the levels and types of technologies produced and subsequently adopted are influenced by changes in relative prices of inputs and outputs. Institutional changes also are induced by changes in relative prices and by technical change.

The logic of the induced technical and institutional change theories and their apparent empirical verification in several countries, particularly along the Pacific rim, give cause for optimism. However, the failure of many countries to follow a path of sustained development has forced economists to broaden the induced innovation theory. This broadening has come by incorporating transactions costs and collective action into the theory.

Transactions costs refer to the costs of information, of adjusting a fixed-asset base, and of negotiating, monitoring, and enforcing contracts. The fact that information is not perfect and is costly to acquire, and the fact that people are willing to exploit their situation at the expense of others, have received particular attention. If one group has greater access to information than another, that group can act collectively to press for policies or new technologies that benefit it at the expense of others.

If a small wealthy elite with large landholdings finds it cheaper to acquire information and act collectively, it may press for technical and institutional changes for personal benefit at the expense of the masses. The elite may press for changes that not only distribute income in its favor, but reduce the agricultural growth rate because the resulting technologies and policies may not be appropriate for the resource base in the country.

Factors that can help reduce transactions costs are those factors that reduce information costs. Improved roads and communications infrastructure are examples. Education is critical. Land reform can help in many countries, as can institutional change to enhance contracting, to improve the legal infrastructure, and to provide certain types of regulations.[2] Freer markets to provide efficient price signals to individual farmers also should help.

Markets are generally held to be the best means of providing signals to actors. In developing countries, however, market imperfections due to transactions costs, unequal asset distributions, and other factors are the norm. Some government involvement is legitimate and necessary to reduce these imperfections and allow the markets to work. Government involvement can be justified to provide ''public goods'' and to redistribute income in accordance with

---

[2] For example, regulations may be needed to reduce externalities. These regulations may be particularly important for avoiding environmental externalities.

Young boys in Guatemala.

society's wishes. Critics of government involvement often maintain that government failures are worse than the market failures that the involvement is designed to correct. Government involvement need not give this result.

Macroeconomic and International Institutional Changes

In the 1950s and 1960s (and to some extent before and after) several economists in developing countries recommended policies that discouraged agricultural exports and encouraged production of goods that would substitute for imports. The argument for these policies was based on potential or perceived exploitation of developing countries by more-developed countries for reasons discussed in Chaps. 6 and 16. However, countries that integrated more closely into international markets tended to develop more rapidly than those that closed or isolated their economies. The more rapid development was due in part to the lower level of rent-seeking behavior and corruption as well as the increased efficiency gains from trade and specialization.

Some of the countries that discriminated against agricultural trade encouraged capital imports. Thus, capital-intensive industries frequently developed in labor-abundant countries. These industries placed a drag on economic development because human resources, freed up by increases in agricultural productivity, were underemployed. This tendency to develop capital-intensive industries may have been induced in part by transactions costs and collective action, but also by a perceived need to imitate more-developed countries.

In recent years, several developing countries have suffered from heavy external indebtedness. This problem has forced some countries to reform their policies in ways that may spur longer-run economic growth. The debt overhang is so large for several Latin American and African countries, however, that unless significant debt reduction takes place on the part of those holding the loans, development will be impeded for years to come. Official debt can be rescheduled through the Paris Club and by multilateral organizations. However, commercial debt reduction will require an improved international oversight facility to reduce the free rider problem that currently exists.

Increased efforts by several developing countries to reduce overvalued exchange rates and to phase out policies such as export taxes will be required to stimulate agricultural growth. Phasing out export taxes, however, will necessitate new mechanisms for generating government revenues, such as land or income taxes. Such taxes become somewhat more feasible as information flows improve in a country. New institutions will be needed along with increased government responsibilities. Reduced trade restrictions by developed countries would also help developing countries. Increased regional economic integration among LDCs can also play a positive role in development.

Foreign Assistance

Economic development assistance can help relieve short-term food crises and can contribute to longer-term development. Emergency food aid is essential for averting famine following natural disasters and major political upheavals. Longer-term financial aid could help to reduce the debt problem in several countries and provide real resources for development.

Aid effectiveness could be improved by longer-term commitments and increased donor coordination. Less tying of aid to factors such as procurement from donor sources but increased tying of aid to institutional changes that eliminate distortions or reduce transactions costs would help. International development agencies should internalize the notion that food aid is a development tool, and not just a means of disposing of developed-country surpluses. These two purposes of food aid need not conflict.

Coordinated international action has been successful in dealing with some very specific development problems. Worldwide immunization efforts, coordinated by WHO, have significantly reduced deaths due to common childhood diseases. Concerted efforts to provide food to famine victims have reduced famine mortalities. Similar international coordination could be effective in reducing debts, providing assistance for policy reforms, and for other specific actions. Because development needs and the impacts of different interventions vary from country to country, international actions to promote growth have tended to be less successful than those used to address specific short-run problems.

In summary, it is clear that many pieces are needed for a country to solve its development puzzle. Enhanced information flows are vitally important for agricultural development. More labor-intensive industrial growth is needed in several countries if the employment problem is to be solved.

ASSESSING FUTURE PROSPECTS

Several countries in Asia have grown at relatively rapid rates for almost two decades, but masses of impoverished people still live in Asia. Latin American countries that grew in the 1960s and 1970s stagnated in the 1980s. Most Sub-Saharan African countries have grown very slowly, stagnated, or declined for the past 30 years. Hunger problems persist despite increased food production per capita in the world over the past 40 years. Environmental problems have grown worse in several countries as well. What does the future hold for reducing hunger, poverty, population growth, and environmental problems? Let's consider some of the underlying forces at work.

Supply and Demand for Food

The real price of food in the world has trended downward for several years as supply growth has outstripped demand growth. The major long-run supply shifters are new technologies, while the major demand shifters are population and income growth. As we look to the future, population will continue to grow, but the *rate* of population growth will continue to fall. Incomes have increased rapidly in several Asian countries, including China with its massive population base. Asia has two-thirds of the world's population and, as a region, the best chance of continued supply increases due to research-induced technical change. Food production per capita will likely continue to increase in Asia as supply shifts outpace demand shifts, although the magnitude of this increase is a bit uncertain (Box 19-1). There will be increased diversification away from rice, however, as diets change with higher incomes.

In Latin America, increased food production per capita is likely, but at the slow rate of the 1980s due to continued debt problems that limit public investments in agriculture. Population growth rates have already declined from their peaks in the 1960s and 1970s, facilitating this per capita increase.

Unfortunately, many Sub-Saharan African countries will continue to experience stagnant per capita growth in food production. Some increased investments in education and in agricultural research systems have been realized, but population growth rates are currently near their peaks in many countries. If small income increases can be realized, population growth may decelerate, but environmental problems appear to have already degraded the resource base in parts of the Sahel to the point of reducing productivity.

Institutional Changes

Improved information technologies and infrastructure development have improved information flows in some developing countries. These improvements may create pressures for political and institutional changes; changes that offer favorable opportunities for development. Reduced transactions costs that result would induce the development of technologies that are better suited to the relative resource scarcities of the countries. More market-oriented policies

---

BOX 19-1

THE PROSPECTS FOR CEREAL TECHNOLOGIES

The spectacular bursts in yield potential from new varieties of rice and wheat that began the Green Revolution have not been repeated. Rice yields on experimental farms have not grown dramatically since the introduction of IR-8 in 1966. However, the difference between yields on the best farms and the yields on experiment stations has shrunk dramatically since 1970, particularly in Asia. This reduced difference is due to widespread irrigation, high application of fertilizer, and good management. Future gains in rice production must come increasingly from rainfed-upland and deep-water areas.

The prospects for wheat and maize are more optimistic. Centro de Mejoramiento de Maiz y Trigo (CIMMYT) reports a continuing increase in the yield potential of wheat of about one percent annually. Substantial progress has been made toward breeding in disease resistance, especially against wheat leaf-rust. Yield growth for wheat in less favorable conditions has been less spectacular. High-yielding varieties for low-rainfall marginal areas are limited, and there are virtually no new varieties for the lowland humid tropics. Major breakthroughs in these areas may pave the way for a technology-driven boom in wheat yields. Maize shows the most promise. There is a large gap between experiment station and farmer's yields, and weed control seems to be the critical problem. Human-based solutions to weed problems provide opportunities for increased employment while increasing maize yields.

In terms of genetic engineering and other biotechnology, the outlook is less certain. It is unlikely that any single experiment is likely to produce a major breakthrough—such as nitrogen fixation among grasses. However, many small improvements, such as increased disease and drought resistance, hold some promise.

Source: Walter P. Falcon, "Future Links Between U.S. Agriculture and the World Food Economy," *Journal of Production Agriculture,* vol. 3(3), 1990, pp. 269–273.

---

may continue to create efficiency gains, as they have in Asia. There is evidence that some governments in Latin America and Africa have laid the groundwork for these types of gains as well.

The willingness of more-developed countries to provide foreign assistance and international institutional changes to help poor countries may be reduced by the large fiscal deficits in the United States and several other developed countries. The fall of communism in Eastern Europe and the breakup of the Soviet Union has reduced political pressures on Western governments to help LDCs for the purpose of keeping those countries out of Soviet influence. The increased aid burden to the Soviet Republics and Eastern Europe may divert assistance away from other regions. Diversion of aid from Latin America and Asia are likely to be the most severe.

The relatively wealthy countries of the world must resist isolationist temptations. Many of the security, income, hunger, and environmental problems require a supranational decision-making process. In order to strengthen the United Nations agencies that could make these decisions, developed countries will need to increase their contributions to official development assistance. If all countries with per capita incomes in excess of $10,000 per year spent 1 percent of their GNP on official development assistance, $140 billion dollars would be available annually to assist developing countries. This amount represents roughly three times the current level of assistance.

HOW YOU CAN HELP

You as individuals can do a great deal to help solve hunger, poverty, ill health, environmental degradation, and other development problems. Some of you can get involved directly through working for grass-roots organizations in developing countries. The U.S. Peace Corps is an example, but there are many others. Spending time living and working in a developing country can greatly improve your understanding of development problems. We are each captive of the pictures in our mind, and living in a developing country provides a more accurate picture of the world.

Getting directly involved in influencing the fortunes of others can bring you a feeling of significance or satisfaction. The frustrations of working with desperately poor people are many. If you are not an optimist, you may not want to try. However, if you are adventurous, flexible, somewhat persistent, and like to bite off more than you can chew, you may want to consider working at a grass-roots level in a developing country. You can gain a certain satisfaction when you chew successfully even a small part of what you bite off.

Some of you can go to graduate school and educate yourselves to become animal scientists, plant breeders, plant pathologists, entomologists, agricultural

People in developing countries can benefit from grass-roots help.

economists, soil scientists, microbiologists, or some other type of agricultural scientist needed to help solve world food, income, and environmental problems. Employment opportunities exist for rewarding careers at universities, in international agricultural research centers, national research centers, and private firms. Until the world's population stabilizes, the battle to keep world food production increasing at roughly 2 to 3 percent per year will continue.

Most of you will take very different career paths, but the opportunity always exists to contribute to solving poverty problems through financial contributions to private voluntary organizations. All of you can strive to keep informed about what is happening in the world outside your state and country. You can try to keep politicians informed and let them know that you support foreign assistance contributions to countries where needs are greatest.

SUMMARY

In this chapter, but also in the whole book, we have stressed the interrelatedness of hunger, population, and poverty problems. There are no panaceas, but a set of interconnected pieces to a development puzzle. We have learned over the years what many of these pieces are. In this chapter we stressed particularly the importance of enhanced-information flows if broad-based development is to occur. Open economies, employment-based industrial policies, and development policies that do not discriminate against agriculture are essential. For developed countries, now is the time for renewed commitment to finding solutions to development problems.

IMPORTANT TERMS AND CONCEPTS

Agricultural scientist
Enhanced information flows
Feeling of significance
Grassroots organization
Interdependence

No panacea
Supply and demand shifters
Supranational decision-making
    process

QUESTIONS FOR DISCUSSION

1 Why might there be room for guarded optimism with respect to future agricultural and economic development?
2 Describe the interconnectedness among the pieces that can contribute to solving the development puzzle.
3 How has the theory of induced technical and institutional innovation been broadened in recent years and why?
4 What factors can help reduce transactions costs?
5 Why have relatively open economies grown more rapidly than relatively closed economies?
6 What factors will determine the long-run future price of food in the world?

7 Why do enhanced information flows offer favorable prospects for development?
8 What might you as an individual do to help solve hunger, poverty, and other development problems?

RECOMMENDED READINGS

Adelman, Irma, "A Poverty-Focused Approach to Development Policy," Chap. 1, in John P. Lewis and Valeriana Kallab, (eds.), *Development Strategies Reconsidered* (New Brunswick, N.J.: Transaction Books, 1986).

Johnston, Bruce F., and William C. Clark, *Redesigning Rural Development: A Strategic Perspective* (Baltimore: Johns Hopkins University Press, 1982), p. 270.

Mellor, John W., "Agricultural Development: Opportunities for the 1990s," International Food Policy Research Institute, Food Policy Statement Number 10, Washington, D.C., June 1989.

Mellor, John W., "Agriculture on the Road to Industrialization," Chap. 2, in John P. Lewis and Valeriana Kallab, (eds.), *Development Strategies Reconsidered* (New Brunswick, N.J.: Transaction Books, 1986).

Stevens, Robert D., and Cathy L. Jabara, *Agricultural Development Principles* (Baltimore: Johns Hopkins University Press, 1988), Chap. 15.

GLOSSARY OF SELECTED TERMS

absolute advantage   When one country's cost of producing a good is lower than the cost in other countries.

agricultural extension   The process of transferring information about improved technologies, practices, or policies to producers, consumers, or policymakers.

agricultural productivity   Level of agricultural output per unit of input.

balance of payments   Difference between receipts from all other countries and payments to them, including all public and private transactions.

bilateral   Two-party or two-country, such as aid from one country to another.

birth rates and death rates   The number of births or deaths per 1000 population in a given year.

bloc-floating exchange-rate system   A system in which the values of major currencies are allowed to change rapidly (float) against each other according to market conditions at the same time several lesser currencies are fixed to the major floating currencies.

buffer stocks   Supplies of a product that are stored and used to moderate price fluctuations. These stocks are sold during periods of rising prices, and purchased when prices fall.

capital accumulation   Investment.

common property   Property for which the rights of use are shared and ownership is not private but communal.

comparative advantage   Ability of a country to produce a good or service at a lower opportunity cost than can another country. The theory of comparative advantage implies that a country should devote its resources not to all lines of production, but to those it produces most efficiently.

concessional   Subsidized, usually used with respect of interest on loans.

debt rescheduling   Extending the repayment period for loans, altering interest rates, forgiving part of the principal, or some combination of the three.

demographic transition   The historical shift of birth and death rates from high to low levels in a population. Death rates usually decline before birth rates, resulting in rapid population growth during the transition period.

dependency theory   The idea that the indigenous elite in developing countries collude with capitalists in more-developed countries to perpetuate the problems in developing countries. The more-developed countries and the elite in developing countries gain economically at the expense of the poor.

economic development   Improvement in the standard of living of an entire population. Development requires rising per capita incomes, eradication of absolute poverty, reduction in inequality over the long term, and increased opportunity of individual choice.

economic or structural transformation of an economy   The increase in the size of the nonagricultural sector relative to agriculture that occurs in all economies as economic growth occurs.

efficiency improvements   Getting more for the same amounts of inputs by allocating them in a better way.

elasticity   A measure of the percentage response of one variable (for example, quantity demanded) to a one percent change in another variable (for example, price).

enhanced information flows   Increased speed and spread of information transmitted.

environmental degradation   The deterioration of the soil, water, air, or biological diversity in a region, country, or world.

experiment station   A center or station at which scientists conduct research.

external debt   Debts owed by the government in one country to creditors in another country.

externality   An economic impact of an activity by an individual or business on other people for which no compensation is paid. Externalities may be positive or negative and are often unintentional.

farming systems research   Research that treats the farm in a holistic manner and considers the various interactions in the system.

food balance sheet   A tool used for nutritional assessment that calculates the availability of food for human consumption by subtracting (exports + animal feed + seed needed for next year's crops + wastage) from (agricultural output + stocks + imports).

foreign assistance or foreign aid   Includes financial, technical, food, and military assistance given by one or several countries to another country. This assistance may be given as a grant or subsidized loan.

foreign exchange rate   The number of units of one currency that it takes to buy a unit of another currency.

free rider   An individual or business that receives the benefits of the actions of another individual or business without having to pay for those benefits.

free trade area   A block of countries that agree to lower or eliminate tariffs and other trade barriers among themselves, but each country maintains its own independent trade policy toward nonmember nations.

fungibility of credit   The degree to which money loaned for one purpose can be used for another.

GATT (General Agreement on Tariffs and Trade)   Multilateral agreement, originally negotiated in 1947, for the reduction of tariffs and other trade barriers. The agreement provides a forum for intergovernmental tariff negotiations.

green revolution   The dramatic increases in wheat and rice harvests that were achieved in the late 1960s, primarily in Asia and Latin America, following the release of fertilizer- and water-responsive, high-yielding, semidwarf varieties of those crops.

high-yielding variety   Varieties of plants that have been improved through agricultural research so that they yield more per amount of input than the traditional varieties.

import substitution   Actions by a government to restrict imports of a commodity to protect (from international competition) and encourage domestic production.

induced innovation theory   A theory that hypothesizes that technical change is induced by changes in relative resource endowments and by growth in product demand; institutional change is induced by changes in relative resource endowments and by technical change.

institutions   Organizations or rules of society. Government policies, regulations, and legal systems, are examples.

integrated pest management   The coordinated use of biological, cultural, and chemical pest control practices to reduce insects, diseases, and weeds. The purpose is to control pests in both an economically and an ecologically sound manner.

international agricultural research centers (IARC)   The set of agricultural research centers supported by a group of public and private funding sources. These centers provide improved technologies and institutional arrangements to help developing countries increase their food production. Funding is coordinated by the Consultative Group on International Agricultural Research (CGIAR).

international capital market   The transfers of capital (money) among countries in response to short- and long-term investment opportunities.

international commodity agreement   A formal agreement among the major producing and consuming countries of a commodity that specifies a mechanism for stabilizing price. An agreement may specify import and export quotas for each country.

International Monetary Fund (IMF)   An international financial institution designed to: (1) promote international monetary coordination; (2) foster international trade; (3) facilitate stabilization of exchange rates; (4) develop mechanisms for multilateral transactions between members; and (5) provide resources for enhanced international financial stability.

land reform   An attempt to change the land tenure system through public policies.

land tenure   The rights and patterns of control over land.

less-developed country (developing country) (LDC)   Generally refers to countries in which per capita incomes are below $6000, although a few countries with higher incomes consider themselves to be less-developed or developing.

market failure   When undistorted markets fail to maximize social welfare.

mixed cropping   Growing more than one crop on the same piece of land at the same time.

money supply   Currency plus money that can be easily withdrawn from checking or savings accounts.

moneylender   An informal lender whose business is to lend money to borrowers, usually at high interest, with little or no collateral or paperwork.

monopoly power   When a single seller or united group of sellers has the power to alter the market price as opposed to having to just accept the market price.

monopsony   A market with a single buyer.

multilateral   Refers to many countries as opposed to two countries (bilateral). Examples are multilateral aid, multilateral trade, and multilateral agreements.

multiple exchange rates   When a country sets different rates between its currency and foreign currencies depending on the class of imports. May be used to control foreign exchange by limiting certain types of imports.

New International Economic Order (NIEO)   A set of principles and a series of proposals formulated and approved in 1974 and 1975 at the Sixth and Seventh Special Sessions of the United Nations General Assembly. These principles and proposals call for a restructuring of economic relations, including trade, between more- and less-developed countries.

Official Development Assistance (ODA)   Foreign assistance that excludes military-related assistance, export credits, and private fund transfers while having at least a 25 percent grant element. The grant element is defined as the excess of the loan or grant's value over the (present) value of repayments calculated with a 10 percent interest rate.

open (as opposed to closed) economy   An economy in which foreign trade is permitted.

opportunity cost of capital   The rate of return on the best alternative use for the funds. It is the cost of alternative investments foregone when a particular investment is made.

overvalued exchange rate   When the official value of a currency is too high given the exchange rate that would otherwise prevail in international money-markets given the supply and demand for the country's currency.

parastatal   An institution, such as a marketing board, that is used by a government to control the production, distribution, international trade, and domestic price of a product. This product might be an agricultural good or an input such as fertilizer.

population density   Population per unit of land area; for example, persons per square kilometer.

pricing policies   Policies used by governments to (1) support prices above the prices that would prevail in a free market, (2) maintain prices below those that would prevail in a free market, or (3) to reduce price instability over time.

production function   Describes, for a given technology, the different output levels that can be obtained from various combinations of inputs or factors of production.

protectionism   A reaction by an industry or a country to foreign competition. That reaction usually is manifest through tariffs, quotas, or other means of reducing imports to shield domestic producers.

public goods   Goods or services that provide benefits to society as a whole but would be supplied in less than the socially desirable amounts by the private sector alone.

Public Law (P.L.) 480   The U.S. Agricultural Trade Development and Assistance Act of 1954 and its subsequent amendments that authorized use of surplus agricultural products as food aid to other countries. The name of the act was changed to Food for Peace in 1966.

scale-neutral technology   A technology that can be employed equally well by any size firm.

structural adjustment program   Government program aimed at adjusting the economy to reduce imbalances between aggregate supply and demand. Structural adjustment programs typically involve: devaluation of the foreign exchange rate to increase exports and reduce imports, reduced government spending, and removal of many government policies that distort prices, including barriers to trade.

subsidized (concessional) credit   Loans made with interest rates below the rates prevailing in the market.

sustainable development Development that meets the needs of the present without compromising the ability of future generations to meet their own needs.[1]

tariff A tax or duty placed on goods imported into a country.

technology The method for producing something. New technologies are often imbedded in inputs, for example seeds or machines. Hence higher yielding seeds or more efficient machines are often referred to as improved technologies. Technological progress occurs when more output is obtained from the same quantity of inputs. Technology transfer occurs when methods (perhaps imbedded in materials) from one location are applied in a second location.

terms of trade The relationship between the prices of two goods that are exchanged; for example, the price of an export good relative to the price of an import goods. When the price of an export good increases relative to the price of an import good, the terms of trade have increased for the export and are said to be favorable.

trade preferences Refers to favorable tariff treatment accorded by one country or group of countries to exports of certain other countries.

transactions costs The costs of adjustment, of information, and of negotiating, monitoring, and enforcing contracts.

United Nations Conference on Trade and Development (UNCTAD) A permanent organization within the United Nations that has developed proposals for trade arrangements that are favorable to developing countries. The organization was formed, in part, because of concerns that the GATT has focused too little on trade problems affecting LDCs.

Uruguay Round The round of multilateral trade negotiations held under the auspices of the GATT in the late 1980s and early 1990s. It was the first round of GATT negotiations to focus heavily on reducing agricultural trade barriers.

World Bank The major multilateral-funded organization that makes loans to developing countries. It contains the International Finance Corporation, the International Bank for Reconstruction and Development, and the International Development Association.

---

[1] World Commission on Environment and Development, *Our Common Future* (New York: Oxford University Press, 1987), p. 43.

AUTHOR INDEX

Page numbers followed by *n* indicate footnotes.

SUBJECT INDEX

Page numbers followed by *f* indicate illustrations.
Page numbers followed by *n* indicate footnotes.
Page numbers followed by *t* indicate tables.

Abject poverty, 109
    See also Poverty and related entries
Abortion
    China, 67
Absolute cost differences, 295
Acquired auto-immune deficiency syndrome
        (AIDS). See AIDS virus
Adaptive research, 274
Administrative costs
    informal money-markets, 234–235
    loan size, 236
Africa
    AIDS virus, 68*n*
    colonialism, 193
    common-property institutions, 217
    debt crisis, 337
    debt relief, 35
    declining growth rate, 105
    desertification, 210
    environmental problems, 12
    free trade area, 311
    hunger/poverty problems, 4–5
    index of per capita food production, 6*f*
    infant mortality, 7, 8*f*
    landholdings, average size, 191, 192*t*
    migration, 137
    pastoral nomadism, 154
    shifting cultivation, 154
    soil erosion, 208–209
    tse-tse fly, 150
    women in farming system, 160
Aggregate versus household data, 46
Agrarian class structure, 191, 195, 196
Agricultural commodities, income elasticities
        of demand, 41, 43*t*
Agricultural development, 112
    assessing future prospects, 375–377
    designing an operational strategy, 181–187
    historical perspective on, 19
    how individuals can help, 377–378
    integrated approach to, 369–374
    international trade/aid in, 4
    theories of, 169–170
        high-payoff inputs, 173
        location and diffusion, 172
        resource exploitation and conservation,
            170–172

Agricultural development (*Cont.*):
    theory of induced innovation, 173–174
        induced institutional change, 176–177
        induced technical innovation, 174–176
        transactions costs and collective action,
            177–181
    trade and, 293–316
    traditional farming and, 141–145
Agricultural extension, 182, 284–287, 350
Agricultural goods, growth of demand, 50*t*
Agricultural linkages, 232
Agricultural mechanization, 230
Agricultural policies, 4, 52–53, 350
Agricultural prices, 242–243
    supply/demand shifts, 52–53
Agricultural production, 4, 9
    improved technologies, 18–19, 105
    increasing, 32, 52
Agricultural productivity, 263–265, 283
Agricultural product prices, 329
Agricultural research, 182, 350
    changes in output, 264*t*
    distributional and nutritional effects of,
        265, 268
        farm size and tenure, 268–269
        land, labor, capital, 270–271
        nutritional implications, 271
        producers and consumers, 269–270
        regional disparities, 269
    environmental effects of, 272
    green revolution, 281
    institutional change, 272
    International Agricultural Research Center
        (IARC), 276–277, 278–279*t*, 280
    modern biotechnology research, 275
    nature, organization, transfer of research,
        274
        categories, 274–276
        organization, 276
        transfer of results, 280–283
    need for farming systems research, 277
    productivity, 263–265
    public versus private sector, 273
    rate of return on investment, 266, 266*t*
    research and environment: case of
        cassava mealybug, 273
    role of, 262–263

388